HOUGHTON MIFFLIN

English

Authors
Robert Rueda
Tina Saldivar
Lynne Shapiro
Shane Templeton
C. Ann Terry
Catherine Valentino
Shelby A. Wolf

Consultants
Jeanneine P. Jones
Monette Coleman McIver
Rojulene Norris

HOUGHTON MIFFLIN   BOSTON • MORRIS PLAINS, NJ

California • Colorado • Georgia • Illinois • New Jersey • Texas

Acknowledgments

For each of the selections listed below, grateful acknowledgment is made for permission to excerpt and/or reprint original or copyrighted material as follows:

Published Models

From "Afraid of the Dark" from *Journey Through a Tropical Jungle* by Adrian Forsyth. Text copyright ©1988 by Adrian Forsyth. Reprinted with permission of Simon & Schuster Books for Young Readers, an imprint of Simon & Schuster Children's Publishing Division and Greey de Pencier Books Inc.

Chiming In on Windchimes by Gary Soto. Copyright © 2000. Used by permission of the Author and Bookstop Literary Agency. All rights reserved.

From *Edmund Hillary* by Timothy R. Gaffney, Chicago: Childrens Press, 1990.

From *Hurricanes and Tornadoes* by Keith Greenberg. Copyright ©1994 by Blackbirch Graphics, Inc. Reprinted by permission of The Millbrook Press.

From "Shortstop" from *Knots in My Yo-Yo String: The Autobiography of a Kid* by Jerry Spinelli. Copyright ©1998 by Jerry Spinelli. Reprinted by permission of Alfred A. Knopf.

Acknowledgments are continued at the back of the book following the last page of the Index.

Copyright © 2001 by Houghton Mifflin Company. All rights reserved.

No part of this work may be reproduced or transmitted in any form or by any means, electronic or mechanical, including photocopying and recording, or by any information storage or retrieval system without the prior written permission of the copyright owner, unless such copying is expressly permitted by federal copyright law. With the exception of nonprofit transcription in Braille, Houghton Mifflin is not authorized to grant permission for further uses of copyrighted selections reprinted in this text without the permission of their owners as identified herein. Address requests for permission to make copies of Houghton Mifflin material to School Permissions, Houghton Mifflin Company, 222 Berkeley Street, Boston, MA 02116.

Printed in the U.S.A.

ISBN: 0-618-03082-4

23456789-VH-06 05 04 03 02 01 00

TABLE OF CONTENTS

Getting Started

Listening, Speaking, and Viewing 1

The Writing Process
  Writing a Description 7

Part 1

Grammar, Usage, and Mechanics

Why Learn Grammar? 30

Unit 1 — The Sentence 31

Lessons
1. What Is a Sentence? 32
2. Four Kinds of Sentences 34
3. Subjects and Predicates 36
4. Simple Subjects 38
5. Simple Predicates 40
6. Subjects in Imperatives 42
7. Conjunctions 44

Revising Strategies: Sentence Fluency
  Writing Good Sentences 46
  • Combining Sentences: Compound Sentences
  • Avoiding Stringy Sentences

8. Run-on Sentences 48

ENRICHMENT 50
CHECKUP 51
TEST PRACTICE 53
EXTRA PRACTICE 55

Table of Contents **iii**

Part 1

Unit 2 — Nouns 63

Lessons
1. What Is a Noun? 64
2. Common and Proper Nouns .. 66

   Revising Strategies: Sentence Fluency
   Writing with Nouns 68
   - Combining Sentences: Compound Subjects
   - Combining Sentences: Telling More About Nouns

3. Singular and Plural Nouns ... 70
4. More Plural Nouns 72
5. Singular Possessive Nouns ... 74
6. Plural Possessive Nouns 76

Revising Strategies: Sentence Fluency
Writing with Nouns 78
- Combining Sentences: Possessive Nouns
- Combining Sentences: Appositives with Possessive Nouns

Revising Strategies: Vocabulary
Using Exact Nouns 80

ENRICHMENT 81
✓ CHECKUP 82
✓ TEST PRACTICE 84
✓ CUMULATIVE REVIEW 87
EXTRA PRACTICE 89

Unit 3 — Verbs 95

Lessons
1. Action Verbs 96
2. Direct Objects 98
3. Main Verbs and Helping Verbs 100
4. Linking Verbs 102
5. Present Tense 104
6. Past Tense 106
7. Future Tense 108

Revising Strategies: Sentence Fluency
Writing with Verbs 110
- Combining Sentences
- Keeping Verbs in the Same Tense

8. Subject-Verb Agreement 112
9. Agreement with *be* and *have* 114
10. Contractions with *not* 116
11. Regular and Irregular Verbs . 118
12. More Irregular Verbs 120
13. Verb Phrases with *have* 122
14. *teach, learn; let, leave* 124
15. *sit, set; can, may* 126

Revising Strategies: Vocabulary
Using Exact Verbs 128

ENRICHMENT 129
CHECKUP 130
TEST PRACTICE 133
EXTRA PRACTICE 136

Unit 4 — Adjectives 151

Lessons
1. What Is an Adjective? 152

Revising Strategies: Sentence Fluency
Writing with Adjectives 154
- Elaborating Sentences
- Combining Sentences

2. Articles and Demonstratives . 156
3. Comparing with Adjectives .. 158
4. Comparing with *good* and *bad* 160
5. Proper Adjectives 162

Revising Strategies: Vocabulary
Choosing Different Adjectives 164

ENRICHMENT 165
CHECKUP 166
TEST PRACTICE 168
CUMULATIVE REVIEW 170
EXTRA PRACTICE 174

Unit 5 — Capitalization and Punctuation 179

Lessons

1 Correct Sentences 180
2 Proper Nouns and Adjectives 182
3 Commas in a Series 184

Revising Strategies: Sentence Fluency

Writing Sentences with Commas 186
- Combining Sentences with a Series of Words or Phrases
- Combining Whole Sentences in a Series

4 More Uses for Commas 188

Revising Strategies: Sentence Fluency

Writing Sentences with Commas 190
- Combining Sentences: Introductory Groups of Words

5 Interjections 192
6 Quotations 194
7 Abbreviations 196
8 Titles 198
ENRICHMENT 200
CHECKUP 201
TEST PRACTICE 204
EXTRA PRACTICE 207

Unit 6 — Pronouns 215

Lessons

1 Subject Pronouns 216
2 Object Pronouns 218
3 Using *I* and *me* 220
4 Possessive Pronouns 222

Revising Strategies: Sentence Fluency

Writing with Pronouns 224
- Using Enough Pronouns
- Writing Clearly with Pronouns

5 Contractions with Pronouns . 226
6 Double Subjects 228
7 Using *we* and *us* with Nouns . 230

Revising Strategies: Vocabulary

Using Homophones Correctly 232
ENRICHMENT 233
CHECKUP 234
TEST PRACTICE 236
EXTRA PRACTICE 238

Unit 7   Adverbs and Prepositions   245

Lessons
1 Adverbs 246

Revising Strategies: Sentence Fluency
Writing with Adverbs 248
- Elaborating Sentences
- Combining Sentences

2 Comparing with Adverbs 250
3 Adjective or Adverb? 252
4 Negatives 254
5 Prepositions 256
6 Prepositional Phrases 258

Revising Strategies: Sentence Fluency
Writing with Prepositions . . . 260
- Elaborating Sentences: Prepositional Phrases
- Combining Sentences: Prepositional Phrases

7 Pronouns in Prepositional Phrases 262
8 Adverb or Preposition? 264

Revising Strategies: Vocabulary
Choosing Different Adverbs . . 266

ENRICHMENT 267
✓ CHECKUP 268
✓ TEST PRACTICE 270
✓ CUMULATIVE REVIEW . . . 272
EXTRA PRACTICE 276

Table of Contents   **vii**

Part 2: Writing, Listening, Speaking, and Viewing

SECTION 1 Narrating and Entertaining

Listening to a Narrative 288
Writing a Narrative Paragraph 289

Unit 8 Writing a Personal Narrative 294

Writing a Personal Narrative
- Published Model:
  "Shortstop,"
  by Jerry Spinelli 295
- What Makes a Great Personal Narrative? 298
- Student Model
  by Mike Jones 299

The Writing Process 304
- Focus Skills
  - Organizing Your Narrative . . 306
  - Good Beginnings 307
  - Writing with Voice 308
  - Good Endings 309
- ✓ Evaluating Your Personal Narrative 310

Revising Strategies 312
- Elaborating: Word Choice
- Elaborating: Details
- Sentence Fluency

Grammar and Spelling Connections 313
- Proper Nouns
- Complete Sentences
- Spelling the |ī| Sound

✓ **WRITING PROMPTS** 315
✓ **TEST PRACTICE** 316

Special Focus on Narrating
  Writing a Friendly Letter 317

Unit 9 Writing a Story 319

Writing a Story
Published Model:
"The Woman Who Outshone the Sun," by Rosalma Zubizarretta, Harriet Rohmer, and David Schecter 320
What Makes a Great Story? 325
Student Model
by Chris Rivera 326

The Writing Process 330
Focus Skills
Planning Characters 331
Planning Setting and Plot .. 332
Developing Characters 333
Developing Your Plot 334
Writing with Voice 336
✓ **Evaluating Your Story** 337

Revising Strategies 339
- Elaborating: Word Choice
- Elaborating: Details
- Sentence Fluency

Grammar and Spelling Connections 340
- Writing Dialogue
- Spelling |ā| and |ē| Sounds

✓ **WRITING PROMPTS** 342
✓ **TEST PRACTICE** 343

Special Focus on Entertaining
Writing a Play 344

Communication Links
Speaking: Dramatizing ... 350
Viewing/Media: Comparing Stories in Print and on Film 352

SECTION 2 Explaining and Informing

Listening for Information 356
Writing Informational Paragraphs 357

Unit 10   Writing to Compare and Contrast 364

Writing to Compare and Contrast
Published Model:
"Hurricanes and Tornadoes,"
by Keith Greenberg 365
What Makes a Great Compare-Contrast Essay? 368
Student Model
by Portia Caldwell 369

The Writing Process 374
Focus Skills
Organizing Your Essay 377
Introductions and
   Conclusions 379
Topic Sentences and
   Transitional Words 380
☑ **Evaluating Your Compare-Contrast Essay** 381

Revising Strategies 383
- Elaborating: Word Choice
- Elaborating: Details
- Sentence Fluency

Grammar and Spelling Connections 384
- Subject-Verb Agreement
- Commas in a Series
- Spelling the |oo| or |yoo| sound

☑ **WRITING PROMPTS** 386
☑ **TEST PRACTICE** 387

Special Focus on Explaining
Writing Instructions 388

Communication Links
Listening/Speaking:
Giving and Following
Instructions 394
Viewing/Media: Comparing
Visual Information 396

Table of Contents

Unit 11 Writing a Research Report 398

Writing a Research Report
Published Model:
"Scaredy Cats,"
by Christina Wilsdon 399
**What Makes a Great
Research Report?** 403
Student Model
by Christina Clark 404

The Writing Process 409
Focus Skills
Finding the Best
Information 412
Writing from an Outline ... 417
Introductions and
Conclusions 419
✓ Evaluating Your Research
Report 420
Revising Strategies 422
- Elaborating: Word Choice
- Elaborating: Details
- Sentence Fluency

**Adding Graphics and
Visuals** 423

Grammar and Spelling
Connections 425
- Proper Nouns and Adjectives
- Spelling the |ô| Sound

✓ **WRITING PROMPTS** 427

Special Focus on Informing
Writing to Solve a Problem ... 428
Writing a News Article 430
Completing a Form 432

Communication Links
Speaking/Viewing/Media:
Giving an Oral Report 434
Viewing/Media:
Evaluating the News 436

Table of Contents **xi**

SECTION 3 Expressing and Influencing

Listening to an Opinion 440
Writing an Opinion Paragraph 441

Unit 12 Writing to Express an Opinion 446

Writing to Express an Opinion

Published Model:
"Why I Love Kwanzaa," by
Angela Shelf Medearis 447

**What Makes a Great
Opinion Essay?** 450

Student Model
by Allison France 451

The Writing Process 455

Focus Skills
Elaborating Your Reasons . . 457
Organizing Your Reasons . . 458
Introductions and
Conclusions 460

✓**Evaluating Your Opinion
Essay** 461

Revising Strategies 463
• Elaborating: Word Choice
• Elaborating: Details
• Sentence Fluency

**Grammar and Spelling
Connections** 464
• Possessive Pronouns
• Interjections
• Spelling the |ō| Sound

✓ **WRITING PROMPTS** 466
✓ **TEST PRACTICE** 467

Special Focus on Expressing
Writing a Book Report 468
Writing a Poem 470

Communication Links
Listening/Speaking: Having
a Panel Discussion 476
Viewing/Media: Finding
Points of View in Visuals . . . 478

xii Table of Contents

Unit 13 — Writing to Persuade 480

Writing to Persuade
Published Model:
"Chiming In on Wind Chimes,"
by Gary Soto 481
**What Makes a Great
Persuasive Essay?** 484
Student Model
by Michael Le 485

The Writing Process 489
Focus Skills
Supporting Your Goal 490
Evaluating Your Reasons . . . 492
Organizing Your Essay 493
Introductions and
 Conclusions 494
Writing with Voice 495
☑ **Evaluating Your Persuasive
 Essay** 496
Revising Strategies 498
 • Elaborating: Word Choice
 • Elaborating: Details
 • Sentence Fluency

Grammar and Spelling
Connections 499
 • Commas in a Series
 • Using Pronouns Clearly
 • Spelling the Final |ər| Sounds
☑ **WRITING PROMPTS** 501
☑ **TEST PRACTICE** 502

Special Focus on Influencing
Writing a Business Letter 503

Communication Links
Listening: Listening for
 Persuasive Tactics 505
Viewing/Media: Watching
 for Persuasive Tactics 507

Tools and Tips

Listening and Speaking Strategies
Taking and Leaving
 Messages H4
Giving a Talk H5
Understanding Nonverbal
 Cues H7
Interviewing H9

Building Vocabulary
Similes and Metaphors H11
Idioms H12
Synonyms H13
Antonyms H14
Word Connotations H15
Prefixes H16
Suffixes H17
Word Roots H18
Regional and Cultural
 Vocabulary H19

Research and Study Strategies
Using a Dictionary H20
Using the Library H23
Using Visuals H26
Research and Study Skills . . . H28

Test-Taking Strategies
Word Analogies H33
Open-Response Questions . . H35

Using Technology
Technology Terms H37
Using E-mail H39
Using a Spelling Tool H40
Computers and the Writing
 Process H41
Using the Internet H45
Creating an Electronic
 Multimedia Presentation . H47

Writer's Tools
Keeping a Learning Log H50
Keeping a Writer's
 Notebook H51
Graphic Organizers H52

Guide to Capitalization, Punctuation, and Usage H57

Spelling Guide
Words Often Misspelled H67
Spelling Guidelines H68

Diagramming Guide H72

Thesaurus Plus H81

Index I-1

Listening, Speaking, and Viewing

Getting Started: Listening, Speaking, Viewing

Learning from Each Other

Each one of you has your own special talents, knowledge, experiences, opinions, and observations. As individuals you're like one-of-a-kind books, full of great information and ideas to share. Together, you're a whole encyclopedia!

Sharing what you know and learning from others will make school—and life—easier and much more fun! You can count on each other to help solve problems, to think of and respond to ideas, and to offer encouragement. How can you do it? LISTEN, SPEAK, and VIEW! Speaking allows you to share what you know. Listening and looking, or viewing, help you to learn from others. Here are some major purposes for speaking, listening, and viewing.

Speaking	Listening and Viewing	Examples
to entertain	for enjoyment	telling or listening to a story, looking at a cartoon, watching a comedy show
to inform	to get information	asking for or giving directions, listening to directions, reading a map
to persuade	to form an opinion	recommending a movie, listening to reasons for doing an activity, watching a commercial

Think and Discuss

- Look back at the pictures on the previous page. What is each student's purpose for listening, speaking, or viewing?
- At what other times do you rely on listening, speaking, and viewing during the day?

Discussion Breakdown

These students are trying to choose items to put in their class time capsule, but they are not using good listening and speaking skills. What's wrong?

Think and Discuss

- What is each student doing wrong in this discussion?
- What could the students do to improve their discussion?

Getting Started: Listening, Speaking, Viewing

Breakthrough Discussion

The students are still planning their time capsule. How have they improved their listening and speaking skills?

Think and Discuss

- What has each student done to improve his or her listening and speaking skills?

Being a Good Listener and Speaker

Whether you are in the classroom, on the field, or at the dinner table, speaking and listening connect you with other people. Here are some basic guidelines to help you keep those connections strong.

When You Listen

- Get rid of barriers to listening. Turn off the television. Close the door to the noisy hallway.
- Face the speaker. Make eye contact.
- Listen attentively. Don't daydream.
- Don't create distractions—no pencil tapping or knuckle cracking!
- Ask questions when you don't understand.
- Silently summarize what you hear.
- If confused, repeat what was said, using your own words. Ask whether you've understood.

When You Speak

- Vary your role—participate, lead, and listen so that others can do the same.
- Make eye contact with your listeners. Speak loudly and clearly enough that others can hear and understand your words.
- Wait your turn. Don't interrupt!
- Share your ideas with the group rather than in side conversations.
- Stick to the subject being discussed. From time to time, summarize the main points of the discussion so far.
- Ask other people for their opinions.
- Respond to the opinions and ideas of others.
- If you disagree, explain why politely.

Try It Out Choose one of the statements below. Decide whether or not you agree with it. Discuss your opinions in small groups.

- The school year is too short.
- Wild animals don't make good pets.
- Movie ratings are a good idea.

Getting Started: Listening, Speaking, Viewing

Being a Good Viewer

You see many things every day, but when you view, or observe carefully, you're using your eyes to learn. Here are some ways you learn through your eyes as well as your ears. What are some other ways?

When You View

Viewing the World Around You
- First, take in all that you can.
- Then focus. What is the most important part of what you're viewing?
- Then refocus. What interesting or important details do you see?

Viewing Others
- Watch for gestures that help explain what someone is saying.
- Watch people's body language for clues to how they feel.
- Watch people's body language for clues to how they are reacting to your words or actions.

Viewing Still or Moving Images
- Look for the main focus of the image. What catches your eye?
- Then look more closely. What details are important? Why?
- Is the image meant to send a message? If so, what message?
- Look for the purpose of the image. Is it to entertain? inform? persuade?
- What audience is the image for? How do you know?
- How might viewers from different age groups or interests respond to this image?

Try It Out With a small group, choose a saying the whole class knows, but don't say what it is. Act out the saying without speaking or using props. Have the rest of the class guess the saying by viewing your hands, faces, and actions.

The Writing Process

A Day in the Life of a Student

What Is the Writing Process?

The writing process helps you move step by step from a blank piece of paper to an interesting piece of writing. The writing process gives you many chances to make your writing better.

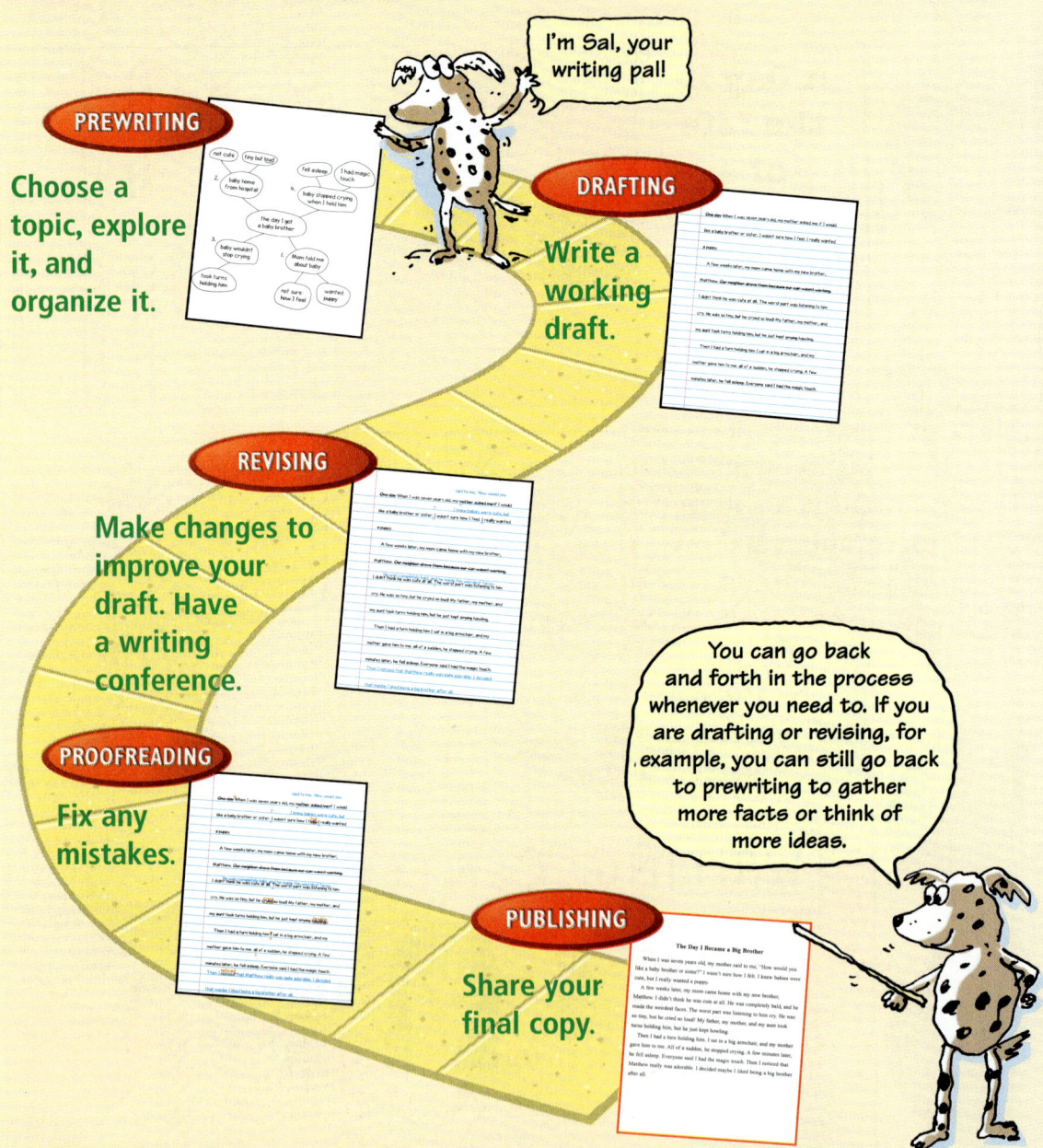

PREWRITING
Choose a topic, explore it, and organize it.

I'm Sal, your writing pal!

DRAFTING
Write a working draft.

REVISING
Make changes to improve your draft. Have a writing conference.

You can go back and forth in the process whenever you need to. If you are drafting or revising, for example, you can still go back to prewriting to gather more facts or think of more ideas.

PROOFREADING
Fix any mistakes.

PUBLISHING
Share your final copy.

Looking Ahead In this section, you will learn about the writing process while writing a description. To get ready, you will first read a description that was published in a book.

Getting Started: Listening, Speaking, Viewing

A Published Model

Adrian Forsyth took a walk through a rain forest at night. Later, he wrote a description of his unusual experience. What sights, sounds, and smells does he describe?

Afraid of the Dark

from *Journey Through a Tropical Jungle*,
by Adrian Forsyth

In Monteverde the sun was my alarm clock. Sunrise set off a chorus of bird songs that made sleeping impossible. It seemed like the liveliest time in the rain forest. But I knew that many of the animals in the jungle actually wake up at sunset and are most active during the night. To really see the wildlife, I would have to visit the forest after sundown. The thought of hiking through the jungle in the dark made me both excited and nervous.

Late one afternoon I packed my headlamp, some spare batteries, my camera and flash, and a chunk of cheese and set off uphill. When I reached the edge of the woods the sun was already sinking toward the golden foothills and the Pacific Ocean. As it slipped below the horizon, I made my way into the forest. A fallen log made a convenient bench and I took a seat, waiting

more ▶

for night to fall. It was like sitting in a deep hole. The clouds above still glowed, but the jungle interior was dissolving into a misty gloom. Soon streaks and spots of cool green light began to pulse in the dark. I knew they were the courting signals of the fireflies and click beetles. But knowing that did not make the flickering lights and the black shapes of trees in the heavy shadows any less eerie.

I was amazed to see that the end of my log was also glowing with a strange green light. But this light did not go out. I bent my head forward and pushed my face right up to the pale shape: mushrooms. I could smell and feel them. Flickering fireflies were familiar, but I couldn't guess why mushrooms would shine in the dark, and so their soft glow added more mystery to the dark.

The forest was also filling up with all kinds of strange sounds. Whistles, whoops, and chirpings were coming from every direction. Without the use of my eyes, my ears seemed much more sensitive. I could hear the swooping bats above me and the whining mosquito circling my head.

There were rustling noises in the leaves beside me. My nose was picking up the heavy perfume of flowers and the earthy scent of decaying leaves. I felt surrounded by invisible activity and sensations.

I wanted to wait as long as possible in the dark, soaking up the sounds, the smells, the feeling of night in the jungle. Then something ran across my hand. I jumped up electrified. It was time to turn on the lights.

I felt for my headlamp and switched on the light. As soon as I looked around, I realized this had been a sensible decision. Right beside me was a large scorpion armed with a long, powerful stinging tail. That was one nighttime sensation I did not want to experience. The scorpion was munching on a katydid, so I left it to enjoy its breakfast without my company.

Reading As a Writer

Think About the Description

- What sights does Adrian Forsyth describe in the second paragraph of his description? In the fourth paragraph, what four exact words describe sounds? In the fifth paragraph, which words describe two smells?
- What details are included in the opening paragraph that tell you the topic of this description?
- In the next-to-last paragraph, what touches the writer's hand?

Think About Writer's Craft

- Why do the words *dissolving into a misty gloom* help you picture nightfall more clearly than a phrase such as *getting dark*?

Think About the Pictures

- What do the photographs add to the selection?

Looking Ahead

Now you are ready to write your own description. Starting on the next page, you will find many ideas to help you. As you go along, you will see how one student, John Coghlan, used the writing process to write a description of his pet lizard.

Getting Started: The Writing Process

Using the Writing Process

What Is Prewriting?

Prewriting has three parts. You choose your topic; you explore your topic; and you organize, or plan, your writing.

Start thinking about **audience** and **purpose**. Who will read or listen to your writing? What kind of paper will you write?

Think about how you are going to **publish** or **share** your paper. This may make a difference in how you write it.

How Do I Choose a Topic?

Here are a few ways to find an idea to write about.

Ways to Think of Topics		
Try this!	**Here's how.**	
Remember your experiences or those of others.	Your birthday cake tipped off the table just before you blew out the candles.	• Write a **personal narrative** about what happened. • Add this event to a **story**. • **Describe** the splattered cake.
Read a book.	You enjoyed a story about saving an injured hawk.	• Write a **research report** about hawks. • **Persuade** people to care for wildlife.
Reread your journal.	You wrote a journal entry about being an only child.	• Turn it into an **opinion essay** about having brothers and sisters. • **Compare and contrast** large and small families.
Use your imagination.	What would it be like to play in a basketball championship?	• Write a **story** about winning the finals. • Write an **opinion essay** about sports.

Description | PREWRITING

Write a Description

Choosing a Description Topic

Learning from a Model John wanted to write a description to put in his grandmother's birthday card as a gift. First, he made a list of ideas and thought about each one.

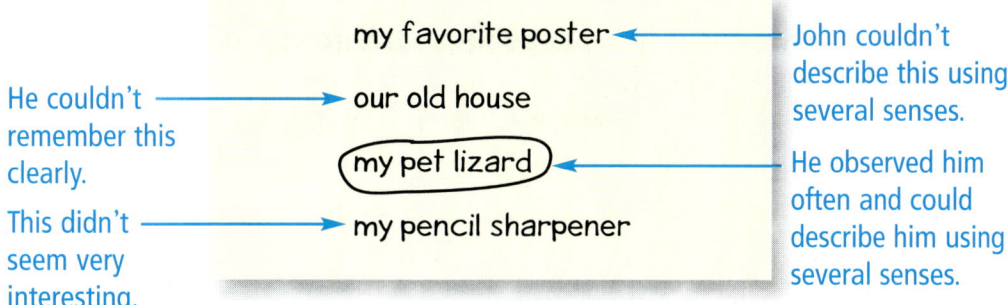

- my favorite poster — John couldn't describe this using several senses.
- our old house — He couldn't remember this clearly.
- my pet lizard (circled) — He observed him often and could describe him using several senses.
- my pencil sharpener — This didn't seem very interesting.

▶ **Choose Your Topic**

As you choose your topic, think about your **purpose**, your **audience**, and how you will **share** or **publish** your description.

❶ **List** five topics that you would enjoy describing, such as a favorite possession, an interesting place, or a special person. Use the chart on page 12 to help you think of ideas.

❷ **Discuss** your topics with a partner. Which ideas does your partner like? Why?

❸ **Ask** yourself these questions about each topic.
- Is this topic about one person, place, or thing?
- Can I observe it before I describe it?
- Can I describe it using at least three senses?
- Which topic would both my audience and I enjoy?

❹ **Circle** the topic you will write about.

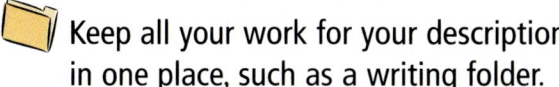 Keep all your work for your description in one place, such as a writing folder.

 **Tech Tip** See page H41 for ideas for using a computer at each stage of the writing process.

Prewriting 13

Getting Started: The Writing Process

What Is Exploring?

Exploring is the second part of prewriting. You remember events, collect facts, and think of details to elaborate, or tell more, about your topic.

How Do I Explore My Topic?

This chart shows different strategies you can use to explore a topic.

Try this!	Exploring Strategies
	Here's how.
Brainstorming a list	**Gray Squirrel** gray fur bushy tail eats berries eats nuts lives in tree hole nervous
Clustering	how they look — KANGAROOS — what they eat — where they live — Australia
Making a chart	**Maple Trees** Touch | rough, scratchy bark Taste | sugary maple syrup
Drawing and labeling	Rain leaked into our tent.
Interviewing with a partner	What does your parrot look like?
Asking *Who? What? When? Where? Why? How?*	**A Class Trip** Where? art museum Why? will learn about sculpture

 See page H52 for more graphic organizers.

Exploring a Description Topic

Learning from a Model John brainstormed a list of details about his lizard.

> yellow eyes   round body
>
> oval head   still hisses
>
> still scratches   long green tail
>
> line from nose to tail

▲ Part of John's list

▶ Explore Your Topic

① **Think** about your topic carefully.

② **Brainstorm** a list of details about it.

③ **Use your five senses** to brainstorm sensory words and details to expand your list. Use the chart below for examples of sense words. Use some of these or think of your own.

Sight	Sound	Smell	Touch	Taste
magenta	crackling	fragrant	velvety	salty
foggy	shriek	smoky	bumpy	minty
scrawny	splash	musty	icy	tangy
oval	slurp	pungent	slick	bitter
blinking	jingle	burnt	gritty	sour
webbed	sizzle	perfumed	grooved	spicy
glistening	hiss	piny	brittle	burnt
baggy	gurgle	fresh	sharp	lemony

If you can't think of details for three of the five senses, you may want to choose another topic.

Prewriting **15**

Getting Started: The Writing Process

What Is Organizing?

Organizing is the third part of prewriting. You select what ideas and details to include, group the ones that belong together, and then put the groups in order.

How Do I Organize My Writing?

Group facts, events, or ideas. Collect related details into separate groups, such as what you heard and what you saw or the steps for making something.

Choose an organization. Present the groups of details in an order that fits your purpose. It often helps to chart, diagram, or outline your plan.

Ways to Organize	
Try this!	Here's how.
Time order First Next Last	Tell events in the order they happen.
Place order	Describe things from top to bottom, bottom to top, right to left, left to right, near to far, or far to near.
Comparison and contrast	Describe how two subjects are alike. Then describe how they are different. You can also tell the differences first and the likenesses next.
Order of importance LEAST / MOST MOST / LEAST	Tell the most important reason first and the least important reason last, or tell them the other way around.
Question and answer Q? A... Q? A...	Ask a question and tell the answer. Then ask another question and answer that.
Logical order	Group details that belong together. Present the groups in an order that makes sense.

16 **Getting Started:** The Writing Process

Organizing a Description

Learning from a Model John needed to figure out how to group the details on his list. He decided to make a cluster.

- First, he circled related details on his list with different colored pens.
- Next, he created categories for each related group of details.
- Then he made a cluster. He numbered the groups in a logical order.
- Finally, he added more details to his cluster.

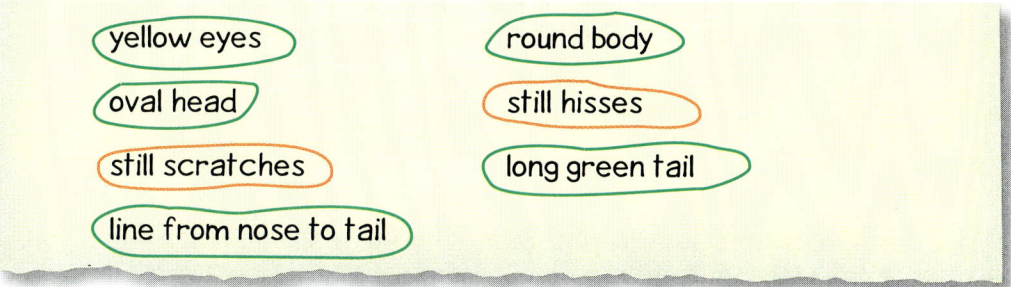

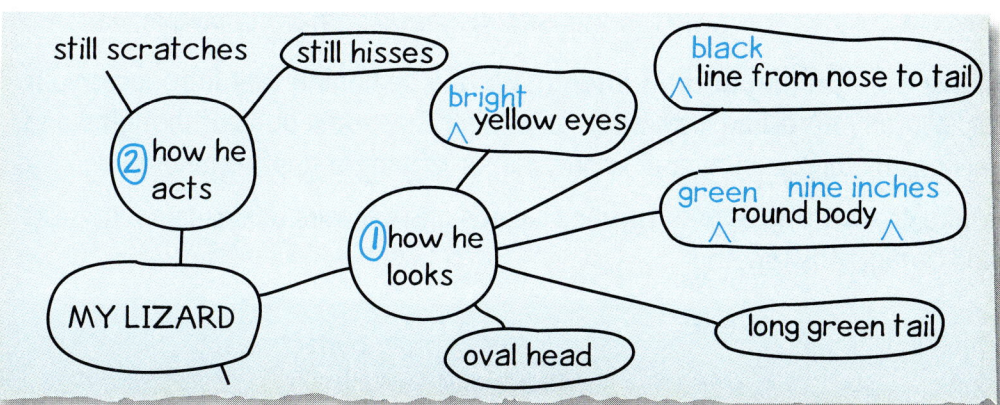

▲ Part of John's cluster

Organize Your Description

1. **Group** the details about your topic that belong together.
2. **Organize** your details. Make a cluster.
3. **Number** your details in the order you will write about them.
4. **Add** any more details you think of. Use exact words.

Go to www.eduplace.com/kids/hme/ for graphic organizers.

Getting Started: The Writing Process

What Is Drafting?

When you draft, you just get your ideas down on paper. Don't worry about mistakes. You can fix them later because this is a **working draft.**

- Think about your purpose and your audience as you write.
- Add more details as you go along. Good ideas can come at any time.
- Write on every other line to leave room for changes.
- If you change your mind, just cross out the parts you don't want. Don't start over. Keep writing!

How Do I Draft My Paper?

Write sentences and paragraphs. Start with the plan you made when you organized your ideas. Turn the words and phrases into sentences. Each section should make at least one paragraph. Most paragraphs will need a topic sentence. The **topic sentence** tells the main idea of the paragraph.

Write a beginning and an ending. Write a beginning that introduces your topic in an interesting way. Write an ending that sums up your thoughts and feelings by telling an overall impression or making a final comment.

Make transitions. Use transitional words and phrases to tie your sentences and paragraphs together.

Ways to Make Transitions	
Try this!	**Look at these examples.**
Use time clues.	before, after, finally, then, next, until, when, often, first, yesterday, at night, Monday
Link causes and effects.	because, as a result, so that, therefore, after, when, if . . . then
Use place clues.	around, down, here, there, beside, inside, outside, over, under
Signal likenesses and differences.	but, however, although, in contrast, similarly
Signal another idea.	also, too, another, in addition

18 Getting Started: The Writing Process

Description

DRAFTING

Drafting a Description

Learning from a Model John wrote his working draft. He introduced his topic in an interesting way. Then he started with the circle he had numbered *1* on his cluster: *how he looks*. He wrote a topic sentence and supporting sentences about how Stripe looked. He used the cluster to write the rest of his draft.

> Stripe is not your avrage lizard. ~~I have~~ He is a Water Dragon.
>
> Stripe looks ~~weird~~ different from other lizards. I named him stripe because he has a black line from his nose to the end of his tail That's not nachural because lizards are supposed to be all green? Stripe has about a nine-inch body thats round. His head is like an oval. His eyes are bright yellow. He has a long green tail.
>
> He still hisses, which most lizards stop doing at three years old. He still gives scratches.
>
> Stripe is pretty old. A water dragon's life span is about ten years. I hope Stripe beats that.

▲ **John's working draft**

▶ Draft Your Description

❶ Write an interesting beginning that introduces your topic.

❷ Use your cluster to help you write your working draft. Skip every other line. Don't worry about mistakes yet.

❸ Think about the main idea of each paragraph, and write a topic sentence. Write other sentences that fill in the details about the main idea.

❹ Write an ending to sum up your thoughts or feelings about your topic.

Getting Started: The Writing Process

What Is Revising?

When you revise, you make changes to make your writing clearer or more interesting. Ask yourself the Big Questions. Don't worry about fixing mistakes at this point.

Revising: The Big Questions
- Did I say what I wanted to say?
- Did I elaborate and use details?
- Did I organize the facts, events, or ideas clearly?
- Did I write in an interesting way that suits my audience?

How Do I Make Revisions?

Don't erase! Make changes on your draft. Don't worry if your paper looks messy. You can make a clean copy later. Here are ways to make your changes.

Ways to Mark Your Revisions	
Try this!	**Look at these examples.**
Cross out parts that you want to change or take out.	I ~~did~~ built a model sailboat with my father.
Use carets to add new words or sentences.	When you walk into my room, the first thing you see is my ^giant stuffed^ giraffe.
Draw circles and arrows to move words, sentences, or paragraphs.	Don't eat one of those cereals that has a lot of sugar in it. (Eat a nutritious kind of cereal.)
Use numbers to show how sentences should be ordered.	③Don't get soap in his eyes. ① First, you get your dog wet. ② Then you rub the shampoo in his fur.
Add wings to show sentences that won't fit on your paper.	When I ran to the garage, I found a pile of broken wood on our car. The roof had fallen down. ^I heard a cracking sound and then a loud bang.^

Revising a Description

Learning from a Model John reread his first draft. To help his grandmother picture Stripe more clearly, he added details and exact words. He also added a topic sentence. He didn't fix mistakes yet.

> Stripe is not your avrage lizard. ~~I have~~ He is a Water Dragon.
>
> Stripe looks ~~weird~~ different from other lizards. I named him stripe because he has a black line from his nose to the end of his tail That's not nachural because lizards are supposed to be all ^lime green? Stripe has about a nine-inch body thats round. His head is like an oval. His eyes are bright yellow ^like ^marbles.
> He has a long green tail ^that sticks up in the air.
> ^For a seven-year-old, Stripe doesn't act his age. For example, He still hisses, which most lizards stop doing at three years old. He still gives scratches ^, which he can't help.
> ^He also has more energy than a dog before an earthquake.

▲ Part of John's revised draft

▶ Revise Your Description

Reread your description. Use the Revising Checklist to help you make changes. Use a thesaurus to find vivid, descriptive words.

Don't worry about fixing any mistakes yet!

Revising Checklist
✔ Did I introduce my topic in an interesting way?
✔ Did I write clear topic sentences? Do my details support them?
✔ Did I order the details so my readers can follow them easily?
✔ Where can I add sensory words or details?
✔ Does my ending sum up my thoughts and feelings about this topic?

📖 See the Thesaurus Plus on page H81.

Getting Started: The Writing Process

What Is a Writing Conference?

In a writing conference, a writer reads his or her paper to a partner or a group. The listeners tell what they like, ask questions, and make suggestions. Your conference partners might be a classmate, a small group, your teacher, or someone who knows about your topic.

How Do I Have a Writing Conference?

In a writing conference, you will be either the writer or the listener. The following guides can help you do your best in either role.

Guides for a Writing Conference	
When You're the Writer . . .	**When You're the Listener . . .**
• Read your paper aloud. • Pay attention to your listeners' comments and suggestions. Keep an open mind. • Take notes to remember any compliments, questions, or suggestions. • Reread your paper after the conference. • Use your notes. Make any other changes you want.	• Look at the writer. • Listen carefully. Don't let your thoughts wander. • Retell what you have heard. • Then tell two things that you like about the paper. • Next, ask questions about things you don't understand. • Finally, give one or two suggestions to help the writer. • Always be positive and polite.

Description

REVISING

Having a Writing Conference

Learning from a Model John had a conference with Sally. She asked him some questions about his description.

▶ Have Your Writing Conference

① **Find** a partner or a small group, and have a writing conference. Use the guides on page 22.

② **Use** your conference notes to make any other changes you want.

Revising **23**

Getting Started: The Writing Process

What Is Proofreading?

When you proofread, you correct any mistakes. You check spelling, capitalization, and punctuation. You also check that you have used words correctly, written complete sentences, and indented paragraphs.

How Do I Proofread?

Choose from these ideas to help you.

- Use proofreading marks.
- Proofread for one skill at a time.
- Read your paper backward so that you focus on the spelling of each word.
- Say each word aloud to yourself.
- Read your paper aloud to a friend. You may notice mistakes when you hear them.
- Circle words that might be misspelled. Check spellings in a dictionary.

Proofreading Tip

Remember **CUPS** when proofreading.
Capitalization
Usage
Punctuation
Spelling

Proofreading Marks

Try this!	Here's when.	Look at these examples.
¶	to begin a new paragraph; to indent the paragraph	¶ We went to an air show last Saturday. Eight jets flew across the sky in the shape of V's, X's, and diamonds.
∧	to add letters, words, or sentences	The leaves were red ∧ orange. (and)
℘	to take out words, sentences, and punctuation marks; to correct spelling	The rain stopped, quickly. The sky is bright blew now. (blue)
/	to change a capital letter to a small letter	My cousin caught ten Fireflies and put them in a jar.
≡	to change a small letter to a capital letter	We drove through the crowded streets of New York city.

24 Getting Started: The Writing Process

Description | PROOFREADING

Proofreading a Description

Learning from a Model John made more changes to his description after talking to Sally. Then he proofread it.

> ¶ Stripe is not your ~~avrage~~ *average* lizard. ~~I have~~ He is a Water Dragon.
>
> Stripe looks ~~weird~~ different from other lizards. I named him stripe because he has a black line from his nose to the end of his tail. That's not ~~nachural~~ *natural* because lizards are supposed to be all green? Stripe has about a nine-inch body that's round. His head is like an ~~oval~~ *egg* lying down, and His eyes are *like* bright yellow *marbles*. He has a long green tail *that sticks up in the air*. *His skin looks scaly and smells like canola oil.*

▲ Part of John's proofread draft

▶ **Proofread Your Description**

Proofread your description, using the Proofreading Checklist shown here. Use the proofreading marks shown on page 24.

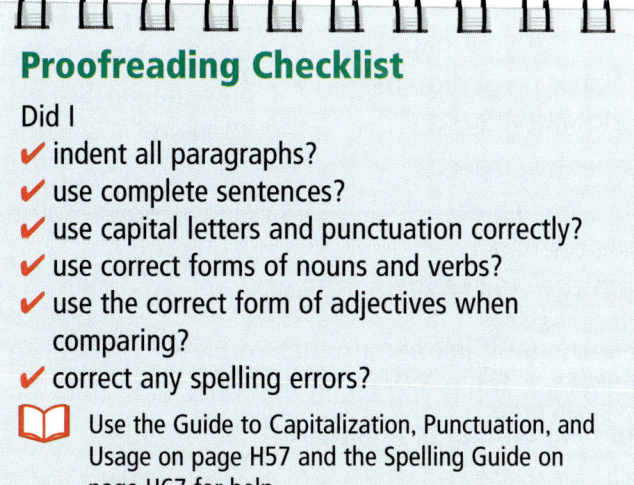

Proofreading Checklist

Did I
- ✔ indent all paragraphs?
- ✔ use complete sentences?
- ✔ use capital letters and punctuation correctly?
- ✔ use correct forms of nouns and verbs?
- ✔ use the correct form of adjectives when comparing?
- ✔ correct any spelling errors?

📖 Use the Guide to Capitalization, Punctuation, and Usage on page H57 and the Spelling Guide on page H67 for help.

Getting Started: The Writing Process

What Is Publishing?

When you publish your writing, you prepare to share it with your audience.

How Do I Publish My Writing?

Here are some ideas for sharing your writing.

Write It
- Send your paper as a letter or an e-mail to friends or family.
- Make your paper into a booklet. Add pictures and a cover.
- Combine your paper with your classmates' to create a collection of writing.
- Send your paper to a magazine, a newspaper, or an Internet site that publishes student writing.

Say It
- Read your paper aloud from the Author's Chair.
- With friends, act out your paper.
- Record your paper on audiotape. Add music or sound effects.
- Read your paper as a speech.

Show It
- Illustrate your work with photographs or drawings.
- Make a comic book showing each step or event in your paper.
- Make a poster to display with your paper.
- Show the main events of your topic on a time line.
- Show slides about your topic to the class while reading your paper aloud.

Tech Tip
Make a multimedia presentation. See page H47 for ideas.

How Do I Reflect on My Writing?

When you reflect, you think about what you have written. You can think about what you did well, what you could do better next time, and what your goals are for your next writing assignment.

 You might want to keep a collection of some of your writing, such as favorite or unusual pieces.

Publishing a Description

Learning from a Model John made a neat, correct final copy of his description. He sent it to his grandmother with a picture of Stripe.

John Coghlan

My Strange Pet
by John Coghlan

Stripe is not your average lizard. He is a water dragon.

Stripe looks different from other lizards. I named him Stripe because he has a black line from his nose to the end of his tail. That's not natural because lizards are supposed to be all lime green. Stripe has about a nine-inch body that's round. His head is like an egg lying down, and his eyes are like bright yellow marbles. He has a long green tail that sticks up in the air. His skin looks scaly and smells like canola oil.

> These comparisons help me picture Stripe clearly.

For a seven-year-old, Stripe doesn't act his age. For example, he still hisses, which most lizards stop doing at three years old. He also has more energy than a dog before an earthquake. He stills gives scratches, which he can't help.

Stripe is pretty old, because a water dragon's life span is about ten years. I hope Stripe beats that. He's not your average lizard!

> Your ending connects to the beginning. This makes your paper feel finished.

▶ Publish Your Description

Make a neat final copy of your description. Give your description a title. Publish or share your description. Look at page 26 for ideas.

 Will you keep this description? Use the paragraph on page 26 to help you reflect on your writing experience.

See www.eduplace.com/kids/hme/ for more examples of student writing.

Part 1

Grammar, Usage, and Mechanics

What You Will Find in This Part:

Unit 1 The Sentence 31

Unit 2 Nouns 63

Unit 3 Verbs 95

Unit 4 Adjectives 151

Unit 5 Capitalization and Punctuation 179

Unit 6 Pronouns 215

Unit 7 Adverbs and Prepositions 245

Why Learn Grammar?

Informal Language

When you're with your friends or in other informal situations, you may not worry about using every word correctly. That's fine.

When you write in your diary or do other personal writing, it doesn't matter if every word or punctuation mark is correct. YOU know what you mean.

Formal Language

In school and in many situations outside of school, though, you need to use more formal language, both for speaking and for writing. This section of the book will help you develop your ability to use formal language when you need it.

Look closely. How many do you count? Together they become a sea of black and white. What a stunning sight they make!

Unit 1

The Sentence

Grammar

1 What Is a Sentence?

One-Minute Warm-Up

Try to make a sentence out of the words in the clouds. Do the words express a complete thought? If not, what words could complete the thought?

- A **sentence** is a group of words that expresses a complete thought. In order to express a complete thought, a sentence must tell *who* or *what*. It must also tell *what is* or *what happens*. A sentence begins with a capital letter and ends with a punctuation mark.

Sentences	
Lightning flashed in the sky.	The alert ranger spotted fire.

- A group of words that does not express a complete thought is called a **sentence fragment**. A fragment is not a sentence.

Sentence Fragments	
Flashed in the sky.	When the tree fell.
The alert ranger.	Soaked by rain.
During the storm.	Thunder in the distance.

Try It Out

Speak Up Which groups of words are sentences? Which groups of words are sentence fragments? Add words to the fragments to make them sentences.

1. A storm was coming.
2. Behind the pine tree.
3. A crack of thunder after the lightning.
4. Because the loud noise surprised us.
5. Luckily, the storm ended quickly.

On Your Own

Write the group of words in each pair that is a sentence.

Example: A tornado in the distance.
A tornado is a violent storm.   *A tornado is a violent storm.*

6. Tornadoes are dangerous.
   Winds of high speed.
7. They spin like tops.
   Often in the Midwest.
8. Can appear very suddenly.
   They appear as funnel-shaped clouds.
9. Such storms can be called waterspouts.
   When they occur over water.
10. Reaching speeds of 300 miles per hour.
    Everything in their path is destroyed.
11. Because of the spinning winds.
    They are more violent than hurricanes.

12–18. These notes on a reporter's laptop computer have seven sentences. Write each sentence.

Example: An approaching tornado.
No one predicted it.   *No one predicted it.*

Tornado Roars Through Town

The air feels heavy. I can't breathe. Suddenly a dark, whirling cloud. It's shaped like a funnel. It is racing across the fields. Toward the town. People point and run. A roar like a freight train. Whirling winds scoop up trees and houses. At last it is over. When people go out. Rubble everywhere.

Writing Wrap-Up WRITING • THINKING • LISTENING • SPEAKING

DESCRIBING

Write a News Report

Write a TV news report describing a bad storm. Use complete sentences. Read your report to a partner. Which details are most vivid?

Grammar/Mechanics
2 Four Kinds of Sentences

One-Minute Warm-Up

What is a penguin doing in the desert? What does the camel think about it? Make up their conversation, using a statement, a question, an order, and an exclamation.

There are four kinds of sentences. Each kind does a different job. All four kinds begin with a capital letter. The end mark varies, however.

 Tip
Use a variety of these sentence types in your writing.

The Four Kinds of Sentences	
A **declarative sentence** tells something. It ends with a period.	Deserts are dry.
An **interrogative sentence** asks something. It ends with a question mark.	Are deserts always hot?
An **imperative sentence** gives an order. It ends with a period.	Always carry water.
An **exclamatory sentence** expresses strong feeling. It ends with an exclamation point.	How hot it was! It was so hot!

Try It Out

Speak Up Identify each sentence as *declarative*, *interrogative*, *imperative*, or *exclamatory*. Which end punctuation would you use?

1. These mounds are called sand dunes
2. Do sand dunes stay in the same place
3. This is a terrible sandstorm
4. Try to protect your eyes from the dust
5. How thick the dust is

34 Unit 1: The Sentence

On Your Own

Write each sentence and add end punctuation. Then label each sentence *declarative, interrogative, imperative,* or *exclamatory.*

Example: The Sahara Desert is in Africa
The Sahara Desert is in Africa.   declarative

6. A program about deserts will be on TV
7. Please watch it
8. Isn't the Sahara the world's largest desert
9. How hot it must be there
10. Look for lots of camels on the program
11. Why are camels so useful in the desert
12. Camels can go for days without water

13–20. Write the eight sentences on this post card. Add end punctuation. Label each sentence *declarative, interrogative, imperative,* or *exclamatory.*

Example: I'm sending a big hello from Arizona
I'm sending a big hello from Arizona.   declarative

> How gorgeous it is here Have you heard of the Painted Desert Look at the picture on the card Can you guess the reason for its name The rocks glow in shades of red, yellow, blue, lavender, and white At times the hazy air looks pink or purple Try to imagine that What an incredible sight it is

Writing Wrap-Up
WRITING • THINKING • LISTENING • SPEAKING

EXPRESSING

Write a Post Card

What is your favorite place to go or thing to do? Write a post card to a friend telling about it and why you like it. Use each of the four kinds of sentences. Read your message to a partner. Have your partner name each kind of sentence.

For Extra Practice see page 56.   Four Kinds of Sentences

Grammar
3 Subjects and Predicates

One-Minute Warm-Up

Which four words tell whom or what this sentence is about? Which seven tell the action?

The early black aviators made a significant contribution to American history.

—from *Flying Free: America's First Black Aviators*, by Philip S. Hart

- Every sentence has two parts. **The subject tells whom or what the sentence is about. The predicate tells what the subject is or does.**

Subject	Predicate
Captain Ortega	is a good pilot.
The large jet	carries many people.

- **All the words in the subject make up the complete subject. All the words in the predicate make up the complete predicate.**
- The complete subject may be either one word or more than one word.

  Pilots waved.
  The pilots of the plane waved.
  The pilot and the copilot waved.

- The complete predicate may also be one word or more than one word.

  Several helicopters landed.
  Several helicopters landed in the field.

Try It Out

Speak Up Find the complete subject and the complete predicate in each sentence.

1. The jungles of Brazil are hot and rainy.
2. Many trees and bushes grow.
3. The Amazon River flows through Brazil.
4. This country has mountains and jungles.

36 Unit 1: The Sentence

On Your Own

Write each sentence. Draw a line between the complete subject and the complete predicate.

Example: Mr. Santos traveled on the Amazon River.
  Mr. Santos | traveled on the Amazon River.

5. He saw many turtles.
6. One of the birds screeched.
7. Another boat passed by.
8. Mr. Santos and the passengers waved.
9. A man near Mr. Santos took photographs.
10. Everyone enjoyed this trip.

11–20. This part of a magazine article has ten sentences. Write the article. Draw a line between each complete subject and complete predicate.

Example: The para nut may sound unfamiliar.
  The para nut | may sound unfamiliar.

Going Nuts!

You may have eaten a para nut without realizing it. *Para nut* and *cream nut* are names for a Brazil nut. This nut grows on trees in the Amazon River basin. The fruit of the tree looks like a coconut. The nuts are its seeds. About twenty nuts lie inside each fruit. Brazil nuts have a hard shell. They do not crack easily. Their taste makes the work worthwhile. They are delicious.

Writing Wrap-Up
WRITING • THINKING • LISTENING • SPEAKING

NARRATING

Write a Story Opening

You are a parrot in a jungle. How do you react when tourists walk below your favorite tree? Write the first paragraph of a story from the parrot's viewpoint. With a partner, check that each sentence has a subject and a predicate.

For Extra Practice see page 57.

Grammar

4 Simple Subjects

One-Minute Warm-Up

What are the complete subjects of these sentences? In each complete subject, which is the main word?

> Most fruit-eating bats find their way and locate food almost entirely by sight. Their large bulging eyes are a sign of their excellent vision.
>
> —from *Bat,* by Caroline Arnold

- You have learned that the complete subject contains all the words in the subject. **Every complete subject has a simple subject, the main word that tells whom or what the sentence is about.**

    Many bats live in caves.
    They sleep during the day.
    The body of the bat is small.
    The bat's wings are very large.

- The simple subject can sometimes be exactly the same as the complete subject.

    Bats look like mice with wings.

- Sometimes the simple subject may be several words that name a person or a place.

    Linda Lee Carver showed us a picture of a bat.
    South America is the home of many bats.

Try It Out

Speak Up The complete subject is underlined in each sentence below. What is the simple subject?

1. Cavefish live in dark underwater caves.
2. Kim Lee told us about cavefish.
3. These fish lack ordinary eyesight.
4. Their other senses take the place of sight.
5. Everyone in my class enjoyed listening to Kim Lee.

38   Unit 1: The Sentence

On Your Own

Write each underlined subject. Draw a line under the simple subject.

Example: The Robins family moved to New Mexico.   *The Robins family*

6. Matt Robins liked his new home.
7. His family visited Carlsbad Caverns.
8. Carlsbad Caverns are caves.
9. Several of the caves are open to the public.
10. Matt's family took a tour.
11. Some of the rocks hung from the ceiling.
12. Others rose from the floor.
13. The pretty colors surprised everyone.

14–22. These tour guidelines have nine sentences. Write the underlined complete subject of each sentence. Then draw a line under the simple subject.

Example: All visitors must show their tickets.   *All visitors*

Welcome to Deep Down Caves

Take Care in Our Caves A visit to a cave is unlike any other tour. These guidelines will help you.

- A pair of comfortable shoes is a must.
- A light jacket is best. It will keep you warm.
- Mike Ryan is your guide and your boss.
- Caves are fragile. A touch can do damage.
- Anything beyond the walkway is off limits.

 WRITING • THINKING • LISTENING • SPEAKING

INFORMING

Write a Speech

If you were guiding a group of new students around your school, what would you tell them? Write your remarks. Read them to a partner. Have your partner ask questions about anything that is unclear.

For Extra Practice see page 58.

Grammar

5 Simple Predicates

One-Minute Warm-Up

Which group of words tells what Sarah Nade did? Which word is the most important? What other words could you replace it with?

> Sarah Nade sang a spectacular song onstage with her brother Lemo Nade.

- You know that the complete predicate contains all the words in the predicate. **In the complete predicate, the simple predicate is the one main word that tells what the subject is or does.** The simple predicate is also called the verb.

    Abigail **runs** to her voice class.
    She **sings**.
    This **is** her favorite activity.

- The simple predicate may be more than one word. There may be a main verb and one or more helping verbs.

    Abigail **has sung** in many musicals.
    She **will be performing** again tonight.
    My favorite musical **was performed** last month.

Try It Out

Speak Up The complete predicate is underlined in each sentence below. What is the simple predicate?

1. Louis Armstrong sang with many jazz bands.
2. He has been called a great singer.
3. He became very famous as a trumpet player.
4. People have been copying his musical style for years.
5. Armstrong was hired by many concert halls.
6. Armstrong played the trumpet brilliantly.
7. His hit songs will be played for a long time.

Unit 1: The Sentence

On Your Own

Each complete predicate is underlined. Write the complete predicate. Then draw a line under the simple predicate.

Example: Bessie Smith sang sad songs.   *sang sad songs*

8. Her songs were called "the blues."
9. Bessie performed in many places.
10. She traveled in a special railroad car.
11. "Queen of the Blues" was written on the car.
12. Blues lovers remain great fans of hers.
13. Thousands have bought her recordings.
14. Fans have been collecting them for years.
15. They are being played still.

16–24. This part of a biography has nine sentences. Write each complete predicate. Then draw a line under the simple predicate.

Example: Stephen Foster wrote more than two hundred songs.
wrote more than two hundred songs.

Music Pioneers

An American Musical Genius

Stephen Foster was born in 1826 in Pennsylvania. He showed musical talent very early. He was playing the clarinet at the age of six. Foster received little formal musical training.

Foster has become a popular American songwriter. "My Old Kentucky Home" is one of his melodies. Foster produced the words and the music for most of his works. This composer would sell his new songs at low prices. Foster created many memorable American songs.

Writing Wrap-Up   WRITING • THINKING • LISTENING • SPEAKING

SUMMARIZING

Write a Biography

Think of a person you admire. Write the first paragraph of his or her biography. Use complete sentences. Read your work to a group. Have listeners list each simple predicate.

For Extra Practice see page 59.

Grammar

6 Subjects in Imperatives

One-Minute Warm-Up

Arrange these words into a sentence that begins with the verb. What is the subject?

tonight   performance   at   the   watch   school

- You have learned that the subject of a sentence tells whom or what the sentence is about.

    Dan is in the play.
    You are going tonight.
    Plays can be fun.

- **In an imperative sentence, *you* is always the subject.** It is usually not stated in the sentence. We say that *you* is the "understood" subject.

    Imperative: **(You)** Please bring your camera.
                      (You) Take lots of pictures.

Try It Out

Speak Up What is the simple subject of each sentence below? Which sentences are imperative?

1. Find three seats.
2. Dac will sit beside me.
3. Watch the blue curtain.
4. Look at that fancy costume.
5. My brother is the king.
6. The audience loves this play.
7. Everyone is sitting very quietly.
8. Please read this name to me.
9. Clap as hard as you can.
10. I really enjoyed that play.

On Your Own

Write the simple subject of each sentence.

Example: Look in the newspaper. *(You)*

11. I want to go to the movies.
12. Movies about real people interest me.
13. Please buy me two tickets.
14. Listen to the exciting music.
15. The hero really climbed that mountain.
16. Tell my sister about this movie.
17. She is interested in mountain climbing.
18. Remember the name of that mountain.

19–28. Write each of the ten sentences in this movie review. Label the sentence *imperative* or *declarative*. Then write the simple subject.

Example: You should read this movie review.
You should read this movie review.   declarative   You

MOVIE REVIEWS

Scrap *Screamers*

My job is to review movies. Otherwise I would not have sat through *Screamers*. My readers do *not* have to suffer. Take my advice. Avoid this movie. Do not even walk past the theater. You might be crushed by movie patrons running out and screaming. The title of *Screamers* describes the audience. Ask some viewers. Listen to them scream.

Writing Wrap-Up   WRITING • THINKING • LISTENING • SPEAKING

EVALUATING

Write a Review

What movie, TV program, or play have you seen? Write a review. Use at least three declarative sentences and two imperative sentences. Read your review to a partner. Compare the performances you wrote about.

Grammar/Usage

7 Conjunctions

One-Minute Warm-Up

Which word joins two number words? two sentences?

Many people think puffins are two or three feet tall, but they are really only about the height of a jug of milk—about ten inches.

—from *Project Puffin: How We Brought Puffins Back to Egg Rock*, by Stephen W. Kress

- **Words that connect other words or groups of words in a sentence are called conjunctions.** Words such as *and, but,* and *or* are conjunctions.
- Conjunctions can connect two subjects, two predicates, or two sentences.

    Gulls and puffins are sea birds.   They swim and dive well.
    Gulls soar, and puffins swim gracefully.

- Conjunctions can also connect other words in a sentence.

    Sam walked quickly but quietly.   He did not see any puffins or gulls.
    He looked on the cliff and near the shore.

- When you write, use the conjunction that best expresses your meaning.

Conjunction	Use	Example
and	joins together	Swans and penguins swim.
but	shows contrast	Swans live on ponds, but penguins do not.
or	shows choice	Penguins slide or waddle.

Try It Out

Speak Up What is the conjunction in each of these sentences?

1. Parrots live in wild places or in zoos.
2. Their beaks and feet are good for climbing.
3. Tame parrots are friendly and loyal to their owners.
4. Most parrots live in jungles, but some live in grasslands.
5. They eat seeds and drink at water holes.

Unit 1: The Sentence

On Your Own

Write each sentence, adding the conjunction that best expresses the meaning shown in parentheses.

Example: Hawks are large, _____ eagles are even bigger. (shows contrast)
Hawks are large, but eagles are even bigger.

6. This bird appears fierce, proud, _____ courageous. (joins together)
7. The eagle has inspired Roman warriors, Russian emperors, _____ United States presidents. (joins together)
8. The bald eagle has white feathers on its head, _____ some think it looks bald. (shows contrast)
9. Eagles build nests on cliffs _____ in tall trees. (shows choice)
10. Eagles soar easily, _____ they walk clumsily. (shows contrast)

11–18. Write this part of a science report. Underline the eight conjunctions. Then write the meaning that each conjunction expresses.

Example: Hummingbirds are tiny but brave.
Hummingbirds are tiny but brave.   shows contrast

The Amazing Hummingbird

Hummingbirds are small and colorful. Their legs are weak, but their wings are strong. The wings beat fast and make a humming sound. The birds can fly up or down, backwards or sideways. They can hang in the air and drink from a flower. They usually lay two eggs, and the babies are featherless. Grass, bark, or cobwebs hold the nest together.

Writing Wrap-Up
WRITING • THINKING • LISTENING • SPEAKING

COMPARING / CONTRASTING

Write a Science Report

Write a science report. In one paragraph, tell how eagles and hummingbirds are alike. In another, tell how they differ. Use one conjunction in each sentence. Ask a partner to question you about anything that is unclear.

Revising Strategies

Writing Good Sentences

Combining Sentences: Compound Sentences To avoid choppy writing, combine two or more short sentences that have related ideas. Place a comma and a conjunction—a connecting word such as *and, but,* or *or*—between the sentences.

Bats make calls in flight.
These sounds bounce off objects in their way.

Bats make calls in flight, and these sounds bounce off objects in their way.

Apply It

1–4. Read these sentences from a Web page. Use the conjunction in parentheses to combine the sentences after each number.

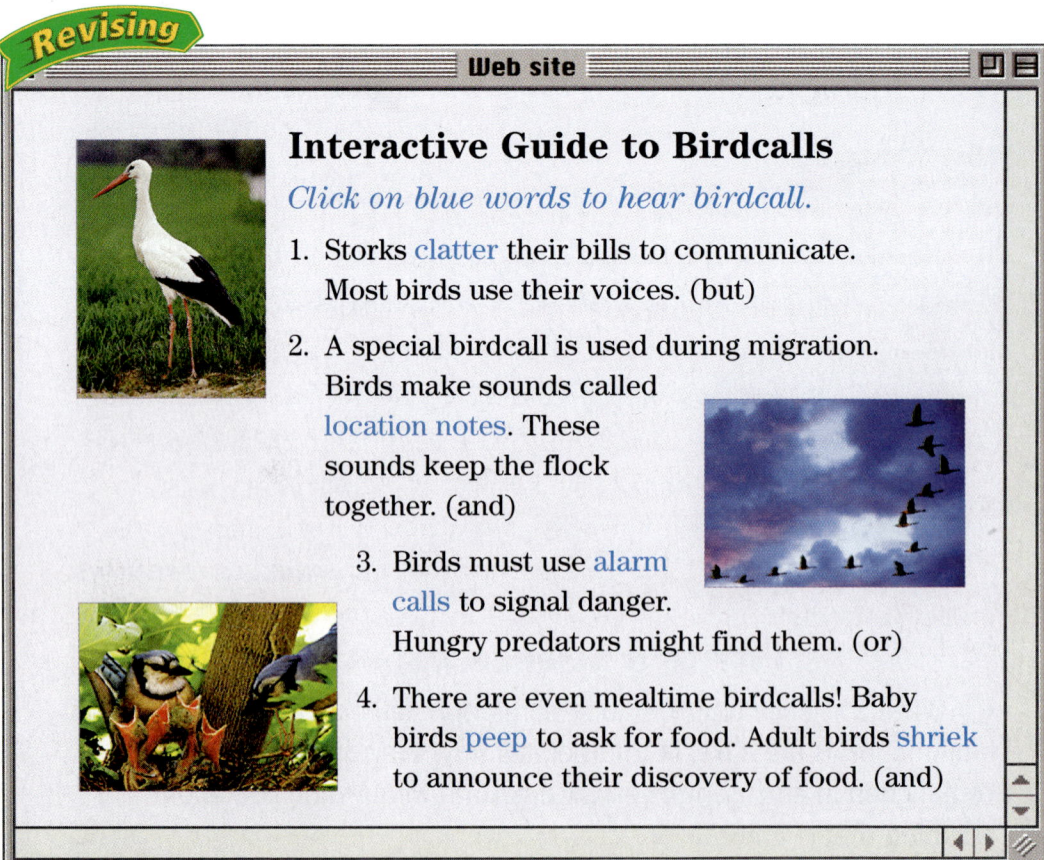

Revising

Interactive Guide to Birdcalls

Click on blue words to hear birdcall.

1. Storks clatter their bills to communicate. Most birds use their voices. (but)

2. A special birdcall is used during migration. Birds make sounds called location notes. These sounds keep the flock together. (and)

3. Birds must use alarm calls to signal danger. Hungry predators might find them. (or)

4. There are even mealtime birdcalls! Baby birds peep to ask for food. Adult birds shriek to announce their discovery of food. (and)

46 Unit 1: The Sentence

Sentence Fluency

Avoiding Stringy Sentences

Stringy sentences go on and on without a pause. Good writers break up stringy sentences by putting related ideas in separate sentences that are easier to read. The new sentences can be short, containing one idea, or compound, containing two ideas.

When you combine two ideas in a compound sentence, use a conjunction, such as *and*, *but*, or *or*, to make the meaning clear!

Swans are graceful water birds and they belong to the same family as ducks and geese and they are more closely related to geese. ⟶ Swans are graceful water birds. They belong to the same family as ducks and geese, but they are more closely related to geese.

Apply It

5–8. Break up the four stringy sentences in this part of a science report. Write single ideas as short sentences, or use conjunctions to write pairs of ideas as compound sentences.

Swans are known for their long, graceful necks and swans have short legs like those of ducks and they have webbed feet too. Swans have white feathers and duck feathers are usually dark and ducks are also smaller than swans.

Swans eat water plants and their bills have jagged edges and their tongues have spines. These features help the swans as they feed on the water plants.

Mute swans are white and they have orange bills and they are quieter than most swans. Mute swans are very common in North America.

Writing Good Sentences 47

Usage/Mechanics

8 Run-on Sentences

One-Minute Warm-Up

What's wrong with the punctuation in this sentence? How can you fix it?

My brother is a diamond cutter he mows the grass at the baseball stadium.

- A **run-on sentence** is two or more sentences that are run together with commas or without any punctuation. One way to correct a run-on sentence is to make it into a compound sentence. You form a compound sentence by using a conjunction, such as *and, but,* or *or* to connect the sentences.

 Tip
Use a comma before the conjunction in a compound sentence.

Run-on: Some jobs require special clothing these clothes provide protection.

Corrected: Some jobs require special clothing, and these clothes provide protection.

- Another way to correct a run-on sentence is to divide it into separate sentences.

Run-on: Electricians often wear rubber gloves, electricity cannot go through rubber.

Corrected: Electricians often wear rubber gloves. Electricity cannot go through rubber.

Try It Out

Speak Up Which sentences are correct, and which are run-ons? What is one way to correct each run-on sentence?

1. Some dancers wear special shoes the toes are stiff.
2. Rita is a police officer, her badge tells her rank.
3. Clowns paint their faces, and they wear funny costumes and colorful wigs.
4. Pete often walks in mud his boots keep his feet dry.
5. Ms. Lam is a judge her robe is black.

48 Unit 1: The Sentence

On Your Own

Rewrite each run-on sentence correctly. Use a comma before each conjunction.

Example: Climbers should wear spiked shoes they might fall.
Climbers should wear spiked shoes, or they might fall.

6. Scuba divers often dive into cold water special rubber suits keep them warm.
7. Lifeguards wear bright bathing suits, these are easily spotted.
8. People fish for trout in deep water high boots keep their legs very dry.
9. Carpenters wear overalls with many pockets, a special belt holds their nails.
10. Pitchers throw baseballs very fast catchers must wear face masks.
11. Astronauts wear space suits these suits let them move in space.
12. Scott is a figure skater he moves like the wind.
13. Jockeys' trousers are white, their jackets are colorful.

14–18. This ad has five run-on sentences. Write the ad correctly.

Example: Put this hat on you won't take it off.
Put this hat on, and you won't take it off.

Proofreading

Whether It's Sunny or Dreary, Put on Your Dearie!

Outdoor workers and walkers should not be without one. Use it in the sun use it in the rain. Wear it at work wear it at play. Put it on when you're at the beach, it will give great protection. What is this new product? It's a Dearie Umbrella Hat. It is practical, it is cute too. Buy two or three keep one with you at all times.

Writing Wrap-Up
WRITING • THINKING • LISTENING • SPEAKING

PERSUADING

Write an Ad

What product would you like to see invented? Write an ad for this amazing invention. Avoid run-on sentences. Read your ad to a classmate, and ask which sentence is most convincing.

Enrichment

Haiku

Pick something that you like in nature, and write a one-sentence haiku on that topic. A haiku is a short Japanese poem. Most haiku have three lines and seventeen syllables. The first line has five syllables, the second line has seven, and the third line has five. Draw a picture to illustrate your haiku.

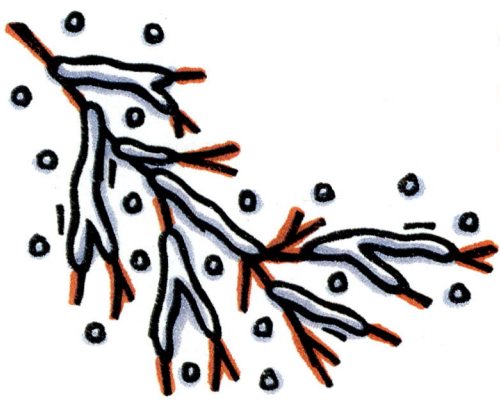

(5) One lacy snowflake
(7) Falls and adds its delicate
(5) Beauty to a branch.

Scrambled Messages

Solve this scrambled message. Match each subject with the right predicate. (Subjects are in order.) *Hint:* The message is from the American Revolution.

Challenge Create your own scrambled message from history. Exchange with a classmate and unscramble each other's message.

> The British soldiers must be protected! Our families and homes should bring a weapon and food to the village green tonight. Every man are coming!

Checkup: Unit 1

1. What Is a Sentence? *(p. 32)*
Write *sentence* or *fragment* for each group of words.

1. A tornado hit the barn.
2. In the middle of the day.
3. Since it happened so fast.
4. I had never seen a twister.
5. Just the noise of the storm alone.
6. Afterward, how still it was!

2. Four Kinds of Sentences
(p. 34) Copy each sentence, and add the correct end punctuation. Then write *declarative, interrogative, imperative,* or *exclamatory* to identify each of the sentences.

7. What an exciting movie we saw
8. It was about the adventures of a brave knight
9. What happened in the movie
10. Listen to the knight's tales
11. He rescued the king's son from many dangers
12. How the crowd cheered
13. What is the movie called

3. Complete Subjects and Predicates *(p. 36)*
Copy each sentence. Draw a line between the complete subject and the complete predicate.

14. A helicopter flies over the city.
15. A reporter observes the traffic.
16. Cars and trucks crawl along.
17. Drivers turn on their radios.
18. The announcer lists any accidents.
19. News about the traffic is helpful.

4. Simple Subjects and Predicates *(pp. 38, 40)*
Copy each sentence. Underline the simple subject once. Underline the simple predicate twice.

20. The parade has started late.
21. Everyone in our band is marching.
22. The musicians play a lively tune.
23. Rosa's instrument is gleaming.
24. A huge float will appear next.
25. Bunches of flowers cover the float.
26. Jen James is waving at us.
27. Several of the children have balloons.

5. Subjects in Imperatives
(p. 42) For each sentence, write *declarative* or *imperative.* Then write the simple subject of the sentence.

28. Buy four tickets for the concert.
29. Ask for seats in the front row.
30. I love banjo music.
31. Jay is my favorite musician.
32. Please don't forget your money.
33. We will get the tickets today.
34. Get to the box office early.

6. Conjunctions *(p. 44)*
Choose the conjunction in parentheses that best fits each sentence. Then write the meaning that each conjunction expresses.

35. Sue (and, but) I were lost.
36. We needed a map (or, but) a good compass.
37. Should we go east (but, or) west?

See www.eduplace.com/kids/hme/ for an online quiz.

Checkup 51

Checkup continued

38. We had water (but, or) no food.
39. Sue was nervous, (but, or) I stayed calm.
40. A park ranger came (and, or) helped us.

7 Run-on Sentences (p. 48)
Correct each of these run-on sentences.

41. Japan's four main islands are Honshu, Hokkaido, Kyushu, and Shikoku the capital of Japan is located on the Kanto Plain on Honshu.
42. Japan is a chain of many islands the islands are covered by hills there are a few flat plains.
43. Japan has very little farmland, some farmers carve out flat areas on hillsides.
44. Some of the fields are flooded with water every year then rice is planted there.
45. Rice is planted in the spring the crop must be tended all summer the harvest is in the fall.
46. Japanese farmers are experts at growing rice they produce large crops.

Mixed Review 47–54. This part of a short story has three incorrect or missing end marks, three incorrect conjunctions, and two run-on sentences. Write the story correctly.

Proofreading Checklist
Look for the following:
✓ incorrect end punctuation
✓ incorrect conjunctions
✓ run-on sentences

Proofreading

Pepe's Most Wonderful Day

The sky had been clear all day, or now some dark clouds were moving in. Was it going to rain. Pepe didn't care he was walking on air a few puddles wouldn't bother him. Still, he had a long way to go, and he began to walk faster

What an absolutely amazing day this had been? It may have been the best day of his whole life. The streets were busy and crowded, and Pepe didn't notice anything around him. He just kept thinking about the day. Had he dreamed the whole thing, and had it really happened? Pepe just couldn't stop smiling then all of a sudden, the rain poured down.

Unit 1: The Sentence

Assessment Link

Test Practice

Write the numbers 1–8 on a sheet of paper. For questions 1–4, read each sentence. Choose the underlined part that is the simple subject of the sentence. Write the letter for that answer.

1. The <u>books</u> on this <u>shelf</u> <u>belong</u> to my <u>sister</u>.
       A   B   C   D

2. <u>Some</u> of the <u>students</u> <u>performed</u> in the <u>talent show</u>.
     F   G   H   J

3. <u>Several friends</u> <u>worked</u> together on this <u>project</u>.
     A   B   C   D

4. That <u>police officer</u> <u>gave</u> us <u>directions</u> to the <u>shopping mall</u>.
         F   G   H   J

For questions 5–8, read each sentence. Choose the underlined part that is the simple predicate of the sentence. Write the letter for that answer.

5. <u>Mr. Bernardo</u> <u>wrote</u> a <u>letter</u> to his <u>grandchildren</u>.
       A   B   C   D

6. The <u>people</u> of our <u>town</u> <u>have voted</u> for a new <u>mayor</u>.
      F   G   H   J

7. Please <u>wipe</u> your <u>feet</u> on the <u>mat</u> beside the <u>door</u>.
      A   B   C   D

8. The <u>woman</u> in the <u>seat</u> behind <u>us</u> <u>was knitting</u>.
      F   G   H   J

✓ Test Practice continued

Now write numbers 9–16 on your paper. Choose the sentence that is written correctly. Write the letter for that answer.

9 A How far are we from the amusement park!
   B We have walked three miles, and my legs are tired.
   C Me and Ian are ready to return.
   D Why didn't we take the bus.

10 F I can't find no wrapping paper for the gift.
   G Please show me how to tie the ribbon.
   H Have you signed you're name on the card yet?
   J This is a great gift Emile will love it.

11 A The moon is closest to Earth than the stars.
   B My father has a telescope I use it sometimes.
   C You can also see Venus, Mercury, and Jupiter.
   D Do you think humans will ever travel to Mars.

12 F Three firetrucks are racing down Green river road.
   G A old barn has caught on fire.
   H Firefighters quick put it out.
   J The cows and horses are safe in a pasture.

13 A Does anyone know where Mom left her glasses.
   B Let's all look she can't drive without them.
   C Mom weared the glasses to the movie theater last night.
   D Robby will look in Mom's bag.

14 F Nell bought a used bike that had a flat tire.
   G She taked off the flat tire and put a patch on it.
   H The brakes were squeaky she oiled them.
   J Now that bike works good.

15 A Their is a computer in our classroom.
   B Students takes turns using it.
   C Our teacher put some great games on the computer.
   D We can play they during recess or quiet time.

16 F The days seem so long in june and july.
   G What time does the sun set.
   H We go to bed later in summer than in winter.
   J Summer don't last long enough for us.

54 Unit 1: The Sentence

Extra Practice

1. What Is a Sentence?
(pages 32–33)

- A **sentence** is a group of words that expresses a complete thought.
- A **sentence fragment** is a group of words that does not express a complete thought.

● Copy the complete sentence in each pair.

Example: The rain ruined our picnic. Ate sandwiches in the car.
The rain ruined our picnic.

1. A very bad storm. The sun came out.
2. Blew across the lake. The breeze made little waves.
3. Yesterday at the cottage. The rain started to fall.
4. When it rained in June. July may bring better weather.
5. The child is afraid of thunder. A bolt of lightning suddenly.

▲ Copy each group of words that is a sentence. Write *sentence fragment* for each group of words that is not a sentence.

Example: The bright sun.   *sentence fragment*

6. We practiced yesterday.
7. During the soccer game.
8. The fog rolled in.
9. Covered the field.
10. We could not see the ball.

■ If the group of words is a sentence, write *sentence*.
If it is a sentence fragment, add words to make it a complete sentence.

Example: On a windy morning.   *I flew a kite on a windy morning.*

11. Last winter in Vermont.
12. I wore boots and a heavy coat.
13. Covered with soft snow.
14. Clouds hung over the mountain.
15. Coldest winter in fifteen years.

Extra Practice

(pages 34–35)

2 Four Kinds of Sentences

- A **declarative** sentence tells something and ends with a period.
- An **interrogative** sentence asks something and ends with a question mark.
- An **imperative** sentence gives an order and ends with a period.
- An **exclamatory** sentence expresses strong feeling and ends with an exclamation point.

● Copy each sentence, and add the correct end punctuation. The kind of sentence is shown in parentheses.

Example: Camels are useful in deserts (declarative)
Camels are useful in deserts.

1. Study a picture of a camel (imperative)
2. How many humps does a camel have (interrogative)
3. Camels may have one or two humps (declarative)
4. What good travelers camels are (exclamatory)

▲ Copy each sentence, and add the correct end punctuation. Label each sentence *declarative, interrogative, imperative,* or *exclamatory.*

Example: Is the Gobi Desert in Asia or Africa
Is the Gobi Desert in Asia or Africa? (interrogative)

5. The Gobi Desert is in northeastern Asia
6. Find it on this map of the world
7. What a huge desert it is
8. How do people live in a desert

■ Answer each question by writing a complete sentence. Write the kind of sentence shown in parentheses.

Example: Do you want to visit a desert? (declarative)
I would love to visit a desert.

9. What should I wear in a desert? (imperative)
10. What will the weather be like? (declarative)
11. Should I take a jug of water? (imperative)
12. How will I find my way? (declarative)

Unit 1: The Sentence

Extra Practice

(pages 36–37)

3 Subjects and Predicates

- A sentence has two parts, a subject and a predicate.
- The **subject** tells whom or what the sentence is about.
- The **predicate** tells what the subject is or does.
- The **complete subject** contains all the words in the subject.
- The **complete predicate** contains all the words in the predicate.

● Copy each sentence. Include the line that separates the complete subject from the complete predicate. Underline the part named in parentheses.

Example: Peru and Chile | are South American countries. (predicate)
Peru and Chile | <u>are South American countries</u>.

1. A large part of Peru | is in the Andes Mountains. (subject)
2. The people in the mountains | live in small villages. (predicate)
3. Their houses | are made from sun-dried bricks. (predicate)
4. Most people | are farmers and shepherds. (subject)

▲ Copy the sentences below. Underline the complete subject once and the complete predicate twice.

Example: Brazil covers nearly half of South America.
<u>Brazil</u> <u>covers nearly half of South America</u>.

5. Portuguese explorers came to Brazil in 1500.
6. This country was a Portuguese colony until 1822.
7. Dom Pedro ruled Brazil from 1822 to 1831.
8. The main language of Brazil is Portuguese.

■ Write complete sentences by adding words to the following subjects and predicates. Use correct capitalization and end punctuation.

Example: the small boats   *The small boats sailed on the river.*

9. the tourists
10. the noisy birds
11. is hiding behind that tree
12. paddled a canoe

Extra Practice

4 Simple Subjects

(pages 38–39)

- The **simple subject** is the main word or words in the complete subject. It tells whom or what the sentence is about.

● Choose a simple subject from the words in the box to complete each sentence. Then write each sentence.

sounds
Grand Canyon
trip
eagle
rocks
Uncle Larry

Example: _____ hiked in the Grand Canyon.
Uncle Larry hiked in the Grand Canyon.

1. His two-day _____ was exciting.
2. An _____ flew above him.
3. Noisy _____ of wildlife filled the night.
4. The _____ was carved out by the Colorado River.
5. The _____ in the Grand Canyon are very colorful.

▲ The complete subject is underlined in each sentence. Copy each complete subject. Then underline the simple subject.

Example: <u>My family</u> went camping in Acadia National Park.   *My family*

6. <u>Acadia National Park</u> is on Mount Desert Island in Maine.
7. <u>The island</u> has seventeen peaks.
8. <u>A long, winding road</u> goes to the top.
9. <u>The view at sunrise</u> is beautiful.
10. <u>Everyone in my family</u> got up early to see it.

■ Write the complete subject of each sentence. Then underline the simple subject.

Example: Hoover Dam is considered a tall dam.   *Hoover Dam*

11. The walls of the dam are steep and very white.
12. The clear water is bright blue against the white walls.
13. Aunt Alice sent us a picture of the dam.
14. This huge dam controls the Colorado River.
15. Towns in a wide area are provided with electric power.
16. Aunt Alice's trip to the Hoover Dam was very interesting.

58   Unit 1: The Sentence

5 Simple Predicates

(pages 40–41)

- The **simple predicate**, or verb, is the main word or words in the complete predicate. It tells what the subject is or does.
- The simple predicate may be more than one word. It may be a main verb and a helping verb.

● Choose a simple predicate from the words in the box to complete each sentence. Then write the sentences.

Example: Jeff _____ onto the stage.   *Jeff walks onto the stage.*

1. The musicians _____ their instruments.
2. Jeff _____ his song.
3. People _____ their hands to the music.
4. They _____ the concert tonight.
5. There _____ a party after the concert.

> are clapping
> will be
> play
> are enjoying
> sings
> walks

▲ The complete predicate is underlined in each sentence. Copy each complete predicate. Then underline the simple predicate.

Example: Our class saw an opera last week.   *saw an opera last week*

6. *Hansel and Gretel* is the name of the opera.
7. The story has been enjoyed for years.
8. Two children are wandering in the woods.
9. A mean woman keeps them in her house.
10. The children finally escape.

■ Write the complete predicate of each sentence. Then underline the simple predicate.

Example: An opera is a musical drama.   *is a musical drama*

11. That woman is singing an aria.
12. An aria is sung by one person.
13. Many operas contain dances and fancy costumes.
14. The opera *Carmen* will run for ten weeks in Atlanta.
15. Janet will be going to the last performance.

Extra Practice

6 Subjects in Imperatives (pages 42–43)

- The subject of an imperative sentence is *you*.
- Usually the word *you* is understood, not stated.

● Four of the sentences below are imperative. Copy each imperative sentence, and put the subject in parentheses.

Example: Come into the theater.   *Come into the theater. (You)*

1. Read the program quietly.
2. Now watch the stage.
3. The Smiths enjoy the dancing.
4. Sit here next to my brother.
5. Remember the first three songs.
6. We will listen to the CD at home.

▲ Label each sentence *declarative* or *imperative*. Then write the subject of each sentence.

Example: Peter is an actor.   *declarative   Peter*

7. Go to one of his films.
8. Listen to his musical voice.
9. One film was a great success.
10. Peter was a clever director.
11. Please tell me the name of that film.
12. You can rent it at the video store.

■ If the sentence is imperative, rewrite it as declarative. If it is declarative, rewrite it as imperative.

Example: Look at this list.   *Marilyn looks at this list.*

13. She is reading it aloud.
14. Count the actors in this play.
15. Eric will play the part of the robot.
16. He moves his arms stiffly.
17. Close the curtain after the last scene.
18. Discuss the play with the audience.

Unit 1: The Sentence

Extra Practice

7 Conjunctions

(pages 44–45)

- A **conjunction** is a word that connects words or groups of words.
- *And, but,* and *or* are conjunctions.

● Write the conjunction in each sentence.

Example: All penguins can swim fast, but none can fly. *but*

1. Penguins paddle with their webbed feet, but they can also walk.
2. Wild storms and high waves hardly bother penguins.
3. Penguins eat all summer, and their fat protects them.
4. One parent or the other sits on the eggs.
5. The newborn chicks are protected and fed.
6. The chicks lose their down and grow feathers.

▲ Write the conjunction that fits each sentence better.

Example: A puffin's wings are short (and, or) stubby. *and*

7. The puffins can dive deep (or, but) swim a long distance.
8. Puffins eat small fish (but, and) shrimp.
9. Some puffins feed on the surface, (or, but) others dive for food.
10. Most birds fly well, (but, or) puffins fly poorly.
11. The puffin's beak (and, but) webbed feet are bright red.
12. Explorers (and, but) sailors have hunted these birds.

■ Complete each sentence, using the conjunction that expresses the meaning in parentheses.

Example: Owls hunt at night _____ rest during the day. (joins together)
Owls hunt at night and rest during the day.

13. The tiny elf owl is the size of a sparrow, _____ the great gray owl is three feet long. (shows contrast)
14. All owls have large eyes _____ excellent vision. (joins together)
15. Owls cannot move their eyes, _____ their heads can turn in almost any direction. (shows contrast)
16. Their feathers have soft edges, _____ their flight is silent. (joins together)

Extra Practice **61**

Extra Practice

8 Run-on Sentences (pages 48–49)

- A **run-on sentence** is two or more sentences that are run together with commas or without any punctuation.
- Correct a run-on sentence by making separate sentences or by making a compound sentence.

● Correct each run-on sentence. Separate each one into two sentences.

Example: Football is dangerous players wear helmets and pads.
Football is dangerous. Players wear helmets and pads.

1. In the past, they wore shorts their legs were not protected.
2. In 1878 heavier uniforms were used pads were required.
3. Most players wore leather helmets, some wore canvas ones.
4. Modern helmets are hard they also have chin straps.
5. Players today also wear heavy pads these pads protect their bodies.

▲ If the sentence is correct, write *correct*. If it is a run-on sentence, rewrite it correctly.

Example: *Peter Pan* is a great play I have seen it many times.
Peter Pan is a great play. I have seen it many times.

6. Peter Pan is not really flying we are fooled by special effects.
7. The actor hangs from wires, and a fan creates wind.
8. Designers build a pirate ship the stage itself becomes a ship's deck.
9. They construct huge rocks out of paper, each weighs only a pound.

■ If the sentence is correct, write *correct*. If it is a run-on sentence, rewrite it correctly.

Example: Beth owns a horse named Rusty he is a great jumper.
Beth owns a horse named Rusty. He is a great jumper.

10. Rusty went to the Olympics he competed against other horses.
11. A man rode Rusty in the Olympics, he wore a red jacket.
12. Rusty won two medals one was a silver medal the other was a gold medal.
13. We could not go to the Olympics we watched Rusty on television.
14. I saw Rusty's picture on a magazine cover I sent it to Beth.

Unit 2

Nouns

Their smiles say it all—the Cyclones are the best players in town!

Grammar
1 What Is a Noun?

One-Minute Warm-Up

It's rhyme time! What rhyming word that names a person, place, thing, or idea can complete each word group?

a big _____   a long _____   a green _____
the main _____   a grand _____   a rare _____

- **A word that names a person, a place, or a thing is called a noun.**

  Pablo lives in a house on my street.

  His grandparents came from Puerto Rico.

- Notice that the noun *Puerto Rico* is two words that name one place. Nouns can be two or more words.

Nouns		
Persons	boy student	writer Tammy Robbins
Places	lake country	field New York City
Things	boat calendar	sweater basketball

- Nouns can also name feelings, thoughts, and ideas.

  excitement   fear   freedom   anger   happiness

Try It Out

Speak Up Which words in each sentence are nouns?

1. The students planned a party.
2. The band played happy, loud music.
3. Excitement filled the air!
4. Pedro Casals won a prize.
5. The bandstand was covered with ribbons.

64 Unit 2: Nouns

On Your Own

Write each noun. Then write whether it names a person, a place, a thing, or an idea.

Example: river   *river   place*

6. candle
7. juggler
8. Statue of Liberty
9. South America
10. friendliness
11. Luisa Perez

Write each noun in these sentences.

Example: Mexico is a beautiful country.   *Mexico   country*

12. Maria Rodrigo and her parents enjoyed the trip.
13. An exciting festival was held in Veracruz.
14. People in colorful costumes filled the streets.
15. The vacation was a great thrill for the Rodrigos.

16–30. This part of a travel brochure has fifteen nouns. Write each noun.

Example: More tourists discover the area every day.
tourists   area   day.

Visit the land of flowers and festivals!

The state of Veracruz in Mexico is a feast for travelers. Visit its beaches and mountains. Learn its fascinating history and culture. Travel from the Gulf of Mexico to the mountains of the Sierra Madre.

Writing Wrap-Up
WRITING • THINKING • LISTENING • SPEAKING

PERSUADING

Write a Travel Brochure

Write a paragraph for a travel brochure about someplace you really enjoyed visiting. Include details that will convince your readers to visit there. In a small group, take turns reading your paragraphs aloud. Did your words convince classmates?

For Extra Practice see page 89.

Grammar/Mechanics
2 Common and Proper Nouns

One-Minute Warm-Up

Which words in this sentence are nouns? Why are some of the nouns capitalized?

> While she was still a toddler, Mae and her family moved to the big city of Chicago, Illinois.
>
> —from *Mae Jemison: Space Scientist*, by Gail Sakurai

- When you talk or write about persons, places, or things in general, you use a **common noun**. When you talk or write about a particular person, place, or thing, you use a **proper noun**.

  Common: Scientists come from many countries.

  Proper: Marie Curie was a scientist from Poland.

- Capitalize every proper noun. If it is more than one word, capitalize only the important words. Do not capitalize words such as *the, of,* or *for*.

Common Nouns	Proper Nouns	Common Nouns	Proper Nouns
street	North Drive	river	Hudson River
city	Vancouver	building	White House
state	Maryland	poet	Emily Dickinson
continent	Asia	holiday	Fourth of July
ocean	Arctic Ocean	month	November
mountain	Mt. McKinley	day	Monday

- When you use the words for family relationships as names, capitalize them. Otherwise, do not capitalize those words.

  A science magazine interviewed Mom.   My dad teaches chemistry.

Try It Out

Speak Up Which words are proper nouns and should be capitalized? Which words are common nouns?

1. august
2. face
3. san diego
4. gulf of mexico
5. program
6. francis scott key

66 Unit 2: Nouns

On Your Own

Write each pair of nouns. Capitalize the proper noun.

Example: thanksgiving day—holiday   *Thanksgiving Day—holiday*

7. india—country
8. president—thomas jefferson
9. statue of liberty—monument
10. author—louisa may alcott
11. avenue of the americas—avenue
12. building—empire state building

13–22. This part of a student report has ten capitalization errors in nouns. Write the report correctly.

Example: In the library, aunt naomi wrote a report on women.
In the library, Aunt Naomi wrote a report on women.

Proofreading

Maria Tallchief is a famous Ballerina. This great dancer performed all over the world, in Cities such as New york and Paris. Among other awards, Tallchief received the Indian Achievement Award.

Marian anderson was a renowned Opera singer. She was the first African American to perform at the metropolitan opera. Anderson was awarded Honors by many countries.

Amelia Earhart was the first woman to fly alone across the atlantic ocean. Her last flight, however, was over the Pacific.

Maria Tallchief

Writing Wrap-Up
WRITING • THINKING • LISTENING • SPEAKING

DESCRIBING

Write a Character Sketch

Write one paragraph of a character sketch. Your character can be from a book you have read or a real person. Include details to help your reader know this person. Use common nouns and proper nouns. Read your sketch to a partner. Then reread it, and have your partner list all the proper nouns. Check your capitalization.

For Extra Practice see page 90.

Common and Proper Nouns

Revising Strategies

Writing with Nouns

Combining Sentences: Compound Subjects You might find sentences in your writing that share the same predicate. Try combining them to create a longer, more interesting sentence. Use a conjunction, such as *and* or *or,* to join the simple subjects.

Stunt fliers brought airplanes to the public's attention.
Exhibition teams brought airplanes to the public's attention.

Stunt fliers and exhibition teams brought airplanes to the public's attention.

Apply It

1–4. Rewrite this section of a history book. Combine four pairs of sentences by making compound subjects.

Revising

1929 Women's Air Derby

It was the first race ever for women pilots. Aviators came to California for the exciting cross-country race. Thrill-seeking spectators came too.

The pilots had to figure out the route. Good maps were scarce. Reliable radios were scarce. The pilots looked at the ground to navigate. Rivers helped them find their way. Railroad tracks helped them find their way.

Amelia Earhart participated in the 1929 Women's Air Derby. Nineteen other pilots participated too. Louise Thaden won.

68 Unit 2: Nouns

Sentence Fluency

Combining Sentences: Telling More About Nouns You can add interesting details to a sentence by elaborating, or telling more, about the nouns. The first sentence below tells only one thing about the subject. The second sentence adds words that tell more.

Valentina Tereshkova was the first woman in space.
Valentina Tereshkova, a Russian cosmonaut, was the first woman in space.

You can also combine sentences to tell more about the nouns. Notice how commas set off the words that tell more in the combined sentence.

Sally Ride was the first U.S. woman in space.
She was an astronaut on the 1983 space shuttle.

Sally Ride, an astronaut on the 1983 space shuttle, was the first U.S. woman in space.

Apply It

5–8. Revise these paragraphs from a report. Combine each pair of underlined sentences.

Revising

Biography of a Woman Astronaut

As a young child, Shannon Lucid dreamed of being an explorer. In 1979 she became an astronaut. She became a space explorer.

Dr. Lucid has an important job on space-shuttle crews. Her job is mission specialist. She has flown on three shuttles. The shuttles were *Discovery, Atlantis,* and *Columbia.* Dr. Lucid set a record of more than three months in orbit. She was the first woman to earn the Congressional Space Medal of Honor. This award is given by the President of the United States.

Writing with Nouns **69**

Grammar
3 Singular and Plural Nouns

One-Minute Warm-Up

Which words in this sentence name people or things? Which of those words show the plural form?

> They bring loads of thatch, potatoes, long radishes, and chili peppers, garlic, scallions, sugar cane, and ginger.
>
> —from *Market!* by Ted Lewin

You have learned that nouns are naming words. A **singular noun** names one person, place, thing, or idea. A **plural noun** names more than one person, place, thing, or idea.

Singular: The farmer drove to the market with the box.

Plural: The farmers drove to the markets with the boxes.

Rules for Forming Plurals	
1. Most singular nouns: Add -s.	street—streets house—houses
2. Nouns ending in *s, x, ch,* or *sh*: Add -es.	dress—dresses ax—axes bench—benches dish—dishes
3. Nouns ending with a vowel and *y*: Add -s.	valley—valleys joy—joys
4. Nouns ending with a consonant and *y*: Change the *y* to *i* and add -es.	city—cities cranberry—cranberries

HELP? Tip

Do not use apostrophe and -s ('s) to show the plural.

Try It Out

Speak Up What is the plural form of each noun?

1. ostrich
2. fox
3. letter
4. alley
5. boss
6. panda
7. porch
8. family
9. holiday

On Your Own

Write the plural forms of each noun.

Example: hobby   *hobbies*

10. glass
11. idea
12. month
13. toy
14. ocean
15. party
16. flute
17. marsh
18. basket
19. doctor
20. body
21. paper
22. picture
23. ranch
24. library
25. business
26. birthday
27. notebook

28–38. This part of a writer's notebook has eleven incorrect plural nouns. Write the notebook correctly.

Example: Waves lapped at the sides of the dockes.
Waves lapped at the sides of the dock*s*.

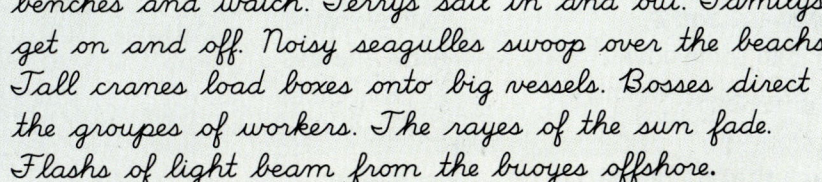

At the City Harbor

Huge ocean lineres arrive. Tiny tugboats pull the giant shipes. Persones young and old sit on benches and watch. Ferrys sail in and out. Familys get on and off. Noisy seagulles swoop over the beachs. Tall cranes load boxes onto big vessels. Bosses direct the groupes of workers. The rayes of the sun fade. Flashs of light beam from the buoyes offshore.

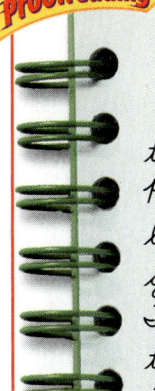

Writing Wrap-Up   WRITING • THINKING • LISTENING • SPEAKING

DESCRIBING

Write a Writer's Notebook Entry

What have you done lately that was memorable? Have you visited a new friend? gotten caught in a storm? gone to a ballpark? Write four or five sentences describing what you saw and heard. Use some plural nouns. Then read your description to a classmate. Which details were most striking to your classmate?

For Extra Practice see page 91.   Singular and Plural Nouns

Grammar

4 More Plural Nouns

One-Minute Warm-Up

How many plural nouns are in the sentence below? Name them.

Children learned the skills and customs of their tribe from their parents, grandparents, aunts, and uncles.

—from *Children of the Wild West*, by Russell Freedman

Many nouns do not become plural according to the regular rules. The chart below shows you the different patterns for forming the plurals of these nouns.

More Rules for Forming Plurals

1. **Nouns ending in *f* or *fe*:** Change the *f* to *v* and add *-es* to some nouns. Add *-s* to other nouns.	life—li**ves** calf—cal**ves** leaf—lea**ves** cliff—cliff**s**
2. **Nouns ending with a vowel and *o*:** Add *-s*.	rodeo—rodeo**s** radio—radio**s** studio—studio**s**
3. **Nouns ending with a consonant and *o*:** Add *-s* to some nouns. Add *-es* to other nouns.	solo—solo**s** piano—piano**s** hero—hero**es** echo—echo**es** tomato—tomato**es**
4. **Nouns that have special plural spellings**	foot—f**ee**t woman—wom**e**n
5. **Nouns that remain the same in the singular and the plural**	trout—trout deer—deer sheep—sheep

 Tip Use your dictionary to check for correct plurals.

Try It Out

Speak Up What is the plural form of each noun? You may use your dictionary to help you.

1. echo
2. cliff
3. radio
4. tooth
5. half
6. hero
7. deer
8. wife
9. giraffe

72 Unit 2: Nouns

On Your Own

Write the plural form of each noun. Use your dictionary to check your spelling.

Example: shelf *shelves*

10. moose
11. sheep
12. belief
13. potato
14. man
15. roof
16. tooth
17. thief
18. mouse
19. child
20. studio
21. cuff

22–28. Each of these seven riddles has an incorrect noun plural. Write the riddles correctly.

Example: When are your tooths like your tongue? *when they chatter*
When are your teeth like your tongue? *when they chatter*

Proofreading

Tickle-A-Rib Riddles

What's worse than giraffes with sore throats? centipedes with sore feets

What two animals go everywhere with you? your calfs

How many sheeps does it take to make a sweater? I didn't know they could knit!

Are tomatos healthy? I never heard one complain.

What famous womans were born in Kansas? None. Only babies are born there.

What happens when gooses collide? goose bumps

How many childrens have six legs? three

Writing Wrap-Up WRITING • THINKING • LISTENING • SPEAKING

CREATING

Write Jokes

Write three jokes or riddles with at least one plural noun from the lesson in each one. Read them to a small group. Ask the group to answer the riddles and to spell the nouns aloud. Did you all agree on the spelling?

For Extra Practice see page 92.

Grammar/Mechanics

5 Singular Possessive Nouns

One-Minute Warm-Up

Two words that show ownership are incorrectly punctuated in this joke. What are they? How can you fix them?

Puffs owner liked to brag about how smart his dog was.

"How much is two minus two?" the dogs' owner asked. Puff said nothing.

- You have learned that a singular noun names one person, place, thing, or idea. A **singular possessive noun shows that one person, place, or thing has or owns something**. To make a singular noun show possession, add an apostrophe and *-s* (*'s*).

    the fur of the dog   the dog's fur
    the collar that the pet has   the pet's collar

- Using possessive nouns is shorter and better than other ways of showing possession.

    Longer: The dog belonging to Joel is barking.
    Better: Joel's dog is barking.

Singular Noun	Singular Possessive Noun
child	child's toy
Tess	Tess's bike
pony	pony's tail
fish	fish's fins

Try It Out

Speak Up Each phrase can be changed to show possession in a shorter way. What is the possessive form of each underlined singular noun?

1. the tail of the <u>fox</u>
2. the pet that the <u>child</u> has
3. the name of the <u>poodle</u>
4. the dog that <u>Alex</u> has
5. the hat of my <u>sister</u>
6. the book that <u>Lee</u> owns

Unit 2: Nouns

On Your Own

Rewrite each phrase to use a singular possessive noun.

Example: the nest of the hamster   *the hamster's nest*

7. the job that Ari has
8. the teeth of the fox
9. the rabbit my friend has
10. the chicks that the hen had
11. the shoes that Liz owns
12. the voice of the boy

13–22. This part of a shooting script for a movie has ten incorrect singular possessive nouns. Write the shooting script correctly.

Example: The camera tracks the kittens steps.
The camera tracks the kitten's steps.

Movie Script

- Zoom in on sign over store: Besss Pet Shop.
- Follow man into store to the sound of a parrots' shriek.
- Pan around store as the customers' voice is heard.
- Zoom in on puppy's tail swishing back and forth.
- Switch from bulldogs wrinkles to huskys' blue eyes.
- Switch to close-up of parakeet brilliant feathers.
- Move to kittens' face as it looks up at parakeet.
- Move to the fishs picture and fox's picture next to it.
- Zoom in on mouses' name below its picture: Alfred.
- Show Bess smiling as she remembers mans name: "Alfred!"

Writing Wrap-Up
WRITING • THINKING • LISTENING • SPEAKING

DESCRIBING

Write a Shooting Script

Find a scene in a book or a play that you like or that you have written. Write a shooting script of this scene for a movie camera crew. Give clear step-by-step instructions. Use singular possessive nouns. Ask a partner to picture the scene as you read the script. Work together to check that you wrote the possessive nouns correctly.

For Extra Practice see page 93.

Singular Possessive Nouns **75**

Grammar/Mechanics

6 Plural Possessive Nouns

One-Minute Warm-Up

Suppose you are an apostrophe or the letter -s. Do you belong in the blanks below? Which ones?

men__suits   designers__clothes   girls__jackets
mice__tails   monkeys__fur   players__uniforms

- A plural noun that shows ownership, or possession, is called a **plural possessive noun**.

    The cars that belong to the teachers are parked here.
    The teachers' cars are parked here.

- When a plural noun ends in -s, add only an apostrophe after the -s (s') to make the noun show possession.

    boys' books   wolves' pups   babies' mothers

- Not all plural nouns end in -s. When a plural noun does not end in -s, add ('s) to form the plural possessive noun.

    shoes of the men   men's shoes   food of the mice   mice's food

Singular	Singular Possessive	Plural	Plural Possessive
girl	girl's	girls	girls'
calf	calf's	calves	calves'
pony	pony's	ponies	ponies'
child	child's	children	children's
mouse	mouse's	mice	mice's

Try It Out

Speak Up Each phrase can show possession in a shorter way. What is the possessive form of each underlined plural noun?

1. the medals of the <u>swimmers</u>
2. the speeds of the <u>runners</u>
3. the skills of the <u>musicians</u>
4. the sports of the <u>women</u>
5. the nails of the <u>carpenters</u>
6. the uniforms of the <u>sailors</u>

76 Unit 2: Nouns

On Your Own

Rewrite each phrase to use a plural possessive noun.

Example: mitts the catchers use   *catchers' mitts*

7. pens the teachers have
8. aprons the cooks wear
9. boots the men own
10. flags of the countries
11. names of the people
12. yards of the neighbors
13. sneakers the joggers wear
14. jackets of the guests

15–22. This part of an online news article has eight underlined phrases. Write each underlined phrase to include a plural possessive noun.

Example: The best players on the teams practice after school
teams' best players

news article

Do the <u>cheers of crowds</u> make teams play better? Sports researchers are looking into the <u>reactions of players</u> to such events. They compared <u>scores of teams</u> when crowds cheered and when crowds were quiet. They also looked at how scores were affected by the following: <u>teams of men</u> playing <u>teams of women</u>, <u>cries of babies</u>, <u>whistles of coaches</u>, and <u>calls of umpires</u>.

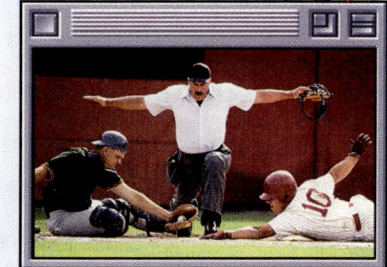

Writing Wrap-Up   WRITING • THINKING • LISTENING • SPEAKING

EXPLAINING

Write a Cause-and-Effect Paragraph

What is your opinion about the effects people and things have on a team's performance? What example have you witnessed that supports your opinion? Write a paragraph stating your views. Identify each cause and its effect on the player. Include at least three plural possessive nouns. Read your paragraph to a few classmates. Does anyone agree with you?

For Extra Practice see page 94.

Revising Strategies

Writing with Nouns

Combining Sentences: Possessive Nouns A possessive noun can replace a whole sentence. Instead of writing two choppy sentences to tell about one noun, try using a possessive noun to combine them into one smooth sentence.

> The national game in Malaysia is sepak takraw.
> The name of this game means "foot ball."

> Malaysia**'s** national game is sepak takraw, which means "foot ball."

Apply It

1–4. Revise these instructions for a sepak takraw game. Combine each pair of underlined sentences, using a possessive noun.

Revising

How To Play Sepak Takraw

1. The rules are similar to those in volleyball. <u>Your kit has a videotape. The videotape explains the rules.</u>

2. <u>Takraw has a grapefruit-sized ball. The ball was originally woven from rattan.</u> The ball in your kit is plastic.

3. You need two teams to play. <u>Each team has four players. The players use their feet to keep the ball in the air.</u> Don't use your hands!

4. <u>The videotape has a demonstration. This demonstration shows kicks, jumps, and spikes.</u> Don't play takraw unless you are physically fit!

78 Unit 2: Nouns

Sentence Fluency

Combining Sentences: Appositives with Possessive Nouns

Instead of using two choppy sentences to elaborate, try combining them by using an appositive. An **appositive** is a word or phrase that describes a noun.

Write the appositive immediately after the noun it explains. Use commas to set it off from the rest of the sentence.

The Porcupines are famous for their roll spike.
The Porcupines are the league's best takraw team.

→ The Porcupines, the league's best takraw team, are famous for their roll spike.

Apply It

5–8. Revise this part of a letter. Combine each set of underlined sentences by changing the sentence with the possessive noun into an appositive.

Revising

Dear Grandma,

The Bigfoots promoted me to the varsity squad. The Bigfoots are my school's takraw team. I'm so happy!

Yesterday was my first practice. We practiced kicks for over an hour. Kicks are takraw's most important move. My legs are sore today! Then Captain Terry showed us some tricks. Captain Terry is the team's best spiker. I think we'll leave the spiking to her and will rely on teamwork to win. Spiking is difficult!

The Middle School Takraw Championship takes place next month. We will play at the Superdome in front of hundreds of spectators. The Superdome is Portland's stadium. Can you come?

Love,
Georgia

Writing with Nouns **79**

Using Exact Nouns

When you write, use exact nouns to name specific people, places, and things. Using exact nouns will help you to create a clear picture in your writing.

Less exact noun:
The dog chased the boy.

More exact noun:
The golden retriever chased the skater.

Apply It

1–6. Rewrite the following letter, replacing the underlined nouns with more exact nouns.

Revising

Dear Mario,

    I can't wait for you to visit! There is a spot by a small, shady tree down by the river that is perfect for fishing. On Sundays my uncle and dad get up early and bring all their fishing stuff with them to fish there. They catch many things in the river, like trout and bass. Sometimes they come back with enough stuff to feed the whole family! Once in a while they sell their catch to this place that cooks fresh fish.

    If you visit in the spring, it might rain, so bring the right stuff to wear. I hope you can come fishing with us soon.

                               Your friend,
                               Justin

Enrichment

Classifying Nouns

Players: 2

Materials: paper, pencils, and a 3-minute timer

To play: Pick a scientific topic, such as the sea, the planets, or the weather. Start the timer. Write down as many nouns as you can think of that have to do with your topic.

Scoring: Each correct noun scores 1 point. The player with the most points after 3 minutes wins the game.

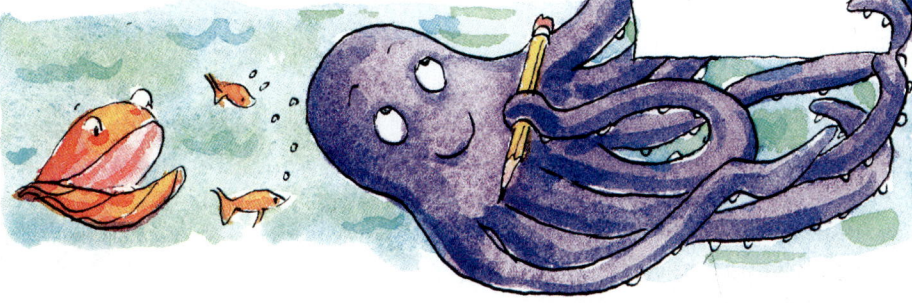

Pet Products

You have invented a new pet product. What is it? What does it do for the animal? Write an ad for the product. Use singular possessive and plural possessive nouns. Underline each singular possessive once and each plural possessive twice. Draw a picture to go with your ad.

Challenge Write one-sentence ads for products for these animals: goose, deer, mouse, fox, pony, calf, sheep. Use the plural possessive form of the animal's name.

Example: Foxy Shampoo keeps <u>foxes'</u> tails fluffy!

Nibble-Gnaw

Nibble-Gnaw keeps <u>hamsters'</u> teeth sharp. A daily serving of Nibble-Gnaw is your <u>hamster's</u> toothbrush.

Checkup: Unit 2

1 What Is a Noun? *(p. 64)* Write each noun in these sentences.

1. Ann visited London in July.
2. London is the capital of England.
3. A trip to London is great fun.
4. Go during the summer.
5. Many buses have two decks.
6. Go to Buckingham Palace to see the royal family.
7. See if the royal flag is flying.
8. It means the Queen is at home.
9. Sit by the Thames River.
10. Look for London Bridge.
11. The Tower of London was a prison.
12. Now a museum is in the tower.

2 Common and Proper Nouns *(p. 66)* Write a list of all the common nouns. List all the proper nouns. List each noun only once.

13. Benjamin Franklin led a useful life.
14. His family lived in Boston.
15. His education came from books.
16. Ben started a newspaper and an almanac.
17. Ben also had a love for science.
18. Ben did many experiments and also invented a stove.
19. Ben organized a library that lent books to people.
20. He started what became the University of Pennsylvania.
21. Franklin was a statesman and lived in England and France.
22. My mom has read many books about this admirable man.

3 Singular and Plural Nouns *(p. 70)* Write the plural form of each underlined noun.

23. Wendell rode the small gray donkey down the trail.
24. He took the path into the forest.
25. The bridge crossed the stream.
26. The moss covered the rock.
27. Soon the boy reached the valley.
28. He knew the secret of the place.
29. A magnificent butterfly lived there.
30. Wendell sat quietly on a bench.
31. The small basket held his lunch.
32. The bread and cheese tasted good.
33. His hungry donkey ate the apple.
34. Then Wendell made the wish.
35. The butterfly flew onto his hand.

4 More Plural Nouns *(p. 72)* Write the plural of each underlined noun.

36. Megan performed at the rodeo.
37. She roped the calf in record time.
38. It was a happy day in her life.
39. Her horse jumped at a leaf.
40. There were stripes on her cuff.
41. Later a man rode the wild horses.
42. He became the hero of the day.
43. Why was a deer in the barn?
44. Did you listen to the radio?
45. The studio had sent reporters.
46. They sat in the row under the roof.
47. A happy child was singing.
48. I liked the sound of his solo.
49. I still hear the echo in my ears.

82 Unit 2: Nouns Go to www.eduplace.com/tales/hme/ for more fun with parts of speech.

5 Singular Possessive Nouns

(p. 74) Rewrite each phrase, using a singular possessive noun.

50. the hat of the ringmaster
51. the pranks of the monkey
52. the roar of the lion
53. the costume of the acrobat
54. the trunk of the elephant
55. the stunts of the clown
56. the bicycle of Carlos
57. the tricks of the dog
58. the dance of the bear
59. the trainer of the horse
60. the excitement of a child
61. the stripes of the tiger
62. the skill of the juggler
63. the cheers of the crowd

6 Plural Possessive Nouns

(p. 76) Rewrite each phrase, using a plural possessive noun.

64. the hoses of the gardeners
65. the tunes of the musicians
66. the laughter of my friends
67. the joy of the dancers
68. the jackets of my cousins
69. the umbrellas of the uncles
70. the necklaces of the women
71. the ears of the calves
72. the bonnets of the babies
73. the smiles of the parents
74. the feathers of the geese
75. the balloons of the children
76. the notebooks of the students
77. the pictures of the moose

Mixed Review 78–85. This poem has three incorrect plural nouns, two incorrect proper nouns, and three incorrect possessive nouns. Write the poem correctly.

Proofreading Checklist
Have you written these correctly?
- ✔ plural nouns
- ✔ proper nouns
- ✔ possessive nouns

Proofreading

A Very Special Room

In Liz' huge room were her favorite things.
There were puzzles and books and stuffed ostrichs with wings.
A bowl with some goldfish sat near two painted blouses.
The fish's glass world contained leaves, rocks, and houses.
Filling the shelfs were childrens' old games and toys.
The radios were Liz's, the stuffed ponys were Roys.
The bench's soft pillows were puffy and full,
And the bed's cozy blankets were made out of wool.
The house was on Main street in a town named roween,
And I'm really Liz, but the room was a dream.

See www.eduplace.com/kids/hme/ for an online quiz.

Assessment Link

✓ Test Practice

Write the numbers 1–10 on a sheet of paper. Read the sentence. Choose the part that needs a capital letter. Write the letter for that answer. If no part needs a capital letter, write the letter for the last answer, "None."

1. My mother / took some photographs / of the White house. / None
      A   B   C   D

2. The children crossed / the street / in the crosswalk. / None
      F   G   H   J

3. Is africa / the biggest continent / in the world? / None
      A   B   C   D

4. The Blake family / lived in texas / for several years. / None
      F   G   H   J

5. In december / we skated at the pond / almost every day. / None
      A   B   C   D

6. The tall girl / in the back row / is my cousin. / None
      F   G   H   J

7. The crew sailed / across the Pacific ocean / on a large ship. / None
      A   B   C   D

8. We saw a parade / and had a cookout / on the fourth of July. / None
      F   G   H   J

9. My father / restores old cars / on saturday. / None
      A   B   C   D

10. The travel club / takes trips to / the Far East. / None
       F   G   H   J

Now write numbers 11–14 on your paper. Use the paragraph to answer the questions. Write the letter for each answer.

> [11]Akiro has two pet mouses. [12]Them names are Paul and Polly. [13]Pauls fur is gray, and Pollys fur is white. [14]Every morning Akiro feeds them Akiro cleans their cage.

11 Which is the best way to write Sentence 11?

  A Akiro has two pet mouse.
  B Akiro has two pet mice.
  C Akiro has two pet mices.
  D Best as it is

12 Which is the best way to write Sentence 12?

  F Their names are Paul and Polly.
  G Theirs names are Paul and Polly.
  H They names are Paul and Polly.
  J Best as it is

13 Which is the best way to write Sentence 13?

  A Pauls' fur is gray, and Pollys' fur is white.
  B Pauls fur is gray, and Pollies fur is white.
  C Paul's fur is gray, and Polly's fur is white.
  D Best as it is

14 Which is the best way to write Sentence 14?

  F Every morning Akiro feeds them and cleans their cage.
  G Every morning Akiro feeds them and Akiro cleans their cage.
  H Every morning Daniel feeds them cleans their cage.
  J Best as it is

Test Practice

✓ Test Practice continued

Now write numbers 15–18 on your paper. Use the paragraph to answer the questions. Write the letter for each answer.

¹⁵Vonda harris had to work late on monday night. ¹⁶Her three childs surprised her by fixing dinner. ¹⁷They picked a few carrots and tomatoes from the garden. ¹⁸Then they made baked chicken rice and salad.

15 Which is the best way to write Sentence 15?

   A Vonda harris had to work late on Monday Night.

   B Vonda Harris had to work late on Monday night.

   C Vonda Harris had to work late on monday Night.

   D Best as it is

16 Which is the best way to write Sentence 16?

   F Her three child surprised her by fixing dinner.

   G Her three childes surprised her by fixing dinner.

   H Her three children surprised her by fixing dinner.

   J Best as it is

17 Which is the best way to write Sentence 17?

   A They picked a few carrot and tomato from the garden.

   B They picked a few carrotses and tomatos from the garden.

   C They picked a few carrotes and tomaties from the garden.

   D Best as it is

18 Which is the best way to write Sentence 18?

   F Then they made baked chicken, rice, and salad.

   G Then they made, baked chicken, rice and, salad.

   H Then they made baked chicken rice, and salad.

   J Best as it is

Cumulative Review

Unit 1: The Sentence

What Is a Sentence? *(p. 32)* Write *sentence* or *fragment* for each of the following groups of words.

1. The Gulf Stream has warm water.
2. The clear, bright blue stream.
3. Is the Gulf of Mexico the source for this current?
4. When boats speed in this water.
5. Flows northeast across the Atlantic.
6. Many kinds of fish are found in this stream.

Four Kinds of Sentences *(p. 34)* Write each sentence and add correct end punctuation. Then write *declarative, interrogative, imperative,* or *exclamatory*.

7. These caves are interesting
8. Have you seen them
9. Bring a good flashlight
10. How strange the rocks are
11. Our guide pointed them out
12. Be careful down there

Complete Subjects and Predicates *(p. 36)* Write each sentence. Draw a line between the complete subject and the complete predicate.

13. Kenya has beautiful plains.
14. Animals in East Africa are wild.
15. National parks protect them.
16. Scientists and travelers visit there.
17. A camera trip can be great fun.
18. Tourists film elephant herds.

Simple Subjects and Predicates *(p. 38, 40)* Write each sentence. Underline simple subjects once and simple predicates twice.

19. The small dog was running fast.
20. A cow with black spots saw it.
21. The dog's owner appeared.
22. Mr. Stratton ran into the pasture.
23. Frisky rushed to him.
24. Nobody on the farm saw the duck.

Subjects in Imperatives *(p. 42)* For each sentence, write *declarative* or *imperative*. Then write the simple subject of the sentence.

25. We will like a harbor boat trip.
26. Please buy two tickets for me.
27. Don't forget your lunch.
28. The harbor is windy sometimes.
29. Bring a warm sweater.
30. Captain Anders is our guide.

Conjunctions *(p. 44)* Choose the conjunction in parentheses that better fits each sentence. How is it used?

31. Wild hamsters are found in Central (and, but) Northern Asia.
32. Some hamsters are pets, (but, or) most live in the wilderness.
33. Bea (and, but) Eva have one.
34. The hamster rests all day (and, or) stays up all night.
35. Bea is bothered by the noise, (but, or) Eva sleeps through it.

See www.eduplace.com/kids/hme/ for a tricky usage or spelling question.

Cumulative Review *continued*

Run-on Sentences *(p. 48)* Write each of the following run-on sentences correctly.

36. Ms. Trill worked in her garden she weeded the flowers.
37. She had waited too long the garden was overgrown.
38. What great care she took weeds were everywhere.
39. Ms. Trill finished her work the garden looked very nice she was proud of it.
40. Some tomatoes were ripe she chose them for dinner they would taste delicious.
41. Ms. Trill picked roses she put them in a vase they smelled lovely.

Unit 2: Nouns

Common and Proper Nouns

(pp. 64, 66) Write the common nouns in a list. Then list all the proper nouns. List each noun only once.

42. Wanda Landowska played the harpsichord.
43. Wanda was born in Warsaw.
44. This performer soon left Poland.
45. Paris was her new city.
46. Landowska started a school.
47. Landowska composed music.
48. This composer also wrote books.
49. Landowska inspired Dad and my teacher.

Plural Nouns *(pp. 70, 72)* Write the plural of each underlined noun.

50. We rode away from the <u>city</u>.
51. I heard the <u>piano</u> on the <u>radio</u>.
52. We saw the <u>deer</u> and the <u>goose</u>.
53. I carried our <u>lunch</u> in the <u>box</u>.
54. Jill cut the <u>loaf</u> in <u>half</u>.
55. We ate the <u>trout</u> and the <u>tomato</u>.
56. We traveled toward the <u>valley</u>.

Possessive Nouns *(pp. 74, 76)* Rewrite each phrase, using a possessive noun.

57. the speeches of the mayors
58. the question of the lawyer
59. the answer of the witness
60. the thoughts of the officers
61. the comments of the boys
62. the decision of the judge
63. the opinions of the players
64. the story of the reporter

88 Unit 2: Nouns

Extra Practice

1. What Is a Noun?

(pages 64–65)

- A **noun** is a word that names a person, a place, a thing, or an idea.
- A noun can be two or more words.

● Each sentence contains two nouns. One noun is underlined. Write the other noun.

Example: Christopher Columbus was born in Italy.
Christopher Columbus

1. Columbus decided to be a sailor.
2. His ships came from the Spanish queen.
3. This explorer traveled to the New World.
4. Central America and South America were reached.
5. A short route to the Far East was never found.

▲ Write each noun in these sentences.

Example: Columbus discovered the island of Puerto Rico.
Columbus   island   Puerto Rico

6. Another explorer set up a Spanish colony.
7. The people planted sugar.
8. This crop is still grown on many farms.
9. Furniture and textiles are other important products.
10. Puerto Ricans are now citizens of the United States.

■ Make four columns labeled *Person, Place, Thing,* and *Idea*. Write each noun in the correct column.

Example: Pat traveled by jet to Jamaica.

Person	Place	Thing	Idea
Pat	Jamaica	jet	

11. Her pen pal lived on that island.
12. Their friendship had grown through their letters.
13. The two friends met at the airport.
14. Ana was wearing a blue hat and a green dress.
15. Ana showed Pat many beautiful cities and beaches.
16. The girls climbed Blue Mountain.

Extra Practice

(pages 66–67)

2 Common and Proper Nouns

- A **common noun** names any person, place, or thing.
- A **proper noun** names a particular person, place, or thing.
- Begin each important word in a proper noun with a capital letter.

● Write each pair of nouns. Capitalize the proper noun.

Example: author—mark twain   *author—Mark Twain*

1. columbus day—holiday
2. state—west virginia
3. robert redford—actor
4. colorado river—river
5. month—november

Mark Twain

▲ Make two columns labeled *Proper* and *Common*. Find each noun, and list it in the correct column.

Example: Legends say Betsy Ross made our flag.

Proper	*Common*
Betsy Ross	*woman*

6. Betsy Ross lived in Philadelphia.
7. Ross was an excellent seamstress.
8. George Washington was elected to lead the Colonial army.
9. Legends say the general asked Ross to make the first flag.
10. The first flag was called the Stars and Stripes.

■ Write each noun, capitalizing proper nouns correctly. Label each noun *common* or *proper*. Then write a proper noun for each common noun and a common noun for each proper noun.

Example: country   *country   common   Norway*

11. pacific ocean
12. movie star
13. king george
14. city
15. bill cosby
16. book
17. july
18. car
19. singer
20. missouri river
21. holiday
22. gwendolyn brooks
23. mountain
24. fernwood drive
25. queen noor

90 Unit 2: Nouns

Extra Practice

3 Singular and Plural Nouns

(pages 70–71)

- A **singular noun** names one person, place, thing, or idea.
- A **plural noun** names more than one person, place, thing, or idea.
- Form the plural of most nouns by adding *-s* or *-es*. Look at the ending of a singular noun to decide how to form the plural.

● Write the plural form of each noun.

Example: horse *horses*

1. storm
2. book
3. folder
4. tax
5. lunch
6. paper
7. wish
8. dress
9. tray
10. jelly
11. window
12. grass
13. branch
14. strawberry
15. baseball

▲ Write the plural form of each underlined noun.

Example: Nantucket is an island far out at sea. *islands seas*

16. I live there with my family in the summer.
17. We drive our car onto a ferry.
18. The bay has calm water.
19. We saw a beautiful boat in the harbor.
20. The beach is five miles from the town.

■ Write each underlined noun. If it is singular, write the plural form. If it is plural, write the singular form.

Example: The museum guide showed me old boxes.
  guide guides   boxes box

21. The ivory piece in a box came from a whale.
22. I saw an interesting dish at the exhibit.
23. A sailor had made it at sea.
24. He had written a message with paint from berries.
25. The message told of his love for his family.

Extra Practice

Extra Practice

(pages 72–73)

4 More Plural Nouns

- To form the plural of some nouns ending in *f* or *fe,* change the *f* to *v* and add *-es*. For others, simply add *-s*.
- To form the plural of nouns ending in *o,* add *-s* or *-es*.
- Some nouns have special plural forms.
- Some nouns have the same singular and plural forms.

● Write the plural form of each of these singular nouns.

Example: cliff *cliffs*

1. piano
2. elk
3. man
4. trout
5. safe
6. auto
7. thief
8. stereo
9. wife
10. moose
11. roof
12. tomato
13. tooth
14. shelf
15. fowl
16. deer
17. child
18. hero

▲ Look at each underlined plural noun. If the noun is spelled correctly, write *correct*. If it is not correct, write it correctly.

Example: We picked <u>tomatos</u> and corn. *tomatoes*

19. We fed bread crumbs to the <u>geese</u>.
20. We caught five large <u>trouts</u> for dinner.
21. His two <u>childrens</u> helped him.
22. The boards were five <u>feet</u> long.
23. Men and <u>woman</u> work hard on farms.

■ Write an answer. Use the plural of a noun in the box.

Example: How do we usually buy bread? *loaves*

24. Where do banks keep money?
25. What do people use for chewing food?
26. Where could you put books?
27. What do we call brave people?
28. What are red and juicy and good in salads?
29. What parts of houses can you see from a plane?
30. What musical instruments have keys?

| hero |
| roof |
| piano |
| loaf |
| tomato |
| shelf |
| safe |
| tooth |

92 Unit 2: Nouns

Extra Practice

(pages 74–75)

5 Singular Possessive Nouns

- A **singular possessive noun** shows that one person, place, or thing has or owns something.
- Form a singular possessive noun by adding an apostrophe and -s ('s) to the singular noun.

● Write each phrase to show possession.

Example: the woman ____ coat   *the woman's coat*

1. the cat ____ tail
2. a baby ____ smile
3. Trish ____ plan
4. Ernesto ____ pen
5. the doctor ____ bag
6. the giraffe ____ neck
7. my aunt ____ apartment
8. Mr. Swartz ____ shoes
9. a child ____ bicycle
10. Tomas ____ idea
11. the prince ____ name
12. Umeko ____ calendar

▲ Rewrite each phrase. Use a singular possessive noun.

Example: the costume that Celie wore   *Celie's costume*

13. the newspaper of the lawyer
14. the guitar of Carlotta
15. the lawn mower that my brother owns
16. the magazine that belongs to Roberta
17. the office of the dentist
18. the journal of the student

■ Rewrite each sentence, using a singular possessive noun.

Example: The cat that belongs to my sister is yellow.
    My sister's cat is yellow.

19. The house that my uncle lives in is gray.
20. The legs of that moose are long.
21. The song that Jill wrote was funny.
22. Did you find the book that belongs to Amy?
23. Have you seen the scarf that Jade owns?
24. The desk of Nita is always piled with papers.
25. The fishing rod that belongs to Jeff was new.

Extra Practice

6 Plural Possessive Nouns (pages 76–77)

- A **plural possessive noun** shows that more than one person, place, or thing owns or has something.
- If a plural noun ends in *s*, add only an apostrophe to form the plural possessive. If a plural noun does not end in *s*, add *'s* to form the plural possessive.

● Write each phrase to show possession.

Example: the children pencils   *the children's pencils*

1. the dancers legs
2. the boys sneakers
3. the men meeting
4. the robins nest
5. the turtles bowl
6. the horses tails
7. the neighbors porch
8. the officers badges
9. the cities taxes
10. the sheep pasture
11. the musicians drums
12. the actors roles

▲ Rewrite each phrase, using a plural possessive noun.

Example: the rugs that the weavers made   *the weavers' rugs*

13. the flowers that my aunts grow
14. the houses of the ladies
15. the suitcases that belong to the women
16. the raincoats of the children
17. the boots that the climbers wear
18. the playroom that my cousins have

■ Write a sentence for each noun, using the form shown.

Example: artist (plural possessive)
Have you seen the sketches in the artists' notebooks?

19. writer (singular possessive)
20. Gus (singular possessive)
21. speaker (singular possessive)
22. woman (plural possessive)
23. voter (singular possessive)
24. secretary (plural possessive)

Unit 3

Verbs

The massive wave curled above me. I tucked my body low and skimmed the inside curve with my board.

Grammar

1 Action Verbs

One-Minute Warm-Up

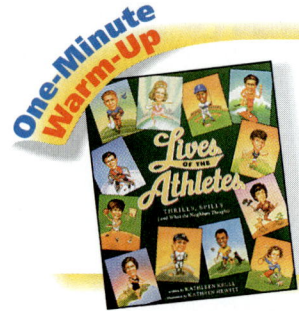

What are the action words, or verbs, in this sentence? What other verbs might you use in other sentences about baseball?

Ruth negotiated his own baseball contracts and drove a hard bargain.

—from *Lives of the Athletes*, by Kathleen Krull

- You have learned that the predicate of a sentence tells what the subject is or does. **The main word in the predicate is the verb.** Most verbs are action verbs. **An action verb shows what the subject does or did.**

    Jill **pitches** the ball.   Roberto **swings** at the ball.

    The ball **flew** over the plate.   Roberto **ran** to first base.

- Action verbs can also show action that you cannot see.

    The coach **thought** about the players in the field.

Try It Out

Speak Up What is the action verb in each of the following sentences?

1. People admire Mildred Ella "Babe" Didrikson as an all-round athlete.
2. At sixteen she joined an excellent women's basketball team.
3. She scored a hundred points in one game!
4. During that same period, she won medals as a swimmer.
5. She also set records as a figure skater.
6. Didrikson entered many track and field events.
7. In the 1932 Olympics, she captured three medals.
8. Sports reporters named her the greatest woman athlete.
9. Didrikson liked golf more than any other sport.
10. She still inspires many golfers today.

On Your Own

Write the action verb in each sentence.

Example: Javed enjoys sports events.   *enjoys*

11. He watches games on television very often.
12. Javed writes about sports for the school newspaper.
13. His news stories cover different kinds of events.
14. One of his stories described a bicycle race.
15. The cyclists raced around the track many times.
16. In another event, runners jumped over hurdles.
17. Team sports excite Javed too.
18. Last night he went to a hockey game.
19. The goalie missed an important shot.
20. Javed describes the exciting details in his article.

21–26. These newspaper headlines are from sports pages. Write the headlines. Underline the six action verbs.

Example: Colts Steal Title from Eagles   *Colts <u>Steal</u> Title from Eagles*

SPORTS
Kwon Li Streaks Across Finish Line

SPORTS
Beloved Pitcher Returns as Coach

SPORTS
Dukes Dribble Their Way to Championship

Cobras Squeeze Victory from Eagles

Sprained Finger Injures Barbosa's Game

SPORTS
Angry Coach Suspends Evans for Season

Writing Wrap-Up
WRITING • THINKING • LISTENING • SPEAKING

SUMMARIZING

Write Headlines

Write five headlines about sports or other events. Use an action verb in each headline. With a partner, take turns reading your headlines aloud. Have your partner tell you which headline of yours is the catchiest. Name each other's action verbs.

For Extra Practice see page 136.

Grammar
2 Direct Objects

One-Minute Warm-Up

Which word is the verb in each sentence? Which word answers the question *What?* after the verb in each sentence? Look at the drawing for a clue to what the captain shouted.

I heard a scream from the deck. The ship's captain shouted something.

- Some sentences express a complete thought with only a subject and an action verb.

   subj. action verb
   The ship sails.

- In other sentences, a direct object is used with the action verb. A **direct object** is a word in the predicate that receives the action of a verb. It can be a noun or a pronoun, a word that takes the place of a noun.

   subj. action verb dir. obj.   subj. action verb dir. obj.
   The captain steers the big ship.   His crew always obeys him.

- A direct object answers the question *What?* or *Whom?* after the verb.

   The captain steers the big ship. *(steers what? the ship)*

   The captain calls the crew. *(calls whom? the crew)*

   The captain praises them. *(praises whom? them)*

Try It Out

Speak Up What are the action verb and the direct object in each sentence?

1. The captain ordered the sailors on deck.
2. Some sailors mopped the deck.
3. Other sailors cooked the stew.
4. A crew member spotted some whales.
5. One sailor climbed the mast to the lookout.
6. He viewed the whales for a long time.
7. He made a sketch of one of the whales.
8. He showed it to another sailor.

A humpback whale

Unit 3: Verbs

On Your Own

Write the action verb in each sentence. Then write the direct object and underline it. If there is no direct object, write *no D.O.*

Example: Scientists study whales.   *study* <u>whales</u>

9. They learn many interesting facts about whales.
10. Some whales sing.
11. The ocean water carries the sound far away.
12. Other whales hear it.
13. Some whales use sound for navigation.
14. They locate various objects by sound.
15. Whales also have very good vision.
16. I heard a recording of actual whale songs.

A whale's flukes

17–28. Write this journal entry. Underline the twelve verbs once. Underline any direct objects twice. If a verb has no direct object, write *no D.O.*

Example: We wore warm clothes for our boat tour.
We <u>wore</u> warm <u>clothes</u> for our boat tour.

April 14

My family and I took a trip on a whale-watching boat. Everyone searched the ocean for whales. At first we saw only other boats. Then a little girl pointed. We spotted three whales in the distance. Many people used their binoculars. The tall waterspouts from the whales' blowholes really impressed me. Amazingly, the huge, graceful creatures approached our ship. Then they dived. The ocean water covered their shiny bodies. They disappeared. Tears filled my eyes.

Writing Wrap-Up
WRITING • THINKING • LISTENING • SPEAKING

REFLECTING

Write a Journal Entry

When have you seen or done something that amazed you? Describe it to another student. Then write one or two paragraphs about it in a journal entry. Use action verbs and direct objects. Read your entry to your partner. Has he or she had a similar experience?

For Extra Practice see page 137.

Grammar

3 Main Verbs and Helping Verbs

One-Minute Warm-Up

Which words are verbs in this sentence? Which verbs tell the action and which only help?

The season had opened last week, and the Otters had lost to the Dolphins 21 to 19.

—from *The Counterfeit Tackle*, by Matt Christopher

A verb may have two parts, a main verb and one or more helping verbs. **The main verb shows the action in the sentence. The helping verb works with the main verb.** Helping verbs do not show action. **The main verb and the helping verb form a verb phrase.**

In these sentences, the helping verbs are in yellow, and the main verbs are in blue.

Fran has passed everyone.
She is winning the race.
She will get the prize.

Common Helping Verbs				
am	are	were	shall	has
is	was	will	have	had

Try It Out

Speak Up What is the main verb in each sentence? What is the helping verb?

1. The Chargers have practiced for months.
2. Their cheerleaders are creating new cheers.
3. The football schedule was planned last summer.
4. The band is rehearsing every day.
5. The students will get their tickets tomorrow.

Unit 3: Verbs

On Your Own

Write the verb or the verb phrase in each sentence.

Example: We are watching the game on television. *are watching*

6. The halfback is tackling the runner.
7. The runner was fumbling the ball.
8. A player is passing the ball.
9. A player on the other team caught it.
10. The quarterback has scored a touchdown.
11. He had waited for the perfect opportunity.
12. His teammates are jumping for joy.
13. I will go to the game next week.
14. I always cheer for my favorite team.

15–20. Each of these six captions for a photo essay has a verb phrase. Write the captions. Underline the helping verbs once and the main verbs twice.

Example: Fans have come for the game. *Fans <u>have</u> <u><u>come</u></u> for the game.*

Photo Essay Captions

A crowd is gathering for the town volleyball game.

Lake Street players are carrying last year's trophy.

Alton Road players were looking confident too.

"Our luck will change this year!"

Players have taken their positions.

The Sutton Volleyball Victory Game is starting.

Writing Wrap-Up
WRITING • THINKING • LISTENING • SPEAKING

DESCRIBING

Write Captions

Recall the events of an exciting trip or gathering. What pictures come to mind? Write five captions describing those pictures, and draw some rough sketches if you like. Use verb phrases. Ask a partner to listen to your captions and tell you which caption is most vivid.

Grammar
4 Linking Verbs

One-Minute Warm-Up

How many sentences can you make out of the lists of words below?

LIST 1: Katie, a swimmer, Peter, the judge, good, faster, winner, tired, strong

LIST 2: is, looked, felt, was, will be, seemed, appeared

You know that some verbs show action and some verbs are helping verbs.

Action Verb: Jennifer runs.   **Helping Verb:** Jennifer is running now.

- A **linking verb** **links the subject of a sentence with a word or words in the predicate.** When a verb is a linking verb, it does not show action, and it is not a helping verb. It is followed by a word in the predicate that names or describes the subject.

    Anna **looks** cheerful.   (*Cheerful* describes *Anna*.)

    Anna **is** a lifeguard.   (*Anna = lifeguard*)

HELP Tip
Linking verbs never have direct objects.

- Some verbs can be either linking verbs or action verbs.

    Action: The crowd looked at the divers.
    Linking: The divers looked tired. (*Tired* describes *divers*.)

Common Linking Verbs					
am	is	are	was	were	will be
look	feel	taste	smell	seem	appear

Try It Out

Speak Up List each linking verb. Which word(s) does it link to the subject?

1. Ray is a swimmer and a diver.
2. He was a winner last week.
3. Ray's parents are coaches.
4. They feel proud of Ray.

102   Unit 3: Verbs

On Your Own

Write the verb in each sentence. Then write *action* or *linking* to describe the verb.

Example: Gertrude Ederle was a fine swimmer.   *was   linking*

5. Gertrude Ederle looked strong and fit.
6. In 1926 she seemed ready for a test of her ability.
7. She was the first woman to swim the English Channel.
8. Ederle swam the distance in fewer than fifteen hours.
9. She set a world record.
10. Ederle will be a champion to swimmers forever.

11–21. This museum display poster has ten verbs. Write the poster. Underline each verb. For each of the seven linking verbs, draw an arrow showing the words the verb links.

Example: Sharks are quite beautiful.   *Sharks are quite beautiful.*

The Truth About SHARKS!

Most people feel afraid of sharks. The shark's streamlined body looks torpedolike. Its many teeth always seem sharp. Some species really are a threat to people. The white shark stretches to twenty feet. It attacks boats and frightens swimmers. Not all sharks are a menace, however. The whale shark is quite harmless. Its diet is small fish and plankton.

Writing Wrap-Up   WRITING • THINKING • LISTENING • SPEAKING

NARRATING

Write a Story Beginning

Imagine that you are an underwater creature at a nearby aquarium. How did you get there? What experiences have you had there? Write the first two paragraphs of a personal narrative. Include at least four linking verbs. Read your story to a small group of classmates. Which detail was fun for them to hear?

For Extra Practice see page 139.

Grammar/Usage

5 Present Tense

One-Minute Warm-Up

Which words show that something is happening in the present?

My mom and I hike on the nearby cliffs. Ben follows.
—from *A Child's Glacier Bay*, by Kimberly Corral with Hannah Corral

- **A verb that tells what its subject is doing right now is in the present tense.** You change the form of a verb in the present tense when a singular noun is the subject. Notice the *-s* added to *see* below.

    The ranger sees the campers.

- You do not change the form of verbs when they are used with plural subjects or with *I* or *you*.

    The campers wave.   I wave.   You wave.

Rules for Forming the Present Tense		
1. Most verbs: Add *-s*.	get—gets	play—plays
2. Verbs ending in *s*, *ch*, *sh*, *x*, and *z*: Add *-es*.	pass—passes push—pushes	punch—punches mix—mixes fizz—fizzes
3. Verbs ending with a consonant and *y*: Change the *y* to *i* and add *-es*.	try—tries	empty—empties

Try It Out

Speak Up What is the correct present tense verb form for each sentence? Use the verb in parentheses.

1. The bird ____. (hatch)
2. The alarm ____. (buzz)
3. The boys ____. (rush)
4. We ____. (talk)
5. Dad ____. (worry)
6. The baby ____. (fuss)

104   Unit 3: Verbs

On Your Own

Write the correct present tense form of each verb in parentheses.

Example: I carefully _____ the weather. (study)   *study*

7. The sun _____ brightly in the blue sky. (shine)
8. Only one cloud _____ overhead. (pass)
9. Roger _____ to the weather report. (listen)
10. "You _____ a picnic lunch," says Mother. (pack)
11. Roger _____ to her request quickly. (reply)
12. We _____ to the center of the lake. (row)
13. Mother _____ from the rowboat. (fish)
14. I _____ a fish on the end of my line. (lose)
15. The others _____ several trout. (catch)

16–25. This part of a schedule has ten incorrect present tense forms. Write the verbs correctly.

Example: The principal watchs out for our safety.   *watches*

Proofreading

Schedule

Schedule for Class Picnic

7:30 Students gatheres at the school. Bus waites.
7:45 Ms. Garcia handes out seat numbers.
8:00 Students take their seats in the bus. Eric carrys the food to the bus and stores it.
8:15 Bus doors closes and bus leaves.
9:30 Bus pass's through park gates and stopes. Ms. Garcia fixs a meeting place for lunch. I organize the games, and you help.
12:00 Leroy rushs to the picnic area and pushs tables together.

Writing Wrap-Up   WRITING • THINKING • LISTENING • SPEAKING

EXPLAINING

Write a Schedule

Choose a three-hour time slot in your day. What do you usually do during that time? Write a schedule. Include specific tasks or details. Use the present tense. Ask a partner to listen to your schedule. Is anything in the schedule unclear? Do you need to correct any verb forms?

For Extra Practice see page 140.

Grammar

6 Past Tense

One-Minute Warm-Up

Which words are verbs in these sentences? When does the action take place? Which two verbs are formed incorrectly?

The pirates hurryed aboard the ship. They had planned badly, however. The gold was heavy, and they almost droped it!

- A verb that shows that something has already happened is in the **past tense**.

    Gino liked his grandmother's story.

- The verb *liked* is in the past tense. It tells that the action in the sentence happened before now.

- Usually the past tense of a verb is formed by adding *-ed*. However, some verbs must undergo a spelling change before you add *-ed*.

Rules for Forming the Past Tense	
1. **Most verbs:** Add *-ed*.	play—played suggest—suggested
2. **Verbs ending with *e*:** Drop the final *e* and add *-ed*.	believe—believed hope—hoped
3. **Verbs ending with a consonant and *y*:** Change the *y* to *i* and add *-ed*.	study—studied hurry—hurried
4. **One-syllable verbs ending with a single vowel and a consonant:** Double the final consonant and add *-ed*.	stop—stopped plan—planned

Try It Out

Speak Up What is the past tense of each verb?

1. watch
2. cry
3. store
4. review
5. dance
6. spray
7. zip
8. yell
9. care
10. marry
11. bake
12. talk
13. scrub
14. shop
15. bury

Unit 3: Verbs

On Your Own

Write the past tense form of each verb in parentheses.

Example: Jo _____ this story about pirates. (share) *shared*

16. A long time ago, a ship _____ a load of gold. (carry)
17. In those days, heavy storms _____ many ships. (destroy)
18. One day a band of pirates _____ the ship. (attack)
19. They _____ the gold and buried it. (grab)
20. They _____ a map showing the gold's location. (create)
21. Years later the captain's son found the map and _____ it. (use)
22. He _____ the treasure from his father's ship. (recover)

23–30. This part of a children's story has eight incorrect past tense forms. Write the verbs correctly.

Example: Dexter walkd to the edge of the forest. *walk**ed***

Proofreading

Dexter the dragon lovd his life. He lived in a beautiful forest, he chewd on leaves and branches for food, and he plaied with the elephants and the mice. Every morning he jumpped out of bed and hurryed joyfully into the forest. Every night he hoped happily into bed. Dexter worryed about just one thing. He feared people. Every once in a while, a knight entered the forest and looked for a dragon to slay. Dexter wonderred why.

Writing Wrap-Up
WRITING • THINKING • LISTENING • SPEAKING

NARRATING

Writing a Children's Story

What stories did you like as a child? real-life stories? tall tales? animal stories? Write a short children's story like the ones you once enjoyed. Use past tense verbs. Read it to a group of classmates. Ask them which part of your story appeals to children most.

Grammar

7 Future Tense

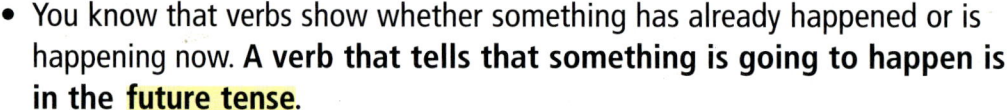

One-Minute Warm-Up

How can you change the two verbs in these sentences so that they tell about future events?

Farmer: I hired birds as my helpers this year.
Visitor: Why?
Farmer: They provide cheep labor!

- You know that verbs show whether something has already happened or is happening now. **A verb that tells that something is going to happen is in the future tense.**

  Derek **will bring** his new book about birds.
  Derek and Gretchen **will look** for some nests.

- To form the future tense of a verb, use the helping verb *will* or *shall* with the main verb. *Shall* is often used with *I* or *we*.

  Shall we invite Melissa?
  She **will** probably come with us.

Try It Out

Speak Up What is the future tense form of each verb?

1. run
2. think
3. talk
4. check
5. spill
6. count
7. whisper
8. tumble

What is the future tense form of each underlined verb?

9. Birds <u>make</u> homes all over the world.
10. Some birds <u>stay</u> near the water.
11. Many shore birds <u>build</u> nests in the Everglades.
12. Bird watchers <u>study</u> how the birds live.
13. They <u>learn</u> about the birds' actions and habits.
14. Two students <u>focus</u> their binoculars.
15. Falcons <u>fascinate</u> most observers.

108 Unit 3: Verbs

On Your Own

Write the name of the tense of each verb. Then write the verb in the future tense.

Example: hurries   *present   will hurry*

16. write
17. stopped
18. swims
19. completed
20. surprises
21. decide
22. deliver
23. recover
24. multiplied

25–36. This part of an online magazine article has twelve verbs. Write the article. Underline each verb. Then write the name of its tense.

Example: Next year the birds will return.
   Next year the birds <u>will return</u>.   future

Magazine Article

Bird Migration Under Close Study

When the fall comes, birds will move to their winter homes. For example, the barn swallow makes its summer home in Alaska. When fall arrives, this bird will journey eight thousand miles to South America. Other birds will search for food during the day on their long trip and will travel at night.

Scientists started a study recently. They wrapped metal bands around the birds' legs. The scientists then will follow each bird throughout its flight and will measure its speed. Next year they will report their findings.

Writing Wrap-Up
WRITING • THINKING • LISTENING • SPEAKING

CREATING

Write a Poem

Imagine you can turn into a bird in flight or any other creature on the run. What will you see? do? feel? Where will you go? Write a poem that tells your adventures. Use the word *I*. Use some future tense verbs. Your poem need not rhyme. With a partner, take turns reading your poems. Compare the experiences you wrote about.

Revising Strategies

Writing with Verbs

Combining Sentences If many sentences in your paragraph repeat the same subject, you could end up sounding like a broken record! Combine these sentences by using a conjunction, such as *and* or *or,* to create a compound predicate.

> When you combine two predicates, you don't need a comma! When you combine three, set off the predicates with commas.

Max peered inside the nest.
Max saw three fuzzy chicks huddled together.

→ Max peered inside the nest and saw three fuzzy chicks huddled together.

Tara cleaned the birdbath.
Tara filled the bird feeder.
Tara watched the goldfinches.

→ Tara cleaned the birdbath, filled the bird feeder, and watched the goldfinches.

Apply It

1–4. Revise this flier by combining the predicates in each set of underlined sentences.

Revising

What to Do If You Find a Baby Bird

1. Leave it alone unless you KNOW its parents aren't returning. Sometimes the parents hunt for food. Sometimes the parents chase away a predator. They may be coming right back!

2. Put a fallen bird back in its nest. Birds have a poor sense of smell. Birds cannot tell that humans have touched their babies.

3. Don't put it back in the wrong nest. Birds take care of only their own young. Birds often harm other babies.

4. Perform basic first aid but be careful! Baby birds overheat easily. Baby birds choke on food. Baby birds need shelter. For serious injuries, call an animal rescue center.

110 Unit 3: Verbs

Sentence Fluency

Keeping Verbs in the Same Tense Your readers will be confused if you shift tense within a paragraph. Show readers whether an event is happening now, has happened in the past, or will happen in the future by choosing the best tense and sticking with it.

A male cardinal **is** about eight inches long.
It **had** bright red feathers.
The crest on top of its head **threatened** enemies.

A male cardinal **is** about eight inches long.
It **has** bright red feathers.
The crest on top of its head **threatens** enemies.

Apply It

5–20. Rewrite the nature-walk journal below. Show that all the action took place in the past. Check each underlined verb for correct tense.

Revising

Nature Walk: Cardinals and Their Nest

As I <u>approached</u> the bushes at the back of the school, I <u>hear</u> some baby birds. A moment later I <u>see</u> a flash of red in the trees—a male cardinal. I <u>listen</u> carefully. A bird <u>sings</u> in a nearby tree—probably the female. Then the babies <u>call</u> again—the same sound I <u>hear</u> before.

When I <u>look</u> inside the bushes, I <u>spotted</u> a nest. The nest <u>seems</u> to be made mostly of twigs, grass, and some colored paper. The paper probably <u>comes</u> from the school. Inside the nest <u>are</u> two baby cardinals and one egg. The babies <u>curl</u> up in a ball. Their feathers <u>appeared</u> wet. The egg <u>is</u> grayish white. It <u>has</u> brown spots and lots of little speckles.

Writing with Verbs **111**

Usage

8 Subject-Verb Agreement

One-Minute Warm-Up

What's wrong with the verb in one of these sentences? How can you fix it?

> Ice and snow can hurt the paws of a dog. In a race, a sled dog wear four little booties.

- A present tense verb and its subject must agree in number. If the subject is singular, use the singular form of the verb. If the subject is plural, use the plural form of the verb.

Rules for Subject-Verb Agreement	
1. **Singular subject:** Add *-s* or *-es* to the verb.	The **driver trains** his dog team. **He teaches** one dog to lead. **He studies** his map.
2. **Plural subject:** Do not add *-s* or *-es* to the verb.	The **dogs pull** the sleds. The **driver** and his **team travel** far. **They work** together.
3. *I* or *you*: Use the plural form of the verb.	**I like** your report on dogs. **You write** well.

- Look at the second example for Rule 2. The compound subject *driver, team* is followed by the plural form of the verb. When the parts of a compound subject are joined by *and,* always use the plural form of the verb.

Try It Out

Speak Up Which verb in parentheses correctly completes each sentence?

1. I (like, likes) dogs very much.
2. They (work, works) with people in many ways.
3. The diner and the factory (keep, keeps) watchdogs.
4. A dog (try, tries) to be an excellent partner.
5. Alex (own, owns) a sheepdog named Charlie.

Unit 3: Verbs

On Your Own

For each sentence, write the present tense form of the verb in parentheses.

Example: Mr. Crosby _____ dogs. (train)   *trains*

6. He and his dogs _____ people who are blind. (help)
7. Mr. Crosby _____ dogs to cross streets safely. (teach)
8. His dog Tilly _____ his commands perfectly. (obey)
9. Many people who are blind _____ trained dogs. (use)
10. You _____ the name for these dogs. (know)
11. We _____ them seeing-eye dogs. (call)

12–22. This part of a business letter has eleven incorrect verb forms. Write the paragraphs correctly.

Example: The dogs obeys.   The *dogs obey.*

Proofreading

Our organization breed and train seeing-eye dogs. The German shepherd and the Labrador retriever makes good guide dogs. Only a smart, gentle, healthy puppy pass the test and become a seeing-eye dog. Our center then match each dog with an owner.

With a seeing-eye dog, people gains more independence. They move freely, and their lives improves. The center and its important work costs money. I asks for your help. Please gives whatever you can.

Writing Wrap-Up
WRITING • THINKING • LISTENING • SPEAKING

PERSUADING

Write a Business Letter

Write a brief letter to a company or a community group, asking for support for a cause that you care about, such as an animal shelter or a clean-up campaign. Use the present tense. Share your letter with classmates. Ask them to name your most convincing sentence. Note: See page 503 for a model of a business letter.

Usage 9: Agreement with *be* and *have*

One-Minute Warm-Up

Use the words in the flowers to complete these riddles.
I _____ eyes, but I can't see. What _____ I?
They _____ ears but can't hear. What _____ they?
It _____ leaves, but it _____ not a plant. What _____ it?

Riddle Answers: a potato, cornstalks, a table

You have already learned that the verbs *be* and *have* can be used as main verbs or as helping verbs. You have also learned that a verb and its subject must agree in number. You must change the forms of the verbs *be* and *have* in special ways to agree with their subjects. The chart below shows the present and past tense forms.

Subject	Form of *be*		Form of *have*	
	Present	Past	Present	Past
Singular subjects:				
I	am	was	have	had
You	are	were	have	had
He, She, It (or singular noun)	is	was	has	had
Plural subjects:				
We	are	were	have	had
You	are	were	have	had
They (or plural noun)	are	were	have	had

Try It Out

Speak Up Which form of *be* or *have* in parentheses correctly completes each sentence?

1. Jeff (is, am) a talented gardener.
2. Becky (has, have) brought us this pumpkin.
3. (Are, Is) you staying for dinner?
4. Molly and Pete (is, are) making pumpkin stew.
5. They (has, have) found an excellent recipe.

On Your Own

Write the verb in parentheses that correctly completes each sentence.

Example: Many fruits (has, have) lots of seeds.   *have*

6. Apple trees (was, were) once tiny seeds.
7. I (has, have) seen big trees grow from tiny seeds.
8. Our apple tree (is, are) huge now.
9. We (have, has) eaten wonderful apples from that tree.
10. The birds (is, are) gathering in our yard today.
11. Many apples (has, have) fallen on the ground.
12. I (is, am) picking the apples as fast as I can.
13. (Have, Has) Sam picked any peaches yet?

14–22. These listings from an online catalog have nine incorrect verb forms. Write the listings correctly.

Example: The roses is unusual.   *The roses are unusual.*

Pansy

Proofreading

Catalog

Gardeners Dig Our Products!

Our new garden catalog have many pleasures and surprises.

* This begonia have shiny leaves and are perfect in a pot.
* The marigolds is a glittery yellow and has gold flecks.
* Has you ever seen a more stunning pansy? Its deep violet color are a standout, and it have velvety petals.
* This tulip was growing strong last year. It were both hardy and pretty, and we are now recommending it.

Writing Wrap-Up
WRITING • THINKING • LISTENING • SPEAKING
PERSUADING

Write Catalog Listings

List items in your classroom, your school, your street, or your room for a catalog. What features, serious or funny, might attract a buyer? Write listings for four items. Use forms of *be* and *have*. Find a partner, and read your listings to each other. Which items sound most appealing?

Grammar/Mechanics

10 Contractions with *not*

One-Minute Warm-Up

When you speak or write informally, you don't always use full words. Which words are shortened in the second sentence? What words do they stand for?

> Aunt Dew stopped rocking hard and turned and looked at him. But he didn't say anything, and she didn't say anything.
>
> —from *The Hundred Penny Box,* by Sharon Bell Mathis

- You can combine some verbs with the word *not* to make contractions. **A contraction is a word formed by joining two words, making one shorter word.** An apostrophe (') takes the place of the letter or letters dropped to shorten the word.

Contractions Made with Verbs Plus *not*

do not	don't	were not	weren't	would not	wouldn't
does not	doesn't	will not	won't	should not	shouldn't
did not	didn't	have not	haven't	cannot	can't
is not	isn't	has not	hasn't	must not	mustn't
are not	aren't	had not	hadn't		
was not	wasn't	could not	couldn't		

- Since *not* is not a verb, it cannot be part of a verb phrase. The *n't* in a contraction is also not part of a verb or a verb phrase.

 Tip
Do not use contractions in formal reports or business letters.

Try It Out

Speak Up What are the contractions for the following words?

1. cannot
2. does not
3. is not
4. should not
5. had not
6. are not
7. were not
8. has not
9. do not
10. will not
11. was not
12. could not
13. must not
14. have not
15. did not

DON'T EVEN THINK OF PARKING HERE!

116 Unit 3: Verbs

On Your Own

Write the word or words that form each contraction.

Example: couldn't   *could not*

16. weren't   **17.** doesn't   **18.** hadn't   **19.** wouldn't

Write the contractions for the underlined words.

Example: Mary Ann is not feeling well.   *isn't*

20. She did not sleep well.
21. Mary Ann cannot go out.
22. She was not able to eat.
23. She could not sit up in bed.
24. We should not worry.
25. She will not be sick for long.
26. She must not get out of bed.
27. We have not visited her yet.

28–35. These health tips have eight incorrect contractions. Write the contractions correctly.

Example: Walk. Dont run.   *Walk. Don't run.*

Proofreading

How to Stifle the Sniffles

These health tips for cold sufferers arent hard to follow.
- Do'nt forget to get plenty of rest. You must'nt tire yourself out.
- You should'nt go out in crowds, and you cann't run.
- Excessive exercise doesn't help. Conserve your energy, or you wont have any strength.
- Fatty, heavy foods aren't good. Junk food isnt either.
- In case you did'nt know, liquids are good for you.

Writing Wrap-Up
WRITING • THINKING • LISTENING • SPEAKING

EXPLAINING

Write Safety Tips

What should you do and not do when you exercise, eat, ride a bus, see a movie? Write some helpful tips for a common activity or event. Be serious or be silly, but use at least four contractions. Read your tips to a small group. Ask them to spell the contractions you used. Did you all agree on the spelling?

Grammar/Usage

11 Regular and Irregular Verbs

One-Minute Warm-Up

What is the past tense of *play*? Look at the list of past tense verbs. Which verbs follow the same pattern as *play*? Which verbs don't?

hoped   wrote   covered   stayed   went   came   worked
thought   walked   ran   used   crossed   made

- You have learned that, for most verbs, you form the past by adding *-ed* to the verb. Verbs that follow this rule are called **regular verbs**.

    plant—planted   dare—dared   cry—cried

 Tip
Use your dictionary when in doubt about spelling.

- For some verbs, you do not form the past by adding *-ed*. **Irregular verbs** have special forms to show the past.

Irregular Verbs		
Verb	**Past Tense**	**Past with Helping Verb**
bring	brought	(has, have, had) brought
come	came	(has, have, had) come
go	went	(has, have, had) gone
make	made	(has, have, had) made
run	ran	(has, have, had) run
say	said	(has, have, had) said
take	took	(has, have, had) taken
think	thought	(has, have, had) thought
write	wrote	(has, have, had) written

Try It Out

Speak Up Which of these past tense verbs are regular? Which are irregular?

1. dressed
2. thought
3. came
4. wrote
5. said
6. tried

What is the past form of each verb above when it is used with the helping verb *have*?

Unit 3: Verbs

On Your Own

Write two forms for each verb: the past tense and the past with *have*.

Example: go   *went, have gone*

7. bring   8. complete   9. take   10. dry   11. come   12. run

Write the correct past form of the verb in parentheses to complete each sentence.

Example: I _____ about a good topic. (think)   *thought*

13. I _____ to the library for books about bears. (go)
14. I had _____ a list of the books. (make)
15. I _____ my report in two hours. (write)
16. I _____ the report to school yesterday. (take)
17. She _____ that my report was great! (say)

18–24. This part of a job interview has seven incorrect past tense forms of verbs. Write this part of the interview correctly.

Example: I runned a book group.   *I ran a book group.*

Proofreading

Central City Library

Q: Why have you come to the library to apply for a job?

A: I apply here before, but I was too young. Now I have took a library course and worked in my school library. Three people have wrote letters of recommendation for me. I have bringed them. I have always love books and have thinked I would be a good librarian. Now others have sayed the same thing.

Writing Wrap-Up

WRITING • THINKING • LISTENING • SPEAKING

REFLECTING

Write an Interview

What after-school or Saturday job could you apply for? dog walker? baby sitter? crossing guard? reporter? Write at least five sentences that answer these interview questions: Why do you want this job? What makes you the right person for the job? Use some verbs in the past. Take turns with a partner reading your interview answers to each other. Compare the reasons and the arguments you used.

Grammar/Usage
12 More Irregular Verbs

Which words are past tense verbs? Which one is regular? Which are irregular?

> Jonathan found a piece of driftwood, yelled, "Moose! Fetch!" and threw it into the lake.
>
> —from *Earthquake Terror,* by Peg Kehret

There are no rules to help you form the past of irregular verbs. However, certain patterns will help you remember the past forms of some irregular verbs.

Irregular Verbs		
Verb	**Past Tense**	**Past with Helping Verb**
ring	rang	(has, have, had) rung
sing	sang	(has, have, had) sung
swim	swam	(has, have, had) swum
begin	began	(has, have, had) begun
tear	tore	(has, have, had) torn
wear	wore	(has, have, had) worn
break	broke	(has, have, had) broken
speak	spoke	(has, have, had) spoken
steal	stole	(has, have, had) stolen
choose	chose	(has, have, had) chosen
freeze	froze	(has, have, had) frozen
blow	blew	(has, have, had) blown
grow	grew	(has, have, had) grown
know	knew	(has, have, had) known
fly	flew	(has, have, had) flown

Try It Out

Speak Up What is the past tense form of each verb? What is the past form with *have*?

1. fly
2. choose
3. ring
4. break
5. begin

120 Unit 3: Verbs

On Your Own

Write the correct past form of the verb in parentheses to complete each sentence.

Example: Eva and Roy _____ warm clothing on the outing. (wear)   *wore*

6. We _____ on the way to the campsite. (sing)
7. The water in the pond had not _____. (freeze)
8. The strong winds have _____ down a tent. (blow)
9. Mulan _____ how to tend the campfire. (know)
10. She had _____ to us about campfire safety. (speak)
11. Mr. and Mrs. Lonzo had _____ the food. (choose)
12. The raccoons had _____ some of it! (steal)

13–22. This electronic news bulletin has ten incorrect past tense verb forms. Write the bulletin correctly.

Example: The fire begun at dawn.   *The fire began at dawn.*

Proofreading

News Bulletin

Forest Devastated by Flames

For more details

Fire alarms rung early this morning, and everyone knew very quickly that this forest fire was serious. Strong winds have tore into the forest and have blowed the flames, and the fire has growed fast. Some creatures of the forest swum or flied to safety. Others began too late. Helicopters have flew above the area to check the damage. Additional firefighters have began to arrive, and many weared their full gear, ready to go to work. Some campers broke down and cried. "This fire has broke my heart," said one.

Writing Wrap-Up
WRITING • THINKING • LISTENING • SPEAKING

COMPARING / CONTRASTING

Write a Letter

Think of two vacations you have had. How were they alike? different? Write the beginning of a letter to a friend. Include one paragraph of likenesses and one of differences. Use irregular verbs. Read your work to a partner. Has he or she had a similar experience?

Usage/Mechanics
13 Verb Phrases with *have*

One-Minute Warm-Up

What's wrong with the verbs in these sentences? How can you fix them?

> The tubas shoulda marched at the end of the band. Then we could of heard the other instruments.

- A main verb can have more than one helping verb. The helping verb *have* is often used with the helping verbs *could, would, should,* and *must.* The two helping verbs and the main verb form a verb phrase.
- These helping verbs are often spoken as contractions.

Helping Verbs	Contractions
could have	could've
would have	would've
should have	should've
must have	must've

- Do not use *of* with *could, would, should,* or *must.*

   Incorrect: You should of seen the parade last weekend.

   Correct: You should have seen the parade last weekend.
   You should've seen the parade last weekend.

Try It Out

Speak Up Is the verb phrase in each sentence correct? If not, what should it be?

1. Jim could of told us about his trip to Utah.
2. Perhaps we should have called him.
3. He must of seen some wonderful places.
4. We would've enjoyed his pictures of the trip.
5. He must'ov put them in an album by now.
6. We shoulda saved Jim's post card.

On Your Own

Write the verb phrase in each sentence. Then rewrite each phrase to include a contraction.

Example: Birdwatchers must have liked this.
<u>must have liked</u>   must've liked

7. They would have learned about wild geese.
8. They could have written about them.
9. Larry and I must have seen fifty wild geese.
10. We would have taken some great pictures.
11. I should have checked in the library.
12. Maybe I would have discovered a good article.

13–20. This script has eight incorrect verb phrases. Write the script correctly.

Example: You shoulda seen it!   *You should've seen it!*

Sara: You must of studied a lot before the hike.
Cory: I wouldve learned more if I could'ave.
Sara: You musta named twenty birds already!
Cory: Well, I couldv'e made some mistakes.
Sara: I should've brought my binoculars.
Cory: I wouldof lent you mine, but I needed them.
Sara: Well, you couldve let me use them just once.
Cory: And *you* could'of remembered yours!

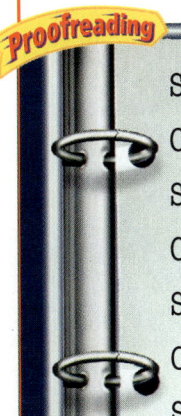

Writing Wrap-Up
WRITING • THINKING • LISTENING • SPEAKING

CREATING

Write a Script

Think of an outdoor scene with two or three characters. Write a script for the scene. Use four verb phrases with *could*, *would*, *should*, or *must* plus *have*. Ask one or two partners to read the scene with you. Work together to check your verb phrases.

Usage 14 teach, learn; let, leave

One-Minute Warm-Up

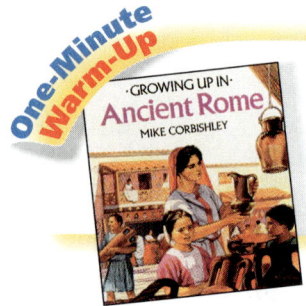

Which word is the verb in this sentence? How can you change the sentence using the verb *learned*?

In early Roman times, families taught their sons at home.

—from *Growing Up in Ancient Rome,* by Mike Corbishley

Do not confuse the verbs *teach* and *learn*. Their meanings are related but not the same. Also be careful not to confuse the verbs *let* and *leave*. They sound similar, but their meanings are different.

Verb	Meaning	Example
teach	to give instruction	He will **teach** us history.
learn	to receive instruction	We will **learn** about Rome.
let	to permit	**Let** Kevin go with us.
leave	to go away from	We will **leave** tomorrow.
	to let remain in place	**Leave** it on the table.

Try It Out

Speak Up Which is correct in each sentence, *teach* or *learn*?

1. How can I _____ more about interesting places to visit in the city?
2. Tour guides will _____ you.
3. This book will _____ you its history.
4. You can also _____ a lot in the museum.

Liberty Bell, Pennsylvania

Which is correct in each sentence, *let* or *leave*?

5. Will you _____ me go to the museum with Nate this morning?
6. We should _____ this crowded train go by.
7. Don't _____ your coat on the bench.
8. Where did I _____ the map?

Unit 3: Verbs

On Your Own

Write the word in parentheses that correctly completes each sentence.

Example: You may (let, leave) your jackets in the coat room.   *leave*

9. We will (teach, learn) about fossils at the museum.
10. Will the guide (let, leave) us use the computers?
11. The guide used to (teach, learn) college students.
12. Please (teach, learn) us about that strange fossil.
13. (Let, Leave) me see it, please.
14. What kind of fossil would this plant (let, leave) behind?
15. Sam, we told your mother we would (let, leave) early.
16. I will (let, leave) you see my notes later.
17. I hope we (teach, learn) more about fossils in school.

18–26. This part of a guide's speech has nine incorrect verbs. Write the speech correctly.

Example: Leave us begin now.   *Let us begin now.*

Proofreading

First, leave me introduce myself. I am Ms. Kim, and I will learn you a little about fossils. You can teach more from the exhibits, so please leave lots of time to look at them. I will also leave you use the museum's computers before you leave. Fossils learn us about early forms of life. They let their outlines in rocks and leave us see them eons later. Leave me show you a fossil that learns us about dinosaurs.

Writing Wrap-Up
WRITING • THINKING • LISTENING • SPEAKING

INFORMING

Write a Speech

If you were to guide a group from another country through your classroom, what would you show them? tell them? Write part of your speech explaining one area or aspect of your classroom. Use some present tense forms of *let, leave, teach,* and *learn.* In a small group, take turns reading your work to each other. How do your speeches differ?

For Extra Practice see page 149.

Usage 15: sit, set; can, may

One-Minute Warm-Up

What does *can* mean in the second sentence? How would the meaning of the sentence change if *may* were used instead?

"Come on Chrissie," Marla called to her. "You can hit it, I know you can!"

—from *Me, Mop, and the Moondance Kid*, by Walter Dean Myers

You have already learned about some frequently confused verbs. Also be careful not to confuse the verbs *sit* and *set*. Their meanings are different. Do not confuse the verbs *can* and *may*. Their meanings are similar but not the same.

Verb	Meaning	Example
sit	to rest	I will sit in the chair.
set	to place or put	Set the book on the table.
can	to be able	I can ride my bike well.
may	to be allowed	May I go to the park?

Try It Out

Speak Up Which is correct in each sentence, *can* or *may*?

1. _____ I invite a friend for lunch?
2. Luke does not live far away. He _____ get here easily.
3. Yes, you _____ invite Alex.
4. Luke, _____ you reach that jar on the shelf?
5. You _____ sit down now. We are ready to eat.

Which is correct in each sentence, *sit* or *set*?

6. Latoya, _____ your gloves on that bench.
7. No one will _____ there until later.
8. Would you like to _____ near Carmen?
9. _____ the puzzle on the worktable.
10. Later you will _____ on the high stools.

126 Unit 3: Verbs

On Your Own

Write the word in parentheses that correctly completes each sentence.

Example: (Can, May) I do that puzzle with you?   *May*

11. Carmen should (sit, set) in the big chair.
12. Alex will (sit, set) a box under her cast.
13. She has to (sit, set) with her foot raised.
14. (Can, May) I use your desk lamp for an hour?
15. Do you think we (can, may) finish this puzzle in an hour?
16. Carmen (can, may) do even hard puzzles quickly.

17–26. This set of instructions has ten incorrect verbs. Write the instructions correctly.

Example: If you may read these rules, you are ready to begin.
*If you **can** read these rules, you are ready to begin.*

Proofreading

- First, set in an uncomfortable chair so you stay awake.
- You cannot work lying down. You'll doze off.
- Sit the puzzle box on the table. You may not begin yet.
- Set still and breathe deeply. Now you can open the box.
- Sit out as many pieces as you may on the table.
- Look for all the edge pieces you may find.
- To make room, you can set other pieces back in the box.
- See how many edge pieces you may fit together.

Writing Wrap-Up
WRITING • THINKING • LISTENING • SPEAKING

EXPLAINING

Write Instructions

Write some instructions for something you know how to do—play chess, for example, or get out of bed in the morning. Use *sit, set, can,* and *may* at least once. Read your instructions to at least two people. Ask them to listen for correct verb usage.

Revising Strategies

Vocabulary

Using Exact Verbs

Most verbs are action words. To make your writing clear and interesting and to avoid repetition, choose exact verbs that describe the action taking place.

Less exact verb: The men moved the piano.
More exact verb: The men hoisted the piano.

Apply It

1–6. Rewrite the sentences from this poster. Use your Thesaurus Plus in the back of your book to find a more exact word for each underlined verb.

Revising

What Can You Do at our Fair?

You and your friends can...

- do puzzles.
- do secret messages.
- do a short play.
- spend a long time looking in mirrors.
- look quickly at tiny scenes inside little boxes.
- laugh quietly at silly cartoons.

128 Unit 3: Verbs

Enrichment

The Time of Your Life

Time lines show the order of events in history. Make a time line of some events in your life. Draw a long line on white paper. Divide the line equally to show the years of your life. Label each year. Then write a short sentence about something important that happened to you or your family that year. Use past tense verbs.

Verb Frenzy

Players: 2 and a caller

Materials: 7 index cards with these pronouns written on them: *I, you, he, she, it, we,* and *they;* for each player, 2 index cards with the verbs *has* and *have.*

To play: The caller shuffles the pronoun cards, picks one, and reads it aloud. Each player tries to be the first to hold up the verb card that correctly follows the pronoun—for example, *she has.*

Scoring: The player who holds up the correct verb first scores a point.

Challenge Write some present tense irregular verbs from pages 118 and 120 on index cards. The player scores another point by adding the correct form of this verb to the first two cards—for example, *she has chosen.*

Checkup: Unit 3

1. Action Verbs (p. 96)
Write the action verb in each sentence.

1. A hurricane struck the island.
2. Waves crashed over the rocks near the shore.
3. The wind blew fiercely.
4. Trees bent in the wind.
5. Then heavy rains fell.
6. The storm passed quickly.
7. Homeowners worry about it.

2. Direct Objects (p. 98)
Write the direct objects.

8. Scientists study the planets.
9. They carefully record their observations.
10. They make vital discoveries.
11. Some own telescopes.
12. Others use cameras with a special lens.
13. They take unusual pictures.
14. The sky at night fascinates them.

3. Main Verbs and Helping Verbs (p. 100)
Write the verb in these sentences. Underline the helping verb once and the main verb twice.

15. The sun has risen over the town.
16. A rooster is crowing in the yard.
17. Birds were calling to each other.
18. The children have awakened because of the noise.
19. They are eating fruit and cereal.
20. The day is beginning slowly.
21. Soon the school bus will come for the children.

4. Linking Verbs (p. 102)
Write each sentence. Underline the linking verb. Draw an arrow to show the words that the verb links.

22. Canaries are delightful pets.
23. My canary is a good singer.
24. Her songs seem very loud.
25. She looks beautiful to me.
26. Her feathers appear yellow.

5. Present Tense (p. 104)
Write the present tense form of each verb.

27. She _____ her face. (wash)
28. Her brother _____ about the rain. (worry)
29. Mom _____ our progress. (watch)
30. I _____ quickly. (dress)
31. Alice _____ her long hair. (fix)
32. The doorbell _____ twice. (buzz)
33. We _____ to the door. (hurry)
34. The graduation party _____. (begin)

6. Past Tense (p. 106)
Write the past tense form of each verb.

35. We _____ the early West. (study)
36. Few doctors _____ there. (move)
37. Some doctors _____ a trip to the West with explorers. (plan)
38. They _____ the wildlife. (observe)
39. They also _____ the sick. (treat)
40. The people _____ for aid. (hope)
41. More patients _____ professional care. (receive)

130 Unit 3: Verbs Go to www.eduplace.com/tales/hme/ for more fun with parts of speech.

7 Future Tense (p. 108) Write the future tense form of each verb.

42. Our club ____ a terrific new game. (create)
43. Liz and I ____ our ideas. (share)
44. Stan ____ the board. (build)
45. Karla ____ the maze. (draw)
46. Alexi ____ the rules. (write)

8 Subject-Verb Agreement (p. 112) Write the present tense of each verb.

47. Jed and I ____ newspapers. (read)
48. I ____ the sports section. (enjoy)
49. You ____ the comics. (prefer)
50. An editor ____ stories. (pick)
51. Reporters ____ articles. (write)
52. A proofreader usually ____ for errors. (check)
53. A computer ____ the page. (fit)
54. Photographers ____ exciting pictures. (take)

9 Agreement with *be* and *have* (p. 114) Write the verb in parentheses that completes each sentence.

55. Hawaii (is, are) made up of many islands.
56. They (was, were) formed long ago by volcanoes.
57. Their beauty (is, are) amazing.
58. Hawaii's mild climate (has, have) attracted many tourists.
59. (Have, Has) you visited Hawaii?
60. I (was, were) there last year.

10 Contractions with *not* (p. 116) Write the word or words that were combined to form each contraction.

61. Aren't you making a sketch?
62. Haven't you seen it yet?
63. Can't you ask about it?
64. The image isn't quite clear.
65. You shouldn't judge so soon.
66. People won't be disappointed.

11 Regular and Irregular Verbs (p. 118) Write each sentence, using the past form of each verb.

67. Carlotta ____ the play. (write)
68. Jay had ____ of it. (think)
69. Gary ____ the stage set. (make)
70. Maria ____ the props. (create)
71. Jessie and Pete have ____ the lights. (fix)
72. We ____ our lines well. (say)
73. Mom ____ Ken to the box office. (take)
74. A large crowd ____. (come)
75. The cast ____ food. (bring)

12 More Irregular Verbs (p. 120) Write the correct past form of each verb.

76. A cold wind ____. (blow)
77. The branches of the trees had ____. (freeze)
78. Some limbs had ____ off. (break)
79. The birds had ____ south. (fly)
80. I had ____ a fall coat. (wear)

See www.eduplace.com/kids/hme/ for an online quiz.

Checkup 131

Checkup continued

13 Verb Phrases with *have*
(p. 122) Write each sentence, using the correct words in parentheses.

81. He (must of, must have) forgotten all about us.
82. He (should've, should of) told them everything.
83. Jo (would of, would have) gone.
84. You (could've, could of) asked her to go.
85. We (would've, would of) had a good time.
86. The phone (must of, must have) rung earlier.
87. Mom (would've, would of) left.
88. Maybe I (could've, could of) reached him.

14 *teach, learn; let, leave; sit, set; can, may*
(pp. 124, 126) Write the word in parentheses that correctly completes the sentence.

89. Ms. Clark will (learn, teach) us.
90. (Set, Sit) the paints on the box.
91. (Set, Sit) on a stool by me.
92. I (may, can) draw well already.
93. (May, Can) I borrow some paper?
94. (Let, Leave) me help you.
95. We will (learn, teach) about paints.
96. We must (let, leave) now.
97. (Leave, Let) your work overnight.

Mixed Review 98–105. This part of a script for a TV documentary has eight incorrect verb forms. Write the script correctly.

Proofreading Checklist
Check these carefully.
✔ subject-verb agreement
✔ past forms
✔ verb phrases with *have*
✔ contractions with *not*
✔ teach/learn

Proofreading

Narrator: Have you ever visited a museum? Perhaps you goed to see art. Perhaps you choosed to visit a collection of butterflies. Museums has existed since ancient days, but early museums weren't for the general public. You could of visited them only as a scholar or as a noble.

Director: We have tryed to make this museum a lively, interesting place open to everyone. Is you young? a parent? a grandparent? Museums are fun. Every visitor learn about art, science, or history.

Test Practice

Write the numbers 1–8 on a sheet of paper. Read each sentence. Choose the best way to write the underlined part. Write the letter for that answer. If there is no mistake, write the letter for the last answer, "No mistakes."

1. Bees <u>has made</u> a hive in the tree.
   A have made
   B has make
   C had make
   D (No mistakes)

2. The reporters <u>are listens</u> to the mayor's speech.
   F is listening
   G has listened
   H are listening
   J (No mistakes)

3. You <u>should of seen</u> the fireworks in the park last night!
   A should of saw
   B should have seen
   C should have saw
   D (No mistakes)

4. Uncle Theo <u>will learn</u> me some Spanish words.
   F can learn
   G are teaching
   H will teach
   J (No mistakes)

5. Our dog <u>has swum</u> across the river.
   A has swimmed
   B has swam
   C have swum
   D (No mistakes)

6. Dr. Sanchez <u>aren't</u> in her office now.
   F isn't
   G wasn't
   H weren't
   J (No mistakes)

7. The workers <u>will sit</u> the ladder on the ground.
   A will set
   B can sets
   C are sitting
   D (No mistakes)

8. The students <u>have wrote</u> letters to their favorite authors.
   F have writed
   G have written
   H has wrote
   J (No mistakes)

Test Practice continued

Now write numbers 9–16 on your paper. Read each paragraph. Choose the line that shows the mistake. Write the letter for that answer. If there is no mistake, write the letter for the last answer, "None."

9 A Stanley should of
   B worn socks and shoes today.
   C It is too cold for sandals.
   D (None)

10 F May I please look at
   G the map of the zoo? The apes
   H and monkies are over there.
   J (None)

11 A There are many
   B famous sights in California.
   C One is the golden gate bridge.
   D (None)

12 F Someone stealed my
   G bike from the bike rack! Who
   H could have done such a thing?
   J (None)

13 A My little brother loves
   B chess. Him and Dad play a
   C game every night before bed.
   D (None)

14 F Hannah is the most
   G graceful dancer in the class.
   H See how she spins and leaps!
   J (None)

15 A Carlos can't mend the
   B rip in his shirt. No one never
   C showed him how to sew.
   D (None)

16 F The children listened
   G good to the directions. They
   H didn't make any mistakes.
   J (None)

Now write numbers 17–24 on your paper. Read each paragraph. Choose the line that shows the mistake. Write the letter for that answer. If there is no mistake, write the letter for the last answer, "None."

17 A You'll find womens'
   B clothes and shoes on the
   C second floor near the stairs.
   D (None)

18 F Why is Pearl watching
   G television. She should be
   H outdoors with her friends.
   J (None)

19 A Zack is almost as tall
   B as his mother. He has growed
   C about four inches this year.
   D (None)

20 F Mr. Lorenz got up
   G early this morning to catch
   H the train to Salt lake city.
   J (None)

21 A Please ask Morey to
   B turn down his music. Their
   C are people trying to sleep.
   D (None)

22 F No, the post office
   G and the library will not be
   H open on the Fourth of July.
   J (None)

23 A Carlita and I just saw
   B Dirk Drago's new movie.
   C What a terrific actor he is?
   D (None)

24 F Grandma said, Please
   G take some photographs of
   H Scott at his birthday party."
   J (None)

Test Practice 135

Extra Practice

1 Action Verbs

(pages 96–97)

- An **action verb** shows what the subject does or did.

• Write an action verb from the box of words to complete each sentence. Use each verb only once.

Example: Carla _____ me for her team.   *chose*

1. I _____ at Allison's joke.
2. Laurie _____ the ball to Tony.
3. Kevin _____ to second base.
4. I _____ over a rock in the field.
5. I _____ a hole in my new jeans.
6. Tony always _____ his bike to the game.
7. After the game, we _____ lunch.
8. We also _____ cold drinks.

| tripped |
| ate |
| tore |
| rides |
| sipped |
| ran |
| laughed |
| chose |
| threw |

▲ Write the action verb in each sentence.

Example: Suzanne Lenglen played tennis well.   *played*

9. She won her first Wimbledon competition in 1919.
10. Lenglen changed the game of women's tennis.
11. She turned it into a more exciting game.
12. Long ago, women tennis players wore long dresses.
13. Lenglen introduced the short tennis dress.
14. She smashed the ball over the net.
15. She captured six championships in seven years.

■ Read each word. If it is an action verb, use it in a sentence. If it is not an action verb, write *not an action verb*.

Example: leaped   *The dancer leaped into the air.*

16. sent
17. twig
18. crawled
19. sing
20. basket
21. hopped
22. sea
23. chased
24. car
25. said
26. raced
27. threw
28. hurried
29. shared
30. constructed

136 Unit 3: Verbs

2 Direct Objects

(pages 98–99)

- A **direct object** is a word in the predicate that receives the action of the verb.
- Direct objects are used with action verbs only.

● Read each sentence. Then write the answer to each question. The answer will be the direct object.

Example: Hard rain hit the roof. The rain hit what?   *roof*

1. Thunder scared Glenn. Thunder scared whom?
2. He shut the windows. He shut what?
3. He read a book. He read what?
4. The storm will not hurt him. The storm will not hurt whom?
5. He will draw pictures of stormy skies. He will draw what?

▲ Make two columns. Label them *Action Verb* and *Direct Object*. Find the action verb and the direct object in each sentence, and write them in the correct columns.

Example: Herman Melville wrote *Moby Dick*.

Action Verb	**Direct Object**
wrote	Moby Dick

6. Melville tells a great story in this book.
7. Men hunt a large white whale.
8. They sail their ship all over the world.
9. They shoot harpoons at the white whale.
10. During the struggle, the whale sinks their ship.

■ Write a sentence, using each action verb below. Include a direct object in each sentence.

Example: made   *Long ago, people made ships out of wood.*

11. search
12. carried
13. gathered
14. chop
15. dragged
16. hold
17. followed
18. build
19. wear
20. covered

Extra Practice **137**

Extra Practice

3 Main Verbs and Helping Verbs

- A **verb phrase** is made up of a main verb and a helping verb.
- The **main verb** shows action.
- The **helping verb** works with the main verb.

(pages 100–101)

● Each sentence contains a helping verb and a main verb. The main verb is underlined. Write the helping verb.

Example: The football team is <u>hoping</u> for a victory.   *is*

1. The players have <u>worked</u> hard this season.
2. It was <u>raining</u> last Saturday.
3. The players were <u>slipping</u> on the muddy field.
4. The quarterback had <u>hurt</u> his shoulder.
5. He will <u>play</u> in the game this afternoon.
6. Joan and I are <u>going</u> to the game.

▲ Write the verb or verb phrase in each sentence.

Example: I am going to every game this season.
   am going

7. The Eagles have won four games this year.
8. The school newspaper has praised them.
9. Last year they had hoped for a winning season.
10. Al was throwing a pass in the last game.
11. The Terriers were charging at him.
12. His fumble resulted in a touchdown for them.
13. I am expecting a victory this year.

■ Use each verb phrase in a sentence.

Example: was hired   *The new coach was hired yesterday.*

14. is choosing
15. had played
16. will miss
17. is buying
18. had gotten
19. have watched
20. were defeated
21. am memorizing
22. was looking
23. have talked
24. are thinking
25. was wondering

138 Unit 3: Verbs

Extra Practice

4 Linking Verbs

(pages 102–103)

- A **linking verb** links the subject with a word or words in the predicate that name or describe the subject.
- A linking verb does not show action.

● Write *action* or *linking* for each underlined verb.

Example: Diana Nyad is a long-distance swimmer.
linking

1. She <u>completed</u> a sixty-mile swim.
2. She <u>began</u> her swim at Bimini Island.
3. The water <u>looked</u> cold and choppy.
4. She <u>swam</u> to Florida.
5. She <u>saw</u> jellyfish and sharks.
6. She <u>was</u> brave.

▲ Write each sentence. Underline the linking verb. Then draw an arrow to connect each subject with the word that names or describes it.

Example: The Olympic Games are exciting.
The Olympic Games <u>are</u> exciting.

7. The athletes are very talented.
8. The first prize in each event is a gold medal.
9. Mark Spitz was famous during the 1972 Olympic Games.
10. His swimming was excellent.
11. He was a winner of seven gold medals.
12. Perhaps you will be a famous winner too.

■ Write sentences with linking verbs. Use each word or group of words below as the subject of a sentence.

Example: Christopher Columbus   *Christopher Columbus was an explorer.*

13. My school
14. An elephant
15. Apples
16. I
17. The weather today
18. Dinosaurs
19. Abraham Lincoln
20. My college major
21. Umbrellas
22. That painting

Extra Practice

5 Present Tense

(pages 104–105)

- A **present tense verb** shows action that happens now.
- Add -s or -es to most verbs to show the present tense if the subject is singular.
- Do not add -s or -es if the subject is *I* or *you* or if it is plural.

● Write the present tense verbs in the sentences below.

Example: Bill collects postage stamps. *collects*

1. I like stamps too.
2. Bill and I often go to stamp shows on weekends.
3. We buy new stamps there.
4. My cousin Ramon sometimes goes with us.
5. Bill watches a show about stamps on television.
6. It teaches him a lot about stamps.

▲ Write the correct present tense form of each verb in parentheses.

Example: My mother _____ old chairs. (fix) *fixes*

7. She _____ new cane seats in them. (put)
8. First, she _____ the strips of cane in water. (soak)
9. Next, she carefully _____ the seat. (weave)
10. Then the cane _____ slowly. (dry)
11. The new seat _____ tightly. (fit)

■ Write each group of sentences, using the correct present tense form of each underlined verb.

Example: <u>dry</u>: Joan ____ the clothes. We ____ the dishes. He ____ his hair.
   Joan dries the clothes. We dry the dishes. He dries his hair.

12. <u>pay</u>: Pat ____ the bill. He ____ attention. We ____ for lunch.
13. <u>toss</u>: We ____ the ball. He ____ the newspaper. I ____ the salad.
14. <u>mix</u>: I ____ the dough. She ____ the cards. Amy ____ the paints.
15. <u>wash</u>: You ____ the car. He ____ the floor. They ____ windows.
16. <u>cry</u>: The babies ____ at night. You ____ out loud. She ____ for help.

Extra Practice

(pages 106–107)

6 Past Tense

- A **past tense verb** shows something that already happened.
- Form the past tense of most verbs by adding *-ed*.
- If a verb ends with *e*, add *-d*. If a verb ends with a consonant and *y*, change the *y* to *i* and add *-ed*. If a verb ends with a vowel and a consonant, double the consonant and add *-ed*.

● Write the past tense verbs in the sentences below.

Example: Bonita walked quickly down the hall.   *walked*

1. Her friends stayed in the classroom.
2. They waited for their turns.
3. Bonita finally reached the cafeteria.
4. Mr. Wong called her to a special table.
5. She picked up the paper with the list of names.
6. She voted for Terry for president of the school.

▲ Write the past tense form of each verb in parentheses.

Example: Inez _____ an adventure on TV. (watch)   *watched*

7. Later she _____ the main character. (describe)
8. People _____ this pirate "Blackbeard." (call)
9. Blackbeard _____ along the coast of Virginia. (sail)
10. He and his men _____ many ships. (rob)
11. The people finally _____ him. (punish)

■ Rewrite these sentences, using verbs in the past tense.

Example: People write many stories about Captain Kidd.
       People wrote many stories about Captain Kidd.

12. Captain Kidd and his men chase pirates.
13. They carry the pirates' treasures back to England.
14. They bury the treasure in a secret place.
15. Captain Kidd dies in 1701.
16. People search for his treasure without success.

Extra Practice

7 Future Tense

(pages 108–109)

- A **future tense verb** tells what is going to happen.
- Use the main verb with the helping verb *will* or *shall* to form the future tense.

● Write the future tense form of each verb below.

Example: cry   *will cry*

1. read
2. hope
3. steal
4. want
5. ride
6. pull
7. come
8. grow
9. begin
10. wish
11. worry
12. catch

▲ Write the verb in each sentence. Then write the future tense form of the verb.

Example: We have fed the birds every winter for many years.
   have fed   will feed

13. We hang pieces of fat in special bags.
14. Chickadees and woodpeckers like this food.
15. Woodpeckers flew to our feeder each winter.
16. The fat kept them warm on cold days.
17. We buy seeds for the cardinals and sparrows.
18. Cardinals have eaten at our feeder many times.
19. Blue jays reach the feeder before the other birds.
20. Sometimes they chase the other birds away.

■ Answer these questions by writing full sentences. Use the future tense form of each underlined verb.

Example: Where are we <u>going</u>?   *We will go to the park.*

21. What birds do people <u>see</u>?
22. Do birds <u>travel</u> south for the winter?
23. What foods do they <u>eat</u>?
24. Is anyone going to <u>bring</u> seeds for them?
25. Have you <u>read</u> any books about birds?
26. Has Ted <u>designed</u> a birdhouse?
27. When is he <u>hanging</u> it in the apple tree?
28. Are you going to <u>help</u> him?

Extra Practice

(pages 112–113)

8 Subject-Verb Agreement

- A present tense verb and its subject must agree in number.
- Add *-s* or *-es* to the verb if the subject is singular.
- Do not add *-s* or *-es* to the verb if the subject is plural or if the subject is *I* or *you*.

● Write whether the subject and the verb in each sentence are *singular* or *plural*.

Example: Some dogs work on farms and ranches.   *plural*

1. They watch the cattle and sheep.
2. Annie Dalton lives on a ranch with her dog.
3. She calls her dog Judd.
4. Annie and Judd work together.
5. Judd takes care of many sheep and cattle.

▲ Write each sentence. Use the correct present tense form of the verb in parentheses.

Example: Some dogs _____ sleds over ice and snow. (pull)
Some dogs pull sleds over ice and snow.

6. The sleds _____ supplies. (carry)
7. My friend in Canada _____ dogsleds. (use)
8. He _____ the sleds out of wood. (make)
9. A person _____ on the back of the sled. (ride)
10. The lead dog _____ the commands of that person. (obey)

■ If the subject and the verb agree in number, write *correct*. If they do not agree, rewrite the sentence correctly.

Example: You knows a lot about working dogs.
You know a lot about working dogs.

11. I read books and articles about them.
12. You and I often goes to the library.
13. The librarian also enjoy books about dogs.
14. She usually puts books about dogs on that shelf.
15. We talks about different kinds of working dogs.

Extra Practice

(pages 114–115)

9 Agreement with *be* and *have*

- Change the forms of the verbs *be* and *have* to make them agree with their subjects.

● The subjects and the verbs agree in the sentences below. For each sentence, write *singular* or *plural*.

Example: Potatoes and carrots are vegetables. *plural*

1. A vegetable is part of a plant.
2. A carrot plant has only one root.
3. I am eating a carrot.
4. This carrot was once a root.
5. We have eaten flower buds too.
6. We were eating cauliflower last night.
7. Most vegetables are delicious.

▲ Write each sentence, using the verb in parentheses that agrees with the subject.

Example: A banana (has, have) seeds. *A banana has seeds.*

8. I (has, have) looked for the seeds in a banana.
9. The banana seeds (was, were) tiny.
10. The watermelon (has, have) many seeds.
11. White seeds and black seeds (is, are) in a watermelon.
12. We (is, are) saving these seeds.
13. I (has, have) planted some in pots already.

■ Read each sentence below. If the subject and the verb agree, write *correct*. If not, rewrite the sentence correctly.

Example: These tomatoes is ripe. *These tomatoes are ripe.*

14. I is going to pick them this afternoon.
15. This morning we has a bad storm.
16. The wind and the rain has damaged my plants.
17. Mom has offered to help in the garden.
18. We is tying the plants to strong stakes.
19. We are protecting them from the wind and the rain.
20. Too much water are bad for plants.

144 Unit 3: Verbs

Extra Practice

10 Contractions with *not*

(pages 116–117)

- A **contraction** is the shortened form of two words. An apostrophe (') takes the place of any dropped letters.

● Write the contraction in each sentence.

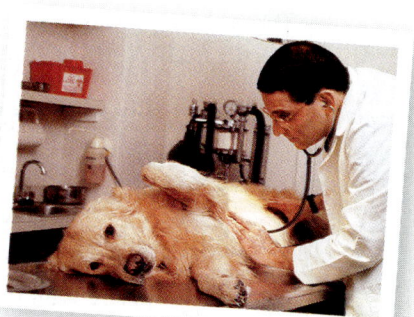

Example: Some doctors don't treat people. *don't*

1. Haven't you ever met an animal doctor?
2. Animals aren't always healthy.
3. I don't like to see my dog sick.
4. Shouldn't you take your cat to the doctor?
5. My dog's doctor isn't far from your house.
6. Why don't you take your cat to Dr. Strong's office?

▲ Write each sentence, using a contraction in place of the underlined word or words.

Example: My cat Molly <u>is not</u> feeling well.
My cat Molly isn't feeling well.

7. Molly <u>has not</u> eaten any food.
8. This morning she <u>did not</u> want to play.
9. She <u>will not</u> stay sick if Dr. Strong treats her.
10. She <u>should not</u> be afraid of Dr. Strong.
11. Thanks to Dr. Strong, she <u>is not</u> sick anymore.

■ Answer each question by writing a sentence that contains a contraction with *not*.

Example: Does your pony have a cold?
My pony doesn't have a cold.

12. Do you know an animal doctor named Dr. Strong?
13. Have you forgotten that dogs need shots every year?
14. Has your cat seen a doctor lately?
15. Has your goldfish stopped coughing yet?
16. Could a lion get the chicken pox?

Extra Practice

11 Regular and Irregular Verbs

(pages 118–119)

- Add *-d* or *-ed* to **regular** verbs to show the past.
- **Irregular** verbs have special forms to show the past.

● Write each verb or verb phrase. Then write *regular* or *irregular* for each one.

Example: have thought   *have thought   irregular*

1. walked
2. has written
3. had stamped
4. said
5. had gone
6. had discovered
7. brought
8. have taken
9. tried
10. had needed

▲ Write each sentence, using the correct form of the verb in parentheses to show past time.

Example: In school we have _____ about deer. (learn)
In school we have learned about deer.

11. People have _____ about them in books. (write)
12. One book _____ the different kinds of deer. (discuss)
13. A deer once _____ past me in the mountains. (run)
14. My teacher _____ that deer rest most of the day. (say)
15. She once _____ several deer in the evening. (follow)
16. She _____ them as they grazed. (watch)

■ Rewrite each sentence, using the past with a helping verb.

Example: The polar bear ran twenty-five miles per hour.
The polar bear has run twenty-five miles per hour.

17. The brown bear gathered acorns and berries.
18. A mother bear brought her cubs to the stream.
19. The black bear searched for honey.
20. Angry bees swarmed around the bear.
21. My teacher wrote a book about bears.
22. In class he said many interesting things about them.

Extra Practice

12 More Irregular Verbs
- Some irregular verbs follow similar patterns in their past tense forms.

(pages 120–121)

● Write the past tense form of each verb below. Then write the form that is used to show the past with a helping verb.

Example: know *knew* *have known*

1. wear
2. fly
3. tear
4. grow
5. freeze
6. swim

▲ Write each sentence, using the correct form of the verb in parentheses to show past time.

Example: I _____ my Tigers hat to the baseball game. (wear)
I wore my Tigers hat to the baseball game.

7. I have _____ into a great fan of the Tigers. (grow)
8. The huge crowd _____ "The Star Spangled Banner" at the game. (sing)
9. Then the game _____. (begin)
10. A great hit _____ into center field. (fly)
11. The next batter _____ a base. (steal)

■ Each sentence below uses the past tense form of a verb. Rewrite these sentences, using the past form with a helping verb.

Example: Strong winds blew over the beach.
Strong winds had blown over the beach.

12. Sand flew against our beach house.
13. Harsh winds tore off the shutters.
14. The door broke in the storm.
15. We knew about all the damage.
16. Jim spoke to us about repairs.

Extra Practice **147**

Extra Practice

(pages 122–123)

13 Verb Phrases with *have*

- A verb phrase can have more than one helping verb. Some helping verbs can be contractions.
- Use *have* or *'ve* with *could, would, should,* and *must.* Do not use *of.*

● Write the verb phrases that are in the sentences below.

Example: You should've seen the lovely sunset last night.   *should've seen*

1. I must have taken five pictures of it.
2. You would've loved the pink clouds.
3. I could have watched that sunset forever.
4. There must've been four shades of red in it.
5. Perhaps I should have taken more pictures.

▲ Write each sentence, using the correct word or words shown in parentheses.

Example: You (should have, should of) seen the movie.
You should have seen the movie.

6. Tim (must of, must have) told you about it.
7. Everyone in the whole school (would've, would of) liked it.
8. We (could have, could of) gone together.
9. Tim (should of, should've) told Ms. Brooks.
10. She (would of, would have) provided a bus for our class.

■ If the verb phrase is incorrect, rewrite the sentence correctly. If the verb phrase is correct, write *correct*.

Example: Karen must of taken a course in photography.
Karen must have taken a course in photography.

11. We should've gone to the course too.
12. We should of looked in the paper for an announcement.
13. The paper would of told us about the course.
14. Perhaps I should have asked Karen about it.
15. She must've gotten a new camera for the course.

148 Unit 3: Verbs

Extra Practice

(pages 124–125)

14 teach, learn; let, leave

- Use *teach* when you mean "to give instruction."
- Use *learn* when you mean "to receive instruction."
- Use *let* when you mean "to permit."
- Use *leave* when you mean "to go away from" or "to let remain in a place."

● Write the correct word to complete each sentence.

Example: (Let, Leave) me use your camera. *Let me use your camera.*

1. Where did Jon (let, leave) the extra film?
2. You can (learn, teach) someone to take good pictures.
3. Did you (learn, teach) from someone?
4. My Aunt Maria (lets, leaves) me use her camera.
5. She can (learn, teach) you about cameras.

▲ If the underlined word is correct, write *correct*. If it is incorrect, write the word that should replace it.

Example: Please <u>learn</u> Paul about photography.
teach

6. It is exciting to <u>learn</u> a new student.
7. <u>Let</u> me show you how to focus.
8. I will <u>let</u> the instructions in your bag.
9. Don't <u>let</u> the lens cap on the camera.
10. <u>Learn</u> us how to use the flash.

■ Answer each question by writing a complete sentence containing one of the words in parentheses.

Example: Where will you put your equipment? (let, leave)
I will leave it in the closet.

11. Are you allowed to take pictures in here? (let, leave)
12. Who will show us how to take portraits? (teach, learn)
13. Are you permitted to use Sara's darkroom? (let, leave)
14. Will you allow Dan to enlarge that photo? (let, leave)
15. What did you find out about taking pictures on very cloudy days? (teach, learn)

Extra Practice

sit, set; can, may (pages 126–127)

- Use *sit* when you mean "to rest."
- Use *set* when you mean "to place or put something."
- Use *can* when you mean "to be able to do something."
- Use *may* when you mean "to be allowed or permitted."

● Write the correct word to complete each sentence.

Example: People (may, can) easily make bookends.
People can easily make bookends.

1. (Sit, Set) the glue bottle on the bench.
2. (May, Can) we use your good saw?
3. Nellie (can, may) cut the wood correctly.
4. Now she will (set, sit) one piece next to the other.
5. You (can, may) watch if you are quiet.

▲ If the underlined word is correct, write *correct*. If it is incorrect, write the word that should replace it.

Example: <u>May</u> you move this heavy chair for me?   *Can*

6. Please do not <u>set</u> anything on that table.
7. Everyone needs to <u>set</u> for a while.
8. Maybe you <u>can</u> find two more chairs.
9. When will <u>you</u> be able to <u>sit</u> down?
10. <u>Can</u> I move to that empty <u>seat</u>?

■ Answer each of the following questions by writing a sentence. Use the word in parentheses that better fits the meaning of your answer.

Example: Where will Arthur put the box? (sit, set)
Arthur will set the box on the green bench.

11. Is she allowed to ride the bus alone? (can, may)
12. How well does Jan read a map? (can, may)
13. Do you know how to get to the movies by bus? (can, may)
14. Where is an empty seat for me? (sit, set)
15. Are people permitted to stand? (can, may)

150 Unit 3: Verbs

The tomato was HOW big?
What did it look like?
What did it taste like?

Unit 4
Adjectives

151

Grammar

1 What Is an Adjective?

One-Minute Warm-Up

Which words in this sentence (besides *a* and *its*) are describing words?

> A captive tamarin lives in a confined space, climbs sturdy poles that don't move, and is served its food in a bowl at regular hours by a familiar keeper.
>
> —from *The Golden Lion Tamarin Comes Home,* by George Ancona

- A word that describes a noun or a pronoun is called an **adjective**.

What kind	**Spotted** fawns were resting. They looked **peaceful**.
How many	**Three** elephants were eating. Monkeys did **several** tricks.

- Adjectives appear in a variety of places in a sentence. They may come before the noun they are describing.

  Powerful lions stared boldly at us.

- Adjectives may also come after a linking verb.

  Giraffes seemed gentle and shy.

- When two or more adjectives are listed together, you should usually use a comma to separate them.

  Large, colorful parrots screeched.

- When one of these adjectives tells how many, do not use a comma.

  Two white geese honked loudly.

Tip

To find which word is an adjective, ask *What kind?* or *How many?* about the noun or the pronoun.

Try It Out

Speak Up What are the adjectives in each sentence? (Do not include *a, an,* or *the*.)

1. The two cubs are small and playful.
2. One enormous hippo swam in deep water.
3. The beautiful, proud peacock has many feathers.
4. The owls have speckled wings and sharp claws.

152 Unit 4: Adjectives

On Your Own

Write each sentence. Underline each adjective. (Do not include *a, an,* or *the.*) Then draw an arrow from the adjective to the noun that it describes.

Example: The famous zoo has many interesting animals.

The <u>famous</u> zoo has <u>many</u> <u>interesting</u> animals.

5. The giraffes have long, knobby legs.
6. Several monkeys are cute and frisky.
7. The heavy elephant has a slow, swaying walk.
8. The snouts of the crocodiles are long and narrow.
9. Three gentle deer graze beneath tall, leafy trees.

10–24. These jokes have fifteen adjectives. Write the jokes. Underline each adjective once. (Do not include *a, an,* or *the.*) Underline the noun it describes twice.

Example: What does a cold octopus wear? a coat of arms

What does a <u>cold</u> <u><u>octopus</u></u> wear? a coat of arms

ANIMALS
What animal is gray, has two large ears, four legs, a long, skinny tail, and a trunk?
(a mouse on vacation)

ANIMALS
What rodent is huge and hairless?
(a hippopota mouse)

ANIMALS
What do big gray hippos have that nothing else has? (They have little gray hippos.)

ANIMALS
I can't phone the main zoo. The lion is busy.

ANIMALS
What has a thousand needles but cannot sew?
(a porcupine)

Writing Wrap-Up
WRITING • THINKING • LISTENING • SPEAKING

CREATING

Write Jokes

Some jokes use different words that sound alike (*line/lion*). Some jokes use a word that has different meanings (*needle*). Write four jokes. These words may help you: *poodle/puddle, soup/soap, bark, fly.* Share jokes with a partner. Then, have your partner list the adjectives you read.

For Extra Practice see page 174.

What Is an Adjective?

Revising Strategies

Writing with Adjectives

Elaborating Sentences Paint a picture for your reader by including adjectives that tell *what kind*, *how many*, and *which one*. Adjectives usually are placed right before the noun they modify, but you can put them in other places too.

This **rare** animal is called the okapi.

Its legs are **striped**.

Its tongue, **long and stretchy**, can pluck leaves from branches.

Apply It

1–4. These labels will be hung on a bulletin board display. Elaborate the sentences with adjectives. Use details from the pictures.

Jaguars have a coat with markings for camouflage.

Peacocks can fan their feathers to make a design.

The macaw uses its claws and bill to climb among branches.

The anteater uses its snout and tongue to feed on ants.

154 Unit 4: Adjectives

Sentence Fluency

Combining Sentences Are there two sentences in your writing that tell about the same noun? To make your writing more concise, combine these sentences, using adjectives. You may need to change a word to its adjective form by adding the ending *-y, -ed,* or *-ing.*

The mayor snipped the ribbon to open the zoo. The ribbon looked like **silk**. } The mayor snipped the **silky** ribbon to open the zoo.

Children hurried through the gates to see the animals. The children were **excited**. } **Excited** children hurried through the gates to see the animals.

Monkeys delighted the crowd with their antics. The monkeys were **chattering**. } **Chattering** monkeys delighted the crowd with their antics.

Apply It

5–10. Use adjectives to combine each set of underlined sentences in this newspaper review. Add *-y, -ed,* or *-ing* to form adjectives, as needed.

Revising

The New Zoo Review
By Dennis Ingemi

Years ago, zoos were designed differently. The animals were trapped in cages. The cages were small. They were made of concrete. When I visited the new Safari Zoo, I saw that zoos have improved.

Modern zoos create habitats. They customize the habitats. Animals, insects, and plants that live together in the wild are in these habitats. One habitat has cliffs for goats to climb. These cliffs are steep. They are also made up of rocks. The exercise keeps them healthy. Another habitat has a pool where hippos can wade. It's there to refresh them. The pool keeps them from overheating. How could any visitor resist the koala bears? They have such charm! I love them! My favorite habitat was the rain forest. It was tropical.

The Safari Zoo gets "two paws up" from this critic!

Revising Strategies **155**

Grammar
2 Articles and Demonstratives

One-Minute Warm-Up

Take turns calling on one another, pointing to one or more items, and saying sentences that use *this*, *that*, *these*, and *those*.

"Please hand me those two pencils (that green book, ...)."

"These pencils?"

"Yes, those pencils."

- *A*, *an*, and *the* are **articles**, a special kind of adjective. *A* and *an* refer to any person, place, or thing. *The* refers to a particular one.

    Let's take **a** trip. (any)   It's time for **the** trip. (particular)

- Use *a* before singular words that begin with a consonant sound. Use *an* before singular words that begin with a vowel sound.

    a jet   **a** high step   **an** engine   **an** hour

- *This*, *that*, *these*, and *those* are demonstrative adjectives. **A demonstrative adjective** tells which one. *This* and *these* refer to nouns close to the speaker or writer. *That* and *those* refer to nouns farther away.

    This trip will be long.   Please pass me **that** book.

- Use *this* or *that* before singular words. Use *these* or *those* before plural words.

    this seat   **those** pens

Try It Out

Speak Up Which word correctly completes each sentence?

1. I am flying in (a, an) huge plane.
2. I don't want (a, an) aisle seat.
3. (Those, That) tall man should fasten his seat belt.
4. We are flying over (a, the) state of New York.
5. (These, Those) clouds are far away.

156   Unit 4: Adjectives

On Your Own

Write the word in parentheses that correctly completes each sentence.

Example: I took (a, an) bus to the train station.   *a*

6. (This, These) new trains travel very fast.
7. I rushed to (a, an) window seat.
8. I sat in (a, the) first car of the train.
9. (Those, These) cars behind me were more crowded.
10. My seat has a better view than (this, that) seat over there.

11–20. This magazine interview between a reporter (R) and a passenger (P) has ten incorrect articles and demonstrative adjectives. Write the interview correctly.

Example: An long line of passengers waited to board the new train.
A long line of passengers waited to board the new train.

Proofreading

Zoom on Track

R: Here I am, on a very first trip of that Zoom Express train. Everyone on these new train is thrilled. Here comes a excited passenger now. Sir, are you enjoying that trip?

P: These train trip? It's okay, I guess.

R: Okay? An trip on a brand new super-speed train is just okay?

P: The train is fast and fancy, but it's just a train.

R: That tickets in your hand were very hard to get.

P: Well, this tickets were an surprise birthday gift from my family.

Writing Wrap-Up
WRITING • THINKING • LISTENING • SPEAKING

INFORMING

Write an Interview

Interview a classmate briefly about a trip or something you both like to do. Now switch roles. Then each write your version of the interview. Be sure to include several articles and demonstrative adjectives.

Usage 3: Comparing with Adjectives

One-Minute Warm-Up

What's wrong with this riddle? How can you fix it?

Why does your nose have to be more short than twelve inches?

Because otherwise it would be a foot.

You know that adjectives describe nouns. One way they describe is by comparing people, places, or things. To compare two people, places, or things, add *-er* to the adjective. To compare three or more, add *-est*.

One person: My brother is tall.

Two persons: My mother is taller than my brother.

Three or more: My father is tallest of all.

Rules for Comparing with Adjectives	
1. One-syllable adjectives Add *-er* or *-est* to the adjective.	bright brighter brightest
2. Adjectives ending with *e* Drop the *e* and add *-er* or *-est*.	safe safer safest
3. Adjectives ending with a consonant and *y* Change the *y* to *i* and add *-er* or *-est*.	busy busier busiest
4. One-syllable adjectives that end with a single vowel and a consonant Double the consonant and add *-er* or *-est*.	flat flatter flattest
5. Some adjectives with two syllables and all adjectives with more than two syllables Use *more* or *most* instead of *-er* or *-est*.	careful more careful most careful
6. All adjectives—when you're talking about less instead of more Use *less* or *least* with the adjective.	brave less brave least brave

Unit 4: Adjectives

Try It Out

Speak Up Which form of each adjective do you use to compare two people, places, or things? Which form do you use to compare more than two?

1. angry 2. strange 3. helpful 4. red 5. old

On Your Own

Write the correct form of the adjective in parentheses to complete each sentence.

Example: Roberto is the _____ artist in my family. (talented)
most talented/least talented

6. Art is the _____ subject of all to me. (enjoyable)
7. My _____ time is when I am painting. (happy)
8. My new poster is _____ than my last one. (large)
9. The lettering is _____ than in the earlier poster. (red)
10. Is that the _____ drawing Maria has ever done? (pretty)

11–16. This part of an art book entry has six incorrect adjective forms. Write the entry correctly.

Example: Some museums are most popular than other museums.
Some museums are more popular than other museums.

Proofreading

Children's Art Museums

Oslo, Norway, has one of the cheeriest museums in the world. Its collection of children's art is more wonderfuler than most art museums. Few museums display paintings created only by the world's most young and talentedest artists. Every wall and ceiling is covered with the brighter, grander, most bold artwork by children that you have ever seen.

Writing Wrap-Up
WRITING • THINKING • LISTENING • SPEAKING

COMPARING / CONTRASTING

Write a Description
Compare and contrast two animals or objects. Write two paragraphs, using adjectives that compare. Discuss your description with a partner.

Usage 4 Comparing with *good* and *bad*

One-Minute Warm-Up

What's wrong with this riddle? How can you fix it?

Why is the goodest musician holding his flute against his head?

He is playing by ear.

The adjectives *good* and *bad* have special forms for making comparisons. These words do not take the endings *-er* and *-est* or use the words *more* and *most* or *less* and *least* to make comparisons.

Good: The dress rehearsal of our play was good.
Our first performance was better.
Our last performance was best of all.

Bad: I had a bad case of stage fright.
It was worse in the second act.
The worst stage fright came just before my entrance.

Comparing with *good* and *bad*		
Describing one person, place, or thing	good	bad
Comparing two persons, places, or things	better	worse
Comparing three or more persons, places, or things	best	worst

Try It Out

Speak Up What is the correct form of *good* or *bad* in each sentence?

1. This play was (better, best) than the last play.
2. Mary had a (bad, worst) cough.
3. Her coughing grew (bad, worse) in the last speech.
4. Her coughing was the (bad, worst) thing that happened onstage.
5. Of the four singers, Merle was the (best, good).

160 Unit 4: Adjectives

On Your Own

Write the correct form of the adjective in parentheses to complete each sentence.

Example: This concert was _____ than the last one. (good) *better*

6. Our seats were _____ than our seats last time. (good)
7. I thought the clarinet section was the _____ of all. (good)
8. Attendance last year was _____ than this year's. (bad)
9. Last year was the orchestra's _____ season of all. (bad)
10. This year, however, everything has been really _____. (good)
11. No concert has gotten a single _____ review. (bad)

12–18. This online concert review has seven incorrect forms of *good* and *bad*. Write the review correctly.

Example: Who was the most good of all the musicians onstage?
Who was the *best* of all the musicians onstage?

Proofreading

Web site

EZ-Rocks Solid

Last night the EZ-Rocks gave the loudest, rockingest, bestest performance of their career. The cheering fans, whose behavior was better than usual, clearly agreed. The band started in best form, and they got gooder and more good. The new guitarist was worser than the old one, but the other EZ-Rocks were so better, it didn't matter. Daren was probably the most goodest of all, but every one of the performers was excited, focused, and happy.

UPCOMING CONCERTS

NEXT REVIEW

BUY IT ON CD

Writing Wrap-Up
WRITING • THINKING • LISTENING • SPEAKING

EVALUATING

Write a Review

Write a two-paragraph review of a song, a concert, or other type of performance. What was good about it? What was bad? Use comparing forms of *good* and *bad*. Have a partner listen to your review.

Grammar
5 Proper Adjectives

One-Minute Warm-Up

Which adjective is made from the proper noun *China*? How many similar adjectives can you think of to replace this one in the sentence?

> Mom befriended a Chinese fruit seller who was honest and kind. One day she told him our problem.
>
> —from *Elena,* by Diane Stanley

- **An adjective formed from a proper noun is called a proper adjective.** Like a proper noun, a proper adjective is capitalized.

  Proper Noun: Those olives are from Greece.

  Proper Adjective: They are Greek olives.

Proper Noun	Proper Adjective
Italy	Italian cooking
Mexico	Mexican rug
Switzerland	Swiss watch
South America	South American bird

- When a proper adjective is two words, such as *South American,* capitalize both words.

Try It Out

Speak Up How would you form a proper adjective from the underlined noun to complete each sentence? Use your dictionary if you need help.

1. Food from Spain is _____ food.
2. People from Russia are _____ people.
3. The _____ Highway runs through Alaska.
4. People in Germany are proud of _____ cars.
5. A company in Japan makes _____ watches.

162 Unit 4: Adjectives

On Your Own

Write the proper adjective that comes from the proper noun in parentheses. Use your dictionary if you need help.

Example: I sent a letter to my _____ pen pal. (Britain)   *British*

6. We rode on a _____ train last summer. (Turkey)
7. Have you ever tasted _____ bread? (Poland)
8. We visited the _____ rain forest. (Puerto Rico)
9. A _____ student named Jette visited our school. (Denmark)
10. Do you sell any _____ baskets? (West Indies)
11. Have you been to the new _____ restaurant? (Vietnam)
12. Do you know any _____ words? (Japan)
13. I have a beautiful _____ robe. (Morocco)

14–24. This part of an airline brochure has eleven incorrect proper adjectives. Write the brochure correctly.

Example: Let us fly you to ancient cambodian ruins.
  Let us fly you to ancient Cambodian ruins.

Proofreading

See the World Properly

See the world on North Atlantic Airlines! North american cities and scenic canadian ports await you. Visit exciting south american cities too, such as the brazilian capital, Rio de Janeiro, and the argentinian capital, Buenos Aires. Dig in ancient israeli sites, climb swiss mountains, or admire the thai temples of Bangkok.

Enjoy swedish meatballs in Stockholm or fresh hawaiian pineapple in Waikiki. See the mysterious Sphinx in the egyptian desert or buy lovely pottery in a Mexican market.

Writing Wrap-Up   WRITING • THINKING • LISTENING • SPEAKING   *CREATING*

Write a Menu

Write a menu of international dishes you want to try. Tell what's in each dish. Name it and give the price. Use at least five proper adjectives. Read your menu to a classmate. Name the proper adjectives together.

Choosing Different Adjectives

Adjectives add important details to your writing. Choose your adjectives carefully. Choosing the wrong adjectives can change the meaning of your sentences. Overusing certain adjectives can make your writing unclear and uninteresting.

The girl was <u>grateful</u> to win second prize.

The girl was <u>disappointed</u> to win second prize.

Apply It

1–8. Rewrite these paragraphs from an article for the school newspaper. Complete each sentence by choosing an adjective to tell whether your summer was hectic and fun, or boring. If necessary, use *an* instead of *a* before the new adjective you use.

Revising ★★★ Washington School Gazette ★★★

I had a _____ summer. My friends and I played _____ sports and went on _____ hikes. I was _____ about returning to school, especially after such a _____ summer vacation. My _____ classmates were _____ to see me and I was _____ to see them.

164 Unit 4: Adjectives

Enrichment

The World's Kitchen

Create a tempting menu for The World's Kitchen, a restaurant that serves food from around the world. List several dishes on the menu, using one proper adjective and at least one regular adjective for each—for example, *Chinese* noodles with *rich, spicy* sauce. Include foods from as many different countries as you can.

Challenge You are a food critic for a newspaper. Write a review of the food at The World's Kitchen. Use the adjectives *good, better, best, bad, worse,* and *worst* in your sentences.

A Few of My Favorite Things

Write a three-verse poem about three of your favorite things. Follow the form below for each verse. If you wish, use some adjectives that rhyme or have similar sounds. Illustrate your poem.

I love (noun),
(adjective) and (adjective),
(adjective) and (adjective).
Is anything
(adjective) than (noun)?

I love fog,
pale and misty,
silent and wispy.
Is anything
more mysterious than fog?

Checkup: Unit 4

1 What Is an Adjective? *(p. 152)*
Write each adjective and the noun or pronoun that it describes. (Do not include *a, an,* or *the.*)

1. Denmark is a small kingdom.
2. It is in northern Europe.
3. Denmark lies between two seas.
4. It has many islands.
5. Denmark has mild, damp weather.
6. Little farms cover the land.
7. Four white houses have red roofs.
8. Beautiful Copenhagen is the capital.
9. It is lively, modern.
10. Danes look cheerful and friendly.
11. Tivoli Gardens is a huge park.
12. It is an exciting place.
13. The park has colorful buildings.
14. They are bright with lights.
15. There is an outdoor stage.
16. Concerts sound delightful.
17. People sail boats on a large lake.
18. Hans Christian Anderson was a famous writer from Denmark.
19. He wrote wonderful tales.
20. People around the world read them in many languages.
21. One character is a little mermaid.
22. There is a charming statue of her.
23. The bronze mermaid sits on a rock.
24. She looks at the great, blue sea.
25. Denmark has lovely beaches.
26. People sometimes stay in pretty cottages at the seashore.
27. Many families take trips there.
28. The blue lakes are also popular.

2 Articles and Demonstratives
(p. 156) Write the word in parentheses that completes each sentence correctly.

29. (A, The) island has a good market.
30. (This, That) is an indoor market over there.
31. I like (this, that) open-air market better than that one.
32. (An, The) island is known for its excellent pottery.
33. (An, A) vase will be a nice gift.
34. Look at (these, those) vases back there.
35. Are they any nicer than (those, these) right here?
36. Here is (an, a) unusual vase.
37. (The, A) one in my hand is lovely.
38. Did you see (that, this) green one on the far table?
39. I still like (that, this) one in my hand the best.

3 Comparing with Adjectives
(p. 158) Write the correct form of each adjective in parentheses.

40. Chimpanzees are (intelligent) than other apes.
41. They are also the (noisy).
42. Gorillas are (big) than other apes.
43. Of all the apes, gorillas are the (gentle).
44. They are (fast) than their enemies.
45. They are also (brave) than most monkeys.

 See www.eduplace.com/kids/hme/ for an online quiz.

166 Unit 4: Adjectives

4 Comparing with *good* and *bad* (p. 160)
Write the correct form of *good* or *bad* for each sentence.

46. My meals are (good) than before.
47. The (good) one of all was ravioli.
48. It was (good) than spaghetti.
49. This dish is the (good) of all.
50. Your salad is (good) than mine.
51. This apple looks very (bad).
52. It is (bad) than that one.
53. That store has very (good) fruit.
54. Are vegetables (good) than fruit?
55. I know a recipe for a very (good) vegetable stew.
56. Joe's Diner is (bad) than Harry's.
57. That's the (bad) place around.

5 Proper Adjectives (p. 162)
Write the proper adjective that comes from the proper noun in parentheses. You may use your dictionary.

58. Can you do any (Israel) dances?
59. The (Africa) continent is large.
60. Liz wore a (Norway) folk dress.
61. I have an (Ireland) sweater.
62. Ben has an (Iceland) blanket.
63. (Scotland) wool feels warm.
64. We saw a (Hungary) folk dance.
65. Is that a (France) perfume?
66. Sue climbed the (South America) mountain.
67. Famous (Austria) horses won.
68. The (China) silk was yellow.

Mixed Review 69–76. This ad has two errors in articles or demonstratives, two errors in proper adjectives, and four errors in comparing with adjectives. Write the ad correctly.

Proofreading Checklist
Are these forms correct?
✔ articles *(a, an, the)*
✔ demonstratives
✔ comparatives, superlatives
✔ comparisons of *good, bad*
✔ proper adjectives

Proofreading

Puppies for Sale

Do you want a adorable pet? We have a litter of five of the beautifulest little dogs you have ever seen. Have a better life with a dog. One of those puppies is for you. They are part German shepherd, part french poodle, and part siberian husky too. One puppy is biger than the others, and one seems shyer than the others. Choose one that is most good for you.

Of all our dogs, the pups' mother is the sweetest. Of course, she would have the most wonderful puppies in the world. From the tinyest to the largest, each one is perfect. Come see these adorable animals. Call Elena Shanji at 555-8173.

Go to www.eduplace.com/tales/ for more fun with parts of speech.

Assessment Link

✓ Test Practice

Write the numbers 1–8 on a sheet of paper. Read each sentence. Choose the best way to write the underlined part. Write the letter for that answer. If there is no mistake, write the letter for the last answer, "No mistakes."

1. We saw <u>three red</u> rings in the box.
   A three, red,
   B three, red
   C three red,
   D (No mistakes)

2. My gift from Marnie is <u>these</u> sweater I'm wearing.
   F those
   G this
   H that
   J (No mistakes)

3. Kim's joke was <u>silliest</u> than Carmen's joke.
   A silly
   B sillier
   C more silliest
   D (No mistakes)

4. What was the <u>more important</u> day of your life?
   F most important
   G more importanter
   H important
   J (No mistakes)

5. Call the doctor if Sam's rash gets <u>badder</u> than it is now.
   A worser
   B worst
   C worse
   D (No mistakes)

6. Brazil and Argentina are <u>south america</u> countries.
   F South American
   G south America
   H South America
   J (No mistakes)

7. Who would like <u>an</u> extra helping?
   A a
   B these
   C those
   D (No mistakes)

8. Our dog is <u>friendly</u> than our cat.
   F most friendlier
   G friendliest
   H friendlier
   J (No mistakes)

168 Unit 4: Adjectives

Now write the numbers 9–14 on a sheet of paper. Look at each underlined part of the paragraph. Choose the correct way to write the underlined part in each numbered line. Write the letter of the answer. If the part is already correct, write the letter for the last answer, "Correct as it is."

(9) People has enjoyed the company of pet cats for thousands of years.
(10) The ancestors of pet cats were small wildcats. These wildcats
(11) lived in asia africa, and europe. The first cat owners may have been the
(12) people of ancient Egypt they kept house cats more than four thousand
(13) years ago. Cats were most important to them than farm animals.
(14) Egyptians believed they're cats had special powers, and they treated them with great respect.

9 A has enjoy
   B have enjoyed
   C have enjoy
   D Correct as it is

10 F An
   G A
   H That
   J Correct as it is

11 A Asia africa, and europe
   B Asia, Africa, and Europe
   C Asia Africa, and, Europe
   D Correct as it is

12 F Egypt. They
   G Egypt, they
   H Egypt, or they
   J Correct as it is

13 A important
   B most importantest
   C more important
   D Correct as it is

14 F them
   G their
   H there
   J Correct as it is

Cumulative Review

Unit 1: The Sentence

Four Kinds of Sentences *(p. 34)* For each sentence, write *declarative, interrogative, imperative,* or *exclamatory*. If a group of words is not a sentence, write *fragment*.

1. Have you ever been to a factory?
2. This afternoon our class.
3. We will learn about paper making.
4. Look at this box of pressed wood.
5. How huge the machines are!

Subjects and Predicates *(pp. 36, 38, 40)* Write each sentence. Draw a line between the complete subject and the complete predicate. Underline the simple subject once and the simple predicate twice.

6. Dragonflies live near fresh water.
7. These insects dart through the air.
8. Their long, thin bodies fly high.
9. Their large eyes will be hunting for insects.
10. Four shiny wings beat rapidly.

Imperative Sentences *(p. 42)* For each sentence, write *declarative* or *imperative*. Then write the simple subject.

11. Eat more carrot sticks.
12. Carrots are good for you.
13. Don't cook carrots too long.
14. Raw carrots taste stronger.

Conjunctions *(p. 44)* Choose the correct conjunction in parentheses.

15. Lively otters swim (and, but) play.
16. They slide on mud (or, but) snow.
17. Cubs are blind at birth, (but, or) their eyes open after a month.
18. Otters (and, or) minks are related.

Run-on Sentences *(p. 48)* Write each of the following run-on sentences correctly.

19. Mallards are wild ducks lakes and rivers are their homes.
20. Plants supply most of their food some plants are found underwater.
21. The male duck has a green head its chest is rust its belly is white.
22. Female ducks look different they are brown.
23. Mallards make nests of grass or weeds and line them with down their eggs are olive green.

Unit 2: Nouns

Common and Proper Nouns *(p. 66)* List common and proper nouns.

24. My dad took a trip to Australia.
25. This continent is an island.
26. Sydney is the largest city.
27. Kangaroos roam the vast plains.
28. Farmers raise sheep and cattle.
29. Australia is in the Southern Hemisphere.

 See www.eduplace.com/kids/hme/ for a tricky usage or spelling question.

Unit 4: Adjectives

Plural Nouns *(pp. 70, 72)* Write the plural of each underlined noun.

30. I made the <u>lunch</u> for the <u>party</u>.
31. I heard the <u>recipe</u> on the <u>radio</u>.
32. First, put the <u>fish</u> in the <u>dish</u>.
33. Add the <u>potato</u> and the <u>peach</u>.
34. Pour the extra <u>juice</u> in the <u>glass</u>.
35. Bake the <u>loaf</u> in the <u>oven</u>.

Possessive Nouns *(pp. 74, 76)* Rewrite each phrase, using a possessive noun.

36. the spots of leopards
37. the size of the gorilla
38. the manes of the lions
39. the feathers of the ostrich
40. the grins of the monkeys

Unit 3: Verbs

Action Verbs *(p. 96)* Write the action verb in each sentence.

41. The colonists fought the British.
42. They won their independence.
43. They called a meeting in 1787.
44. The members argued all summer.
45. Finally, they formed a new nation.

Direct Objects *(p. 98)* Write the direct objects.

46. Dr. Fossey studied gorillas.
47. This scientist watched their interesting behavior.
48. She describes them in books.
49. Each gorilla has a personality.
50. They eat nothing but plants.

Main Verbs and Helping Verbs *(p. 100)* Write the verbs in these sentences. Underline the helping verbs once and the main verbs twice.

51. I am starting a stamp collection.
52. I will collect stamps from many countries.
53. The first stamps were sold in 1840.
54. Some stamps have become extremely valuable.
55. A very rare stamp was sold for one million dollars in 1981.

Linking Verbs *(p. 102)* Write each sentence and underline the linking verb. Then draw an arrow showing the words the verb links.

56. This beach is my favorite place in the summer.
57. The blue ocean looks calm today.
58. The gentle waves sound pleasant.
59. The cool breeze smells fresh.
60. I am an excellent swimmer.

Cumulative Review *continued*

Verb Tenses *(pp. 104, 106, 108)*
Change each underlined verb to the tense shown in parentheses. Write the new sentences.

61. Leah will study notes. (past)
62. She asked a question. (present)
63. She hopes for an answer. (past)
64. Leah planned a complex experiment. (present)
65. She has mixed chemicals. (past)
66. The chemicals fizzed. (present)
67. Leah discovers something. (future)

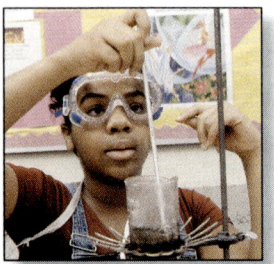

Subject-Verb Agreement *(p. 112)*
Write the correct present tense form of each verb in parentheses.

68. A wolf (look) like a skinny dog.
69. I (hear) its sad cry.
70. Wolves (roam) the Arctic hills.
71. Their fur (keep) them warm.
72. They (live) in family groups.

Agreement with *be* and *have*
(p. 114) Write the verb in parentheses that correctly completes each sentence.

73. My relatives (is, are) visiting.
74. We (have, has) visited them.
75. Uncle Jake (is, are) an athlete.
76. His stories (is, are) exciting.
77. His bike club (have, has) races.
78. He (have, has) crossed the Alps.

Contractions with *not* *(p. 116)*
Write the contraction for the underlined word or words below.

79. Sam has not arrived yet.
80. I cannot imagine where he is.
81. We should not start the meeting.
82. We do not have his notes.
83. His bus was not on time.
84. Do not call his office.
85. He will not still be there.

Irregular Verbs *(pp. 118, 120)* Write the correct forms of the verbs in parentheses to show the past.

86. Joe (run) for club president.
87. He had (run) once before.
88. Joe (speak) to the members.
89. Joe (make) many promises.
90. The members (choose) Joe.
91. Soon Joe (know) his mistake.
92. He had (make) too many promises.

Verb Phrases with *have* *(p. 122)*
Write the correct words to complete these sentences.

93. Mom (must of, must have) heard our noise.
94. I (should have, should of) asked her first.
95. Dad (could've, could of) told her.
96. Then she (might of, might've) agreed to it.

172 Unit 4: Adjectives

97. We (should of, should've) talked about it before.
98. We (would've, would of) laughed hard.

teach, learn; let, leave; sit, set; can, may *(pp. 124, 126)* Write the word in parentheses that correctly completes each sentence.

99. (Can, May) you play chess?
100. I will (teach, learn) you to play.
101. Please (sit, set) the board here.
102. I will (sit, set) over there.
103. (Let, Leave) the box here.
104. This time (let, leave) me have the white pieces.
105. I (learn, teach) games from Jo.

Unit 4: Adjectives

What Is an Adjective? *(p. 152)*
Write each sentence. Underline each adjective. Then draw an arrow from the adjective to the noun it describes.

106. Java is a tropical island.
107. The climate is warm and wet.
108. Java has wide, fertile plains.
109. Healthy plants grow in rich soil.
110. The main crop is rice.

Articles and Demonstratives
(p. 156) Write the word in parentheses that correctly completes each sentence.

111. (A, An) ivy plant is a nice gift.
112. I like (these, those) right here.
113. Look at (those, these) back there.
114. I'll buy (a, the) one in my hand.
115. (This, That) plant across the room is for my aunt.

Comparing with Adjectives
(p. 158) Write the correct form of each adjective in parentheses.

116. Al's voice is (low) than mine.
117. He has the (deep) voice of all.
118. Flo's solo is (funny) than Bob's.
119. Mine is the (simple) of all.
120. This is our (nice) show ever.

Comparing with *good* and *bad*
(p. 160) Write the correct form of *good* and *bad*.

121. I've had a (bad) cold.
122. This is the (bad) time of year.
123. Your cold is (bad) than mine.
124. I'm (good) than I was yesterday.
125. Soup is the (good) cure of all.

Proper Adjectives *(p. 162)* Write the proper adjective that comes from the proper noun in parentheses. You may use your dictionary.

126. One man wore an (Africa) robe.
127. The (Poland) acrobat has talent.
128. The (Austria) mountains are high.
129. That (Finland) knit hat is warm.
130. I love spicy (India) foods.

Extra Practice

1. What Is an Adjective?

(pages 152–153)

- An **adjective** is a word that describes a noun or a pronoun.
- An adjective tells what kind or how many.

● Write the adjectives in the sentences below. (Do not include *a*, *an*, or *the*.)

Example: Lions have large teeth and loud roars.   *large   loud*

1. Male lions have thick manes.
2. They look proud and fierce.
3. Female lions are gentle mothers.
4. They take good care of the little cubs.
5. The cubs have pretty, spotted coats.

▲ Write these sentences. Underline the adjectives. Then draw an arrow from the adjectives to the nouns or pronouns described.

Example: Many wild animals play funny games.

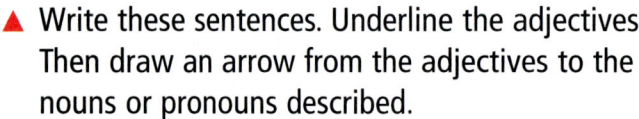

6. Young raccoons play with small pieces of wood.
7. Black bears roll down the steep hills.
8. Old, gray otters slide down the muddy banks.
9. Two squirrels enjoy a fast game of tag.
10. Four lively elephants play with a large ball of clay.

■ Rewrite each sentence, adding two or more adjectives. Draw an arrow from the adjectives to the noun described.

Example: Alligators have bodies and teeth.
   Alligators have long, green bodies and sharp teeth.

11. The snakes ran through the grass.
12. A monkey swings from a tree.
13. A giraffe nibbles leaves.
14. The bird made a nest out of twigs.
15. The robin finds a worm in the ground.

174   Unit 4: Adjectives

Extra Practice

(pages 156–157)

2 Articles and Demonstratives

- *A, an,* and *the* are special adjectives called **articles**. *A* and *an* refer to any person, place, or thing. *The* refers to a particular person, place, or thing.
- *This, that, these,* and *those* are **demonstrative adjectives**. They tell which one.

● Copy the sentences below. Underline the articles once and the demonstrative adjectives twice. Not every sentence contains both articles and demonstrative adjectives.

Example: We took that airplane to the city of Boston.
We took that airplane to the city of Boston.

1. The sky was bright blue outside the window.
2. I saw a group of puffy clouds.
3. Those clouds looked like cotton.
4. I fastened the seat belt before the flight.
5. During that flight, I tried to read a book.

▲ Write the word in parentheses that correctly completes each sentence.

Example: Boston is (a, an) interesting city. *an*

6. I am having (a, an) good visit in Boston.
7. We are riding in one of (the, a) swan boats.
8. The driver pedals the boat like (a, an) bicycle.
9. I will remember (this, those) day in Boston for a long time.

■ To complete each sentence, write an article or a demonstrative adjective as indicated in parentheses.

Example: May I look at _____ book on the shelf above you?
(demonstrative adjective) *that*

10. Are _____ books on your desk mysteries? (article)
11. Please hand me _____ mystery books. (demonstrative adjective)
12. _____ book is very heavy. (demonstrative adjective)
13. _____ books are neatly stacked here. (demonstrative adjective)
14. Is there _____ book cart in this room? (article)

Extra Practice **175**

Extra Practice

(pages 158–159)

3 Comparing with Adjectives
- Add *-er* to one-syllable adjectives to compare two.
- Add *-est* to one-syllable adjectives to compare more than two.
- Use *more* and *most*, *less* and *least*, not *-er* and *-est*, with most longer adjectives.

● Complete each sentence by writing the correct form of the adjective in parentheses.

Example: Crows are _____ than robins. (loud) *louder*

1. A peacock is _____ than a turkey. (colorful)
2. Swans are _____ than ducks. (large)
3. Geese are _____ than swans. (noisy)
4. Hummingbirds are the _____ birds of all. (small)
5. Eagles are _____ than hawks. (powerful)

▲ Complete each sentence by writing the correct form of the adjective in parentheses.

Example: Bees are _____ than wasps. (chunky) *chunkier*

6. They are _____ than ants. (large)
7. They are _____ than flies. (interesting)
8. Bees are the _____ insects of all. (busy)
9. They are also the _____. (helpful)

■ Write an adjective to complete each sentence. Include adjectives that take *-er* and *-est* and adjectives that use *more* and *most*. If the adjective compares two, write *two*. If it compares more than two, write *more than two*.

Example: This book is the _____ of all.
   This book is the hardest of all.   *more than two*

10. Your calendar is _____ than mine.
11. Of all the chairs, this one is the _____.
12. Joseph's desk is _____ than Pauline's desk.
13. That is the _____ bulletin board in the school.
14. This invention is the _____ of all.

176   Unit 4: Adjectives

Extra Practice

(pages 160–161)

4 Comparing with *good* and *bad*

- The adjectives *good* and *bad* have special forms for making comparisons.
- Use *better* and *worse* to compare two.
- Use *best* and *worst* to compare more than two.

● Read each sentence below. If the underlined adjective compares two, write *two*. If it compares more than two, write *more than two*. Write *none* if the sentence contains no comparison.

Example: Rob is a good trumpet player. *none*

1. Rob practices every day, and he loves good music.
2. Yesterday was a very bad day for Rob.
3. The afternoon was worse than the morning.
4. Rob took his best trumpet to school in the morning.
5. He had a bad fall after lunch.
6. It was Rob's worst fall, and he dented his trumpet.

▲ Write the adjective that correctly completes each sentence.

Example: Our band is the (better, best) school band. *best*

7. It is (better, best) than the Oak School band.
8. We have several (good, best) musicians in the band.
9. We are (better, best) musicians than marchers.
10. We are very (bad, worst) marchers.
11. I am the (worse, worst) marcher of all.

■ Write full sentences to compare each pair of items. Use a form of *good* or *bad* in each sentence.

Example: a sweater and a jacket
   On a cold day, a jacket is better than a sweater.

12. cats and dogs
13. today's weather and yesterday's weather
14. your favorite book and all other books
15. this morning and this afternoon
16. swimming and diving

Extra Practice

(pages 162–163)

5 Proper Adjectives

- A **proper adjective** is formed from a proper noun.
- A proper adjective begins with a capital letter.

● Write each phrase, using a proper adjective made from the noun in parentheses.

Example: hotel (Germany)   *German hotel*

1. dance (Mexico)
2. village (England)
3. poetry (Greece)
4. desert (Africa)
5. castle (Austria)
6. seacoast (Ireland)
7. food (Japan)

Sushi from Japan

▲ Write each sentence, using a proper adjective made from the noun in parentheses. Use your dictionary if you need help.

Example: Oslo is the _____ capital. (Norway)
Oslo is the Norwegian capital.

8. Paris is the _____ capital. (France)
9. New Delhi is the _____ capital. (India)
10. Bern is the _____ capital. (Switzerland)
11. Lima is the _____ capital. (Peru)
12. Stockholm is the _____ capital. (Sweden)

India Gate, Delhi

■ Answer each question by writing a sentence that contains a proper adjective. Use your dictionary if you need help.

Example: Have you ever been to a beach in Puerto Rico?
I went to a Puerto Rican beach last year.

13. Do you have a sweater from Denmark?
14. Have you met my cousin from Poland?
15. Have you ever heard music from Ireland?
16. Do you have a pen pal from South America?
17. Have you ever seen any paintings by artists from Italy?
18. Have you hiked through the wilderness of Canada?

178 Unit 4: Adjectives

Unit 5

Capitalization and Punctuation

No statue in the world compares in size to the carved faces of United States Presidents George Washington, Thomas Jefferson, Theodore Roosevelt, and Abraham Lincoln.

Mechanics

1 Correct Sentences

One-Minute Warm-Up

The author used an exclamation point to end this sentence. Why?

Now she would be stuck with a younger brother with a terrible ear for music!

—from *Yang the Second and Her Secret Admirers*, by Lensey Namioka

- You know that every sentence must begin with a capital letter and end with an end mark. Without capital letters and end marks, sentences run together. With them, your reader knows where one sentence ends and another begins.

    Incorrect: we will join you later we are waiting for Cory
    Correct: We will join you later. We are waiting for Cory.

- End marks tell whether you are making a statement (.), asking a question (?), giving a command (.), or showing strong feeling (!).

    Declarative: The concert is on Sunday.
    Interrogative: Are you going?
    Imperative: Buy your tickets early.
    Exclamatory: What a terrific band we have!

Try It Out

Speak Up How should these sentences be written correctly? Be sure to separate any run-on sentences.

1. the chorus is practicing our school song is new.
2. will you come to our concert
3. our music teacher wrote the song listen to us sing
4. what a funny song that is has he written any others
5. he also wrote the music for the school play
6. what talent he has
7. the concert is on Tuesday we will be ready
8. please buy me two tickets my sister will go with me

On Your Own

Write each sentence. Separate run-on sentences. Add capital letters and end marks.

Example: open your music books can you sing this song
Open your music books. Can you sing this song?

9. the band played a march
10. how lively the band looks
11. aren't those songs from the musical *The Music Man*
12. how many trombone players are in our band there are six
13. do you know any other marching songs look in the book
14. we can play "Stars and Stripes Forever" what a great march that is

15–26. This closed-caption script for a television news show has twelve sentence errors. Write the announcement correctly.

Example: here comes the band can you hear it
Here comes the band. Can you hear it?

Proofreading

Hello, I'm here at the reviewing stand on Main Street this year's Labor Day parade is just beginning. What a great sight it is Have you ever watched it if not, you've really missed something. Hurry down now. it's not too late.
Here comes the school band. what a sight they are in their bright red uniforms How amazing they look can you hear that marching music? Don't you feel like marching along I do

Writing Wrap-Up
WRITING • THINKING • LISTENING • SPEAKING
SUMMARIZING

Write a Radio Announcement

Think of an upcoming event at your school such as a parade, a concert, or a sports event. Write a radio announcement. Use all four kinds of sentences. Read it aloud to a partner who tells you from your voice which punctuation mark you used.

Mechanics
2 Proper Nouns and Adjectives

Which words are proper nouns or adjectives in this sentence? How can you tell? Which one is more than one word?

Leopold and Anna Maria Mozart lived in the Austrian town of Salzburg.

—from *Introducing Mozart,* by Roland Vernon

- As you know, **proper nouns** name specific persons, places, and things. Always capitalize a proper noun. If a proper noun is two words, capitalize both words. If it is three or more words, capitalize only the important words.

Capitalizing Proper Nouns		
People	Queen Victoria	Lewis Carroll
Places	Norway Lake Ontario	Wisconsin Avenue Gulf of Mexico
Things	Rosetta Stone	Mayflower Compact
Days, months, and holidays	Monday Columbus Day	July New Year's Day
Buildings and companies	Langley Company	Fogg Art Museum

- **Proper adjectives** are adjectives made from proper nouns. Like proper nouns, proper adjectives begin with capital letters. If a proper adjective is two words, capitalize both words.

Japan   Japanese painting   South America   South American music

Try It Out

Speak Up Which nouns and adjectives should be capitalized?

1. wolfgang mozart was a famous austrian composer.
2. He was born in January 1756 in the city of salzburg.
3. He and his sister anna maria were gifted pianists.
4. His father, leopold, took them on european concert tours.
5. Young wolfgang performed for empress maria theresa.

Young Mozart

On Your Own

Write the proper nouns and the proper adjectives. Capitalize them correctly.

Example: In austria the composer johann strauss was famous.
Austria   Johann Strauss

6. At nineteen strauss conducted his own orchestra in vienna.
7. The austrian people loved his waltz music.
8. One fan was the german composer named johannes brahms.
9. News of strauss traveled across the atlantic ocean.
10. The american people wanted to hear his waltzes.
11. Like european countries, the united states has good concert halls.
12. In boston there is symphony hall.
13. In new york city, musicians love carnegie hall and lincoln center.
14. Special concerts are held on december 31, new year's eve.

15–32. This part of a travel brochure has eighteen errors in the use of proper nouns and adjectives. Write the proper nouns and adjectives correctly.

Example: Welcome to vienna!   *Welcome to Vienna!*

Proofreading

Classic Vienna Awaits You!

This august, visit Vienna, the capital of austria, for its beauty, history, and music. It was home to great european composers such as haydn, mozart, and schubert. Float on the Danube river. Visit st. peter's church. On a Saturday, see a performance at the state opera house.

Call acme travel agency after the fourth of july for more information.

Writing Wrap-Up   WRITING • THINKING • LISTENING • SPEAKING

EVALUATING

Write a Music Review

Write a review of a song of your favorite musician. Describe the music, and then tell your opinion of it. Use proper nouns and proper adjectives. Read it to a few classmates. Do they agree with your review?

For Extra Practice see page 208.

Mechanics

3 Commas in a Series

One-Minute Warm-Up

How many kinds of instruments are woodwinds in this sentence? What punctuation mark tells you the answer?

The woodwind section includes clarinets, bass clarinets, oboes, saxophones, flutes, piccolos, English horns, bassoons, and double bassoons.

—from *A Very Young Musician,* by Jill Krementz

- An end mark tells your reader where to stop. **A comma (,) tells your reader where to pause.** Commas help make the meaning of a sentence clear. Commas may also change the meaning of a sentence.

    Beth, Ann, John, Paul, and I are in the same class.
    Beth Ann, John Paul, and I are in the same class.

- Each sentence above contains a series. **A series is a list of three or more items in a sentence.** A comma is used after each item except the last. A conjunction, such as *and* or *or,* is used before the last item in a series.

    Sara writes poems, short stories, and plays.
    Her newest play will have two, three, or four characters.
    The play takes place under a tree, on a porch, and in a classroom.

- Do not use a comma if a sentence lists only two items, for the sentence does not contain a series.

    Sara writes poems and short stories.

Try It Out

Speak Up Where are commas needed in the following sentences?

1. My class has written directed and produced a musical.
2. Everyone will sing dance or play an instrument.
3. The performances will be on Thursday Friday and Saturday.
4. Karl and Peter found props made scenery and planned the costumes.

On Your Own

Write each sentence that includes a series. Add commas where they are needed. For each sentence that does not have a series, write *none*.

Example: The play is about a child a detective and a gold ring.
The play is about a child, a detective, and a gold ring.

5. Costumes props and lights were planned by the art teacher.
6. Marci or Miguel will control the lights.
7. Ted wears glasses and a black beard.
8. A magnifying glass a ring a book and a hatbox are props.
9. We rehearsed in classrooms in homes or on the stage.
10. The cast joins hands steps forward and bows at the end.
11. The audience will applaud the actors dancers, and musicians.

12–20. This e-mail has nine comma errors. Write the letter correctly.

Example: The school has classes in art set design and lighting.
The school has classes in art, set design, and lighting.

proofreading

e-mail

Yoshiko and I visited a school for the performing arts. It was so wonderful and exciting! Students sing dance or act. They learn ballet tap folk and jazz. Students paint scenery build sets or sew costumes. They also take courses in English science, history and math.

Writing Wrap-Up
WRITING • THINKING • LISTENING • SPEAKING

REFLECTING

Write a Letter

Have you had a part in a play, a concert, or other team effort? Write a letter to a friend, telling what you did and how you felt. Include at least four sentences with series. Read each other's letters aloud to check the commas in a series. Note: See Unit 8 for a model of a friendly letter.

Revising Strategies

Writing Sentences with Commas

Combining Sentences with a Series of Words or Phrases You have learned that a list of three or more items in a sentence is called a series.

Julie**,** Rico**,** **and** Hannah practiced for the school musical.

Use a series to combine two or three sentences into one smooth, elaborated sentence that tells more. The series can consist of single words or of phrases (groups of words).

The dedicated students practiced **before school**. They also practiced **after school** and **on weekends**.	**Incorrect:**	The dedicated students practiced before school, after school, and **they practiced on weekends too**.
	Correct:	The dedicated students practiced before school**,** after school**,** **and** on weekends.

Apply It

1–4. Revise this memo. Combine each set of sentences to make a series.

Revising

To: Chorus, Band Members, and Actors
Subject: School Musical

- Chorus members should arrive at 11:00 A.M. Band members should arrive at 11:00 A.M. Actors should arrive at 11:00 A.M.

- All band and chorus members must wear white shirts. All band and chorus members must wear black pants. All band and chorus members must wear black shoes.

- Chorus members will help set up chairs. Chorus members will also collect tickets and hand out programs.

- After the musical, band members should collect sheet music and store music stands. Band members should stack chairs.

186 Unit 5: Capitalization and Punctuation

Sentence Fluency

Combining Whole Sentences in a Series Sometimes a related group of choppy sentences can be combined in a series. Remember to separate the combined sentences in your series with commas and a conjunction.

I take piano lessons.
My brother Paul studies guitar.
My brother Steve likes to listen.

I take piano lessons**,** my brother Paul studies guitar**, and** my brother Steve likes to listen.

Apply It

5–10. Rewrite each classified advertisement by combining sentences to form a series. Remember to choose conjunctions that fit the meaning of your sentences, such as *and* and *or.*

Revising

Pianos for Sale!

- **Well Loved** The piano is old. The stool is worn. The keys practically play themselves.
- **Just Fixed** Every key was polished. All the strings were tightened. Each note was tuned.
- **Player Piano** You will hear a variety of music. Your children will be fascinated. Your party guests will be entertained for hours.
- **Real Steal** We paid ten thousand dollars. A dealer valued it at eight thousand dollars. You can steal it for six thousand dollars.
- **Fixer-Upper** A fire damaged the finish. The movers lost the bench. Humidity warped the legs.
- **Crowd Pleaser** A student could learn on it. A good player could practice on it. A concert pianist could use it for performances.

Writing Sentences with Commas

Mechanics

4 More Uses for Commas

One-Minute Warm-Up

Where would you pause in these sentences?
How can you show the pauses?

How do you like being a drummer Trent?
Well it's hard to beat.

- **Words such as *yes, well,* and *no* are called introductory words when they begin a sentence.** Always use a comma after an introductory word.

    Yes, I play the drums.   Well, will you play for us?

- **The name of a person who is spoken to, or addressed, is called a noun in direct address**. Use a comma or commas to set off a noun in direct address from the rest of the sentence.

    Maria, will you play the piano for us?
    Place your sheet music here, Maria.
    Thank you, Maria, for doing a good job.

- Sometimes you may use introductory words and nouns in direct address in the same sentence.

    Yes, Maria, you are ready for the concert.

Try It Out

Speak Up Where are commas needed in the following sentences?

1. No I don't know which instrument I should play Jo.
2. Well do you like the trumpet?
3. Yes I like the trumpet.
4. I think Pedro that you should try it.
5. Well Jo the music room is closed today.
6. I have permission Pedro to use it.
7. Ilona what instrument do you play?
8. I play the piano Pedro.

188   Unit 5: Capitalization and Punctuation

On Your Own

Write each sentence correctly. Add commas where they are needed.

Example: Yes Cindy you play the piano very well.
Yes, Cindy, you play the piano very well.

9. Mother may I take piano lessons?
10. Well I took piano lessons in the first grade.
11. Yes I will let you take lessons.
12. Kim you must promise to practice.
13. Yes Mother I will practice every day.
14. Do you think Kim that this music is too hard?
15. No Mrs. Jacobs I am learning it.

16–25. This interview with a tuba has ten comma errors. Write the interview correctly.

Example: No tuba players are not all alike Carlos.
No, tuba players are not all alike, Carlos.

Proofreading

Carlos: Well yesterday we spoke with a clarinet. Today listeners we'll hear from the tuba. Mr. Tuba how are you?
Tuba: I'm fine Carlos.
Carlos: Glad to hear that, Mr. Tuba. You're known Mr. Tuba for your mellow sound. Are you always mellow?
Tuba: No Carlos that really depends on the player.
Carlos: Do you have a close relationship with all players?
Tuba: Well we do tend to get wrapped up in each other.

Writing Wrap-Up   WRITING • THINKING • LISTENING • SPEAKING

CREATING

Write an Interview

Write an interview with a musical instrument. Use introductory words and nouns in direct address. Act out the interview with a partner. Pause at the commas.

For Extra Practice see page 210.

Revising Strategies

Writing Sentences with Commas

Combining Sentences: Introductory Groups of Words A phrase, or group of words, that begins a sentence is called an **introductory phrase**. Use introductory phrases to combine sentences in your own writing when you want to vary sentence length. Set off such phrases with a comma.

Noy was reading a music magazine. } Reading a music magazine,
She found an advice column.   Noy found an advice column.

Incorrect:
Reading a music magazine,
an advice column caught Noy's eye.

Help prevent silly sentences! Make sure that an introductory phrase relates to the noun that follows it.

Apply It

1–5. Revise these questions from an advice column before it goes to print. Combine each pair of underlined sentences by changing one sentence into an introductory phrase.

I was polishing my piano. I sprayed the strings with sticky polish by mistake. Now some notes sound funny. Will the strings dry out?

My family was living in Florida. We noticed that our piano went out of tune quickly. Was the climate responsible?

My aunt is hoping to keep her piano in good shape. She plans to move it away from the window. Would sunlight really fade the wood?

My brother was eating chocolate while he practiced. He got the keys dirty. How can we clean it before our parents notice?

I was trying to save some money. I tuned my piano with a kitchen fork. Do you have any tips for straightening out bent wires?

190   Unit 5: Capitalization and Punctuation

Sentence Fluency

Sometimes the ideas in two separate sentences are related. You can combine such sentences by using a special conjunction called a **subordinating conjunction**. A subordinating conjunction will help show the relationship between the two sentences.

Noy practiced her clarinet solo every day. She memorized the whole piece.

}

Because Noy practiced her clarinet solo every day, she memorized the whole piece.

Common Subordinating Conjunctions

after	as	before	since	when
although	because	if	until	while

Apply It

6–10. Rewrite this part of an e-mail. Combine each pair of underlined sentences, using a subordinate conjunction from above that fits the meaning.

Revising

e-mail

To: Lisa@watersschool.edu

I can't come over tomorrow. Our marching band is playing in the Town Day Parade. We are practicing every afternoon. It's a lot of work! We all can play our instruments well. We are still learning how to march.

Today we rehearsed in front of the whole school. The woodwind section marched and played. Everyone clapped and whistled. Noy's solo was great. The whole band began to play. The crowd went crazy. Our bandleader was beaming. Then the brass section marched into the woodwind section! They got back on track quickly. I hope that doesn't happen during the parade!

Writing Sentences with Commas **191**

Mechanics

5 Interjections

One-Minute Warm-Up

Who's saying what? Decide which word goes with each person.

Ah   Hey!   Oops!

- An **interjection** is a word or words that show feeling or emotion.

Common Interjections			
Hurray	Hey	Oh, no	Well
Good grief	Ah	Oops	Whew
Okay	Oh	Ouch	Wow

- If the interjection shows strong feeling, it stands alone and is followed by an exclamation point.

   Wow! That boat is big! **Good grief!** The sails are huge!

- If the interjection shows mild feeling, it begins the sentence and is followed by a comma.

   Ah, the breeze is nice. **Well,** let's go sailing!

Try It Out

Speak Up What is the interjection in each sentence?

1. Hey, this boat needs a few repairs.
2. Good grief! Can we repair it in time for the race?
3. Oh, I hope so!
4. Oops! The sail is torn!
5. Whew! Someone remembered to bring the sewing box.
6. Ouch! That needle is sharp!
7. Hurray! The sail is as good as new!
8. Oh, no! Here's another rip we missed!

192   Unit 5: Capitalization and Punctuation

On Your Own

Write each sentence. Add the punctuation after each interjection.

Example: Whew The big day is here at last!
Whew! The big day is here at last!

9. Ah there's nothing like a windy day for a race!
10. Well let's get everything ready.
11. Oh, no The race begins in an hour!
12. Hurray The jackets are in the boat!
13. Okay Now we don't have to go back.
14. Hey it's getting windier.

15–22. Eight interjections are punctuated incorrectly in this poem. Write it correctly.

Example: Ah don't you just love sailing?   *Ah, don't you just love sailing?*

The Wind and the Sail

Ah! the race is beginning at last.
Hey, Kevin's boat is moving so fast.
Oops, There's the wind. Oh! it's shifting around.
Oh, no, Is that boat going aground?
Whew, Now the boats are just sailing along.
Wow What a sight when the wind's blowing strong!
Ouch, Did something just hit Kevin's mast?
Oh, well! it's the fifth year that he's come in last.

Writing Wrap-Up   WRITING • THINKING • LISTENING • SPEAKING

EXPRESSING

Write a Poem

Write a short poem about your experience outdoors. It could be a kite-flying day with no wind or a walk in the sun. Begin each line with an interjection. Make it rhyme if you wish. Then read your poem to a small group. Match your voice to the punctuation for each interjection.

For Extra Practice see page 211.

Mechanics

6 Quotations

One-Minute Warm-Up

Which words make up Bosco's question? Which punctuation marks signal the beginning and the end of his spoken words?

"See any wolves yet?" Bosco asks Dad.

—from *On Call Back Mountain*, by Eve Bunting

- In written conversation, a **direct quotation** gives a speaker's exact words. Set it off with **quotation marks** and capitalize the first word.

- Use a comma to set off a direct quotation from the other words in a sentence. Place the comma *outside* the quotation marks at the beginning of a quotation and *inside* the quotation marks at the end of a quotation.

   Hannah announced, "My aunt works in a fire tower."
   "Tell me what she does," said Henry.

- If the quotation is a question or an exclamation, place a question mark or an exclamation point, instead of a comma, inside the quotation marks.

   "What a great job she has!" exclaimed Henry.

- Sometimes a quotation is divided and each part is in quotation marks. If the second part of the divided quotation continues the original sentence, begin it with a small letter. If it starts a new sentence, use a capital letter.

   "Do you think," asked Henry, "that we could see the tower?"
   "I know that we can," replied Hanah. "Let's call my aunt."

Try It Out

Speak Up Where would you use capital letters and punctuation marks in these sentences?

1. Jean asked was there a terrible earthquake in 1906
2. Peter replied yes, it happened in San Francisco
3. over the years said Jean the city has been rebuilt
4. how beautiful San Francisco is now exclaimed Sara

194   Unit 5: Capitalization and Punctuation

On Your Own

Write each sentence. Use punctuation marks and capital letters correctly.

Example: did you see the fire on Tenth Street asked Holly
   "Did you see the fire on Tenth Street?" asked Holly.

5. Ralph said ten fire engines arrived in fifteen minutes
6. Ira exclaimed it destroyed an entire block of buildings
7. wasn't a firefighter slightly injured asked Holly
8. "yes, but the people in the buildings escaped unhurt said Ira
9. it was the biggest fire I've ever seen exclaimed Ralph
10. the street was blocked off said Holly how did you see it
11. well said Ralph we watched from Eighth Street

12–22. This part of a story has eleven punctuation and capitalization errors. Write the story part correctly.

Example: Help me with the salad Kim said to Lee. And with beverages
   "Help me with the salad," Kim said to Lee, "and with beverages."

PUTTING DINNER OUT

"Go easy on the onions" Kim said to Lee. "you always use too many. Lee replied, "and you always make a mess."

"Not true" Kim exclaimed! "Mom and Dad loved last week's dinner."

"That Lee said is because they pretended to like burnt burgers. By the way, you didn't put our burgers too close to the broiler, did you?"

"Uh uh," Kim said, "they're. . . . Oh, no! It's smoke!"

"Quick! Get the fire extinguisher!" Yelled Lee.

Writing Wrap-Up
WRITING • THINKING • LISTENING • SPEAKING

EXPRESSING

Write Dialogue

Fire can make a warm campfire, or it can destroy a forest. Write a dialogue between two people on whether fire is helpful or harmful. Start a new paragraph for each new speaker. Include your opinion. Ask classmates to act it out and follow your punctuation cues.

For Extra Practice see page 212.

Mechanics

7 Abbreviations

One-Minute Warm-Up

On May 1, Detective Chang received this note. What does it say?

On Wed. Apr. 30 Mr. A. E. Hill Jr., of Pans, Inc., left his apt. on Elm Ave., drove down Rte. 2 toward NJ, and disappeared.

- **An abbreviation is a shortened form of a word.** An abbreviation usually begins with a capital letter and ends with a period. Use abbreviations only in special kinds of writing, such as addresses and lists.

Common Abbreviations				
Titles	Mr.	Mister	Dr.	Doctor
	Mrs.	married woman	Jr.	Junior
	Ms.	any woman	Sr.	Senior
Businesses	Co.	Company	Ltd.	Limited
	Corp.	Corporation	Inc.	Incorporated
Days	Tues.	Tuesday	Wed.	Wednesday
Months	Feb.	February	Aug.	August
Addresses	Ave.	Avenue	Rte.	Route
	Apt.	Apartment	P. O.	Post Office
States	CA	California	TX	Texas

- **Initials are a special kind of abbreviation.** An initial most often stands for a person's first or middle name. Some names have two initials.

    E. B. White wrote *Charlotte's Web*. (E. B. = Elwyn Brooks)

Try It Out

Speak Up What abbreviations and initials would you use below?

1. Doctor Ann Hubb
2. Adam Lee Junior
3. 132 Oak Street
4. Honolulu, Hawaii 96815
5. Friday, April 5, 1928
6. Mister Alan Wells Blake

Unit 5: Capitalization and Punctuation

On Your Own

Write each group of words, using the correct abbreviations and initials for the underlined words.

Example: 325 University <u>Road</u>   325 University Rd.

7. <u>Mister</u> Barnett
8. Davis <u>Corporation</u>
9. Ellis, <u>Kansas</u> 67637
10. <u>Apartment</u> 2
11. 184 Pine <u>Avenue</u>
12. Jay, <u>Florida</u> 32565
13. Monaco <u>Incorporated</u>
14. <u>Post Office</u> Box 36
15. Sunday, <u>October</u> 3, 1935
16. Richard Greene <u>Senior</u>
17. Modern Designs, <u>Limited</u>
18. Sunset <u>Boulevard</u>
19. <u>Thomas James</u> Carey
20. San Antonio, <u>Texas</u> 78239
21. Cooper Stamp <u>Company</u>
22. <u>Mister</u> <u>Ronald Gary</u> Payne

23–32. This to-do list has ten abbreviation errors. Write the list correctly.

Example: Meet Kim on East Boul.   Meet Kim on East *Blvd.*

Proofreading

Forget-Me-Nots
- Call Doc. Gomes on Wednes., Aug. 3
- Write to Ms. Adriana Dalpos
  Jay Tweed Comp.
  1420 Cary St
  Lexington, Mass. 02420
- Buy card for Mist. Martin's birthday, Mon., Spt. 4
- Pick up map of Rt. 1 in N.Y.
- Get phone number for A C Sultan in TX

Writing Wrap-Up   WRITING • THINKING • LISTENING • SPEAKING

INFORMING

Write a To-Do List

Do you usually have to remind yourself to buy tickets? write a letter? make a dentist appointment? Write a to-do list with at least six words or phrases to be abbreviated. Read your list to a partner. Then ask your partner to tell you the abbreviations.

For Extra Practice see page 213.

Abbreviations   **197**

Mechanics

8 Titles

One-Minute Warm-Up

Which is a book? Which is a short story? How do you know?

<u>All About Fish</u>, by Gil Scales
"The Happy Amphibian," by Sal A. Mander

- There are special ways for writing the titles of books, poems, and other written works. Capitalize the first, the last, and all important words. Do not capitalize words such as *a, in, and, of,* and *the* unless they begin or end a title.

  "The Ways of Trains"   <u>The Treasure Is the Rose</u>

- When titles of books, magazines, newspapers, and movies are used in printed materials, they appear in italics: *Prince Caspian*. Because you cannot write in italics, in your writing you should always underline these titles.

  My sister reads <u>The Washington Post</u> every morning.

  Have you finished the book <u>Mom's Best Friend</u>?

- Some titles are set off by quotation marks. Put quotation marks around the titles of short stories, songs, articles, book chapters, and most poems.

  I recited the poem "Take Sky."
  My sister showed me the article "Wonder of Words."

Try It Out

Speak Up How would you write these titles?

1. cricket (magazine)
2. water life (book chapter)
3. my side of the mountain (book)
4. this old man (song)
5. the los angeles times (newspaper)
6. the black stallion (movie)
7. rudolph is tired of the city (poem)
8. endangered animals (article)

On Your Own

Write each title correctly.

Example: the wind has wings (poem)   *"The Wind Has Wings"*

9. cobblestone (magazine)
10. animals with pouches (book chapter)
11. the rocky mountain news (newspaper)
12. the time of your life (song)
13. the air we breathe (article)
14. the last piece of light (short story)
15. national velvet (movie)
16. now is your time (book)
17. thirteen ways of looking at a blackbird (poem)

18–25. This part of a library list has eight incorrect titles. Write the list correctly.

Example: Look Both Ways, by Jay Walker (article)
        "Look Both Ways," by Jay Walker

Proofreading

- "The Newton Train Crash" by Dee Rail (book)
- "a Guide to Old Furniture" by Ann Teak (newspaper article)
- That Old Car and Road Fever by Otto Mobeel (song)
- Shall We Meet Again? by Mae B. Sew (poem)
- Government Review edited by Polly Ticks (magazine)
- the Plumbers' Daily edited by Rusty Pipes (newspaper)
- "Numbers and Sums" by Adam Upp (book chapter)
- "Wham!" directed by Dinah Might (movie)
- "The big winners" by Jack Potts (short story)

Writing Wrap-Up
WRITING • THINKING • LISTENING • SPEAKING

PERSUADING

Write a List

If you were going to a desert island for three months, what would you take to pass the time? List at least five different items. Include a book, a story, a poem, a magazine, a movie video, and a song. Explain each choice. Compare lists with a small group of classmates. Which titles match in the group?

For Extra Practice see page 214.

Enrichment

Capitalization! Punctuation!

License Plates

Players: 3

Materials: paper and pencil

To play: Pretend you are on a car trip. On the way, you see license plates from different states. The first player calls out a state. The second player must spell the state correctly on paper. The third player must write the correct abbreviation for the state. Then the second player calls out a new state.

Scoring: Players earn 1 point for naming a state, 2 points for spelling the name correctly, and 5 points for writing the correct abbreviation. The player with the most points wins.

What Do You Say?

What do you think Dara might be saying? How about Will, Maxie, and Aunt Zina? Draw a speech balloon for each person and write what he or she might be saying. Use one of the interjections below in each speech balloon. Be sure to punctuate correctly.

Ouch	Hurray	Hey	Oh, no	Good grief	Ah
Wow	Whew	Oh	Okay	Oops	Well

Aunt Zina　　Dara　　Maxie　　Will

Challenge Instead of using speech balloons, write each person's words as a quotation. Use a phrase such as *Aunt Zina said* or *said Maxie*.

Checkup: Unit 5

1 Correct Sentences (p. 180)
Write each sentence. Separate any run-on sentences.

1. Everglades National Park is a swamp it is in Florida
2. have you ever visited a swamp
3. how remarkable it is
4. small clumps of high land are called hummocks they are covered with trees
5. take a nature walk with a ranger observe the unusual birds
6. what a great time you will have
7. go to the Ten Thousand Islands you can reach the area by boat
8. do you smell the salt air
9. what a pleasant view this is

2 Proper Nouns and Adjectives (p. 182)
Write the proper nouns and the proper adjectives. Capitalize them correctly.

10. Last may I read about john muir.
11. He was an american who loved nature and wildlife.
12. He came to the united states from scotland.
13. He attended the university of wisconsin.
14. The sierra nevada thrilled him.
15. He crossed the alaskan glaciers.
16. He went with his dog, stickeen.
17. He persuaded president roosevelt to protect the wilderness.
18. He helped set up yosemite national park in California.

3 Commas in a Series (p. 184)
Write each sentence. Use commas to separate the items in a series.

19. Men women and children enjoy the Rocky Mountains in Colorado.
20. The mountains lakes and glaciers are beautiful.
21. Many people fish mountain climb and ski in Colorado.
22. Once people hunted buffalo deer and elk there.
23. Arrowheads pots and tools remain.
24. The slopes are cold windy and dry.
25. Moss primroses and sunflowers grow there.
26. Chipmunks squirrels and gophers live there too.
27. Beavers build dams make lodges and gather food.
28. You might see bluebirds hawks owls or meadowlarks.
29. You can find wildlife in the lakes on the mountainside or in the forest.
30. The Colorado Rockies are exciting majestic and rugged.
31. Mount Evans Pikes Peak and Longs Peak are on the east side.
32. You can climb Pikes Peak by automobile toll road on horseback by cog railway or on foot.
33. The Rockies also stretch through Utah Wyoming New Mexico Idaho and Montana.

Go to www.eduplace.com/kids/hme/ for more fun with parts of speech.

Checkup continued

4 More Uses for Commas
(p. 188) Write each sentence. Add commas where needed.

34. Well here we are in speech class.
35. Fred please give your speech first.
36. Is it about the Ritz Theater Fred?
37. Yes Mr. Stone it is.
38. No it won't be torn down.
39. Do you like the idea Fred?
40. Fred stand up straight.
41. Yes look at the audience.
42. Well remember to speak clearly.
43. That speech Fred was very good.
44. Jane do you agree with Fred?
45. No Mr. Stone I don't.
46. A restoration is too costly Fred.
47. Thank you Jane for your opinion.

5 Interjections
(p. 192) Write each sentence. Underline the interjections. Add the correct punctuation after each interjection.

48. Hurray The parade boats are beginning to come down the river!
49. Hey Look at the variety of boats!
50. Ah how I'd love to cruise around on one of them.
51. Okay Now the boats are right in front of us.
52. Oh no That isn't sturdy enough.
53. Oh let's pick our favorite boat.
54. Good grief That one is as big as a house!
55. Well it's a houseboat.
56. Wow Wouldn't it be fun to live on the water?

6 Quotations
(p. 194) Write each sentence. Use punctuation marks and capital letters correctly.

57. Don asked have you read about the volcano
58. no answered Tony what happened
59. Mt. Ridley blew up said Don
60. were people hurt asked Tony
61. it happened in a wilderness area replied Jo no one was hurt
62. several campers got out just in time she added
63. what a miracle that was cried Tony
64. mud flowed down the Jones River Jo added it flooded
65. help is on its way she added
66. rescue workers are in the area said Don families are out of danger
67. was it scary Rory wondered
68. do you think asked Jo that the ground felt hot underfoot
69. stay back screeched Tony
70. Don explained an active volcano is dangerous
71. it produces extreme heat agreed Tony
72. one volcano is in sicily replied Tony it is still active.
73. when it erupts said Don lava smoke and gases flow out of the craters
74. are volcanoes ever helpful Jo asked
75. Tony responded volcanic steam can run a power plant

202 Unit 5: Capitalization and Punctuation

7 Abbreviations (p. 196)
Write these groups of words, using initials or abbreviations for the underlined words.

76. Duxbury, Massachusetts 02332
77. Post Office Box 35
78. Friday, March 14, 2003
79. Doctor Peter Denny
80. Richard Allman Senior
81. Revere Corporation
82. Anna Christina Smithson
83. Mister James William Carson
84. 33 Cleary Boulevard
85. Apartment 2B
86. San Antonio, Texas 78284
87. 11221 Vista Drive
88. Durham, North Carolina 27108

8 Titles (p. 198)
Write each of the following titles correctly.

89. pioneer press (newspaper)
90. children of the year (article)
91. julie of the wolves (book)
92. the goat well (short story)
93. popular science (magazine)
94. how to eat a poem (poem)
95. mary poppins (movie)
96. a new age begins (chapter)
97. sports illustrated (magazine)
98. georgia on my mind (song)
99. the new york times (newspaper)
100. ode to my library (poem)

Mixed Review 101–110. This thank-you note has seven punctuation errors and three capitalization errors. Write the note correctly.

Proofreading Checklist
Check capitalization and punctuation in
- ✓ sentences
- ✓ proper nouns, proper adjectives
- ✓ quotations
- ✓ abbreviations and titles

Aug. 10
Dear Mr. Ortega,
    Today I received a letter a magazine, and a package. Yes, the package was from you, Mr. Ortega. Wow What a wonderful surprise it was!
    "It's a book from Mr. Ortega" I said to my father and mother, "and it's by Jean craighead George." Then I added, "she's a really wonderful writer"
    I'm sure that "My Side of the Mountain" will be great fun to read. I loved Julie of The Wolves. That book is by Ms George too. Have you read it.
    Thank you again for the wonderful gift.
        Sincerely,
        Jackie

See www.eduplace.com/kids/hme/ for an online quiz.

Assessment Link

Test Practice

Write the numbers 1–10 on a sheet of paper. Read the sentence. Choose the part that needs a capital letter. Write the letter for that answer. If no part needs a capital letter, write the letter for the last answer, "None."

1. Will the city bus / stop in front / of the grocery store? / None
    A   B   C   D

2. My cousins arrived / at our apartment / on New Year's day. / None
    F   G   H   J

3. A boy raised his hand / and asked, "may I / sharpen my pencil?" / None
    A   B   C   D

4. The tourist guide / booked us rooms at / the Brunswick hotel. / None
    F   G   H   J

5. Cassie sang a song / called "Stars in the sky" / to her baby sister. / None
    A   B   C   D

6. My teacher found / an italian violin / in his grandfather's attic. / None
    F   G   H   J

7. The cherry trees in / the park will bloom / in early spring. / None
    A   B   C   D

8. In Utah I climbed / a mountain and saw / the Great Salt lake. / None
    F   G   H   J

9. We usually celebrate / Columbus day / as a holiday. / None
    A   B   C   D

10. Both my sisters / majored in mathematics / at Howard university. / None
    F   G   H   J

Now write numbers 11–14 on your paper. Use the paragraph to answer the questions. Write the letter for each answer.

¹¹Frank Lloyd Wright, a famous American architect, was born on june 8, 1867. ¹²He designed houses churches museums and skyscrapers. ¹³Wright was more daring than other architects of his time. ¹⁴Many people disliked Wright's unusual buildings he never doubted himself.

11 Which is the best way to write Sentence 11?

  A Frank Lloyd Wright, a famous American architect, was born on June 8, 1867.

  B Frank Lloyd Wright a famous American Architect, was born on June 8, 1867.

  C Frank Lloyd Wright, a Famous American architect was born on June 8, 1867.

  D Best as it is

12 Which is the best way to write Sentence 12?

  F He designed houses churches museums, and skyscrapers.

  G He designed houses, churches, museums, and skyscrapers.

  H He designed houses, churches museums and, skyscrapers.

  J Best as it is

13 Which is the best way to write Sentence 13?

  A Wright was daring than other architects of his time.

  B Wright was the most daring than other architects of his time.

  C Wright was more daringest than other architects of his time.

  D Best as it is

14 Which is the best way to write Sentence 14?

  F Many people disliked Wright's unusual buildings, but he never doubted himself.

  G Many people disliked Wright's unusual buildings or, he never doubted himself.

  H Many people disliked Wright's unusual buildings, he never doubted himself.

  J Best as it is

Test Practice

✓ Test Practice *continued*

Now write numbers 15–18 on your paper. Use the paragraph to answer the questions. Write the letter for each answer.

¹⁵Last night I watched the Wizard of oz on television. ¹⁶What, a horrible mistake that was? ¹⁷All night I dreamed about witchs and flying monkies. ¹⁸In the morning, I said to Mom, "It was my worst sleep ever!"

15 Which is the best way to write Sentence 15?

  A Last night I watched The wizard of Oz on television.

  B Last night I watched The Wizard of Oz on television.

  C Last night I watched The Wizard Of Oz on television.

  D Best as it is

16 Which is the best way to write Sentence 16?

  F What a horrible mistake that was!

  G What! a horrible mistake that was.

  H What, An horrible mistake that was!

  J Best as it is

17 Which is the best way to write Sentence 17?

  A All night I dreamed about witchs and flying monkeys.

  B All night I dreamed about witches and flying monkeys.

  C All night I dreamed about witchses and flying monkies.

  D Best as it is

18 Which is the best way to write Sentence 18?

  F In the morning, I said to mom, "It was my worser sleep ever!"

  G In the morning, I said to mom "it was my most worst sleep ever!"

  H In the morning, I said to Mom, It was my worse sleep ever!

  J Best as it is

Extra Practice

(pages 180–181)

1. Correct Sentences

- Begin every sentence with a capital letter.
- Use a **period** to end a declarative sentence or an imperative sentence.
- Use a **question mark** to end an interrogative sentence.
- Use an **exclamation point** to end an exclamatory sentence.

● Each sentence is missing a capital letter or an end mark. Write each sentence correctly.

Example: How hard we practice   *How hard we practice!*

1. The spring concert is in just two weeks
2. will you sing any new songs?
3. Who will try out for the solo parts
4. What a lovely voice Rita has
5. please sing the last verse one more time.

▲ Write the sentences correctly. Separate run-on sentences.

Example: contact Allan he has details about the concert
   Contact Allan. He has details about the concert.

6. the concert will be held on Saturday
7. how many school bands will we hear
8. we heard thirty-five bands last year
9. how the music filled the air what a great concert that was
10. don't miss the concert buy your tickets now

■ Rewrite each sentence below as the kind of sentence shown in parentheses. Write the new sentences correctly.

Example: The tickets were sold quickly. (exclamatory)
   How quickly the tickets were sold!

11. Will the concert begin on time? (declarative)
12. The audience is large tonight. (exclamatory)
13. Will Mr. Case record the entire concert? (declarative)
14. How well the chorus performed! (interrogative)
15. Did you listen to the words of our class song? (imperative)

Extra Practice **207**

Extra Practice

2 Proper Nouns and Adjectives
(pages 182–183)

- Capitalize proper nouns and proper adjectives.
- If a proper noun is two words, capitalize both words. If it is three or more words, capitalize each important word.
- If a proper adjective is two words, capitalize both words.

● Write the underlined proper nouns and proper adjectives. Capitalize them correctly.

Example: Are these paintings by <u>mary cassatt</u>?   *Mary Cassatt*

1. She was an <u>american artist</u>.
2. She was born in <u>pittsburgh</u>.
3. Her art education began in the <u>united states</u>.
4. Later she went to <u>europe</u>.
5. She studied with <u>italian</u> and <u>spanish</u> artists.

▲ Write the proper nouns and the proper adjectives. Capitalize them correctly.

Example: When was the artist pablo picasso born?   *Pablo Picasso*

6. He was born on october 25, 1881.
7. He spent his childhood in the spanish city of barcelona.
8. The academy of arts was his first art school.
9. Later he studied art in madrid.
10. When did picasso move to paris?
11. He moved to paris in 1903.

■ Write each sentence, using capital letters correctly.

Example: The city of lakeville is sponsoring an art contest.
The city of Lakeville is sponsoring an art contest.

12. I read about it in a newsletter from the blake art museum.
13. Paintings must be turned in by the first monday in may.
14. The judges are franco pallo and maria romano.
15. They are well-known italian artists.
16. First prize is a scholarship to the hamilton school of art.

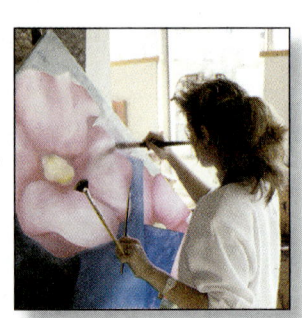

Extra Practice

3 Commas in a Series

(pages 184–185)

- A **series** is a list of three or more items in a sentence.
- Use commas to separate the items in a series. Put a comma after each item except the last one.
- Use *and* or *or* before the last item in a series.

● Copy the sentence that is correct in each pair.

Example: The show was held on Monday Tuesday and Wednesday.
The show was held on Monday, Tuesday, and Wednesday.
The show was held on Monday, Tuesday, and Wednesday.

1. We watched laughed and clapped.
   We watched, laughed, and clapped.
2. We saw string puppets, finger puppets, and hand puppets.
   We saw string puppets finger puppets and hand puppets.
3. Jack Rita and I played with the string puppets.
   Jack, Rita, and I played with the string puppets.

▲ Write these sentences correctly.

Example: Choose between The Wizard of Oz, and Peter Pan.
Choose between The Wizard of Oz and Peter Pan.

4. Will you play the Tin Man the Lion or the Scarecrow?
5. You can try out for the play on Sunday Monday or Tuesday.
6. Memorize your lines learn the songs and be on time.
7. Relax smile and enjoy yourself on the stage.

■ Rewrite each sentence to include a series. Use commas correctly in your sentences.

Example: Use music and movement in your performance.
Use music, movement, and costumes in your performance.

8. Actors and dancers work long hours.
9. Courage and hard work can lead to success.
10. The day of the performance was windy and cold.
11. People wore rubber boots and heavy coats.
12. The auditorium was filled with cheers and joy.

Extra Practice

(pages 188–189)

4 More Uses for Commas

- **Introductory words** are words such as *yes, no,* and *well* when they begin a sentence. Use a comma after these words.
- A **noun in direct address** is the name of a person who is spoken to. Use commas to set off a noun in direct address.

● Copy each sentence. Then underline the introductory word or the noun in direct address and the commas.

Example: You play the piano well, Carla.
You play the piano well, <u>Carla</u>.

1. Your flute has a beautiful sound, Leo.
2. Matt, do you also play the flute?
3. Yes, the flute is an easy instrument to learn.
4. I think, Amy, that we should play together.

▲ Write the sentences. Add commas where they are needed.

Example: Yes Olivia I would like to play in a band.
Yes, Olivia, I would like to play in a band.

5. Yes it would be a lot of fun.
6. What instrument would you choose Tia?
7. Well I would choose a guitar like my dad's.
8. I think Scott that my dad will let me use his guitar.
9. No he told me it is out of tune.

■ Write the sentences. Add commas where needed. Underline introductory words once and nouns in direct address twice.

Example: No Becky I have never been to the ballet.
<u>No</u>, <u><u>Becky</u></u>, I have never been to the ballet.

10. My grandfather took me to the ballet last year Linda.
11. Yes Linda the dancers are very graceful.
12. Louis would you like to square-dance tonight?
13. How do you know which steps to do Meryl?
14. Well Lenny one person calls out directions.

 **Extra Practice**

(pages 192–193)

5 Interjections

- An **interjection** is a word or words that show feeling or emotion.
- Use an exclamation point or a comma after an interjection.

● Copy each sentence. Then underline the interjection and the punctuation that follows it.

Example: Hey! Look under that bush!
Hey! Look under that bush!

1. Oh no! The bird flew away!
2. Goodness! What do you think it was?
3. Oh, I think it might have been a lark.
4. Oops! I forgot to bring my binoculars!
5. Ah, that's too bad.

▲ Write the sentences. Add the correct punctuation after each interjection.

Example: Ouch I just got a splinter from this birdhouse.
Ouch! I just got a splinter from this birdhouse.

6. Goodness The woodpeckers will love it!
7. Oh it's just a hollowed-out log with a roof.
8. Well it will seem cozy to a bird.
9. Oh, no I forgot to add a perch!
10. Hurray It's finished!

■ Write the sentences, using the interjection in parentheses. Add the correct punctuation after the interjection.

Example: An ostrich can run extremely fast! (Goodness)
Goodness! An ostrich can run extremely fast!

11. _____ it can run faster than I can! (Well)
12. _____ That's good, because it can't fly. (Whew)
13. _____ Can you imagine the size of an ostrich egg? (Hey)
14. _____ it must be enormous! (Oh)
15. _____ what a scrambled egg that would make! (Ah)

Extra Practice **211**

Extra Practice

6 Quotations (pages 194–195)

- A **direct quotation** gives a speaker's exact words.
- Set off a quotation with quotation marks. Begin each quotation with a capital letter. Place end punctuation inside the quotation marks. Use commas to separate most quotations from the rest of the sentence.

● Write each sentence correctly. Use capital letters and quotation marks where they are needed.

Example: do you know any riddles? asked Lois.
"Do you know any riddles?" asked Lois.

1. Tim answered, what is black, white, and read all over?
2. it is a blushing zebra, guessed Lois.
3. that's not right, but it's a good guess, said Tim.
4. Tim exclaimed, it's a newspaper!
5. next time I'll fool you! exclaimed Lois.

▲ Write each sentence correctly. Use punctuation marks and capital letters where they are needed.

Example: our town has a volunteer fire department said Norma
"Our town has a volunteer fire department," said Norma.

6. Seth added my father is a volunteer firefighter
7. how does he know when there is a fire asked Jean
8. the volunteers use a phone chain answered Seth
9. Jean asked are there many big fires in your town
10. we're lucky said Norma that we've never had a big fire

■ Rewrite each sentence. Move the speaker's name to the position shown in parentheses.

Example: Jo asked, "Is volunteer firefighting a new idea?" (end)
"Is volunteer firefighting a new idea?" asked Jo.

11. Lee said, "Volunteers were used in ancient Egypt." (end)
12. "They were also used in early America," he added. (beginning)
13. Stan asked, "Were there big fires then?" (end)
14. "Yes," answered Sue, "they often destroyed towns." (end)

Extra Practice

(pages 196–197)

7 Abbreviations

- An **abbreviation** is a shortened form of a word.
- An abbreviation usually begins with a capital letter and ends with a period.

● Write the words that the underlined abbreviations stand for.

Example: 465 Highland Ave.   *Avenue*

1. Orlando, FL 32859
2. Wed., Dec. 3, 1835
3. Dr. Linda Chang
4. DeMarco Tire Co.
5. 36 Park Dr.
6. Aug. 25, 1912
7. Frank Dolan Jr.
8. Rte. 114
9. P. O. Box 50
10. Mr. Peter Jackson
11. Healthy Foods, Inc.
12. Birmingham, AL 35294

▲ Rewrite these groups of words, using abbreviations or initials for the underlined words.

Example: 139 Palmer Road, Sherwood, Connecticut 06143
139 Palmer Rd., Sherwood, CT 06143

13. Post Office Box 15, Hattiesburg, Mississippi 39406
14. Sunday, January 7, 1949
15. Mister Benjamin Montgomery Thompson Junior
16. Doctor Maria Carmen Perez
17. Maxwell Hamilton Photo Color Company
18. 14 Hamlet Street, Apartment 7, Ithaca, New York 14853

■ Follow the directions for each item. You may make up some of the information. Use abbreviations and initials.

Example: Write the name of your best friend's father.
Mr. S. D. Merrick Sr.

19. Write your complete home address.
20. Write the name of a company that makes computers.
21. Mark Rand Sr. has a son with the same name. Write his name.
22. Write the day and date of your birthday this year.
23. Write the address of one of your friends.
24. Write the day and date that school began this year.

Extra Practice   **213**

Extra Practice

(pages 198–199)

8 Titles

- Capitalize the first, last, and all important words in a title.
- Underline the titles of books, magazines, newspapers, and movies.
- Put quotation marks around the titles of short stories, songs, articles, book chapters, and most poems.

● Each title below should be underlined or enclosed in quotation marks. Write the titles correctly.

Example: The White Horse (poem)   "The White Horse"

1. Treasure Island (movie)
2. The Borrowers (book)
3. Oklahoma! (song)
4. Dreams (poem)
5. Boys' Life (magazine)
6. Summertime (chapter)
7. The Necklace (short story)
8. The New Yorker (magazine)
9. Autumn Woods (poem)
10. Miami News (newspaper)
11. A Clever Judge (short story)
12. The Yearling (book)

▲ Write these titles correctly.

Example: on a night of snow (poem) "On a Night of Snow"

13. how thor found his hammer (short story)
14. home on the range (song)
15. the philadelphia inquirer (newspaper)
16. the wizard of oz (movie)
17. justin morgan had a horse (book)

■ Rewrite each sentence, correcting the title.

Example: I just finished the article life in the mountains.
   I just finished the article "Life in the Mountains."

18. My favorite chapter is called in the pasture.
19. The magazine national geographic has interesting articles.
20. On our camping trip, we sang this land is your land.
21. Alexandra and I just saw the movie the sound of music.
22. I will write my book report on the incident at hawk's hill.

214   Unit 5: Capitalization and Punctuation

Unit 6

Pronouns

Our counselors gave us one last reminder—getting lost was *not* a good idea. We campers should follow their directions exactly!

Grammar/Usage

1 Subject Pronouns

One-Minute Warm-Up

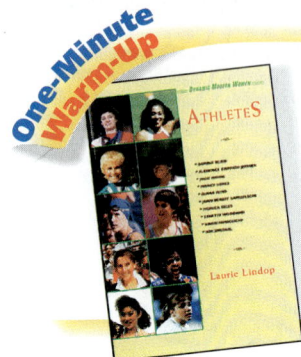

Which two words in this sentence replace *Diana*? Which one of them could be used as the subject of a sentence? What similar words do you know?

> Diana knew that on her swim to Florida she would probably become delirious.
>
> —from *AthleteS*, by Laurie Lindop

- You know that a noun names a person, a place, or a thing. A **pronoun** is a word that takes the place of a noun. A **subject pronoun** takes the place of a noun as the subject of a sentence.

Noun	Subject Pronoun
Carl watches the swimmers.	**He** watches the swimmers.
Rope divides the lanes.	**It** divides the lanes.
Jean and Susan practice.	**They** practice.

- Subject pronouns also follow forms of the linking verb *be*.

    The lifeguard today is **he**.
    Yesterday the lifeguards were **Tara and I**.

Subject Pronouns	
Singular	**Plural**
I	we
you	you
he, she, it	they

Try It Out

Speak Up What subject pronouns could replace the underlined words?

1. <u>Leo and Emily</u> cooked.
2. <u>Leo</u> bought the fruit.
3. <u>Emily</u> served egg rolls.
4. <u>The chicken</u> was broiled.
5. <u>Bill and I</u> ate the most.
6. The dishwashers were <u>Kiran</u> and <u>Pa</u>.

Unit 6: Pronouns

On Your Own

Write these sentences, using subject pronouns to replace the underlined words.

Example: Mark swims in swim meets.   *He swims in swim meets.*

7. Last year Arnie was the lifeguard.
8. The new lifeguard is Jenny.
9. Conrad, Sally, and I played water basketball.
10. Leroy threw the ball through the floating hoop.
11. The floating hoop fell over.
12. Did Deena put the hoop back in place?
13. The best players were Conrad and Tina.
14. Volunteers for cleanup were Nicola and Alan.

15–22. This swim coach's evaluation has eight underlined subjects. Write the evaluation, replacing the underlined words with subject pronouns.

Example: Paul and Alex have shown great team spirit.
They have shown great team spirit.

Swimmer's Progress Report: Alex Sachs

I am proud to have been Alex's swim coach this year. Ron White and Alex have worked hard. Ms. Pinza has told me she gets to school early and sees Alex at the pool. The pool is already busy. There Alex is, doing laps. Who noticed the backstroke flaw? That was Ms. Pinza. Alex and I worked together, and Alex improved. Alex is a fine team player. The strongest swimmers on our team are Ron and Alex. The team unanimously chose Alex Sachs as their captain.

Writing Wrap-Up
WRITING • THINKING • LISTENING • SPEAKING

EXPLAINING

Write an Award Certificate

Write a certificate for an award for someone who has helped you or for a national hero. Explain the reasons for the award. Use at least four subject pronouns. Read it to a classmate. Read it again, and ask the classmate to list the subject pronouns.

Grammar/Usage
2 Object Pronouns

One-Minute Warm-Up

What makes this joke a joke?
- Teacher: Franklin, name an object pronoun.
- Franklin: You mean me?
- Teacher: Correct!

- **Object pronouns** can replace nouns used after action verbs or after the words *to, for, with, in,* or *at*. The object pronouns are *me, him, her, us,* and *them*. *You* and *it* can be either subject pronouns or object pronouns.

Noun	Object Pronoun
Mrs. Stone drove Clyde.	Mrs. Stone drove him.

- Do not use an object pronoun when you need a subject pronoun.

  Incorrect: Him and me like that car.   The drivers were Dad and her.
  Correct: He and I like that car.   The drivers were Dad and she.

- A pronoun after an action verb or after words such as *to, for, with, in,* or *at* is always an object pronoun even when there is more than one object.

  Mary thanked him and Mrs. Stone. (not *he and Mrs. Stone*)
  Alice waited with Mary and her. (not *Mary and she*)

Subject Pronouns:	I	we	**Object Pronouns:**	me	us
	you	you		you	you
	she, he, it	they		her, him, it	them

Try It Out

Speak Up Which pronoun in parentheses is correct? Is it a subject pronoun or an object pronoun?

1. Adam sketched Liz and (I, me).
2. (He, Him) can draw people's faces well.
3. Liz asked (we, us) for suggestions.
4. Adam drew Liz and (they, them) too.

Unit 6: Pronouns

On Your Own

Write each sentence, using the correct pronoun.

Example: Lois and Tony planned a camping trip for (us, we).
Lois and Tony planned a camping trip for us.

5. Beth went with (we, us) to buy supplies.
6. Max showed (I, me) the area on a map.
7. (We, Us) drove with (they, them) to the mountains.
8. I helped (her, she) with the tent.
9. (They, Them) had chosen a spot high in the mountains.
10. (We, Us) pitched the tent for a good view of (they, them).
11. The next night Paul played his guitar for (us, we).
12. We all complimented (he, him) on his playing.

13–20. This part of a story has eight underlined nouns and pronouns. Write this part of the story, replacing the underlined word or words with the correct pronoun.

Example: What scared Pat and <u>she</u>? *What scared Pat and her?*

Web site

The Dreaded Woods

Tom looked around. Was something watching <u>Maria, Pat, and him</u>? The woods seemed dark and scary to Maria and <u>he</u> but not to his sister Pat. <u>Maria, Pat, and he</u> were lost, but <u>Pat</u> didn't look nervous. Maria and Tom were shaking. Why did the mysterious noise not frighten <u>Pat</u>?

Why had Mom and Dad taken <u>Maria, Pat, and Tom</u> to a camp for the first time? The strange noise was growing louder and closer. Was some wild animal coming at <u>Maria, Pat, and him</u>? Ah, it was Dad! <u>Dad</u> had found them!

Writing Wrap-Up   WRITING • THINKING • LISTENING • SPEAKING

NARRATING

Write a Story

Write the first two paragraphs of a story about a time when you were in a new place. Where were you? Why? How did you feel? Read it to a partner. How does your partner think your story might end?

For Extra Practice see page 239.

Object Pronouns **219**

Grammar/Usage

3 Using *I* and *me*

One-Minute Warm-Up

Welcome, my friend.
How clean you'll soon be!
You'll love this bath
With the bubbles and _____.

Which pronoun, *I* or *me*, would you use to end this poem? (Let the rhyme of the poem help you.) Explain your choice.

- You have learned to use the subject pronoun *I* as a subject or after forms of the linking verb *be*. You have also learned to use the object pronoun *me* after action verbs or words such as *to, for, with, in,* or *at*. You may have trouble, however, deciding whether to use *I* or *me* when they are joined with nouns or other pronouns. To help you decide, say the sentence with only *I* or *me*.

With a Noun or Another Pronoun	**With *I* or *me* Only**
Diana and I ride the bus.	I ride the bus.
The winners were Dave and I.	The winner was I.
Who chose Carol and me?	Who chose me?
Is Leo coming with him and me?	Is Leo coming with me?

- When you use *I* or *me* with nouns or other pronouns, always name yourself last.

Scott and I invited Rosa.	Rosa met Scott and me.
He and I saw Rosa.	Rosa waited for him and me.

Try It Out

Speak Up Which words in parentheses correctly complete each of these sentences?

1. (Lisa and I, Me and Lisa) are visiting Daria.
2. Daria teaches a game to (Lisa and me, Lisa and I).
3. Lisa shows (Daria and I, Daria and me) another game.
4. (Daria and I, I and Daria) have played it in school.
5. (Lisa and I, Lisa and me) love playing games.
6. Daria invites (me and Lisa, Lisa and me) for lunch.

Unit 6: Pronouns

On Your Own

Write these sentences, using the correct words in parentheses.

Example: Nate and (I, me) practice our skating every week.
Nate and I practice our skating every week.

7. Nate and (me, I) always ride our bikes to the rink.
8. Kate called to (Nate and me, me and Nate).
9. Kate asked Nate and (me, I) about our progress.
10. (He and I, I and he) laughed about our falls.
11. (I and Lennie, Lennie and I) wear the same skates.
12. The best skaters are (Kate and me, Kate and I).

13–20. Write this invitation and change the eight incorrect uses of *I* or *me*.

Example: Please call Earl or I. *Please call Earl or me.*

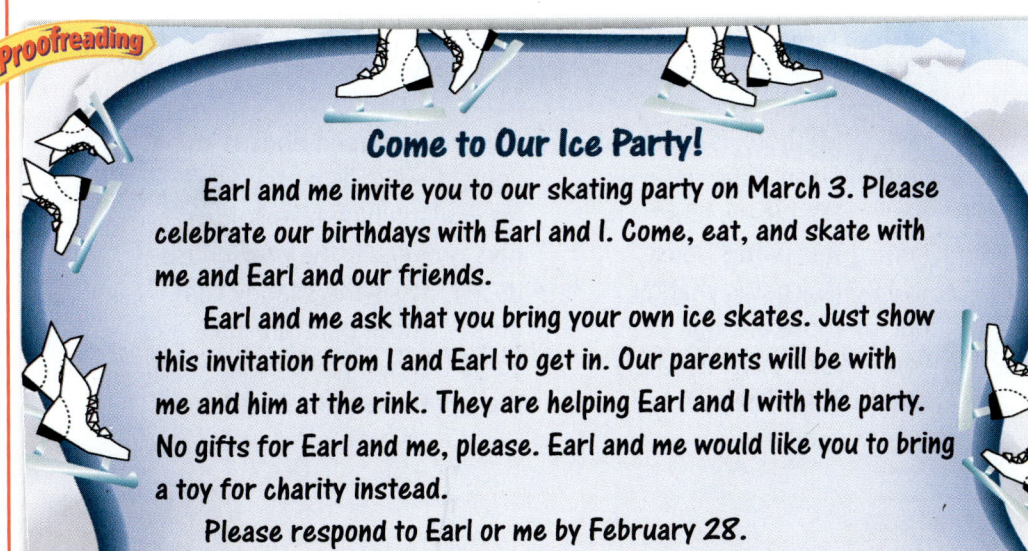

Come to Our Ice Party!

Earl and me invite you to our skating party on March 3. Please celebrate our birthdays with Earl and I. Come, eat, and skate with me and Earl and our friends.

Earl and me ask that you bring your own ice skates. Just show this invitation from I and Earl to get in. Our parents will be with me and him at the rink. They are helping Earl and I with the party. No gifts for Earl and me, please. Earl and me would like you to bring a toy for charity instead.

Please respond to Earl or me by February 28.

Writing Wrap-Up
WRITING • THINKING • LISTENING • SPEAKING

EXPRESSING

Write a Thank-you Note

Write a thank-you note for you and a friend. Express gratitude for a favor someone did for both of you. Use *I* and *me* with other nouns at least three times. Read your note to a partner. Have your partner tell you which sentence most convincingly expresses your gratitude.

Grammar/Usage

4 Possessive Pronouns

One-Minute Warm-Up

Which pronouns are the subject? Which pronoun tells whose chair it is?

> He got up from his chair and fell heavily across the bed. He tried to clear his mind, to think of something else for a while instead of the article.
>
> —from *Darnell Rock Reporting*, by Walter Dean Myers

As you know, possessive nouns show ownership. **A possessive pronoun can replace a possessive noun.** Some possessive pronouns appear before a noun. Other possessive pronouns stand alone.

Possessive Pronouns Used with Nouns		Possessive Pronouns That Stand Alone	
my	My book is green.	mine	The green book is mine.
your	Clean your desk.	yours	Yours is messy.
his	His bike is blue.	his	The blue bike is his.
her	This is her house.	hers	Hers is the gray house.
its	Its coat is shaggy.	its	Its is the shaggy coat.
our	Those are our pens.	ours	Those pens are ours.
your	Take your sweaters.	yours	Leave yours here.
their	Their hats are red.	theirs	Those hats are theirs.

Try It Out

Speak Up Which possessive pronoun in parentheses correctly completes each sentence?

1. The students finished (their, theirs) reports.
2. Is the report about Carlsbad Caverns (your, yours)?
3. (Her, Hers) is about a visit to the museum.
4. The eagle is the subject of (my, mine) report.
5. (Its, It's) is a wide wingspan.

222 Unit 6: Pronouns

On Your Own

Write each sentence, using the correct pronoun in parentheses.

Example: (My, Mine) class is publishing a newspaper.
My class is publishing a newspaper.

6. (It, Its) title is *The Ridley Roundup*.
7. The article about the Special Olympics will be (your, yours).
8. Michele is an artist, and the cartoons are (her, hers).
9. (Her, Hers) story about the bird feeder is on page two.
10. The story about the woodcarvings is (mine, my).
11. Kiki and Toby wrote (their, theirs) story about butterflies.
12. The article on subways was also (theirs, their).

13–22. Write the ten possessive pronouns in this flyer.

Example: Read our new newspaper, and enjoy its stories. *our   its*

The Ridley Roundup

In the first issue:
Articles About Your Friends by Your Friends

- Mario writes about his class's biology project.
- Nan and Pedro make a discovery. The scoop is theirs.
- Mia covers her basketball game and its exciting ending.
- Ernest interviews his music teachers.
- We the editors give our opinions and ask you for yours.

Read the issue and say, "This is really mine!"

WRITING • THINKING • LISTENING • SPEAKING

DESCRIBING

Write a Newspaper Article

Write an article for the school newspaper describing a school event. Be sure to include vivid details. Use at least five possessive pronouns. Read your article to a partner. Then read it again, and have your partner raise a hand when you read a possessive pronoun.

For Extra Practice see page 241.

Revising Strategies

Writing with Pronouns

Using Enough Pronouns To avoid repeating the same noun again and again, you can replace it with a pronoun. Do this with care! It is easy to repeat the same pronoun too many times.

Noun overload: Anna writes for the school newspaper. Anna writes sports articles, and Anna attends every home game. Anna is a real sports fan.

Improved with pronouns: Anna writes for the school newspaper. She writes sports articles, and she attends every home game. Anna is a real sports fan.

Apply It

1–4. Revise these sports highlights for a school newspaper. In each paragraph, use the correct pronouns to replace nouns that are repeated too often.

Lincoln School SPORTS

This Year's Sports Highlights!

Scott Hall scored twenty touchdowns! The league chose Scott Hall as most valuable player. Scott's coach promoted Scott to captain.

Claire Markham joined the City Ballet. Claire is the youngest dancer there! This was Claire's first season with the dance company, and Claire is truly both an artist and an athlete.

The tennis players took part in the championship match. Last year the tennis players lost the championship match. This year the tennis players took back the trophy. The trophy is now in the trophy's rightful place!

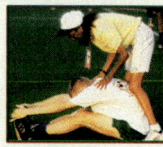
Coach Bernard won the award for top field hockey coach. It is the second time Coach Bernard has won. The award is no surprise to Coach Bernard's players, who appreciate Coach Bernard's skill. Congratulations to Coach Bernard!

Unit 6: Pronouns

Sentence Fluency

Writing Clearly with Pronouns When you use pronouns in your writing, make sure that it is clear which noun a pronoun stands for. If it is unclear, replace the pronoun with a noun.

Unclear: Our school newspaper created a Web site. Nolan likes to write about sports. It often features his writing.

Clear: Our school newspaper created a Web site. Nolan likes to write about sports. The Web site often features his writing.

Does the newspaper or the Web site feature his writing? Which noun does the pronoun stand for?

Don't get carried away with using pronouns! Using the same one again and again can be boring. Instead, include a mix of nouns and pronouns to make your writing interesting and clear.

Apply It

5–10. This article for a Web site has pronouns that are used too much and used unclearly. Revise the article by replacing the underlined pronouns with nouns.

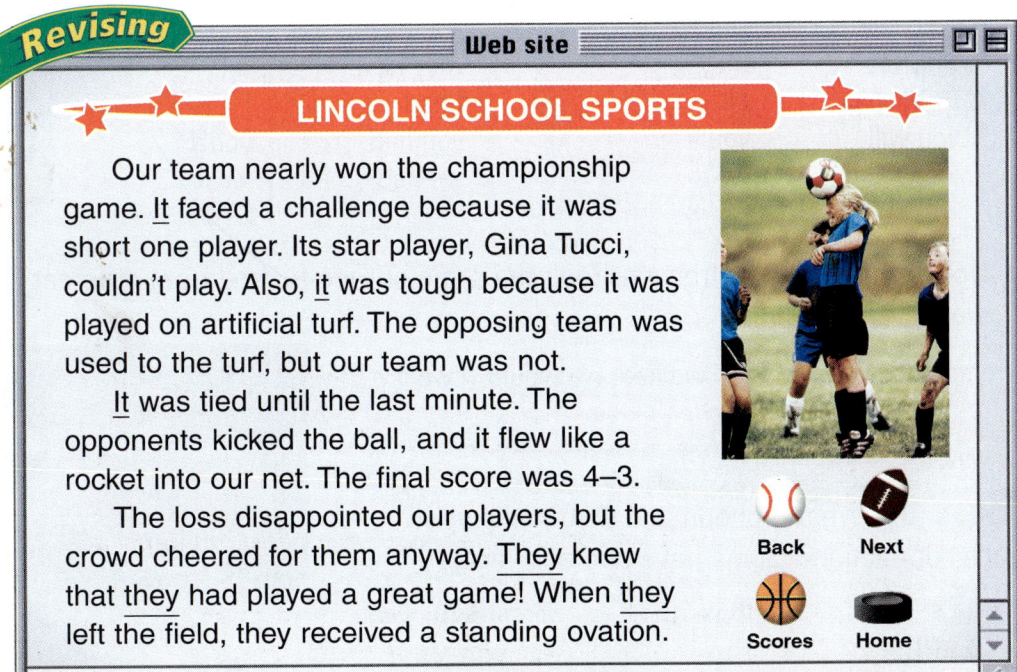

Revising

Web site

LINCOLN SCHOOL SPORTS

Our team nearly won the championship game. <u>It</u> faced a challenge because it was short one player. Its star player, Gina Tucci, couldn't play. Also, <u>it</u> was tough because it was played on artificial turf. The opposing team was used to the turf, but our team was not.

<u>It</u> was tied until the last minute. The opponents kicked the ball, and it flew like a rocket into our net. The final score was 4–3.

The loss disappointed our players, but the crowd cheered for them anyway. <u>They</u> knew that <u>they</u> had played a great game! When <u>they</u> left the field, they received a standing ovation.

Writing with Pronouns **225**

Grammar/Mechanics

5 Contractions with Pronouns

One-Minute Warm-Up

Which words are contractions? What words make them up?

I'm McBroom. Josh McBroom. I'll explain about the watermelons in a minute.

—from *McBroom Tells the Truth*, by Sid Fleischman

- You have learned that a contraction is a shortened form of two words. An apostrophe (') replaces any letters dropped when the words are combined.
- You can make contractions by combining pronouns and the verbs *am, are, is, will, would, have, has,* and *had.* Study the following charts of contractions.

Pronoun +Verb	Contraction
I am	I'm
he is	he's
it is	it's
you are	you're
they are	they're
I will/shall	I'll
you will	you'll
we would	we'd

Pronoun +Verb	Contraction
I have	I've
he has	he's
it has	it's
you have	you've
they have	they've
I had	I'd
you had	you'd
we had	we'd

- Notice that some contractions look the same but are formed from different words.

    he is, he has = he's   we had, we would = we'd

Try It Out

Speak Up What pronoun and verb make up each contraction? (Some have two answers.)

1. he's
2. you'll
3. they're
4. I'm
5. she'd
6. you've

226 Unit 6: **Pronouns**

On Your Own

Write contractions by combining these pronouns and verbs.

Example: you had   *you'd*

7. I shall
8. he had
9. we have
10. it has
11. you have
12. he will
13. they would
14. we had
15. he would
16. we would
17. they have
18. you would

19–30. This diary entry has twelve incorrect contractions. Write the diary entry correctly.

Example: Wer'e visiting my grandparents.
We're visiting my grandparents.

Proofreading

July 11

Im at my grandparents' farm at last. We're here every summer, of course, but its always great to be back. Dad and Mom are busy already. Their happy to be here too. Dad woke up early, and hes working in the corn field. Mom is in the kitchen now, but she'll be out in the field soon. Id be there too, but I'am waiting for Pete. Ive already helped him milk the cows. Hes' been doing it practically all his life. "When your my age, youll be an expert too," he says. Tonight w'll probably have a huge supper, sing songs, and collapse into bed. I'de rather be here than anyplace else on earth!

Writing Wrap-Up
WRITING • THINKING • LISTENING • SPEAKING

REFLECTING

Write a Letter

Write a letter to a friend telling how you spent one summer or one special day. What did you do? What was memorable? Use at least four pronoun and verb contractions. Find a partner. Take turns reading your letters and check together that each contraction is written correctly.

Grammar/Usage

6 Double Subjects

One-Minute Warm-Up

What's incorrect about the sentences in this joke? How can you fix them?

The shoemaker he opened his own shoe store.
Why?
This shoemaker he wanted to be the sole owner.

- You know that every sentence must have a subject. Sometimes people incorrectly use a double subject—a noun and a pronoun—to name the same person, place, or thing.

Incorrect	Correct
Mary she is my sister.	Mary is my sister.
	She is my sister.
Her hat it is pretty.	Her hat is pretty.
	It is pretty.

- *Mary* and *she* should not both be used as subjects. The subject *hat* should not be used with *it*. Use only a noun or a pronoun to name a subject.

Try It Out

Speak Up Which word is unnecessary in each sentence?

1. My parents they own a shoe store.
2. My father he waits on customers.
3. My mother she writes our newspaper ads.
4. People they like our store.
5. My brother and sister they work there too.
6. Our shop it is open six days a week.
7. The shoes they are beautiful.
8. The window display it shows dress shoes.
9. Uncle Ted he helps at the store.
10. My sister she arranges the shoes.

Unit 6: Pronouns

On Your Own

Each sentence has a double subject. Write the sentence correctly.

Example: Paul Newman and Joanne Woodward they are married.
Paul Newman and Joanne Woodward are married.

11. Paul Newman he is an actor.
12. *See How She Runs* it was the name of the movie.
13. Joanne Woodward she starred in that movie.
14. Joanne and Paul they filmed the movie in Boston.
15. The movie it was about the Boston Marathon.
16. Ozzie Nelson and Harriet Nelson they worked together too.
17. The Nelsons they had a show on television.

18–25. This part of an online magazine article has eight double subjects. Write the article correctly.

Example: Old radio shows they can be fun.   *Old radio shows can be fun.*

Proofreading

Web site

Comedy Couple

George Burns he was a comedian, and Gracie Allen acted, sang, and danced. In the 1920s Gracie she teamed up with George, and they created a comedy act. Gracie and George they married, and the Burnses they started a radio show.

In the 1950s, television grew popular. Gracie and George they decided to do the radio show on television. Their show it was on twice a week. Audiences they loved it. Sadly, Gracie she died in the 1960s. George died in 1996 at the age of 100.

Writing Wrap-Up WRITING • THINKING • LISTENING • SPEAKING

Write a Magazine Article

COMPARING / CONTRASTING

How do old TV programs compare with newer shows? Write a two-paragraph article comparing and contrasting an older and a newer TV show, a movie and the book it is based on, or two other works. Avoid double subjects. Compare your choices with those of a partner.

Grammar/Usage
7 Using *we* and *us* with Nouns

One-Minute Warm-Up

Both the girls' soccer team and the boys' soccer team just won championships at your school. What might the girls' captain say to the boys' captain at an awards banquet? Take turns making up sentences using *we girls* and *us boys*.

- Sometimes you use a noun with the pronoun *we* or *us* to make clear whom you are talking about.

    We girls took our places on the field.

- Use the same pronoun as you would if the noun were not there. Use *we* with noun subjects or after linking verbs.

    We girls threw the ball.   The best players are **we girls**.

- Use the pronoun *us* with a noun that follows an action verb or a word such as *to, for, with,* or *at*.

    The girls threw it to **us boys**.   They will not beat **us boys**.

- To decide whether *we* or *us* is correct, read the sentence without the noun.

    We friends watch the game.   **We** watch the game.
    The coach talks to **us players**.   The coach talks to **us**.

Try It Out

Speak Up Which word is correct in each sentence?

1. Mr. Locke invited (we, us) neighbors.
2. (We, Us) friends played softball.
3. The winners were (us, we) girls.
4. Steve came with (we, us) boys.
5. The cooks were (we, us) brothers.
6. (Us, We) girls brought our dog.
7. (Us, We) boys helped Mr. Locke put the chairs away.
8. Mr. Locke reminded (we, us) girls about our dog.

Unit 6: Pronouns

On Your Own

Write each sentence, using *we* or *us*.

Example: The show was planned by _____ girls.
The show was planned by us girls.

9. The girls wrote songs for _____ singers.
10. _____ singers practiced all week.
11. Lois chose _____ dancers.
12. The actors were _____ boys.
13. Were _____ friends the last to arrive?
14. They laughed at _____ clowns.
15. The next performers were _____ singers.

16–20. This letter to the editor in a school newspaper has five incorrect pronouns. Write the letter correctly.

Example: Please help we performers.   *Please help us performers.*

Proofreading

Your Opinions Matter!

Dear Editor:

   The drama club will perform a show in May, and us club members need help. Us students invite YOU to join us members. We organizers need actors, designers, musicians, and more.

   Sign up and have fun! Us show people work hard and have fun too. A big party is planned for we workers after our show. Contact we members today.

   Todd Pitt, Drama Club president

Writing Wrap-Up
WRITING • THINKING • LISTENING • SPEAKING

PERSUADING

Write a Letter to the Editor

Write a letter to the school paper asking students for help with a play or a sale. Give strong reasons for them to say yes. Use *we* and *us* with nouns at least three times. Read the letter to a small group. Did you persuade them? Do they agree with your *we* and *us* usage?

For Extra Practice see page 244.   Using *we* and *us* with Nouns   **231**

Revising Strategies　　　　　　　　　　　　　　　　　　　　Vocabulary

Using Homophones Correctly

Ewe and *you* are **homophones**. The words sound the same, but they have different spellings and different meanings. Whenever you write, be careful to use the homophone that has the correct meaning.

for	shows the receiver of an action	**know**	to understand to be true
four	the number 4	**no**	used to express refusal or denial
hear	to listen	**to**	in the direction of
here	at this place	**too**	also
hour	one of 24 equal parts of a day	**two**	the number 2
our	belonging to us		

Apply It

1–7. Rewrite the sentences from this invitation, correcting the homophones. Use the list of homophones and their definitions in the box for help.

We're having a party four Anthony. He'll be moving two Canada in June. You no we'll all miss him!

The party will be at hour house. Plan to come at too. Please call only if you must say know. I'm sure Anthony will want you to be hear.

232 Unit 6: Pronouns

Enrichment

Healthy Riddles

Design a poster to encourage students to eat healthy food. First, make up a riddle about a healthy food. Use the homophones *its* and *it's*. Try to use each word twice. If you wish, you can make your riddle rhyme. Then write your finished riddle on a poster. Draw pictures as clues, but don't give away the answer.

It's large and round.
Its big leaves have crunch.
In coleslaw it's found.
You'll enjoy its taste at lunch.

Challenge Write a healthy food riddle using the homophones *they're*, *their*, and *there*.

A World Without Pronouns

Choose a paragraph from a short story or novel you have read recently. Reread the paragraph and notice how many pronouns are used. Then rewrite the paragraph, replacing each pronoun with the correct noun. (You may need to change the form of some verbs to agree with their new subjects.) Finally, write a few sentences telling which version of the paragraph is better and why.

Checkup: Unit 6

1. Subject Pronouns (p. 216)
Write subject pronouns to replace the underlined words.

1. <u>Todd and I</u> are studying dinosaurs.
2. <u>A dinosaur</u> could be very large.
3. <u>Jody and Carrie</u> drew pictures.
4. <u>You and Sue</u> visited a museum.
5. The museum guide was <u>Mr. Ross</u>.
6. <u>The dinosaurs</u> mysteriously disappeared from Earth.

2. Object Pronouns (p. 218)
Replace underlined words with pronouns.

7. Kristin spoke to <u>Chet</u> in Swedish.
8. I asked <u>Kristin</u> about the words.
9. Chet said hello to <u>Tim and me</u>.
10. Then he said <u>a word</u> in Dutch.
11. Paul read <u>some French poems</u>.
12. We asked <u>Paul</u> about the meaning.
13. I'll speak Dutch to you and <u>Tanya</u>.
14. I just saw Eleni with <u>Lucy</u>.

3. Using I and me (p. 220)
Write the words that correctly complete these sentences.

15. (Me, I) love to play table tennis.
16. (Lu and I, I and Lu) entered a contest last week.
17. The first and second games went to (me and her, her and me).
18. Rosa kept score for her and (I, me).
19. The champions were Lu and (me, I).

4. Possessive Pronouns (p. 222)
Write the possessive pronoun that correctly completes each sentence.

20. Al and Lily rode (their, theirs) bikes in the race.
21. We rode (our, ours) too.
22. The green bike is (my, mine).
23. (Your, Yours) bike is blue.
24. (Her, Hers) has a silver seat.
25. The red bikes are (their, theirs).
26. (My, Mine) bike passed the test.
27. The safety award was (him, his).
28. Is this repair kit (your, yours)?

5. Contractions with Pronouns (p. 226)
Write the words that were combined to form each contraction.

29. We've come to Washington, D.C.
30. We're at the Air and Space Museum.
31. I've studied Lindbergh before.
32. He'd flown across the ocean.
33. You'd love his airplane.
34. It's called *The Spirit of St. Louis*.
35. I'd like to see the special show.
36. You'd like Dr. Hernando.
37. He's used many special effects.
38. We'll sit in a special dark room.
39. You'll see the volcano on Mars.

6. Double Subjects (p. 228)
Each sentence has one unnecessary subject. Write each sentence correctly.

40. Dr. Lee she is an animal doctor.
41. Pet owners they bring their animals to her.

 Go to www.eduplace.com/tales/hme/ for more fun with parts of speech.

42. Pets they need checkups.
43. A hurt animal it needs treatment.
44. Dr. Snow he works at the animal hospital.
45. The doctors they work together.
46. My mother and I we found Andi.
47. Andi he had a hurt paw.
48. Dr. Lee she put a cast on it.
49. Andi and the doctor they like each other very much.
50. The cast it will be removed soon.
51. Soon Andi he will be well again.

7 Using *we* and *us* with Nouns
(p. 230) Write *we* or *us* to correctly complete each sentence.

52. _____ performers are ready.
53. Those blue costumes are for _____ actors.
54. _____ actors know our lines.
55. The singers are _____ children.
56. Get the armor for _____ knights.
57. _____ royal guards stand here.
58. Are there hats for _____ ladies?
59. _____ musicians go to the ball.
60. Play music for _____ princesses.
61. When do _____ princes arrive?
62. Follow _____ queens on the stage.
63. Everyone watches _____ jugglers.
64. _____ kings sit near the queens.
65. How great _____ dancers will be!
66. Look at _____ kings.

Mixed Review 67–76. This part of a book review has ten mistakes in pronouns. Write the review correctly.

Proofreading Checklist
Have you written these correctly?
✓ subject pronouns
✓ object pronouns
✓ possessive pronouns
✓ contractions with pronouns

Special Book by Katherine Paterson

What are you're favorite books? All of us have our special books. *Bridge to Terabithia* by Katherine Paterson is one of my. I and my brother have both read it many times. In fact, its starting to fall apart from too much handling. For we brothers, it's definitely the book to take to a desert island.

It's two main characters are Jess and Leslie. Theyre very different in certain ways. Still, him and her become close friends. Soon the two of they create a secret kingdom called Terabithia, and their friendship grows. Katherine Paterson really brings her characters to life.

Assessment Link

Test Practice

Write the numbers 1–8 on a sheet of paper. Read each group of sentences. Choose the sentence in which pronouns are used correctly. Write the letter for that answer.

1 **A** The audience clapped for we.
   B Them will be the next act.
   C The singer in the band was me.
   D She peeked out from behind the curtains.

2 **F** These puzzles belong to we.
   G Maybe Jerry can borrow some cards from them.
   H Her will use the jump rope.
   J Sue returned the skates to he.

3 **A** Hannah and I ate our lunch at the round table.
   B Sometimes I and Conrad sit with Nick.
   C Mrs. Gibbons gave me and Ed some napkins.
   D Will and me were the slowest eaters at the table.

4 **F** The biggest raincoat in the closet is your.
   G Hers coat is blue with tan trim.
   H The mittens must be theirs.
   J The boots and shoes in the corner are our.

5 **A** I and Lee are on the same softball team.
   B Me and Henry played catch before the game.
   C My parents cheered for my brother and me.
   D The coach gave Rosa and I new uniforms.

6 **F** Us students are in a play.
   G Mr. Herman he is the director.
   H The props they are ready.
   J Today we actors will practice.

7 **A** Theirs grocery cart is full.
   B The toast and jam are mine.
   C Where is ours shopping list?
   D Did you remember the film for yours camera?

8 **F** Dad took I to his old tree house.
   G Aunt Lizzie and he built it twenty years ago.
   H Them spent many summer days there.
   J Grandma let they sleep there on hot nights.

Now write numbers 9–12 on your paper. Read the passage all the way through once. Then look at the underlined parts. Decide if they need to be changed or if they are fine as they are. Choose the best answer from the choices given. Write the letter for each answer.

Mrs. Burt teaches a baby-sitting class for boys and girls in our town. Many young people <u>has took</u> (9) the class. The boys and girls attend six lessons. By the last lesson, the students can <u>hold dress</u> (10) <u>and feed</u> a baby.

9 A has taked
   B have taken
   C have took
   D (No change)

10 F hold dress, and feed,
    G hold dress, and, feed
    H hold, dress, and feed
    J (No change)

Parents know about Mrs. Burt and her baby-sitting students. They trust <u>she and they</u>. (11)

11 A her and them
   B she and they
   C hers and their
   D (No change)

Many parents say, "Mrs. Burt's students are <u>the goodest</u> baby (12) sitters in town."

12 F the gooder
    G the best
    H the more better
    J (No change)

Test Practice

Extra Practice

(pages 216–217)

1 Subject Pronouns

- A **pronoun** is a word that replaces a noun.
- The **subject pronouns** are *I, you, he, she, it, we,* and *they.*
- Use subject pronouns to replace subject nouns and with all forms of the verb *be.*

● Copy these sentences. Then underline the subject pronouns.

Example: I went to the cookout with Becky and Diego.
I went to the cookout with Becky and Diego.

1. First, we swam in the pool with Gina and Andrew.
2. Then Diego and I made a fruit salad.
3. It was full of watermelon, apples, and pears.
4. We ate, and then Becky suggested a game of softball.
5. The best hitters were she and Maggie.

▲ Write these sentences. Use subject pronouns to replace the underlined words.

Example: <u>Secretariat</u> was a famous racehorse.
He was a famous racehorse.

6. <u>Secretariat</u> won the 1973 Triple Crown of horseracing.
7. <u>The Triple Crown</u> is made up of three races.
8. <u>Fans</u> think Secretariat is one of the greatest racehorses ever.
9. <u>His nickname</u> was "Big Red."
10. The fastest horse ever to race one and one-half miles is <u>Secretariat</u>.

■ Write these sentences. Use subject pronouns to fill in the blanks.

Example: Lars and _____ often watch sports on TV.
Lars and she often watch sports on TV.

11. _____ watched the first Olympic softball competition in 1996.
12. Did _____ see the U.S. women's team win the gold medal?
13. _____ were led to victory by their shortstop.
14. The player who hit the winning two-run homer was _____.
15. _____ saw them defeat China for the gold medal.

238 Unit 6: Pronouns

Extra Practice

(pages 218–219)

2 Object Pronouns

- The **object pronouns** are *me, you, him, her, it, us,* and *them.*
- Use object pronouns after action verbs and after words such as *to* and *for.*
- *It* and *you* may be subject pronouns or object pronouns.

● Complete the second sentence in each pair. Write it correctly. (Use the object pronoun that replaces the underlined word or words in the first sentence.)

Example: I camped with <u>Alex and Carlos</u>. I camped with _____.
I camped with them.

1. We slept in <u>a tent</u>. We slept in _____.
2. Alex gave oranges to <u>Carlos and me</u>. Alex gave oranges to _____.
3. We peeled and ate <u>the oranges</u>. We peeled and ate _____.
4. I found <u>an interesting rock</u>. I found _____.
5. I saved the rock for <u>my sister</u>. I saved the rock for _____.

▲ Write these sentences, using the correct pronouns.

Example: We took Bob and (she, her) on a camping trip.
We took Bob and her on a camping trip.

6. Last night, the rangers showed a film to (we, us).
7. Leah thanked (them, they) for the show.
8. They gave some maps to Bob and (she, her).
9. The maps showed (we, us) interesting places in the park.
10. Bob asked (them, they) about Old Faithful, the geyser.

Old Faithful

■ Write these sentences, replacing the words in parentheses with pronouns.

Example: (The students) met (Gustave and me). *They met us.*

11. (Gustave) questioned (the students) about their bicycle trip.
12. Their answers will help (Gustave) with his own trip.
13. (Gustave's sister) will go with (Gustave).
14. Gustave and his sister will invite (several friends).
15. Have you known Gustave and (his sister) for a long time?

Extra Practice

(pages 220–221)

3 Using *I* and *me*

- Use *I* as the subject of a sentence and after forms of *be*.
- Use *me* after action verbs or words like *to*, *in*, and *for*.
- When using the pronouns *I* and *me* with nouns or other pronouns, name yourself last.

● Use *I* or *me* to complete the second sentence in each pair. Then write the second sentence.

Example: We washed Dad's car. Eva and _____ washed Dad's car.
Eva and I washed Dad's car.

1. The water splashed us. The water splashed Eva and _____.
2. We did not say a word. Eva and _____ did not say a word.
3. The quietest helpers were we. The quietest were Eva and _____.
4. We had surprised him! Eva and _____ had surprised him!
5. Dad thanked us. Dad thanked Eva and _____.

▲ Write each sentence, using *I* or *me* correctly.

Example: My brother and _____ built a doghouse for Willy.
My brother and I built a doghouse for Willy.

6. Willy was happy, and Tom and _____ were proud.
7. Willy used to sleep with my brother and _____.
8. My bed is too narrow for a big dog and _____.
9. Willy and _____ barely fit in.
10. Tom and _____ were happy Willy could sleep in the doghouse.

■ Rewrite each incorrect sentence. If a sentence contains no mistakes, write *correct*.

Example: Me and Larry like to take pictures of animals.
Larry and I like to take pictures of animals.

11. May Larry and I take a picture of your dog?
12. Will your dog pose for I and Larry?
13. I and some other students took these pictures.
14. My sister took this picture for Larry and me.
15. In the picture are Larry and I.

240 Unit 6: Pronouns

Extra Practice

4 Possessive Pronouns

(pages 222–223)

- A **possessive pronoun** shows ownership.
- Use *my, your, his, her, its, our,* and *their* before nouns.
- Use *mine, yours, his, hers, its, ours,* and *theirs* to replace nouns in a sentence.

● Copy the sentences. Then underline the possessive pronouns.

Example: Your report on the school play is excellent.
Your report on the school play is excellent.

1. In fact, yours was the best report in the class.
2. The librarians in our town are having a puppet show.
3. Will you write a report on their puppet show?
4. You can write about the story and its characters.
5. My neighbor is one of the women in charge of the show.
6. Her job is to sell tickets.

▲ Write these sentences, using the correct possessive pronouns.

Example: (My, Mine) aunt works for a newspaper.
My aunt works for a newspaper.

7. Many people in (our, ours) city read that newspaper.
8. Please let me borrow (your, yours) copy of the paper.
9. Samantha is reading (my, mine).
10. Hoshi and Umeko took (their, theirs) to the beach.
11. My aunt's name appears with (her, hers) stories.
12. The story on the front page is (her, hers).

■ Rewrite these sentences, using possessive pronouns.

Example: The students' news stories are written carefully.
Their news stories are written carefully.

13. Our newspaper is the best school paper in the city.
14. Hernando and Shani work on the newspaper's staff.
15. Shani's photographs often appear with Hernando's stories.
16. This photograph of the baseball team is Shani's.
17. Hernando's story comes before my story.
18. Azami and Bret wrote about Azami and Bret's class trip.

Extra Practice

Extra Practice

(pages 226–227)

5 Contractions with Pronouns

- You can combine pronouns with the verbs *am, is, are, will, would, have, has,* and *had* to form contractions.
- Use an apostrophe in place of the dropped letter or letters.

● Write the pronouns and verbs that make up these contractions.

Example: I'd   *I had   I would*

1. she'll
2. I'm
3. I've
4. you'll
5. I'll
6. you've
7. we're
8. they'll
9. you're
10. they've
11. it's
12. you'd
13. they're
14. we'd
15. he's

▲ Write the contractions in these sentences. Then write the words that make up each contraction.

Example: She'll have a great summer.   *She'll   She will*

16. She's at a farm camp.
17. Perhaps you've heard of the camp.
18. It's called Longacre Farm.
19. I'll tell you about the camp.
20. You'll want to know about the staff members.

■ Write contractions that combine these pronouns and verbs. Then write a sentence, using each contraction.

Example: we have   *we've   We've made a colorful poster.*

21. you are
22. they will
23. I am
24. they had
25. he is
26. I had
27. we are
28. she is
29. I will
30. they would
31. I have
32. you will
33. it is
34. he would
35. we will

242   Unit 6: Pronouns

(pages 228–229)

6 Double Subjects
- Do not use a double subject—a noun and a pronoun—to name the same person, place, or thing.

● Write the word that should not appear in each sentence.

Example: Jane Goodall she is a famous scientist. *she*

1. This scientist she worked with her mother at first.
2. Jane and her mother they were a good team.
3. Their work it took them to Africa.
4. Jane she learned a lot about chimpanzees.
5. A photographer he came to Africa.
6. He and Jane they worked together.

▲ Each sentence has a double subject. Write each of the sentences using the noun correctly.

Example: Robert Browning he was a poet.
Robert Browning was a poet.

7. His home it was in England.
8. Elizabeth Barrett she was an English poet too.
9. Robert Browning he wrote her a letter in 1845.
10. The letter it praised her poetry.
11. Elizabeth and Robert they became good friends.
12. In 1846 Robert he was married to Elizabeth.

■ Rewrite each sentence that has a double subject. If a sentence is correct, write *correct*.

Example: Franklin Roosevelt he became President in 1933.
Franklin Roosevelt became President in 1933.

13. His wife she was named Eleanor.
14. The Roosevelts worked together.
15. Eleanor she traveled all over the world to help people.
16. Her goal it was to give all people equal rights.
17. President Roosevelt worked for human rights too.
18. Many people they have written books about the Roosevelts.

Extra Practice **243**

Extra Practice

7 Using *we* and *us* with Nouns (pages 230–231)

- Use *we* with a noun subject or after a linking verb.
- Use *us* with a noun that follows an action verb or a word such as *to, for, with,* or *at*.

● Copy each sentence. Then underline the pronoun and the noun that are used together.

Example: The school supports us athletes.
The school supports <u>us athletes</u>.

1. We girls play basketball every Wednesday afternoon.
2. The reporter talked to us coaches about the teams.
3. We teammates help each other.
4. Last week we boys joined the drama club.
5. Mr. Diaz spoke to us beginners.
6. We students learned about the coming events.

▲ Write each sentence, using the correct word in parentheses.

Example: (We, Us) friends have a club. *We friends have a club.*

7. Jog with (we, us) girls in the park.
8. (Us, We) boys will meet you near the bridge.
9. (We, Us) people will ride bikes around the pond.
10. (Us, We) girls are excellent divers.
11. Beth followed (we, us) skiers downhill.
12. (We, Us) skiers compete locally.

■ Write the sentences, using *we* or *us* with the underlined words.

Example: The girls will debate the <u>boys</u> on Friday.
The girls will debate us boys on Friday.

13. The <u>club members</u> spoke to Mr. Alessi.
14. Mr. Alessi gave advice to the <u>students</u>.
15. The <u>debaters</u> took opposing views of the issue.
16. They tried to persuade the <u>listeners</u>.
17. The <u>boys</u> argued well.
18. The <u>speakers</u> were evenly matched.

Unit 7

Adverbs and Prepositions

Fly away, fly away
In the bowl of the sky.
Fly quickly, fly truly,
Then fly back to me!

Grammar
1 Adverbs

Matthew happily boarded the airplane.
What other emotions might someone feel when starting out on a trip? Replace the word *happily* with adverbs that express other feelings.

- You have learned that an adjective describes a noun or a pronoun. **A word that describes a verb is an adverb.** Adverbs tell how, when, or where an action happens.

    How: The plane landed smoothly at the airport.

    When: Soon Jeff would see his grandparents at the gate.

    Where: They were waiting for him there.

- Many adverbs end with *-ly*. Some are included in these lists of common adverbs.

How	When	Where
fast	tomorrow	here
hard	later	inside
together	again	far
happily	often	upstairs
quietly	first	downtown
secretly	next	somewhere
slowly	then	forward

Try It Out

Speak Up What adverb describes the underlined verb in each sentence? Does it tell how, when, or where?

1. Keith and Tina <u>hurried</u> downtown.
2. They easily <u>found</u> Grove Street Park.
3. Then they <u>watched</u> the parade from the corner.
4. A robot <u>walked</u> awkwardly toward them.
5. Tina and Keith immediately <u>recognized</u> Stan.

On Your Own

Write the adverbs in the sentences below. Then write whether the adverb tells *how*, *when*, or *where*.

Example: Mrs. Janis often visits the art museum. *often   when*

6. Yesterday she took Ramiz and Leslie.
7. The bus traveled far.
8. Finally, they reached the museum.
9. Ramiz went downstairs for an art class.
10. In class he worked carefully and skillfully.
11. His artwork was recently exhibited at the museum.

12–20. This poem has nine adverbs. Write each adverb. Then write the verb it describes.

Example: The conductor stepped forward and took a bow. *forward   stepped*

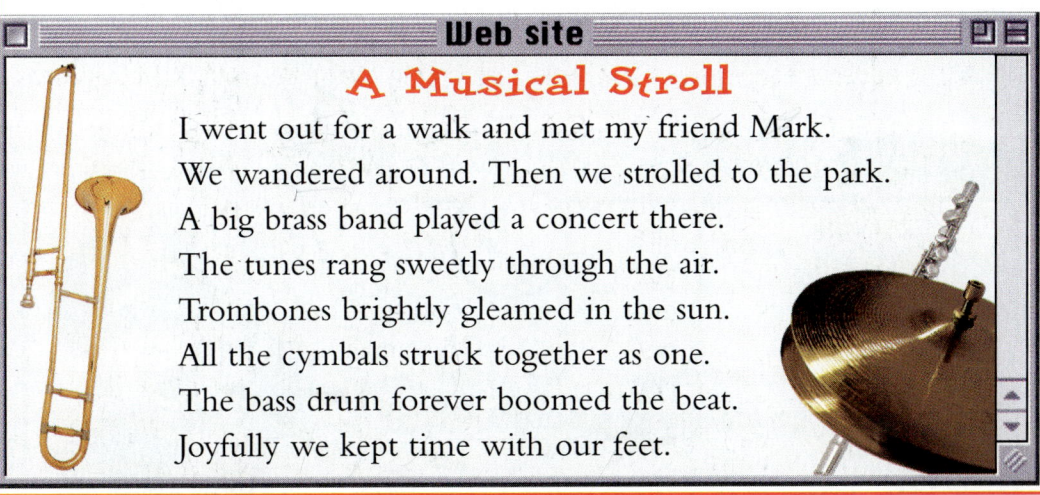

Web site

A Musical Stroll

I went out for a walk and met my friend Mark.
We wandered around. Then we strolled to the park.
A big brass band played a concert there.
The tunes rang sweetly through the air.
Trombones brightly gleamed in the sun.
All the cymbals struck together as one.
The bass drum forever boomed the beat.
Joyfully we kept time with our feet.

Writing Wrap-Up
WRITING • THINKING • LISTENING • SPEAKING

CREATING

Write a Poem

Does music cheer you up? relax you? make you want to dance? Write a poem about how music makes you feel. Your poem doesn't have to rhyme. Just describe the music and your reaction to it. Use several adverbs. Then, with one or two classmates, take turns reading your poems. Ask them which detail in your poem is most striking.

For Extra Practice see page 276.

Revising Strategies

Writing with Adverbs

Elaborating Sentences You can elaborate your sentences by adding adverbs that answer the questions *When? Where?* and *How?* Remember, adverbs don't just follow verbs. Use them in different parts of your sentences to make your writing more interesting.

We are going to a concert.	**Tonight** we are going to a concert.
The band will play.	The band will play **outside**.
Listen to the weather forecast!	Listen **carefully** to the weather forecast!

Apply It

1–8. This bossy bandleader's instructions are incomplete! Add adverbs that tell *when, where,* or *how* to elaborate each underlined sentence. Have at least two sentences in which the adverbs do not directly follow after the verb.

Revising

Meet at the bandstand. <u>We will practice.</u> <u>Dress for the outdoor event.</u>

Band members will sit, and the chorus will stand. <u>We will begin the performance.</u>

<u>Brass section, sway as you play!</u> <u>Chorus, smile while you sing!</u> <u>Woodwind section, don't rustle your sheet music when you turn the pages!</u>

<u>Bow to the audience when they applaud.</u> <u>Pick up your instruments, and leave the stage.</u>

248 Unit 7: Adverbs and Prepositions

Sentence Fluency

Combining Sentences Do you sometimes write one sentence to tell what happened and another to tell *how, when,* or *where* it happened? Try combining such sentences by moving the adverb to the first sentence or by changing an adjective into an adverb.

> The band began to play.
> They were quiet.

> **Quietly** the band began to play.

Remember that many, but not all, words make their adverb form by adding the ending -ly.

Apply It

9–16. Revise this newspaper article. Combine each set of underlined sentences, using adverbs.

Revising

Washington School Times   Volume 1, No. 6

Moony Tunes

Family and friends spread their blankets on the grass. They spread them smoothly. It was a perfect evening! The full moon shone. It was bright. The lawn was packed! The crowd shared food and conversation. They were happy.

The band filed onto the stage at exactly 9:00. They moved slowly. The musicians took their places. They tuned their instruments and prepared to play. They were noisy.

The crowd became quiet. They packed their picnic baskets. They were quick. Everyone settled down to enjoy the music. Most people stretched out under the stars. They looked comfortable.

The band played for one hour. It was beautiful. What an outstanding evening everyone had!

Writing with Adverbs   **249**

Usage 2: Comparing with Adverbs

One-Minute Warm-Up

In this sentence, how did the chicken run? What two other forms of this adverb do you know? When do you use each one?

> Nothing worked. The monster chicken just looked madder and ran at us **faster**.
>
> —from *Summer Reading Is Killing Me!* by Jon Scieszka

You know that you can use adjectives to compare people, places, or things. You can use adverbs to compare actions. Like adjectives, adverbs have special forms for comparisons. To compare two actions, add *-er* to most short adverbs. To compare three or more actions, add *-est* to most short adverbs.

 Tip
Use *less/least* in the same way you use *more/most*.

One action:	Amy will finish the book **soon**.
Two actions:	Amy will finish **sooner** than Jessie will.
Three or more:	Amy will finish **soonest** of all.

Rules for Comparing with Adverbs

1. **Most short adverbs:** Add *-er* or *-est* to the adverb.	late lat**er** lat**est**	early earli**er** earli**est**
2. **Most adverbs of two or more syllables:** Use *more* or *most* with the adverb.	often **more** often **most** often	quickly **more** quickly **most** quickly

Try It Out

Speak Up What form of each word compares two actions? What form compares three or more actions?

1. loudly
2. near
3. cleverly
4. powerfully

Unit 7: Adverbs and Prepositions

On Your Own

Write each sentence using the correct form of the adverb.

Example: Matt lives _____ to the pond than Jon does. (near)
Matt lives nearer to the pond than Jon does.

5. Does Adam swim _____ than Barb does? (often)
6. I get into the water _____ of all my friends. (slowly)
7. Josh always swims _____ than Kyle does. (straight)
8. I do the side stroke _____ than I do the crawl. (easily)
9. Arlene dives _____ of all the swimmers. (skillfully)
10. Tom swam _____ than I did in the race. (swiftly)
11. Of everyone, Alex swam _____. (fast)
12. Gail and Beth stayed in the water _____ of all. (long)

13–20. This part of an e-mail thank-you note has eight incorrect adverb forms. Write the thank-you note correctly.

Example: Now I skate <u>boldlier</u> than I did before.
Now I skate more boldly than I did before.

Proofreading

e-mail

Rapid Mail Delivery

Thank you so much for the in-line skates. Of everything I wished for, I wanted skates more badly. My friend Estella has been skating longest than I have, so she is teaching me. I'm learning more easily than I learned ice-skating. At first I skated awkwardlier than I do now. I fell oftenest of all our friends, but I also tried the most hard! Each day I skate gracefulier than I did the day before. Estella says I'm improving most fast of all the beginners and can be the better skater.

Writing Wrap-Up
WRITING • THINKING • LISTENING • SPEAKING

COMPARING / CONTRASTING

Write an Essay

Write a brief essay about learning a skill such as skating or drawing. Use adverbs to compare your skill as a beginner with your skill as you improved. Which skills stayed the same? Ask a partner to listen to your essay. Work together to check your adverb forms.

For Extra Practice see page 277.

Comparing with Adverbs

Usage

3 Adjective or Adverb?

One-Minute Warm-Up

Be an art critic. Make comments about this painting. Use each of the following adjectives and adverbs: *good, well, skillful, skillfully*.

- Many adverbs are formed by adding *-ly* to an adjective. These words look similar and are easy to confuse. Be careful to use them correctly in a sentence.

    Incorrect: Robert writes clear. (adjective)
    Correct: Robert writes clearly. (adverb)

- Remember to use an adjective to describe a noun or a pronoun. Use an adverb to describe a verb.

    Adjective: Lee made quick moves.   **Adverb:** She moves quickly.

- The words *good* and *well* are also often confused. *Good* is always an adjective. Use *good* before a noun or after a linking verb. Do not use *good* when you mean "healthy."

    Adjective: Sam has a good vocabulary. His stories are good.

- Use *well* as an adverb to describe a verb. Use it as an adjective to mean "healthy."

    Adverb: Sam describes buildings well.
    Adjective: Because Todd ate too fast, he is not well now.

Try It Out

Speak Up Which word in parentheses correctly completes each sentence? Which word does it describe?

1. The ballet company performed (good, well).
2. The dancers' movements were (graceful, gracefully).
3. The star ballerina spun (rapid, rapidly) on her toes.
4. The audience clapped (loud, loudly) at the end.

252   Unit 7: Adverbs and Prepositions

On Your Own

Write the adjective or the adverb in parentheses that correctly completes each sentence. Then write the word or words that it describes.

Example: James is carving a wooden lion (careful, carefully).
carefully   is carving

5. His (expert, expertly) skill is the result of experience.
6. James cut the wood (good, well).
7. The lion took shape (slow, slowly).
8. The surface of the wood was (smooth, smoothly).
9. The finished statue looked (good, well).

10–18. This part of a book review has nine errors in the use of adverbs. Write the book report correctly.

Example: The story characters speak very natural.
The story characters speak very naturally.

Proofreading

Do you like realistic stories? Then you sure will like *Ali Baba Bernstein, Lost and Found*. The author, Johanna Hurwitz, writes very good. She tells her stories both humorously and suspenseful. Her plots hold your attention good, and she describes everything very clearly. You can picture the characters and events easy.

In one story a boy named Ali Baba Bernstein wants a dog bad. When his neighbors go away, Ali Baba takes care of their dog, Slipper. He does his job very responsible, but Slipper disappears. Ali Baba must find him quick! Does the story end good? Read the book to find out.

Writing Wrap-Up
WRITING • THINKING • LISTENING • SPEAKING

PERSUADING

Write a Book Review

Can you persuade your classmates to read or not to read a book? Write a brief review of a book you liked or disliked reading. Tell why. Be careful to use adjectives and adverbs correctly. With a classmate, take turns reading your reviews aloud. Ask if she or he is convinced.

Usage
4 Negatives

There isn't no greater show on Earth!

What's wrong with the sentence on the circus banner? How can you fix it?

- **Words that mean "no" or "not" are negatives.**

    She has no more tickets.   There are none left.

- You have learned to form a contraction from a verb and *not*. These contractions are also negatives. The letters *n't* stand for *not*. The word *not* is an adverb.

    We won't be able to go.   She couldn't get tickets.

- Here is a list of some other common negatives.

not	nowhere	nobody	aren't	haven't
never	nothing	no one	doesn't	wouldn't

- A sentence should have only one negative. Using double negatives in a sentence is usually incorrect.

Incorrect	Correct
Ralph hasn't no homework.	Ralph hasn't any homework.
	Ralph has no homework.
Isn't nobody at home?	Isn't anybody at home?
	Is nobody at home?

Try It Out

Speak Up Which word in parentheses correctly completes each sentence?

1. Didn't you (ever, never) see a three-ring circus?
2. Isn't (anybody, nobody) watching the high-wire act?
3. There isn't (anything, nothing) underneath the wire.
4. Our friends at home (had, hadn't) none of the fun.

254 Unit 7: Adverbs and Prepositions

On Your Own

Write the sentences correctly. Underline the negative word.

Example: My friends haven't (any, no) extra money.
My friends <u>haven't</u> any extra money.

5. They (have, haven't) nothing to spend.
6. Isn't (anyone, no one) working this summer?
7. There (is, isn't) no work in the neighborhood.
8. Can't you think of (any, no) ideas for earning money?
9. We haven't (ever, never) tried.

10–18. This ad for an electronic bulletin board has nine double negatives. Write the ad correctly.

Example: There aren't no harder workers than Kids for Hire.
There *are* no harder workers than Kids for Hire.

Proofreading

Bulletin Board

Kids for Hire

Are you spending hours cleaning and weeding?
Those jobs aren't fun for nobody.
Haven't you nothing better to do?

Kids for Hire can help!

No job isn't too big, small, or dirty for us. Nobody can make your home cleaner or your garden neater. You won't never do those boring chores again. Don't bother looking nowhere else for better help. You can't find none. You won't find no one cheaper, either. Don't wait no longer. Call us at 555-6789. We won't never disappoint you.

Writing Wrap-Up WRITING • THINKING • LISTENING • SPEAKING

PERSUADING

Write an Ad

Think of ways to earn money, both practical and far-fetched. Select an idea and write an ad for it. Use several negatives. Read your ad to a partner. Then read it together to check for double negatives.

For Extra Practice see page 279.

Grammar

5 Prepositions

One-Minute Warm-Up

Which group of three words tells where the stripes were? What other similar group of three words is there?

> As we drew closer, I knew from the stripes on the cloth that it was probably a mummy bundle.
>
> —from *Discovering the Inca Ice Maiden: My Adventures on Ampato,*
> by Johan Reinhard

Small words can make a big difference in meaning.

Sula found it **on** the shelf.   Sula found it **under** the shelf.

- The words *on* and *under* show very different relationships between *found* and *shelf*. **The words that show these relationships are prepositions.**

Common Prepositions						
about	around	beside	for	near	outside	under
above	at	by	from	of	over	until
across	before	down	in	off	past	up
after	behind	during	inside	on	through	with
along	below	except	into	out	to	without

- A preposition relates another word in the sentence to the noun or the pronoun that follows the preposition. **The noun or the pronoun that follows a preposition is the object of the preposition.**

I liked the book **with** the blue **cover**.   Sula gave it **to** **me**.

Try It Out

Speak Up The object of the preposition is underlined in each sentence. What is the preposition?

1. Scientists study tools from the ancient past.
2. When was the tool used by people?
3. Was it made for a special purpose?
4. What does the tool tell us about them?

On Your Own

Write the preposition in each sentence.

Example: Scientists seek clues about the past. *about*

5. They have found dolls in their special searches.
6. These dolls were made from corn cobs.
7. Ancient people must have lived near these sites.
8. Their children probably played with the small dolls.
9. The dolls can be seen at several museums.

10–18. Write this sign for a museum of the future. Underline the nine prepositions once and any objects of the preposition twice.

Example: The objects had been buried for centuries.
The objects had been buried <u>for</u> <u>centuries</u>.

Leather Glove, A.D. 2000

This large glove was found on Earth. People lived there until the fourth millennium. Such gloves were often worn by ancient people. They were probably used during very cold weather. The size of the glove showed an amazing fact about our ancestors. Archaeologists used the glove for clues to the people's height. Our ancestors must have been over eight feet!

Writing Wrap-Up
WRITING • THINKING • LISTENING • SPEAKING

DESCRIBING

Write a Museum Sign

Suppose future scientists find a skateboard from A.D. 2000. Tell what mistaken ideas they might have about its use. Write a museum sign about it. Use at least five prepositions. Then read your sign to one or two classmates. Have them question what is unclear.

For Extra Practice see page 280.

Grammar
6 Prepositional Phrases

One-Minute Warm-Up

What preposition do you find in this passage? what object of the preposition? The preposition and its object relate to which other word in the passage?

Look! A song sparrow nestled on her eggs.
—from *Crinkleroot's Guide to Walking in Wild Places*, by Jim Arnosky

- You have learned that a preposition is always followed by an object. **A prepositional phrase is made up of a preposition, the object of the preposition, and all the words between them.** A prepositional phrase describes another word in the sentence.

    We packed the fruit in our knapsacks.

- The object of the preposition can be a compound object.

    We took enough oranges for Manuel and Anita.

- A prepositional phrase can be at the beginning, in the middle, or at the end of a sentence.

    At dawn we began our walk.
    The map of the area was helpful.
    The path went by a forest and a large lake.

Try It Out

Speak Up The preposition is underlined in each sentence. What is the prepositional phrase?

1. How would you travel across a river?
2. You might cross at a shallow place or a rocky spot.
3. Bridges are a better solution to the problem.
4. On bridges, traffic moves safely and easily.
5. The George Washington Bridge is used by many travelers.
6. It is an important connection between New York and New Jersey.

On Your Own

Write the prepositional phrase in each sentence. Then underline the preposition.

Example: People in every age have built bridges.   *in every age*

7. The oldest bridge was found in England.
8. Piles of rock form the bridge.
9. The Romans used wood for their bridges.
10. During the Middle Ages, stone bridges were built.
11. The bridges were lined with shops and dwellings.
12. The first iron bridge was built in the eighteenth century.
13. In the United States, covered bridges were once popular.
14. People drove wagons and rode horses through them.

15–24. This report has ten prepositional phrases. Write each prepositional phrase, and underline each object of the preposition.

Example: In jungles and mountains, rope bridges are still used.
   In jungles and mountains

String Bridges the Gap

The Inca people of Peru built amazing rope bridges over deep canyons. How did they do it? First, they tied a long string to an arrow. They shot it to someone across the canyon. Then a rope was tied to the end of the string and pulled across. In this way, four rope cables were pulled across. Branches were tied between two ropes for the floor. The other two ropes were handrails.

Writing Wrap-Up   WRITING • THINKING • LISTENING • SPEAKING

EXPLAINING

Write Instructions

You plan to build a toy bridge from toothpicks. Choose a partner and each write brief step-by-step instructions. Use at least five prepositional phrases. Read aloud and compare your instructions.

Writing with Prepositions

Elaborating Sentences: Prepositional Phrases Prepositional phrases can add meaning and detail to your sentences.

Another name is a drawbridge. } Another name for a bascule bridge is a drawbridge.

When prepositional phrases appear in the wrong places, they can make a sentence unclear or silly. Write the phrase as close as possible to the noun or the verb it describes.

Incorrect: The signal tells the captain to cross on the side of the bridge.
Correct: The signal on the side of the bridge tells the captain to cross.

Apply It

1–8. Revise each sentence in this diagram. Add prepositional phrases to sentences that need more detail. Move prepositional phrases that are written in the wrong place. Use the picture for help.

A A bascule bridge on strong supports rests. Sections can be raised.

B Most bascule bridges have traffic lights. The lights show when boats can pass.

C Automobile drivers must pay attention. If they don't, they could cause an accident.

D Bridge tenders open the bridge. They into port let ships.

260 Unit 7: Adverbs and Prepositions

Sentence Fluency

Combining Sentences: Prepositional Phrases When you need to vary sentence length, try using prepositional phrases to combine two sentences. Turn a related sentence into a prepositional phrase. Add it to the beginning, to the middle, or to the end of the first sentence. Be sure it makes sense!

To help your reader, use a comma after an introductory phrase of three or more words.

I cross the footbridge.	I cross the footbridge **on my way to school**.
I cross it on my way to school.	or **On my way to school,** I cross the footbridge.

Sometimes you'll need to change the wording of a sentence to turn it into a prepositional phrase.

Students like to use the bridge. It is a shortcut.	Students like to use the bridge **as a shortcut**.

Apply It

9–14. Revise this petition. Use prepositional phrases to combine each set of underlined sentences.

Revising

Save Our Bridge!

Students walk over the footbridge. They walk over it on their way to school. It's a time-saver! By using it, we avoid a problem. We avoid crossing a busy intersection. We get to school more quickly and safely.

The bridge needs major repairs. Years of wear and tear have made repairs necessary. Some of the floor planks look rotten. People get splinters. The splinters come from the old railing.

We want the town to repair the footbridge. The summer is a good time to repair it. Please don't tear down the bridge! Sign this petition. The town council will receive it. They need to know what we think!

Name   Address   Phone Number

Usage 7: Pronouns in Prepositional Phrases

One-Minute Warm-Up

The word *toward* is a preposition in this sentence. What pronoun is the object of this preposition? Could the pronoun *she* ever be used instead? Why?

> Matthew groaned in spirit as he turned about and shuffled gently down the platform toward her.
>
> —from *Anne of Green Gables*, by L.M. Montgomery

- You have learned that the object of a preposition is the noun or the pronoun that follows the preposition. When the object of the preposition is a pronoun, use an object pronoun. Object pronouns are *me, you, him, her, it, us,* and *them.*

 Tip

Never use a subject pronoun (like *I* or *he*) after a preposition.

- People sometimes get confused when the pronoun is part of a compound object. To see whether the pronoun is correct, remove the other object and check the pronoun alone.

    I gave a picture to Tom and her.   I gave a picture to her.

Try It Out

Speak Up Which pronoun in parentheses correctly completes each sentence?

1. My brothers wouldn't clean the house without my sisters and (I, me).
2. Cleaning the garage was a good job for Marcy and (he, him).
3. In the garage, an old toy box was found by Marcy and (I, me).
4. The toys had belonged to Karen and (him, he).
5. With Larry and (she, her), I carried the box to the yard.
6. Larry looked at the toys with Ken and (she, her).
7. Mom told me to clean the porch with (she, her) and Dad.
8. The boards below Dan and (us, we) needed a new coat of paint.

On Your Own

Write each prepositional phrase. Underline the object pronoun.

Example: I went to the bike race with Jim and her.   with Jim and <u>her</u>

9. The judge showed the starting line to us.
10. Jim sat with Sally and me.
11. Pete, Alonso, and Rita waved to Sally and us.
12. Jim focused his camera on Pete and them.
13. When the race started, Pete and Rita sped past Alonso and them.
14. Behind Pete and her, the remaining riders formed a line.
15. Suddenly Alonso rode by Pete and her.
16. The victory belonged to him!

17–22. This part of an e-mail invitation has six incorrect pronoun forms. Write the letter correctly.

Example: The bike route was planned by my uncle and I.
The bike route was planned by my uncle and me.

Proofreading

e-mail

Kim, please come!

Can you and Jeremy go biking with my family and I on Saturday? My mom will rent bikes for you and we. Uncle Steven gave some excellent bike-trail maps to Dad and she. Last summer my sister and I went with Uncle Steven and they on a long bike ride. That's why I thought of you and Jeremy. With you and he along, it would be even more fun. Ask your mom. Please talk to your dad and she.

Writing Wrap-Up   WRITING • THINKING • LISTENING • SPEAKING

COMPARING / CONTRASTING

Write an Invitation

Write an invitation to a friend to join you and your family on a family outing. Tell why this trip will be better than your last outing together. Use object pronouns after prepositions. Ask a classmate to listen to your invitation and choose the most convincing sentence.

For Extra Practice see page 282.

Usage
8 Adverb or Preposition?

One-Minute Warm-Up

How can you turn the adverb *off* into a preposition?

Hint: Add two words to the sentence.

- Some words can be used as either an adverb or a preposition.

  Adverb: Susan ran inside.

  Preposition: Her hat was inside the store.

  Adverb: The shopkeeper looked up.

  Preposition: Susan raced up the stairs.

- You can tell the difference between an adverb and a preposition if you look carefully at how the word is used in the sentence. If the word begins a prepositional phrase, it is a preposition. Otherwise, it is an adverb.

  Here are some words that can be used as either adverbs or prepositions.

above	below	in	off	outside
along	by	inside	over	under
around	down	near	out	up

Try It Out

Speak Up Is the underlined word an adverb or a preposition? If it is a preposition, give the prepositional phrase.

1. Anita looked around the button shop.
2. Her large blue button had fallen off.
3. Buttons were displayed along the counter.
4. She saw the right button under the glass.
5. A salesperson took the button from the case.
6. Anita took her wallet out and paid the salesperson.

264 Unit 7: Adverbs and Prepositions

On Your Own

If the sentence has an adverb, write the adverb. If it has a preposition, write the prepositional phrase and underline the preposition.

Example: Sarah peeked inside the attic.   *inside the attic*

7. She was curious and went in.
8. In every corner, she saw strange, wonderful things.
9. Sarah walked around.
10. A wooden box beside the vase caught Sarah's attention.
11. Near the bed was an old rocking chair.
12. Sarah sat down.

13–24. This part of a story has twelve adverbs and prepositions. Write the story. If a sentence has an adverb, underline the adverb. If a sentence has a prepositional phrase, underline the phrase once and the preposition twice.

Example: Would the lid come off the box?
Would the lid come off the box?

An Uncovered Mystery

The dusty box in Sarah's lap was locked. She wiped the dust off. Someone had carved a design into the lid. Sarah turned the box over. There was nothing on the bottom. She turned the box around. Along the back, something was loose. A piece of the box moved. It slid to one side and revealed a little drawer. Shivers went up Sarah's spine. She pulled the drawer out. A tiny key lay inside.

Writing Wrap-Up
WRITING • THINKING • LISTENING • SPEAKING

NARRATING

Write a Story

What happened next with Sarah and the key? Write the next paragraph of the story. Use adverbs and prepositional phrases. Find a partner and take turns reading your stories. Which parts created suspense?

Revising Strategies | **Vocabulary**

Choosing Different Adverbs

Adverbs describe verbs. They tell *how*, *when*, or *where* an action happened. By choosing a different adverb, you can change the meaning of a sentence.

Jenna waited <u>eagerly</u> for the bus to summer camp.

Jenna waited <u>anxiously</u> for the bus to summer camp.

Apply It

1–8. Rewrite the message in this e-mail. Complete each sentence by choosing an adverb from the word box.

diligently	extremely
rapidly	confidently
gradually	certainly
really	definitely

Revising

e-mail

VIRTUAL MAIL

To: Aunt Lucy
From: Jenna
Subject: Summer Camps

    Thanks for the information in your last e-mail. It arrived _____. All the camps you talked about _____ sound like fun. I am _____ getting less nervous about going into the water. I _____ want to learn how to swim so I am _____ interested in the programs that teach swimming. I think I'll have fun in the pool once I can swim _____.

    My friend Tasha is _____ going to be the head counselor in a sports camp because she is a great athlete. I want a varied program so I'm looking _____ for a camp that also has arts and crafts and free time.

266 Unit 7: Adverbs and Prepositions

Enrichment

Prepositions

Treasure Mapping

Think of a good location for hidden treasure. Then draw a map on the left half of a large piece of paper. Label compass directions, streets, and important places. Don't mark where the treasure is! On the right half of the paper, write directions for the treasure hunter. Use prepositional phrases, and underline each preposition. Exchange maps with a classmate. Can you follow each other's directions to the hidden treasure?

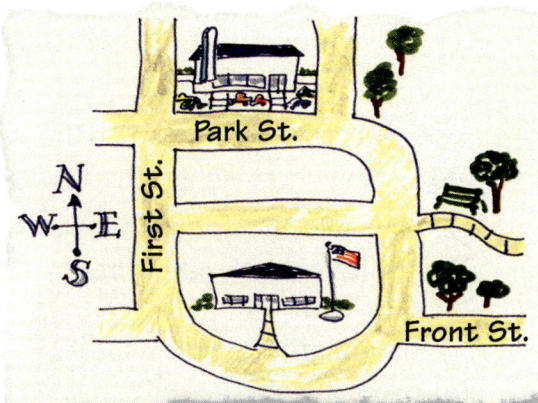

Begin <u>at</u> the corner <u>of</u> First St. and Park St. Go south <u>on</u> First St. until you come <u>to</u> Front St. . . .

Adverb Puns

A pun is a joke based on the double meanings of words. Can you see the humor in the puns below? (What double meanings do the underlined adverbs suggest?)

"These hot dogs are great!" she said <u>frankly</u>.

"Hand me the pencil," he said <u>pointedly</u>.

Try writing three more puns that follow the form above. Use these adverbs: *sweetly, coldly, brightly*.

"I have too many lemons!" she said bitterly.

Challenge Think of some more adverbs you can use to make puns. Write your puns in an Adverb Joke Book.

Checkup: Unit 7

1 Adverbs *(p. 246)* Write each sentence. Underline the adverb and draw an arrow to the verb that it describes.

1. Some animals travel often.
2. Whole herds move together.
3. Deer live quietly in the hills.
4. Sheep frequently roam on cliffs.
5. They go down to the valleys in the early fall.
6. Many plants grow well in the valleys.

2 Comparing with Adverbs *(p. 250)* For each sentence, write the correct form of the adverb in parentheses.

7. Klaus paints _____ this year than last year. (often)
8. Chandra paints _____ of the three girls. (skillfully)
9. Danielle mixes paint _____ than Elise does. (fast)
10. Maida finished her painting _____ of all. (soon)

3 Adjective or Adverb? *(p. 252)* Write the word in parentheses that correctly completes each sentence. Then write whether it is an adjective or an adverb in the sentence.

11. Last week I had a cold, but now I am (good, well).
12. These roses will look (beautiful, beautifully) in our yard.
13. The ice thaws (slow, slowly).
14. The rains are (heavily, heavy).
15. Her photos are (well, good).

4 Negatives *(p. 254)* Rewrite each sentence so that there is only one negative.

16. Isn't nobody in the library?
17. I don't have nowhere to go.
18. I haven't read nothing today.
19. You haven't read no plays lately.
20. Don't you never read newspapers?
21. Won't none of you lend me a book?

5 Prepositions *(p. 256)* Write each sentence. Underline the preposition once and its object twice.

22. Sam will fly his kite in the park.
23. It flies over the tallest trees.
24. Sam and I will go past the enormous white farmhouse.
25. We will go near the farm hands.
26. My kite dropped near them.
27. Before dark we should head home.

6 Prepositional Phrases *(p. 258)* Write the prepositional phrase in each sentence. Then underline the object of the preposition.

28. I went by bus and train.
29. At the museum, I saw beautiful and unusual pearls.
30. Some pearls are made in Japan.
31. A bead is placed inside an oyster.
32. The oyster covers the bead with a thin coating.
33. A pearl is removed from the oyster.

268 Unit 6: Pronouns Go to www.eduplace.com/tales/hme/ for more fun with parts of speech.

7 Pronouns in Prepositional Phrases
(p. 262) Choose the correct pronoun in parentheses.

34. I waited for Bill and (she, her).
35. I take a class with (they, them).
36. Jay was a model for Al and (me, I).
37. Mia drew a picture of (he, him).
38. Sue stood right behind Tom and (her, she).
39. I sat near Manuel and (they, them).
40. My picture looks very good to Manuel and (I, me).
41. Our teacher is happy with (we, us).
42. We have always worked hard for (he, him).

8 Adverb or Preposition?
(p. 264) Write each adverb or prepositional phrase. Underline each preposition.

43. It was dark outside.
44. Tina stepped inside the door.
45. She looked around the ice rink.
46. Bright lights were shining above.
47. White ice sparkled below.
48. Tina climbed up the steps.
49. She sat down and watched.
50. Skaters appeared in red costumes.
51. A clown skated by and fell.
52. People around Tina laughed.
53. Was the time for the final act drawing near?

Mixed Review 54–60. These safety guidelines have three errors with adverbs, two errors with negatives, and two errors with pronouns after prepositions. Write the guidelines correctly.

Proofreading Checklist
Pay special attention to these forms:
- ✔ comparatives and superlatives
- ✔ adjectives and adverbs
- ✔ negatives
- ✔ pronouns after prepositions

Proofreading
Watch That Dog!

People are bitten by dogs oftener than ever. Behave carefully near dogs.

Don't never approach a strange dog. A sweet-looking dog isn't always sweet. Shy or frightened dogs don't behave well. Stay away from them. In fact, try to keep several feet between you and they.

Dogs usually don't want nobody near when they eat or sleep.

Don't approach a dog too quick. Furthermore, don't run from a dangerous dog. The dog can always run fastest. Stand very still, and don't look at he directly.

See www.eduplace.com/kids/hme/ for an online quiz.

Assessment Link

✓ Test Practice

Write the numbers 1–8 on a sheet of paper. Read each paragraph. Choose the line that shows the mistake in the way words are used. Write the letter for that answer. If there is no mistake, write the letter for the last answer, "No mistakes."

1. A Meg gently rocked the
   B baby. Soon he was asleep. He
   C napped peaceful for an hour.
   D (No mistakes)

2. F Dad told a greatly
   G joke at the party tonight. All
   H the guests laughed loudly.
   J (No mistakes)

3. A Yesterday Lucas ran
   B faster of all the racers. John
   C ran more slowly than I did.
   D (No mistakes)

4. F Grant ate nothing for
   G dinner. We had no fruit. He
   H didn't never try the spaghetti.
   J (No mistakes)

5. A The Olsens drove by
   B in a green car. Mrs. Olsen
   C waved to Brenda and me.
   D (No mistakes)

6. F Teddy draws good.
   G He holds his pencil correctly,
   H and he works carefully.
   J (No mistakes)

7. A Mom worked longer
   B than the boys did. They got
   C tired most easily than she did.
   D (No mistakes)

8. F I have no money. I
   G can't find my purse.
   H Hasn't anyone seen it?
   J (No mistakes)

Unit 7: Adverbs and Prepositions

Now write the numbers 9–12 on your paper. Read the underlined sentences. Then choose the answer that best combines them into one sentence. Write the letter for that answer.

9 I couldn't call you last night.
   Dad was on the phone for hours.

   A Dad was on the phone for hours, or I couldn't call you last night.
   B Dad was on the phone for hours before I couldn't call you last night.
   C I couldn't call you last night because Dad was on the phone for hours.
   D I couldn't call you last night, or Dad was on the phone for hours.

10 Mom grew up in Houston, Texas.
   She has happy memories of her childhood.

   F Mom has happy memories of her childhood in Houston, Texas.
   G Mom grew up in Houston, Texas, because she has happy memories of her childhood.
   H Mom has happy memories in her childhood of Houston, Texas.
   J In Houston, Texas, Mom grew up, and has happy childhood memories.

11 Jeremy is wearing a sweater.
   His sweater is yellow.

   A Jeremy is wearing a sweater, but his sweater is yellow.
   B Jeremy is wearing a yellow sweater.
   C Jeremy's sweater that he is wearing is yellow.
   D A yellow sweater Jeremy is wearing is his.

12 Tod swept the floor.
   Tod dusted the furniture.
   Tod washed the windows.

   F Tod swept, dusted, and washed the floor, furniture, and windows.
   G Tod swept the floor, and he dusted and washed the furniture and windows.
   H Tod swept the floor, dusted the furniture, and washed the windows.
   J Tod swept the floor, dusted the furniture, or washed the windows.

Test Practice

Cumulative Review

Unit 1: The Sentence

Four Kinds of Sentences *(pp. 32, 34)* Label each fragment. For each complete sentence, write *declarative, interrogative, imperative,* or *exclamatory*.

1. What a great telephone you have!
2. Listen for the dial tone.
3. Who invented the telephone?
4. Alexander Graham Bell.
5. He also taught deaf children.

Subjects and Predicates *(pp. 36, 38, 40)* Write each simple subject and simple predicate.

6. Mr. Jackson is a scientist.
7. This scientist has invented a robot.
8. The small robot does many things.
9. It talks with a low voice.
10. Get a robot soon.

Run-on Sentences *(p. 48)* Rewrite each pair of run-on sentences correctly.

11. Mow the grass short watch out for stones.
12. Jeff mowed the grass Iris trimmed the shrubs.
13. Brad will rake the leaves he will put them in a bag.
14. Rosa will weed the garden who will help her?
15. It was hard work they finished in one day.

Unit 2: Nouns

Common and Proper Nouns *(pp. 64, 66)* Write a list of the common nouns and proper nouns.

16. My dad visited Sweden last June.
17. This country is in northern Europe.
18. Forests grow on its mountains.
19. The government is in Stockholm.
20. Jenny Lind, the famous singer, was born in that city.

Plural Nouns and Possessive Nouns *(pp. 70, 72, 74, 76)* Rewrite these phrases, using the plural forms of the underlined nouns. Then rewrite the new phrases, using plural possessives.

21. the <u>toy</u> of the <u>baby</u>
22. the <u>watch</u> belonging to the <u>man</u>
23. the <u>tail</u> of the <u>fox</u>
24. the <u>radio</u> belonging to the <u>girl</u>
25. the <u>scarf</u> belonging to the <u>child</u>

Unit 3: Verbs

Action Verbs and Direct Objects *(pp. 96, 98)* Write the action verb and the direct object in each.

26. Leo's class visited two factories.
27. One factory manufactures bicycles.
28. The other factory makes paper.
29. The guide answered questions.
30. Their hospitality surprised me.
31. Finally, we returned home.

See www.eduplace.com/kids/hme/ for a tricky usage or spelling question.

Main Verbs and Helping Verbs

(p. 100) Write the verbs in these sentences. Underline the main verb once and the helping verb twice.

32. The Gordons have flown to China.
33. They are planning day trips.
34. The first trip will start in Beijing.
35. Steve is taking his camera along.
36. He will develop the film himself.

Linking Verbs *(p. 102)*

Write each sentence, and underline the linking verb. Draw an arrow connecting the words that the verb links.

37. The car seems very old.
38. It is a Model T.
39. I feel excited about it.
40. My brother is the new owner.
41. The Lees were also collectors.

Verb Tenses *(pp. 104, 106, 108)*

Write underlined verbs in the tense shown.

42. Jody <u>studies</u> for the test. (past)
43. He <u>outlined</u> the topics. (present)
44. The test <u>lasted</u> one hour. (future)
45. Mrs. Angelo <u>graded</u> it. (present)
46. Jody <u>has passed</u> the test. (future)

Subject-Verb Agreement

(pp. 112, 114) Write the correct verbs.

47. Bryce Canyon (are, is) beautiful.
48. Lin and I (take, takes) a tour.
49. I (see, sees) a fossil in the rocks!
50. We (has, have) warm jackets.
51. It (gets, get) cold at night.

Contractions with *not* *(p. 116)*

Write the words that have been combined to form these contractions.

52. won't
53. didn't
54. shouldn't
55. hasn't
56. couldn't
57. aren't

Irregular Verbs *(pp. 118, 120)*

Write the past form of each verb.

58. I had (make) a box kite.
59. I (run) across the field with it.
60. The kite (fly) high in the sky.
61. Suddenly a strong wind (blow).
62. My kite had (break) in two.

Confusing Verbs *(pp. 122, 124, 126)*

Write the correct word or words.

63. (May, Can) you drive us?
64. We should (let, leave) now.
65. Try to (set, sit) near the stage.
66. Will the speaker (teach, learn) us about different kinds of cats?
67. Lei (should of, should've) come.

Unit 4: Adjectives

What Is an Adjective? *(p. 152)*

Write each sentence, underlining the adjectives. Draw an arrow from each adjective to the noun it describes.

68. Oysters live in shallow water.
69. They have heavy shells.
70. Many oysters produce pearls.
71. White pearls are common.
72. Black pearls are rare and costly.

Cumulative Review continued

Articles and Demonstratives

(p. 156) Write the correct word in parentheses.

73. Every year (a, an) unusually severe hurricane hits there.
74. (Those, These) houses over there were damaged last year.
75. (The, A) winds uprooted trees.
76. (This, That) river near us flooded.

Comparing with Adjectives

(pp. 158, 160) Write the correct form of each adjective.

77. Your shirt is (pretty) than mine.
78. Tina's shirt is (nice) of all.
79. His belt looks (good) than hers.
80. Of all the belts, yours looks (good).

Proper Adjectives

(p. 162) Write the proper adjective that is made from the noun in parentheses.

81. Dad won a (Switzerland) watch.
82. I like to read (Japan) poetry.
83. That (Africa) monkey is playful.
84. Is this (Spain) city Madrid?

Unit 5: Capitalization and Punctuation

Correct Sentences

(pp. 180, 182, 184, 188, 192) Write each sentence. Use capital letters and commas correctly, and add end punctuation as needed.

85. ann which sports do you like
86. I like tennis golf and hockey
87. do not forget lori to wear a belt sara will bring the gloves
88. yes ted your cousin plays well
89. what a great run that was lennie

Quotations

(p. 194) Write each sentence. Use punctuation marks and capital letters correctly.

90. what did you like best about your trip to Arizona asked Carrie
91. I saw a cactus that was over forty feet tall exclaimed Suki
92. she added it's a Giant Cactus
93. did it have flowers asked Carrie
94. in the spring replied Suki flowers blossom on its stem

Abbreviations

(p. 196) Rewrite these groups of words, using abbreviations for the underlined words.

95. Memphis, <u>Tennessee</u> 38115
96. Sunshine Box <u>Company</u>
97. <u>Monday</u>, <u>August</u> 29, 1922
98. Philip <u>Alan</u> Burke <u>Junior</u>
99. 129 Essex <u>Road</u>, Austin, <u>Texas</u>

Titles

(p. 198) Write each of the titles correctly.

100. i am the mummy (book)
101. drops of rain (poem)
102. the shaggy dog (movie)
103. fame or fortune (book chapter)
104. los angeles times (newspaper)

Unit 7: Adverbs and Prepositions

Unit 6: Pronouns

Subject Pronouns, Object Pronouns, and Possessive Pronouns *(pp. 216, 218, 220, 222)* Write each sentence correctly.

105. Holly attended the safety patrol meeting with Maria and (I, me).
106. (Us, We) elected a president.
107. (Our, Ours) votes go to Maria.
108. The new president is (her, she).
109. Maria thanked Lu and (me, I).

Double Subjects *(p. 228)* Write each sentence correctly.

110. The Chens they own a shop.
111. My dad and I we work there.
112. Mrs. Chen she locks up.
113. Fred he is our last customer.
114. His job it makes him late.

***we* and *us* with Nouns** *(p. 230)* Write each sentence, using *we* or *us*.

115. The crowd saw ____ swimmers.
116. ____ students cheered loudly.
117. The winners were ____ friends.
118. The coach praised ____ winners.
119. ____ reporters made notes.

Unit 7: Adverbs and Prepositions

Adjective or Adverb? *(pp. 246, 250, 252)* Write the correct word.

120. Al prepared (careful, carefully).
121. He spoke quite (clear, clearly).
122. The speech went (good, well).
123. Mrs. Lee smiled (proud, proudly).
124. She said he had done (good, well).

Negatives *(p. 254)* Rewrite each sentence, using only one negative.

125. Hasn't nobody seen my sneakers?
126. I don't never clean my room.
127. I can't find no hangers.
128. There isn't no room in my closet.
129. Won't no one help me?

Prepositional Phrases *(pp. 256, 258, 262)* Write the prepositional phrase. Underline the preposition once and its object twice.

130. We learned about *Twelfth Night*.
131. This comedy by Shakespeare is fun.
132. Who plays the part of Viola?
133. Viola dresses in men's clothing.
134. People are fooled by her.

Adverb or Preposition? *(p. 264)* Copy the underlined word, and label it *adverb* or *preposition*.

135. People heard a noise <u>above</u> them.
136. They looked <u>up</u> curiously.
137. <u>In</u> the sky was a glider.
138. It landed <u>near</u> the lake.
139. The pilot stepped <u>out</u> proudly.
140. Reporters walked <u>over</u>.

Cumulative Review

Extra Practice

(pages 246–247)

1 Adverbs

- An **adverb** is a word that tells *how*, *when*, or *where*.
- Adverbs can describe verbs.
- Many adverbs end with *-ly*.

● Write the adverb that describes each underlined verb.

Example: Joy <u>waited</u> impatiently.   *impatiently*

1. Her parents carefully <u>planned</u> the trip.
2. They all <u>boarded</u> the train eagerly.
3. The train <u>arrived</u> at the station early.
4. They <u>traveled</u> far to the hotel.
5. Joy excitedly <u>looked</u> at all the sights.
6. The tired travelers <u>would unpack</u> later.

▲ Write the adverb that describes the underlined verb in each sentence. Then write whether it tells *how*, *when*, or *where*.

Example: Dan recently <u>visited</u> Washington, D.C.   *recently   when*

7. His friend Russ <u>lives</u> there.
8. Russ and Dan <u>took</u> the bus downtown.
9. They immediately <u>headed</u> for the Air and Space Museum.
10. First, they <u>watched</u> the museum's film on flying.
11. Afterward, the boys <u>ate</u> lunch in the cafeteria.
12. Russ sadly <u>waved</u> good-bye to Dan at the train station.

■ Write each sentence, using an adverb. The word in parentheses tells what kind of adverb to write.

Example: _____ an inch of rain fell in one hour. (when)
   Yesterday an inch of rain fell in one hour.

13. The rain hammered _____ on the roof. (how)
14. _____ we were dry and warm. (where)
15. Cars moved _____ along the wet roads. (how)
16. Sections of School Street were _____ closed. (when)
17. We hoped that Dad was not stuck _____. (where)
18. _____ he told us what had happened. (when)

276 Unit 7: Adverbs and Prepositions

Extra Practice

2 Comparing with Adverbs

(pages 250–251)

- To compare two actions, use *-er* or *more* with an adverb.
- To compare three or more actions, use *-est* or *most*.
- Use *-er* and *-est* with most one-syllable adverbs.
- Use *more* and *most* with most adverbs of two or more syllables.

● Copy the correct form of the adverb for each sentence.

Example: Jon arrived (sooner, soonest) than Neil.   *sooner*

1. Leah skates (more often, most often) than Rita does.
2. Of the four, Neil tries (harder, hardest).
3. Rita skates (more smoothly, most smoothly) of all.
4. I can lace my skates (faster, fastest) than Leah can.
5. She glides (more gracefully, most gracefully) than I.

▲ Write each sentence, using the correct form of the adverb in parentheses.

Example: Joe swims _____ of all the children. (smoothly)
   Joe swims most smoothly of all the children.

6. Lori can float _____ of all the girls. (long)
7. Al climbed into the pool _____ than Joe did. (slowly)
8. Henry swam the two laps _____ of all the swimmers. (quickly)
9. Move your arms up and down _____ than I did. (gently)
10. Of everyone, Wayne swims _____. (straight)

■ Rewrite each sentence, using the kind of comparison shown.

Example: Charlie listens to the coach carefully. (two actions)
   Charlie listens to the coach more carefully than I do.

11. After hitting the ball, Kelly runs swiftly. (two actions)
12. Sal practices tirelessly. (three or more actions)
13. Toby comes early to practice. (two actions)
14. Alex stays at the field late. (three or more actions)
15. Charlie swings a bat confidently. (two actions)
16. Ben plays enthusiastically. (two actions)
17. The crowd arrived at the game early. (three or more actions)
18. The coach speaks kindly to each player. (two actions)

Extra Practice

3 Adjective or Adverb?

(pages 252–253)

- Use adjectives to describe nouns or pronouns. Use adverbs to describe verbs.
- Do not confuse *good* and *well*. *Good* is always an adjective. *Well* is an adverb unless it means "healthy."

● Write *adjective* or *adverb* to name each underlined word.

Example: Our teacher paints landscapes <u>well</u>.   *adverb*

1. Our teacher is giving a <u>good</u> lesson in watercolor.
2. He painted a landscape with <u>dark</u> thunderclouds.
3. First, he <u>lightly</u> sketched the landscape on paper.
4. Then he spread a <u>thin</u> coat of water over the sky.
5. He <u>swiftly</u> brushed paint across the wet area.

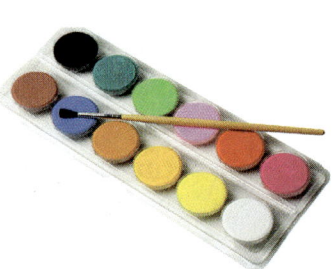

▲ Write each sentence, using the correct word. Label it *adjective* or *adverb*.

Example: Mindy had the flu, but now she is (good, well).
        Mindy had the flu, but now she is well.   *adjective*

6. Mindy and Sue's day at the museum was quite (good, well).
7. They looked (careful, carefully) at a Mary Cassatt painting.
8. The mother holds the child (gentle, gently) in her arms.
9. The child watches the father (curious, curiously).
10. Cassatt painted scenes of family life (good, well).

■ Write the word in parentheses that correctly completes each sentence. Then write a sentence, using the other word in parentheses correctly.

Example: Sandy draws landscapes (skillful, skillfully).
        skillfully   As an artist, Sandy is skillful.

11. Today she works (happy, happily) in the park.
12. The sun is shining (bright, brightly).
13. Ducks swim in the pond (quiet, quietly).
14. Two boats sail (swift, swiftly) across the water.
15. Sandy (quick, quickly) makes a sketch.

278   Unit 7: Adverbs and Prepositions

 **Extra Practice**

(pages 254–255)

4 Negatives

- A **negative** is a word that means "no" or "not."
- Do not use double negatives in a sentence.

● If the sentence has a double negative, write the two negatives. If the sentence is correct, write *correct.*

Example: Al had never been to no circus before.   *never   no*

1. The circus wasn't really in a big tent.
2. I didn't see no man with the peanuts.
3. None of the clowns could skate very well.
4. The juggler didn't drop none of his props.
5. The woman had no more balloons.
6. Nobody wanted to stay for the whole show.

▲ Write each sentence, using the correct word.

Example: Doesn't (anyone, no one) want to see the elephants?
Doesn't anyone want to see the elephants?

7. Those two elephants (have, haven't) no riders.
8. We can't find (any, no) seats in this section.
9. I've never been (anywhere, nowhere) like the circus.
10. Isn't (anybody, nobody) holding on to the rope?
11. Wasn't there (anyone, no one) to catch her?
12. I (will, won't) never forget the excitement.

■ Write a negative statement to answer each question. Use a different negative in each sentence.

Example: Do you need to earn money this summer?
I don't need to earn money this summer.

13. How can you earn money in your neighborhood this summer?
14. Is selling juice at a sidewalk stand a good idea?
15. Did you ever think of having a circus?
16. Would any of your friends help you?
17. Is there anyone who can make costumes?
18. Will you have enough time to get ready?

Extra Practice

(pages 256–257)

5 Prepositions

- A **preposition** relates the noun or the pronoun that follows it to another word in the sentence.
- The **object of the preposition** is the noun or the pronoun that follows the preposition.

● Write the preposition in each sentence.

Example: The ship had disappeared without a trace.   *without*

1. What had happened to the crew?
2. The answers were hidden in the ship.
3. No one except the diver had seen the ship.
4. She dove skillfully into the deep water.
5. What would she discover at the bottom?
6. The mystery would be solved by the diver.

▲ Copy each sentence. Underline the preposition once and the object twice.

Example: Scientists were studying the ruins of an old city.
   Scientists were studying the ruins of an old city.

7. Ashes from a volcano had buried the city.
8. The people had escaped before the disaster.
9. Now scientists were digging around the area.
10. Their discoveries explained daily life in the city.
11. They discovered different kinds of buildings.
12. The houses had beautiful paintings on the walls.

■ Rewrite each sentence. Change the preposition, the object of the preposition, or both.

Example: Kim worked for the city.   *Kim worked in a store.*

13. Kim kept careful records about the city's history.
14. Once she spent a whole day looking for clues.
15. Suddenly she noticed something colorful in the soil.
16. She had discovered an old piece of pottery.
17. The pottery was from the Chicago World's Fair.
18. This colorful dish had been made in 1892!

6 Prepositional Phrases

(pages 258–259)

- A **prepositional phrase** is made up of a preposition, its object, and all the words between them.

● The preposition is underlined in each sentence. Write the prepositional phrase.

Example: Water covers a large part <u>of</u> the earth's surface.

of the earth's surface

1. The ocean floor lies <u>under</u> the water.
2. Many maps have been made <u>of</u> the ocean floor.
3. These maps are often used <u>by</u> sailors.
4. The maps guide them <u>over</u> dangerous rocks.
5. Their ships can travel safely <u>through</u> narrow places.
6. <u>During</u> their explorations, they use maps.

▲ Write the prepositional phrase in each sentence. Then underline the preposition once and the object twice.

Example: In the past, people drew maps.   <u>In</u> the <u>past</u>

7. Today some maps are made by special computers.
8. Spacecraft take pictures of the earth and other planets.
9. Information from these spectacular pictures is stored.
10. On the computer screen, a detailed picture appears.
11. The mapmaker presses a few keys on his keyboard.
12. Maps in beautiful colors are often produced.

■ Write each sentence, using a prepositional phrase.

Example: I found a pencil _____.

I found a pencil in my green knapsack.

13. I sketched a map _____.
14. It showed the way _____.
15. I drew a line _____.
16. I made a circle _____.
17. I gave the map _____.
18. We would meet _____.

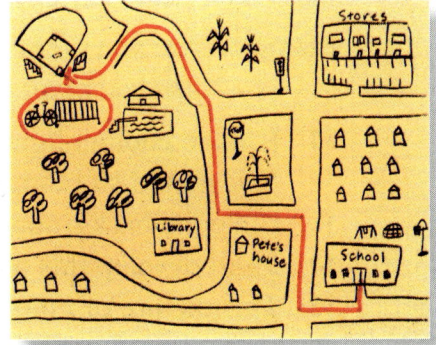

Extra Practice   **281**

Extra Practice

7 Pronouns in Prepositional Phrases

(pages 262–263)

- Use object pronouns as objects in prepositional phrases.
- Check the pronoun in a compound object by removing the other object.

● Copy each prepositional phrase. Underline the object pronoun.

Example: Ansel Adams loved nature and took pictures of it.   *of it*

1. Yosemite National Park was special to him.
2. He photographed many parts of it.
3. His pictures have famous scenery in them.
4. Many photographers have learned from him.
5. For them, his pictures are excellent examples.

▲ Choose the pronoun in parentheses that correctly completes each sentence. Write the sentences.

Example: When Chirp landed, I took a picture of (he, him).
    When Chirp landed, I took a picture of him.

6. Chirp and the other sparrows were familiar to (me, I).
7. I was writing an article about the robins and (they, them).
8. Sometimes I took pictures of (they, them).
9. The birds were not upset by (I, me).
10. I watched from a shed near (they, them).

■ Rewrite each incorrect sentence correctly. For each sentence that is correct, write *correct*.

Example: Are you taking a picture of your sister and he?
    Are you taking a picture of your sister and him?

11. Is there enough light to take a picture of Cal and her?
12. You should sit between Lily and I on the couch.
13. I like the background behind David and them.
14. I will develop this picture for Katie and she.
15. This picture of Frank and he at the beach is excellent.

Extra Practice

8 Adverb or Preposition?

(pages 264–265)

- Do not confuse adverbs with prepositions. Prepositions introduce prepositional phrases. Adverbs do not.

● Write the underlined word. Label it *adverb* or *preposition*.

Example: Doug pulled a book <u>off</u> the shelf.   *off   preposition*

1. Something slipped <u>over</u> the edge.
2. It fell <u>on</u> the floor.
3. Doug picked it <u>up</u>.
4. He held the arrowhead <u>in</u> his hand.
5. Doug loved exploring <u>outside</u>.
6. He was often lucky <u>in</u> his explorations.

▲ Write each adverb or prepositional phrase. Underline each preposition.

Example: The model train raced along the track.   <u>along</u> the track

7. The long, metal track looped around.
8. The electric train clattered by.
9. Suddenly it disappeared into a dark tunnel.
10. Inside the tunnel, the conductor blew the whistle.
11. The train passed through the large mountain.
12. Then it rushed out, and the engine roared.

■ Each sentence below has an adverb. Write another sentence, using that same word as a preposition.

Example: Alexander hurried inside.
      I left my bicycle inside the cluttered garage.

13. Linda skipped along.
14. Stan leaped across.
15. Gina marched around.
16. Carlos jumped up.
17. Anna climbed down.
18. Ted stayed outside.

Extra Practice **283**

Part 2

Writing, Listening, Speaking, and Viewing

What You Will Find in This Part:

Section 1 **Narrating and Entertaining** . . 286

Unit 8 Writing a Personal Narrative . . . 294

Unit 9 Writing a Story 319

Section 2 **Explaining and Informing** 354

Unit 10 Writing to Compare
and Contrast 364

Unit 11 Writing a Research Report 398

Section 3 **Expressing and Influencing** . . . 438

Unit 12 Writing to Express an Opinion . . 446

Unit 13 Writing to Persuade 480

Section 1
Narrating and Entertaining

What You Will Find in This Section:

- **Listening to a Narrative** 288
- **Writing a Narrative Paragraph** 289

Unit 8 **Writing a Personal Narrative** 294
Special Focus on Narrating
Writing a Friendly Letter 317

Unit 9

Writing a Story 319

Special Focus on Entertaining
Writing a Play 344

Communication Links
Speaking: Dramatizing 350
Viewing/Media: Comparing Stories
in Print and on Film 352

Getting Started: Listening

Listening to a Narrative

A **narrative** is a story, either real or imagined. Listening to a narrative is different from listening to instructions or a report. The general purpose for listening to a narrative is enjoyment. Use these guidelines to help you listen well.

Guidelines for Listening to a Narrative

▶ Listen for the one big idea. What is the narrative about?
▶ Listen for the setting. Where and when does the narrative take place?
▶ Identify the important people. What are they like?
▶ Notice the main events. What happens? In what order are events told?
▶ Listen for the author's purpose. Does the author want to entertain? teach? share?

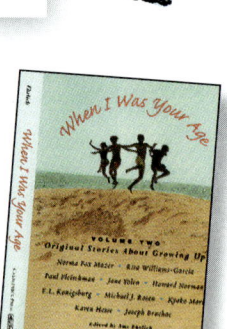

Try It Out Listen as your teacher reads aloud from "Learning to Swim," a true narrative by Kyoko Mori about a frightening incident. Listen for details that answer the questions below.

- What is the narrative about?
- Where does the narrative take place? Who are the important people?
- What are the individual events that Kyoko Mori describes? Tell them in order.
- Why do you think the author wrote this story?

288 Section 1: Narrating and Entertaining

See www.eduplace.com/kids/ for information about Kyoko Mori.

Getting Started: Paragraphs

Writing a Narrative Paragraph

A **paragraph** is a group of sentences that work together to tell about one main idea. A paragraph has a topic and a main idea. The **topic** is the subject of the paragraph. The **main idea** is what the author wants to say about the subject. The first sentence is indented.

A paragraph that tells a real or imagined story is called a **narrative paragraph**. What is the topic of the narrative paragraph below? What is the main idea?

Indent

Lead sentence

Supporting sentences

Concluding sentence

> My sister thought my idea for the Silly Pet Trick Contest was dumb, but I knew I would win easily. I had taught my dog, Sugar, to lick an envelope and seal it with his paw. On the day of the contest, five dogs fetched. A hamster ran backward on its wheel. Two cats waved. The crowd looked bored until Sugar's turn came. When I held up the sealed envelope, the crowd went crazy. I couldn't help but smile at my sister as the judge handed us a gigantic blue ribbon.

The topic is the Silly Pet Trick Contest. The main idea is that winning the contest was easy. Which sentence states the topic and the main idea?

The labels show the three parts of a narrative paragraph.

- The **lead sentence** introduces the topic and hints at the main idea.
- The **supporting sentences** give details that tell what happens.
- The **concluding sentence** ends the paragraph and finishes the narrative.

Think and Discuss What details does the writer include in the supporting sentences in the paragraph above?

Getting Started: Narrative Paragraphs

Getting Started: Paragraphs

The Lead Sentence

Most paragraphs have one sentence, often called the topic sentence, that presents the topic and the main idea. In a narrative paragraph, this sentence is called the **lead sentence**. It introduces the story and may give a hint about what happens or tell what the writer feels or felt.

                  Topic   Writer's feelings

Examples: When I found the baby bird out of its nest, I wasn't sure what to do!

               Hint   Topic

"Are we forgetting something?" Dad asked as we left on vacation.

What do you think narratives with these lead sentences might be about?

- "I hope you like heights," the instructor said with a chuckle.
- The minute I saw the judge's face, I knew I had misspelled *triumphant*.

Try It Out Read the paragraphs below. Each is missing the lead sentence. On your own or with a partner, write the topic and the main idea of each paragraph. Then write two possible lead sentences for each.

1. _____Lead sentence_____. For what seemed like hours, I measured and mixed according to the recipe. I beat and blended. I poured and patted. Finally, my creation was ready. Everyone took a bite. "Yuck!" they all groaned. "This tastes awful!" My proud smile faded fast. I had forgotten to add the sugar!

2. _____Lead sentence_____. First, we made a list of our favorite books, sports, and music. Then we collected pictures of famous people we liked. Finally, we made a collage of newspaper headlines. When we gave our contributions to the principal, he explained that the time capsule would remain sealed for twenty-five years!

Section 1: Narrating and Entertaining

Supporting Sentences

Supporting sentences follow the lead sentence. They give details that support the main idea. **Factual** and **sensory details** may answer the questions *Who? What? Where? When? Why?* or *How?* about the main idea. They can also tell how things look, sound, smell, taste, or feel. In the paragraph about the pet trick contest on page 289, the supporting sentences explain why winning the contest was easy.

Try It Out On your own or with a partner, choose one of the lead sentences below. List at least four details to support it. Then use these details to write at least three supporting sentences.

1. When I heard the lifeguard's whistle, I knew something was wrong.
2. This year, my team was determined to beat our rivals and five-time sand-sculpture champs, the Sand Fleas.

GRAMMAR TIP Check the punctuation in your sentences. Be sure to write end punctuation, commas, and apostrophes correctly.

Keeping to the Main Idea Supporting sentences should give only details that help to tell about the main idea.

Think and Discuss Read the paragraph below. What is the main idea? Which sentence does not belong?

> There on the kitchen table sat a huge, mysterious box with my name on it. First, I picked it up and gave it a shake. It didn't make a sound. Then I squeezed it. That gave me no clue either. Finally, I ripped off the paper. To my surprise, I found only a picture of a fluffy white kitten and a hand-written note inside. The note said to go to the garage. We had just gotten a new garage door because the old one was broken. Can you guess what was waiting for me there?

more ▶

Getting Started: Paragraphs

Ordering Details Supporting sentences are usually arranged in an order that makes sense. Events in a narrative paragraph are often told in the order they happened. **Time-clue words and phrases**, such as *first, next,* and *after dinner,* are signals that tell when things take place.

 See page 18 for more time-clue words and phrases.

Think and Discuss Which two sentences are out of order? How do you know? Tell where they belong.

If anything could have gone wrong in the talent show, it did. I was so nervous I started hiccupping right as I went on stage. Then, in the middle of my Irish step dance, my shoe flew off. It landed with a splash in the punch bowl on the refreshment table. I couldn't wait to get off the stage after my memorable performance! Just before the dance was done, I heard the cassette player crash to the floor.

The Concluding Sentence

 A **concluding sentence** can repeat the main idea in a new way, explain how the writer felt, or tell a last event that wraps up the paragraph. In the pet-trick paragraph on page 289, the concluding sentence tells how the contest worked out. What does it tell in the talent show paragraph above?

Try It Out Read the paragraph below. It is missing the concluding sentence. On your own or with a partner, write two different concluding sentences.

My day fishing with Uncle Lo had an unexpected twist. At dawn, we launched the canoe into the dark, icy lake. By midday we had each reeled in several shimmering trout from the pebbly bottom. On what turned out to be my final cast, my hook caught in a clump of thick grass at the bottom of the lake. While trying to free it, I felt myself slip overboard. _____*Concluding sentence*_____.

292 Section 1: Narrating and Entertaining

Write Your Own Narrative Paragraph

 Now it's time to write your own narrative paragraph. First, think about an experience that made you laugh until you cried, shiver with fear, or turn red with embarrassment. Then picture what happened, and make a list of details. After you have practiced telling your story to a partner, you will be ready to write!

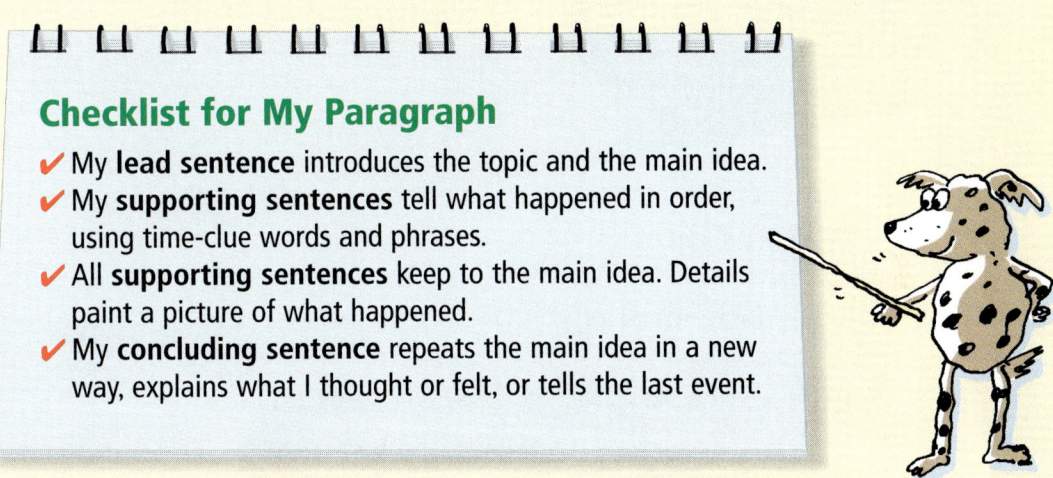

Checklist for My Paragraph
- ✔ My **lead sentence** introduces the topic and the main idea.
- ✔ My **supporting sentences** tell what happened in order, using time-clue words and phrases.
- ✔ All **supporting sentences** keep to the main idea. Details paint a picture of what happened.
- ✔ My **concluding sentence** repeats the main idea in a new way, explains what I thought or felt, or tells the last event.

Looking Ahead

When you know how to write a narrative paragraph, writing a longer narrative is easy! The diagram below shows how the parts of a one-paragraph narrative do the same jobs as the parts of a longer piece.

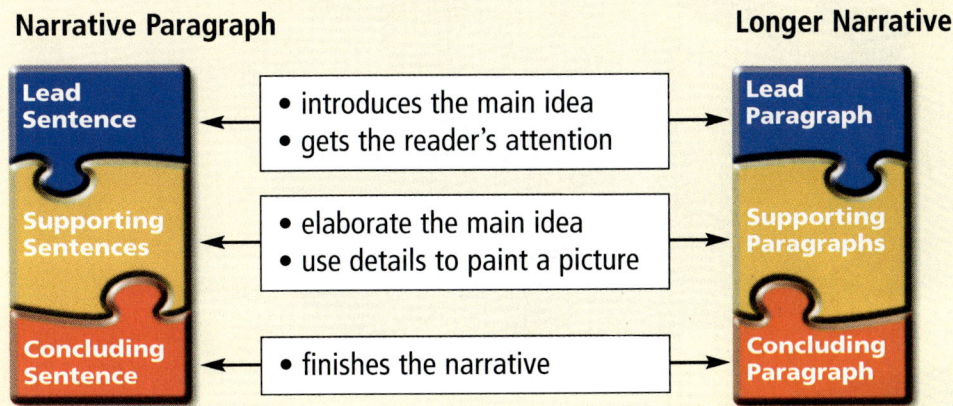

Narrative Paragraph / **Longer Narrative**

Lead Sentence / Lead Paragraph	• introduces the main idea • gets the reader's attention
Supporting Sentences / Supporting Paragraphs	• elaborate the main idea • use details to paint a picture
Concluding Sentence / Concluding Paragraph	• finishes the narrative

Unit 8

Writing a Personal Narrative

I should have known better than to underestimate this amazing dog.

Jerry Spinelli wrote a personal narrative about a memorable baseball game. What important lesson did he learn?

Shortstop

from *Knots in My Yo-yo String,* by Jerry Spinelli

From ages eleven to sixteen, if someone asked me what I wanted to be when I grew up, I gave one of two answers: "A baseball player" or "A shortstop."

Major league baseball—that was the life for me. And I wanted to live it only as a shortstop. When I trotted onto a diamond, I instinctively headed for the dusty plain between second and third. I never wanted to play any other position. When we got up sandlot games, no one else occupied shortstop. They knew it was mine.

I was eleven when I first played Little League baseball. To give as many kids as possible a chance to participate, the Little League declared that some of us would share uniforms with others. And so the season was exactly half over when I pedaled my bike up to Albert Pascavage's house to pick up his uniform: green socks, green cap, gray woolen shirt, and pants with green trim. I packed my precious cargo into my bike basket and drove it carefully home. I was a member of the Green Sox.

During one game in that half season I played second base—apparently no one told the manager I was going to be a major league shortstop. Our opponent was the Red Sox. The batter hit a ground ball right at me. I crouched, feet spread, glove ready, as I had been taught in the *Times Herald* baseball school. I could hear the ball crunching along the sandy ground. It hit my glove—but not the pocket. Instead it glanced off the fat leather thumb and rolled on behind me.

My first error!

I was heartbroken. I stomped my foot. I pounded my fist into the stupid glove.

When the inning was over and I slunk to the Green Sox bench, the manager was waiting for me. I thought he was going to console me. I thought he would say, "Tough luck, Jerry. Nice try," and then tousle my hair.

That's not what happened.

What he really did was glare angrily at me, and what he really said was, "Don't you ever do that again." He pointed out that while I was standing there pounding my glove, two Red Sox runs had scored. "Next time you miss the ball, you turn around and chase it down. You don't just stand there feeling sorry for yourself. Understand?"

I nodded. And I never forgot.

Reading As a Writer

Think About the Personal Narrative
- What did this experience teach Jerry Spinelli?
- From whose point of view is the story told? Which word helps you know this?
- What is the main part of the story?
- What details help you to see Jerry Spinelli's uniform?

Think About Writer's Craft
- Think about the differences between Jerry's dream and what really happened. How does the author show this contrast in the story?

Think About the Picture
- The author selected the photograph on page 296 for his story. Why do you think he chose it?

Responding

Write responses to these questions.

- **Personal Response** What do you think about the manager's reaction? Should he have handled the situation differently?
- **Critical Thinking** Why was the error more upsetting for Jerry Spinelli than it might have been for another player?

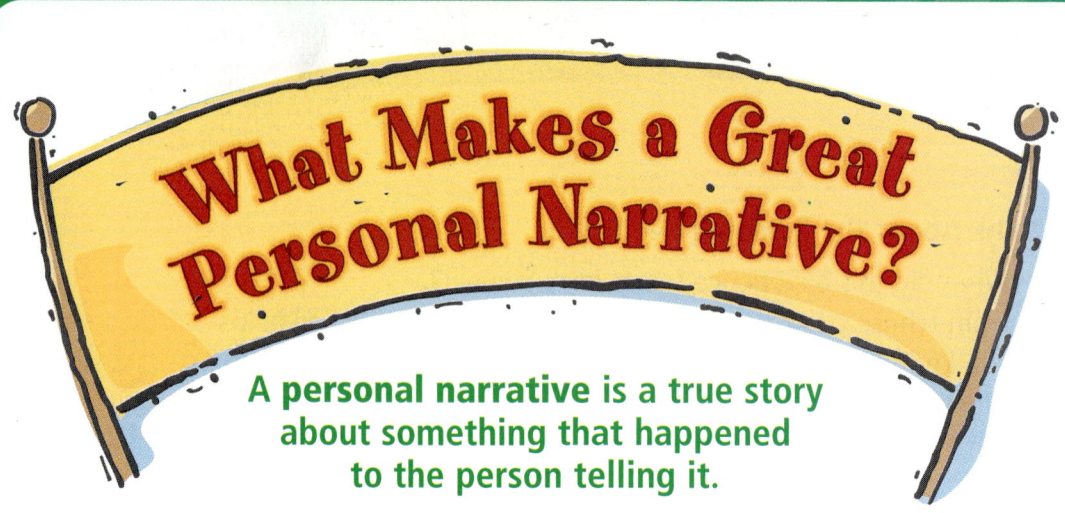

What Makes a Great Personal Narrative?

A personal narrative is a true story about something that happened to the person telling it.

Remember to follow these guidelines when you write your personal narrative.

▶ Grab your readers' attention at the beginning.

▶ Use the pronoun *I*.

▶ Tell only important events, and tell them in order.

▶ Use details, including dialogue, that help readers picture what happened.

▶ Write in a way that sounds like you.

▶ Write an ending that tells how the experience worked out, how you felt, or what you learned.

GRAMMAR CHECK

Avoid fragments. Check that every sentence has a subject and a predicate.

Student Model

WORKING DRAFT

Mike Jones wrote a personal narrative about a fishing trip with his grandfather. He chose this topic because he wanted to describe a special time he had with a very special family member.

Mike Jones

Do you know what I do when I'm feeling blue? I always think about ~~what I've done~~ special times I've had with my grandpa. He is a great person. ~~Do you ever have good times with your grandpa?~~ I think the best time I ever had with my grandpa was on my birthday. For my present he took me fishing.

This is an interesting beginning.

We rented our boat and bought some bait. We ~~left~~ went off on one of the greatest adventures I have ever experienced. Since I was just ten, Grandpa put a hook on my line and put a big, fat, juicy worm on the end of the hook. I pushed the button and let the line fly. I waited forever.

I decided to bring in my line and try casting again, but as soon as I began winding the reel, I felt a little tug. Then I felt a stronger tug. Suddenly, the bobber disappeared

more

Student Model continued

under the water, and my line, ~~looking like a plane on the runway,~~ stretched as tight as a tightrope, raced away from the boat.

> Your second comparison does a much better job of describing how the line looked.

I started screaming at the top of my lungs. My throat got all sore and scratchy. It felt like the time I had tonsillitis in third grade. Even though I got to eat lots of ice cream, it still wasn't much fun being stuck in bed for a week!

> Why is this part important to the story?

My grandpa told me to keep it steady. That fish was strong, and it was really moving! It pulled on the rod so hard, I was afraid I'd lose my grip. I yelled to Grandpa, asking him what I should do. He calmly said to tire the fish out, and give it some line to take.

I fought that fish for ten long minutes. Grandpa just

kept telling me to keep it steady. I was the one getting tired, not the fish, but I was determined to get it into the boat.

> Can you use dialogue?

Finally, I saw it! As I wound in my line, I got splashed by the tail flying up and down out of the water.

After I got the fish into the boat, a sigh of relief came out of my mouth.

Reading As a Writer

- What did Sal like? What questions did Sal have? What revisions might Mike want to make?
- What details describe what happened to the line when the fish bit?
- What questions do you still have for Mike? Where could he add this information?

Student Model

Mike revised his personal narrative after discussing it with classmates. Read his final copy to see what changes and improvements he made.

The Great Birthday Catch
by Mike Jones

Do you know what I do when I'm feeling blue? I always think about special times I've had with my grandpa. He is a great person. I think the best time I ever had with my grandpa was on my tenth birthday. For my present he took me fishing on the mighty St. Johns River in Florida.

We rented our boat and bought some bait. We went off on one of the greatest adventures I have ever experienced. Since I was just ten, Grandpa put a hook on my line and put a big, fat, juicy worm on the end of the hook. I pushed the button and let the line fly. I waited and waited and WAITED until I just couldn't wait anymore. My head was about to explode!

This is great! Your voice really comes through!

I decided to bring in my line and try casting again, but as soon as I began winding the reel, I felt a little tug. Then I felt a stronger tug. Suddenly, the bobber disappeared under the water, and my line, stretched as tight as a tightrope, raced away from the boat.

I started screaming at the top of my lungs, "I've got something!"

"Keep it steady, son," my grandpa said.

That fish was strong, and it was really moving! It pulled so hard on the rod, I was afraid I'd lose my grip. I yelled to Grandpa in a panicky voice, "What do I do now?"

302 Unit 8: Personal Narrative

> That helps me hear your grandpa's voice!

He answered calmly, "Tire the fish out, and give it some line to take."

I fought that fish for ten long minutes. Grandpa just kept saying, "Keep it steady. Keep it steady." I was the one getting tired, not the fish, but I was determined to get it into the boat.

> I can really picture this part!

Finally, I saw it! The fish was right next to the boat and only about six inches from the surface. It was so close I could see the greenish black scales on its back. As I wound in my line, I got splashed by the tail flying up and down out of the water.

After I got the fish into the boat, a sigh of relief came out of my mouth. My grandpa set the fish on the scale and said proudly, "Ten pounds and two ounces!" Here's the best part. Not only did I get to spend the day with my grandpa, but he saw me catch a huge fish. He helped me celebrate my tenth birthday in a big way!

Reading As a Writer

- How did Mike respond to Sal's questions about his working draft?
- What detail did Mike add about where they fished? about the fish he caught?
- Read the last two sentences of the second paragraph. How does Mike let you know he felt impatient?
- Where did Mike add dialogue? Why does it make the story better?
- Why does Mike's new ending finish the story more effectively?

See www.eduplace.com/kids/hme/ for more examples of student writing.

The Writing Process

PREWRITING · DRAFTING · REVISING · PROOFREADING · PUBLISHING

Write a Personal Narrative

▶ Start Thinking

 Make a writing folder for your personal narrative. Copy the questions in bold print, and put the paper in your folder. Write your answers as you think about and choose your topic.

- **Who will be my audience?** Will it be my friends? a grandparent? a younger brother or sister?
- **What will be my purpose?** Do I want to make readers laugh? share something I learned? tell about something special I did?
- **How will I publish or share my story?** Will I make it into a book? record it for the listening center? act it out for my class?

▶ Choose Your Story Idea

Stuck for an Idea?
List emotions to make an experience web.

See page 315 for more ideas.

① **List** five experiences you could write about.

② **Discuss** your ideas with a partner.
- Which experience does your partner like best? Why?
- Does any idea seem too big? Could you break it into smaller pieces? Look at how Mike narrowed his topic.

> summer vacation
> visiting my grandparents
> fishing with Grandpa
> (fishing on my 10th birthday)

③ **Ask** yourself these questions about each idea. Then choose one idea to write about.
- Which idea can I remember well?
- Which idea would my audience enjoy most?
- Which idea am I eager to write about?

304 Unit 8: Personal Narrative

Explore Your Story Idea

1 **Think** about your experience as pictures in a photo album. Close your eyes, and turn the pages in your mind. Which pictures show the most important events?

- Enlarge these pictures in your mind. What details do you see?

2 **Sketch** each important event on a large index card or half a piece of paper. (Stick figures are okay!) With each sketch, make notes about what happened. Here's one of Mike's sketches with his notes.

Stuck for Details?
If you can't think of many details, choose another story idea.

3 **Add** more details to your index cards. Use these questions to help.

- **Who** was there? **What** happened? **What** did people say and do?
- **Where** and **when** did this experience take place?
- **Why** was it memorable? **How** did this experience look, feel, taste, sound, or smell?

See page 14 for other ideas for exploring your topic.

The Writing Process

PREWRITING · DRAFTING · REVISING · PROOFREADING · PUBLISHING

Focus Skill

Organizing Your Narrative

Tell events in the order they happened. Readers shouldn't have to jump around the page to follow your story.

Stick to your topic. Keep only the events or details that help your audience understand the important parts.

Use time clue words. Time clues signal when events happened.

> Use time clue words and phrases to link sentences in a paragraph and to link one paragraph to another.

Time Clue Words	Time Clue Phrases
first, next, later, after, when, while, early, tomorrow, Tuesday, until	by the time, later that evening, before long, at daybreak, after the game, last summer

Think and Discuss Look at Jerry Spinelli's story on pages 295–296.

- In what order does the author present story events?
- What time clue words or phrases tell when these events took place?

▶ ## Plan Your Narrative

Review the pictures on your index cards. Put aside cards showing unimportant events. Arrange the remaining cards so that the events are in order. Number each card. Mike organized his cards and took out an event.

306   Unit 8: Personal Narrative

PREWRITING **DRAFTING** REVISING PROOFREADING PUBLISHING

Good Beginnings

A good beginning is like bait—it attracts readers and creates curiosity. Here are three ways to get your reader hooked.

Make a surprising or dramatic statement. Say something unexpected.

Weak Beginning	Strong Beginning
My muscles were sore from hiking.	As I struggled up the stairs, I gasped, "I will NEVER go hiking again!"

Ask a question. A question makes your readers want to know the answer.

Weak Beginning	Strong Beginning
Grandma and I used lots of paint to paint her garage that week.	What takes two people, seven days, and ten gallons of paint?

Describe a setting or a sensory impression. Let your readers see, hear, taste, smell, and feel your experience.

Weak Beginning	Strong Beginning
We walked through the busy market, trying not to bump into crates of produce.	Farmers shouted back and forth as we dodged around the crates piled high with corn, squash, and apples.

Try It Out

- Work in groups to rewrite each weak beginning above. Ask a question for the first beginning, describe a setting or sensory impression for the second, and make a surprising or dramatic statement for the third.

▶ Draft Your Beginning

Write three beginnings for your narrative, using a surprising statement, a question, and a description. Choose the beginning that you like best.

Drafting **307**

The Writing Process

PREWRITING — **DRAFTING** — REVISING — PROOFREADING — PUBLISHING

Writing with Voice

When you express yourself, make sure your words and language sound like you. Writing without voice will make your narrative sound flat or awkward. Compare the weak examples below with the strong excerpts from Jerry Spinelli's autobiographical story, "Shortstop."

Weak Voice	Strong Voice
I made my first error and felt disappointed. I hit the ground with my foot. I hit my glove with my hand.	My first error! I was heartbroken. I stomped my foot. I pounded my fist into the stupid glove.

Big words aren't always better! They can sound unnatural.

Weak Voice	Strong Voice
Prior to adulthood, whenever someone inquired about my career ambitions, I retorted, "Baseball is my objective."	From ages eleven to sixteen, if someone asked me what I wanted to be when I grew up, I gave one of two answers: "A baseball player" or "A shortstop."

Think and Discuss Compare the weak and strong voices in each chart.

- Which words in the first strong model help to show the author's feelings?
- Why does the second strong model sound more like someone talking than the second weak model?

▶ Draft Your Narrative

❶ **Write** the rest of your narrative. Skip every other line so that you have room to make changes. Don't worry about mistakes. Just write!

❷ **Follow your index cards.** Make your story come alive by adding new details as you think of them. Use time clues to make the sequence clear.

❸ **Be yourself.** Let your audience hear your voice.

Unit 8: Personal Narrative

Good Endings

If your story stops short, your readers will feel cheated. Here are some strategies to make your ending more satisfying.

Tell how the experience worked out. Don't just stop with the final event.

Weak Ending	Strong Ending
Grandma and I finally finished painting her garage. Then we cleaned the paint off our brushes. That paint was stubborn! Our clothes never did get clean.	Grandma tried stain remover and bleach, but she never managed to get the paint off my favorite jeans. Now whenever I wear them, I think about Grandma and our great painting adventure!

Share your thoughts or describe your feelings about the experience. Choose details and exact words that support what you say.

Weak Ending	Strong Ending
Leaving Grandma and Grandpa at the end of summer was hard. My dad picked me up, and I waved as we drove away.	When Dad and I drove away, I waved to Grandma and Grandpa so hard I thought my arm would break! Then I turned around, slumped in my seat, and pulled my cap down low so that Dad wouldn't see the tears in my eyes. I already missed them!

Think and Discuss

- Why are the strong endings better?
- Why is Mike's ending in his final copy on page 303 better than the one in his working draft on page 301?

▸ Draft Your Ending

Write two different endings for your narrative. Choose the ending you like better.

Drafting   **309**

Evaluating Your Personal Narrative

▶ **Reread** your narrative. Which parts need improvement? Use this rubric to help you decide. Write the sentences that describe your personal narrative.

Rings the Bell!

- ☐ The story starts with a surprising statement, a question, or a description.
- ☐ I used dialogue and other details that highlight the five senses.
- ☐ Every event is important to the story and is told in order.
- ☐ I can hear my voice. My writing sounds like me.
- ☐ The ending ties my story ideas together in a satisfying way.
- ☐ There are very few mistakes.

Getting Stronger

- ☐ The beginning needs more spark.
- ☐ More details are needed to make this experience come alive.
- ☐ Some sentences aren't important. More time clues are needed.
- ☐ My voice could be stronger. It doesn't always sound like me.
- ☐ The ending doesn't tie things together.
- ☐ Mistakes make my story hard to follow in some places.

Try Harder

- ☐ The beginning is dull.
- ☐ Where are the details? It's hard to picture what happened.
- ☐ Some events are unimportant or are told out of order.
- ☐ I can't hear my voice at all.
- ☐ The story just stops. There is no ending.
- ☐ There are a lot of mistakes.

 See www.eduplace.com/kids/hme/ to interact with this rubric.

PREWRITING DRAFTING **REVISING** PROOFREADING PUBLISHING

Revise Your Narrative

❶ Revise your narrative. Use the list of sentences you wrote from the rubric. Work on the parts that you described with sentences from "Getting Stronger" and "Try Harder."

 Paragraph Tip
Check the details in each paragraph. Are they related to the topic sentence? presented in a logical order?

❷ Meet with a partner for a writing conference.

When You're the Writer
Read your narrative to your partner. Discuss any questions or problems you are having with it. Take notes to help you remember your partner's comments.

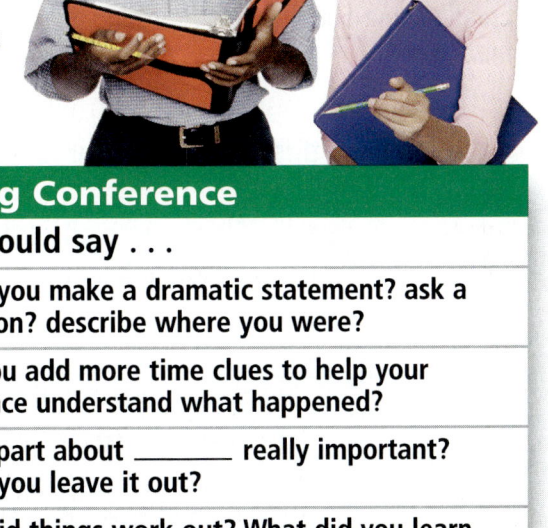

When You're the Listener
Tell at least two things you like about the narrative. Ask questions about anything that is unclear.

The Writing Conference	
If you're thinking . . .	*You could say . . .*
The beginning doesn't get my attention.	Could you make a dramatic statement? ask a question? describe where you were?
I can't tell when things happened.	Can you add more time clues to help your audience understand what happened?
This part doesn't seem important to the story.	Is the part about _____ really important? Could you leave it out?
The ending leaves things up in the air.	How did things work out? What did you learn from this experience?
This part doesn't sound natural.	Can you write so that it sounds like you?

❸ Make additional revisions. Use your writing conference notes and the Revising Strategies on the next page.

Revising **311**

Revising Strategies

Elaborating: Word Choice You can paint pictures for your readers, using similes and metaphors. A **simile** compares two different things, using *like* or *as*. A **metaphor** compares without using *like* or *as*.

Similes	The giant turtle plodded along like a tired elephant. Mom's lasagna was as heavy as a brick in my stomach.
Metaphor	Her lively little brother is a whirling cyclone.

▶ Find at least one place in your narrative where you can use a simile or a metaphor.   See also page H11.

Elaborating: Details Insert details within a sentence, or write more sentences.

Few Details	Elaborated with Details
As I slid on the ice, I made some people fall.	As I lost my balance on the ice, my arms swung around like windmills. My legs did a split and caused three skaters to tumble down right on top of me.

▶ Find at least three places in your narrative where you can add more details.

Sentence Fluency Don't write all sentences the same way. Try writing sentences different ways while keeping the meaning the same. Which way best expresses your voice?

Two sentences	I watched the movie. I munched on some popcorn.
Combined with *and*	I watched the movie, and I munched on some popcorn.
Combined with *as*	As I watched the movie, I munched on some popcorn.
Changed order	I munched on some popcorn as I watched the movie.

▶ Write at least two sentences of your narrative in a different way, or use *and* or *as* to combine two related sentences.

GRAMMAR LINK See also pages 46 and 190.

PREWRITING DRAFTING REVISING **PROOFREADING** PUBLISHING

▶ Proofread Your Narrative

Proofread your narrative, using the Proofreading Checklist and the Grammar and Spelling Connections. Proofread for one skill at a time. Refer to a class dictionary to check spellings.

Proofreading Checklist
Did I
- ✔ indent all paragraphs?
- ✔ correct sentence fragments or run-ons?
- ✔ capitalize proper nouns?
- ✔ punctuate possessive nouns correctly?
- ✔ spell all words correctly?

📖 Use the Guide to Capitalization, Punctuation, and Usage on page H57.

Proofreading Marks
- ¶ Indent
- ∧ Add
- ⌒ Delete
- ≡ Capital letter
- / Small letter

Tech Tip
A spelling tool won't identify a plural possessive noun missing its apostrophe.

Grammar and Spelling Connections

Proper Nouns The name of a particular person, place, or thing begins with a capital letter.

Common nouns	grandpa, river, team
Proper nouns	Grandpa (when used as a name), St. Johns River, Green Sox

GRAMMAR LINK ▶ See also pages 66 and 182.

Complete Sentences
A complete sentence expresses a complete thought and begins with a capital letter. A fragment is not a sentence.

Complete sentence	The umpire called a strike.
Fragment	Called a strike.

GRAMMAR LINK ▶ See also page 32.

Spelling the |ī| Sound The |ī| sound is often spelled *i*, *igh*, or *i-consonant-e*. ch**i**ld, br**igh**t, t**i**me

📖 See the Spelling Guide on page H67.

 Go to www.eduplace.com/kids/hme/ for proofreading practice.

The Writing Process

PREWRITING · DRAFTING · REVISING · PROOFREADING · **PUBLISHING**

▶ Publish Your Narrative

❶ **Make a neat final copy** of your narrative. Be sure you fixed all mistakes.

❷ **Add a title** to your narrative. Write a title that will make your audience curious, such as "Topsy-turvy" instead of "My Ice-skating Party."

GRAMMAR TIP ▶ *Capitalize the first, the last, and each important word in your title.*

❸ **Publish** or share your narrative in a way that suits your audience.

Tips for Making Springy Pop-up Illustrations

- Draw pictures from your story on construction paper. Cut them out.
- Glue two strips of construction paper into an *L* and fold one strip over the other again and again.
- Glue one end of the spring to the illustration and the other to the page. You can add background illustrations to the page.

Ideas for Sharing

Write It
- Send your story in a letter or an e-mail. See pages 317 and H39 for tips.
- ★ Make your story into a pop-up booklet for the Reading Center.

Say It
- Act it out for classmates, friends, or family. See page 350 for tips.
- Record it on audio or videotape.

Show It
- Make your story into a photo essay.

▶ Reflect

Write about your writing experience. Use these questions to get started.

- What part of your personal narrative do you like best?
- What will you do differently the next time you write?
- How does this paper compare with other papers you have written?

Assessment Link

Writing Prompts

Use these prompts as personal narrative topics or to practice for a test. Some of them connect to other subjects you study. Decide who your audience will be, and write your narrative in a way they will understand and enjoy.

1 Write a personal narrative about your first day at school or in some other new place. What happened?

2 Write about a time when you solved a problem. Write about what you did and what you learned.

3 Write about a special time with a friend or a family member. What did you do? What made it special?

4 What is the silliest thing you've ever done? Write about the experience, telling what you did and why you did it.

Writing Across the Curriculum

5 **MATH**
Write about an experience when numbers—clocks, phone numbers, birthdays, dates, piggy banks, and so on—made a big difference.

6 **PHYSICAL EDUCATION**
Think of a game or a sport that you enjoy. Write about something exciting that happened when you played the game.

7 **SCIENCE**
What machine or invention is important to you? Write about a time when the machine made something better or easier for you.

8 **LITERATURE**
Have you ever thought that the main character in a book was like you? Write about an experience you had that was similar to that character's.

See www.eduplace.com/kids/hme/ for more prompts.

Assessment Link

✓ Test Practice

This prompt to write a personal narrative is like ones you might find on a writing test. Read the prompt.

> **What is the silliest thing you've ever done? Write about the experience, telling what you did and why you did it.**

Here are some strategies to help you do a good job responding to a prompt like this.

Remember that a personal narrative is a story about something that happened to the writer.

❶ Look for clue words that tell what to write about. What clue words are in the prompt above?

❷ Choose a topic that fits the clue words. Write the clue words and your topic.

Clue Words	My Topic
silliest thing you've ever done, experience, telling what you did and why you did it	I will write about the time I played a dancing pickle in the school play.

❸ Plan your writing. Use a Time-Order Chart.

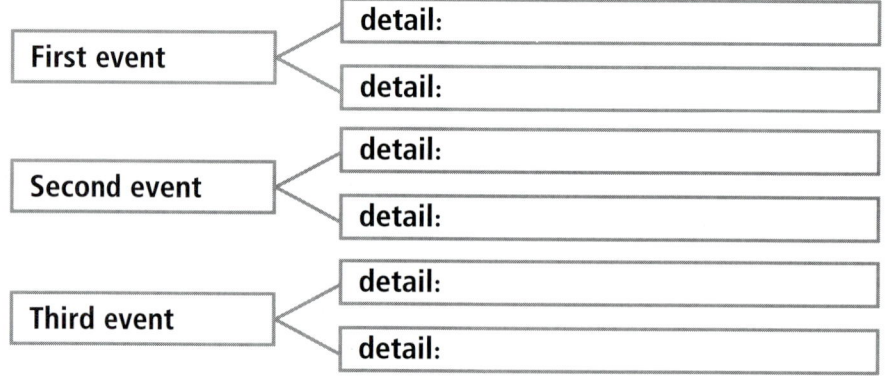

❹ You will get a good score if you remember the description of the personal narrative that rings the bell in the rubric on page 310.

Special Focus on Narrating

Writing a Friendly Letter

A **friendly letter** is written to someone you know well. It is a way of sharing news or just saying "hello." You use informal language in a friendly letter. Read Ben's letter.

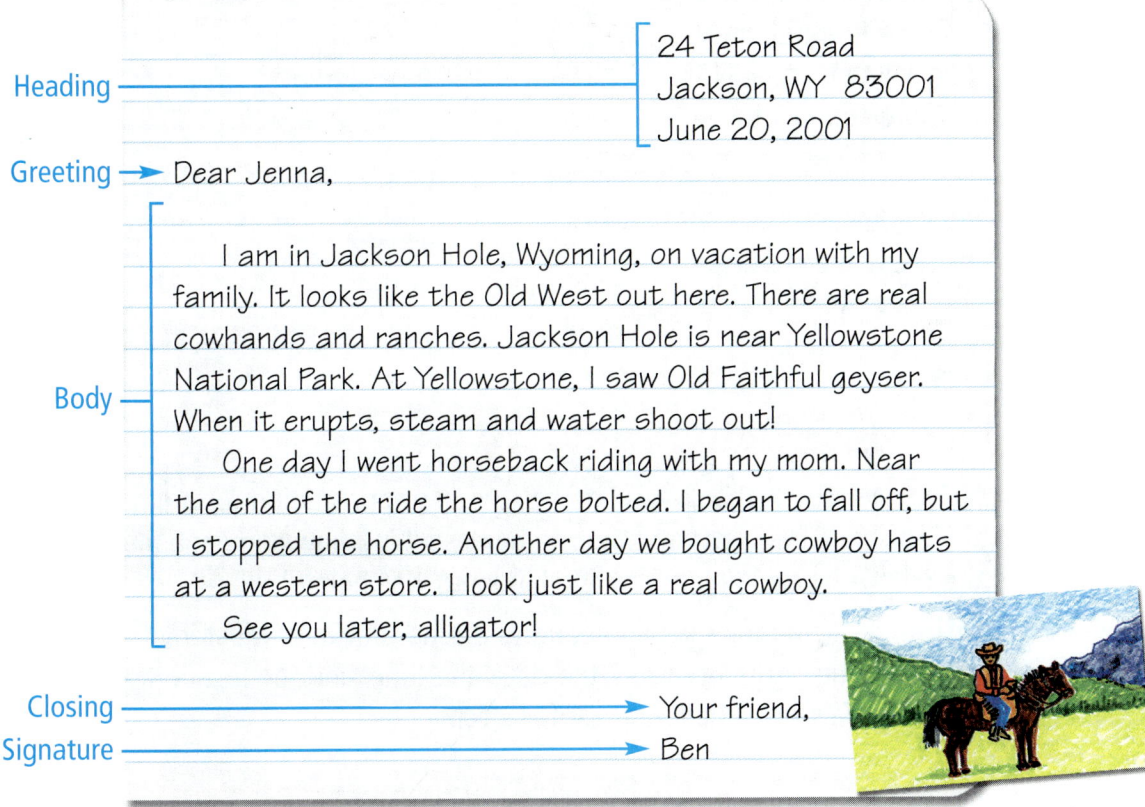

Heading
24 Teton Road
Jackson, WY 83001
June 20, 2001

Greeting → Dear Jenna,

Body
I am in Jackson Hole, Wyoming, on vacation with my family. It looks like the Old West out here. There are real cowhands and ranches. Jackson Hole is near Yellowstone National Park. At Yellowstone, I saw Old Faithful geyser. When it erupts, steam and water shoot out!

One day I went horseback riding with my mom. Near the end of the ride the horse bolted. I began to fall off, but I stopped the horse. Another day we bought cowboy hats at a western store. I look just like a real cowboy.

See you later, alligator!

Closing → Your friend,
Signature → Ben

Reading As a Writer

- The **heading** appears in the upper right corner and contains the writer's address and the current date. *What information belongs on each line?*
- The **greeting** usually begins with the word *Dear* and the name of the person to whom the letter is written. *To whom is Ben writing?*
- The **body** of the letter contains the message and has more than one paragraph. *What did Ben tell Jenna about?*
- The **closing**, such as *Sincerely* or *Yours truly*, completes the letter. It is followed by a comma. *What closing did Ben use?*
- The **signature** is the writer's name. *Where did Ben write his name?*

more ▶

Special Focus continued

How to Write a Friendly Letter

1. **Decide** what you want to write about.
2. **Organize** your thoughts and jot down ideas.
3. **Write** your letter. Be sure to include all five parts.
4. **Proofread** for mistakes. Use the Proofreading Checklist on page 313. Use a dictionary to check spellings.
5. **Make** a neat final copy.
6. **Address** the envelope. Put a stamp on it and mail your letter.

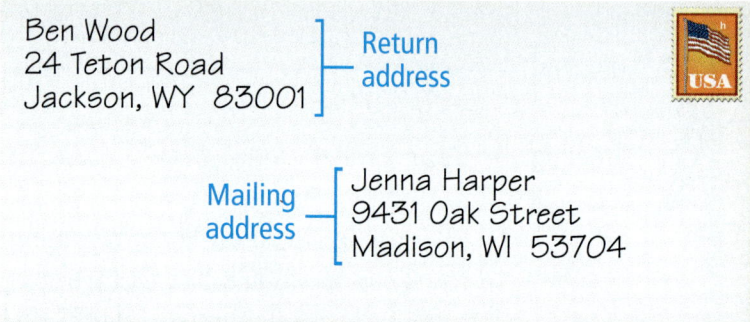

Types of Friendly Letters

Thank-you Letter A thank-you letter expresses appreciation for a gift or an act of kindness. Often, letters elaborate by describing how someone plans to use the gift, or by explaining how the kindness was helpful.

Invitation An invitation asks someone to attend an event. Most invitations include the name of the occasion, the date, the time, and the location. An invitation may also include a request for a reply.

318 Unit 8: Personal Narrative

Unit 9

Writing a Story

Their captain promised a calm and safe voyage, and it was— for the first month.

A Published Model

The legend of Lucia Zenteno is a folktale told by the Zapotec Indians in Mexico. This story retells the folktale. What lesson does the story teach?

The Woman Who Outshone the Sun

by Rosalma Zubizarreta, Harriet Rohmer, and David Schecter

The day Lucia Zenteno arrived, everyone in the village was astonished. No one knew where she came from. Yet they all saw that she was amazingly beautiful, and that she brought thousands of dancing butterflies and brightly-colored flowers on her skirts. She walked softly yet with quiet dignity, her long, unbraided hair flowing behind her. A loyal iguana walked at her side.

No one knew who she was, but they did know that nothing shone as brightly as Lucia Zenteno. Some people said that Lucia Zenteno outshone the sun. Others said that her glorious hair seemed to block out the light.

Everyone felt a little afraid of someone so wonderful and yet so strange.

There used to be a river that ran by the town, almost the same river that runs by there now. And people said that when Lucia Zenteno went there to bathe, the river fell in love with her. The water rose from its bed and began to flow through her shining black hair.

When Lucia finished bathing, she would sit by the river and comb out her hair with a comb made from the wood of the mesquite tree. And when she did, the water, the fishes, and the otters would flow out of her hair and return to the river once more.

The old people of the village said that although Lucia was different from them, she should be honored and treated with respect. She understood the ways of nature, they said.

But some people did not listen to the elders. They were afraid of Lucia's powers, which they did not understand. And so they refused to answer Lucia's greetings, or offer their friendship. They called her cruel names and spied on her day and night.

Lucia did not return the meanness of the people. She kept to herself and continued to walk with her head held high.

Her quiet dignity angered some of the people. They whispered that Lucia must be trying to harm them. People became more afraid of Lucia and so they treated her more cruelly. Finally, they drove her from the village.

Lucia went down to the river one last time to say good-bye. As always, the water rose to greet her and began to flow through her glorious hair. But this time when she tried to comb the river out of her hair, the river would not leave her.

And so, when Lucia Zenteno left the village, the river and the fishes and the otters went with her, leaving only a dry, winding riverbed, a serpent of sand where the water had been.

Everyone saw that Lucia Zenteno was leaving and that the river, the fishes, and the otters were leaving with her. The people were filled with despair. They had never imagined that their beautiful river would ever leave them, no matter what they did.

Where once there had been green trees and cool breezes, now no more rain fell, no birds sang, no otters played. The people and their animals suffered from thirst. People began to understand, as never before, how much the river, the fishes, the otters, even the trees and birds had meant to the village. They began to understand how much the river had loved Lucia Zenteno.

The elders said that everyone must search for Lucia and beg her forgiveness. Some people did not want to. They were too afraid. But when the drought continued, everyone finally agreed to follow the elders' advice. And so the whole village set out in search of Lucia.

After many days of walking, the people found the iguana cave where Lucia had gone to seek refuge. Lucia was waiting for them, but they could not see her face. She had turned her back to the people.

At first no one dared say a word. Then two children called out, "Lucia, we have come to ask your forgiveness. Please have mercy on us and return our river!"

Lucia Zenteno turned and looked at the people. She saw their frightened, tired faces, and she felt compassion for them. At last she spoke. "I will ask the river to return to you," she said. "But just as the river gives water to all who are thirsty, no matter who they are, so you must learn to treat everyone with kindness, even those who seem different from you."

The people remembered how they had treated Lucia, and they hung their heads in shame.

Seeing that the people were truly sorry for what they had done, Lucia returned with them to the village and began to comb out her hair. She combed out the water, she combed out the fishes, she combed out the otters, and she kept on combing until the river had returned once more to where it belonged.

The people were overjoyed to have their river again. They poured water over themselves and over their animals, they jumped into the river, and they laughed and cried with happiness.

In all the excitement, no one noticed at first that Lucia had disappeared again. When the children asked the elders where she had gone, the elders replied that Lucia had not really left them. Though they would not be able to see her, she would always be there, guiding and protecting them, helping them to live with love and understanding in their hearts.

Reading As a Writer

Think About the Story

- A folktale often teaches a lesson. What lesson does this one teach? Who teaches the lesson?
- What do you learn in the first paragraph on page 320 about characters and setting?
- What is the problem, or conflict, in the story?
- At what point do the story events change for the better?
- What is the solution to the problem?

Think About Writer's Craft

- Folktales are often about characters and events that are "bigger than life." Find at least three examples of exaggeration or fantasy in this folktale.

Think About the Pictures

- The illustrations in this story are done in a folk art style, showing fantastic events such as the river riding in Lucia's hair. Another feature of this style is that Lucia is shown in different sizes. Why do you think she looks so small in the picture on page 321? Why do you think she looks so large in the picture on page 322?

Responding

Write responses to these questions.

- **Personal Response** What did you like best about this story? What parts did you find interesting or unusual? Explain your answers.
- **Critical Thinking** Why did Lucia decide to return to the village? What is your opinion about her decision?

What Makes a Great Story?

A story is an original narrative made up by the author.

Remember to follow these guidelines when you tell or write a story.

▶ Develop a plot with a beginning, a middle, and an end.

▶ Decide what voice you will use to tell your story. Use it to create your story's mood.

▶ Introduce the main characters, the setting, and the problem in the beginning in an interesting way.

▶ Show how characters deal with the problem in the middle of your story. Explain how things work out at the end.

▶ Tell only the important events. Present them in an order that makes sense.

▶ Use colorful details and meaningful dialogue to show rather than tell about the characters, events, and setting.

GRAMMAR CHECK

Put quotation marks around a speaker's exact words. Put end punctuation inside the last set of quotation marks.

Student Model

WORKING DRAFT

Sometimes an interesting character can help you to think of a plot. Chris Rivera invented a dog who wants to fly! He decided to write a fable about this unusual dog. Here is Chris's first draft.

Chris Rivera

Hound Dog

Let me tell you a story about Hound Dog. One day near his cabin in the forest, Hound Dog was watching some birds flying. They were having such fun! One of them landed on his neighbor's bird feeder. It ate and ate until a squirrel scared it away. He thought it would be great to be free as a bird and do whatever he wanted while peering down as if he were on top of the world. So Hound Dog ~~decides~~ decided to make his new dream come true.

Hound Dog was no ordinary dog. When he wanted a cabin, he built it. When he wanted a garden, he planted it. He thought he could do anything.

Hound Dog ran across his backyard as fast as his ~~legs~~ big powerful paws could carry him and took a big leap. Just as he started flapping his wings, the wind hit his face, and he crashed right into some bushes.

This situation is clever! I can't wait to see if he succeeds.

Your beginning is good, but would this make a better beginning?

Where did these wings come from, and who is Tom Cat? Can you add more details?

326 Unit 9: Story

Tom Cat shook his head and asked Hound Dog what he was doing.

~~Tom Cat went inside. He drank some milk and combed his whiskers. Then he went back outside.~~

Hound Dog was still there. He was not discouraged. He decided to start out a little higher on his next try. Hound Dog climbed up into a tree, flapped his wings faster and faster, and then leaped off the branch! This time he landed on some flowers. Tom Cat asked Hound Dog again what he was doing.

"Higher," Hound Dog whispered before he fainted.

When he woke up, he climbed onto the roof of his cabin and jumped off, flapping his wings. He ~~flew~~ glided smoothly for a second but then fell with a thud in his garden. A familiar voice asked what he was going to do. Hound Dog decided to quit.

> The story events occur in perfect order. Good!

> Can you say more to wrap up the story?

Reading As a Writer

- What questions and comments did Sal have? What might Chris do to revise his story?
- Where could Chris add dialogue to let you hear the story characters?
- Why did Chris cut the fourth paragraph? What sentences should he cut in the first paragraph?

Student Model

FINAL COPY

Chris revised his story after discussing it in a writing conference. Read his final copy to see what changes he made to improve his story.

Hound Dog's Weird Ups and Downs
by Chris Rivera

Hound Dog was no ordinary dog. When he wanted a cabin, he built it. When he wanted a garden, he planted it. He thought he could do anything.

One day near his cabin in the forest, Hound Dog was watching some birds flying. They were soaring and swooping and looping around as if they were playing tag. They were having such fun! He thought it would be great to be free as a bird and do whatever he wanted while peering down as if he were on top of the world. So Hound Dog decided to make his new dream come true.

First, he made wings by gluing feathers from his pillows to cardboard cut from an old box in the attic. When he finished, he attached his new wings to his front paws with rubber bands. Then he decided to try out his new wings in his back yard.

Hound Dog ran across his backyard as fast as his big powerful paws could carry him and took a big leap. Just as he started flapping his wings, the wind hit his face, and he crashed right into some prickly rosebushes he had just planted. His neighbor, Tom Cat, shook his head and shouted, "What are you going to do NOW, Hound Dog?"

> Nice details. Now I can really picture Hound Dog's wings.

Hound Dog was not discouraged. He decided to start out a little higher on his next try. Hound Dog climbed up into an oak tree he had planted, flapped his wings faster and faster, and then leaped off the branch! This time he landed on a bed of his prize orchids. "What are you going to do NOW, Hound Dog?" cackled Tom Cat.

"Higher," Hound Dog whispered before he fainted.

When he woke up, he climbed onto the roof of his cabin and jumped off, flapping his wings. He glided smoothly for a second but then fell with a thud into his pumpkin patch. A familiar voice hollered, "And what are you going to do NOW, Hound Dog?"

Hound Dog inspected his bruises and scratches. Then he looked at his dented rosebushes, crushed orchids, and smashed pumpkins. Finally, he threw his wings in the compost pile and shouted back to Tom Cat, "NOW I'm going to be me!"

For the rest of his days, Hound Dog went on with his hobby of gardening, enjoying who he was.

Moral: Dogs were just not meant to fly!

> The dialogue you added throughout the story really shows the personality of each character.

> Your new ending makes the story feel finished.

Reading As a Writer

- How did Chris respond to Sal's questions?
- Where did Chris add dialogue to his story? What does the new dialogue tell you about Tom Cat?
- What new details did Chris add to describe where Hound Dog crashed? What do these details tell you about Hound Dog?

See www.eduplace.com/kids/hme/ for more examples of student writing.

Student Model

The Writing Process

PREWRITING · DRAFTING · REVISING · PROOFREADING · PUBLISHING

Write a Story

▶ Start Thinking

 Make a writing folder for your story. Copy the questions in bold print, and put the paper in your folder. Write your answers as you think about and choose your topic.

- **Who will be my audience?** Will it be my friends? my teacher? children at a daycare center?
- **What will be my purpose?** Do I want to give my readers goose bumps? show them the future? make them laugh?
- **How will I publish or share my story?** Will I make it into a book? submit it to a literary magazine? record it?

 Stuck for an Idea?

Try one of these:
- Dogs run the world.
- You develop bionic hearing.
- It snows for a month.

See page 342 for more ideas.

▶ Choose Your Story Idea

❶ **Brainstorm** five story ideas. Make a story chart. Mix and match the items to help you think of more story ideas. Here is part of Chris's chart.

Main Character | Setting | Problem/Situation
a talking dog | a modern city | finds an unusual object
a time traveler | the woods | tries to fly
a shrunken kid | the beach | solves a mystery

❷ **Discuss** your ideas with a partner. Which ones does your partner like best? Why? Which characters, settings, and problems go together best?

❸ **Ask** yourself these questions about each idea. Then choose one idea to write about.
- Do I have enough ideas for this story?
- Can I write an interesting beginning, middle, and end?
- Will my audience enjoy reading about this?

330 Unit 9: Story

Go to www.eduplace.com/kids/hme/ for graphic organizers.

PREWRITING DRAFTING REVISING PROOFREADING PUBLISHING

Focus Skill

Planning Characters

Readers will experience your story through the words, actions, and emotions of the people in it. Give your story at least one **main character** and one or more **minor characters.**

Use details. Flat, colorless characters can make your story flop, even if your plot is great. Use details to create convincing, three-dimensional characters that pop right off the page!

Appearance
Does your character wear glasses? have freckles? look worried?

Actions
Is your character always late? often reading? sometimes clumsy?

Feelings
Is your character confused? excited? disappointed?

Interests
Does your character like old movies? collect marbles? play the tuba?

Speech
Does your character mumble? ask a lot of questions? tell bad jokes?

Personality
Is your character curious? serious? outgoing?

Try It Out

- With a partner, use your imagination and the categories above to describe the pictured character. Make notes about your ideas. Share your ideas with a small group. Discuss how your ideas are alike and different.

▶ Explore Your Story

Create two main characters that you might like to write about. Sketch pictures of these characters. Keep in mind the categories above to tell what each one is like. Choose the one you like better.

HELP ? See page 14 for other ideas for exploring your topic.

Prewriting   **331**

The Writing Process

PREWRITING · DRAFTING · REVISING · PROOFREADING · PUBLISHING

Focus Skill

Planning Setting and Plot

Decide where and when your story takes place. The setting could be a colonial village, a desert, or an imaginary place. The time might be long ago, today, or in the future.

Focus on a situation or a problem. A plot must have a beginning, a middle, and an end that focuses on this situation or problem. Look at the story map of *The Woman Who Outshone the Sun*.

Sometimes it takes several paragraphs to introduce the setting, characters, and problem.

Beginning: introduces setting, main characters, problem	Lucia, a newcomer, is different from the other villagers. Everyone is a little afraid of her. The old people respect Lucia, but fearful villagers drive her away. The river leaves with her, causing a drought.
Middle: shows how characters deal with problem	The drought continues. Finally, the villagers find Lucia, beg for forgiveness, and ask her to return the river.
End: explains how problem is resolved	Lucia forgives them, teaches them a lesson, and returns the river.

Think and Discuss

- What is the problem in Chris's story on pages 328–329? How does Hound Dog try to deal with the problem?

▶ Plan Your Story

Make a story map. Plan the beginning, the middle, and the end of your story. Include details that describe the setting and the characters. List the main events in the order in which they happen.

332 Unit 9: Story   Go to www.eduplace.com/kids/hme/ for graphic organizers.

PREWRITING | **DRAFTING** | REVISING | PROOFREADING | PUBLISHING

Focus Skill

Developing Characters

Once you have planned your characters, how can you make them seem real?

Include details. Using exact, colorful words can help the audience picture a character.

Few Details	Elaborated with Details
The dog, a yellow puppy, fell.	The puppy, a fluffy bundle of yellow fur, tripped clumsily over his giant paws.

Show characters through their actions. Telling about them is less convincing.

Telling	Showing
The salesclerk was a lazy man who hated to work.	With a scowl on his face, the clerk put down his book and shuffled slowly to the cash register.

Show characters through their dialogue. The words of your characters reveal their thoughts and attitudes.

Without Dialogue	With Dialogue
The house was dirty. Paula expected her parents shortly.	"This house is a mess!" Paula gasped in a panicky voice. "My parents will be back in fifteen minutes!"

Try It Out

- With a partner, write two or three sentences of dialogue for the clerk in the example above. Then describe some actions that reveal more about Paula. Share your work with the class.

▶ Draft Some Dialogue

Write dialogue that shows what the main character in your story is like.

Drafting **333**

The Writing Process

PREWRITING · **DRAFTING** · REVISING · PROOFREADING · PUBLISHING

Focus Skill

Developing Your Plot

The Beginning

Use the first sentence to grab your audience's attention. Warning: Starting your story with *I'm going to write about ...* has been proven to put readers to sleep! Here are three different ways to begin.

Describe the setting.	A herd of cows lay in the pasture under a blanket of angry storm clouds.
Describe an action.	The rotting drawbridge swung open, and hundreds of mice scampered to find shelter.
Use dialogue.	"Where were you at midnight?" Detective Sanders demanded.

The Middle

Include only the events important to the main idea. If your story is about a Fourth of July parade, tell only about the parade. Don't tell everything that happened to the characters before, during, and after the parade.

Tell the events in time order. Use time clue words and phrases, such as *first, later, that morning, hundreds of years ago,* and *at midnight,* so that the sequence of events is clear.

Tell events through dialogue. Coming from your characters, dialogue makes events seem more real. *Dad shouted, "Ruth, get the cows in the barn! A storm is coming!"*

Paragraph Tip

You can use order words to link sentences in a paragraph and also to move from one paragraph to the next.

 Whenever the speaker changes in dialogue, begin a new paragraph.

334 Unit 9: Story

The Ending

Show how the problem is solved or how the situation turns out. These sentences come near the end of a story about Ruth, the girl who rescued the cows from the storm.

Can't Solve the Problem?

If you can't think of a good ending, think of a different problem for your story.

> She finally managed to shove the last stubborn cow into the barn and dragged the door shut, making sure the latch was bolted tight. Exhausted, she raced toward the house.

If the story had ended there, you might have wondered, *Did the storm ever hit?* The last two sentences tell you. They make the story feel complete.

> As she leaped up the stairs, the first giant raindrops began to batter the porch roof. The violent storm raged for hours, but she slept well, knowing she had done her part to keep the cows safe.

Try It Out

- List some possible main events for one or two of the story beginnings on page 334?
- Work with a small group of classmates to write a different ending for *The Woman Who Outshone the Sun.* Compare your ending with ones written by other groups.

▶ Draft Your Beginning

❶ **Write** three different beginnings for your story. Try writing dialogue or describing the setting or an action.

❷ **Choose** the beginning you like best.

Drafting **335**

The Writing Process

PREWRITING · DRAFTING · REVISING · PROOFREADING · PUBLISHING

Focus Skill

Writing with Voice

When an author creates characters, he or she gives each a voice, a way that character sounds. A character's voice is heard through dialogue, as you learned in the previous lesson.

The author uses another voice, the **narrative voice**, to tell (narrate) the story. That voice sets the story's **mood**—spooky, silly, sad, or any way the author chooses to make it sound!

Compare the first example with the sentences from *The Woman Who Outshone the Sun*.

First Mood	Second Mood
Some folks thought Lucia was downright snooty, and they didn't take very kindly to that. They got to gossiping like a bunch of magpies, spreading nasty rumors and such. The more they thought Lucia meant them harm, the meaner they got. Fed up, they finally ran Lucia off.	Her quiet dignity angered some of the people. They whispered that Lucia must be trying to harm them. People became more afraid of Lucia and so they treated her more cruelly. Finally, they drove her from the village.

Think and Discuss

- How does the voice sound in the first paragraph? in the second?
- Which words make each paragraph sound the way it does?

▶ Draft Your Story

❶ **Decide** how you want your story to sound. Will it be suspenseful? dramatic? funny?

❷ **Collect** your story map and any dialogue, beginnings, or endings you have written and wish to include.

❸ **Write** the rest of your story. Skip every other line on your paper, and don't worry about mistakes.

Remember to start a new paragraph for a new event or when the setting changes.

336 Unit 9: Story

Evaluating Your Story

▶ **Reread** your story. Use this rubric to help you decide which parts need improvement. Write the sentences that describe your story.

Rings the Bell!

- ☐ An interesting beginning introduces the characters, the setting, and the problem or situation.
- ☐ The middle shows how the characters deal with the problem. Events are in order.
- ☐ The ending shows how the problem is solved or the situation turns out.
- ☐ Dialogue and details make characters, events, and setting real.
- ☐ The mood I chose for my story comes through loud and clear!
- ☐ I made very few mistakes in capitalization, punctuation, or spelling.

Getting Stronger

- ☐ The beginning could be more interesting.
- ☐ The problem is not clear until the middle of the story.
- ☐ Some events in the plot seem to be mixed up.
- ☐ The ending isn't satisfying—I want to know more.
- ☐ I often tell the story instead of showing in details and dialogue.
- ☐ My story has a mood, but it's not the one I wanted!
- ☐ Mistakes make the story confusing in some places.

Try Harder

- ☐ The beginning is dull and uninteresting.
- ☐ There is no clear problem in the story.
- ☐ Many story events are missing or told out of order.
- ☐ The story just stops without telling how the problem worked out.
- ☐ I haven't included enough details. There is no dialogue.
- ☐ My story has no mood. It sounds flat and robotic.
- ☐ There are a lot of mistakes in capitalization, punctuation, or spelling.

See www.eduplace.com/kids/hme/ to interact with this rubric.

The Writing Process

PREWRITING · DRAFTING · **REVISING** · PROOFREADING · PUBLISHING

▶ Revise Your Story

❶ Revise your story. Use the list of sentences you wrote from the rubric. Work on the parts that you described with sentences from "Getting Stronger" and "Try Harder."

❷ Have a writing conference.

When You're the Writer Read your story to a partner. Share the questions or problems you are having with it. Take notes to remember your partner's comments.

When You're the Listener Tell at least two things you like about the story. Ask questions about anything that is unclear.

Revising Tip
Highlight dialogue in your story. When appropriate, replace *said* with a more exact verb, such as *shouted* or *whispered*.

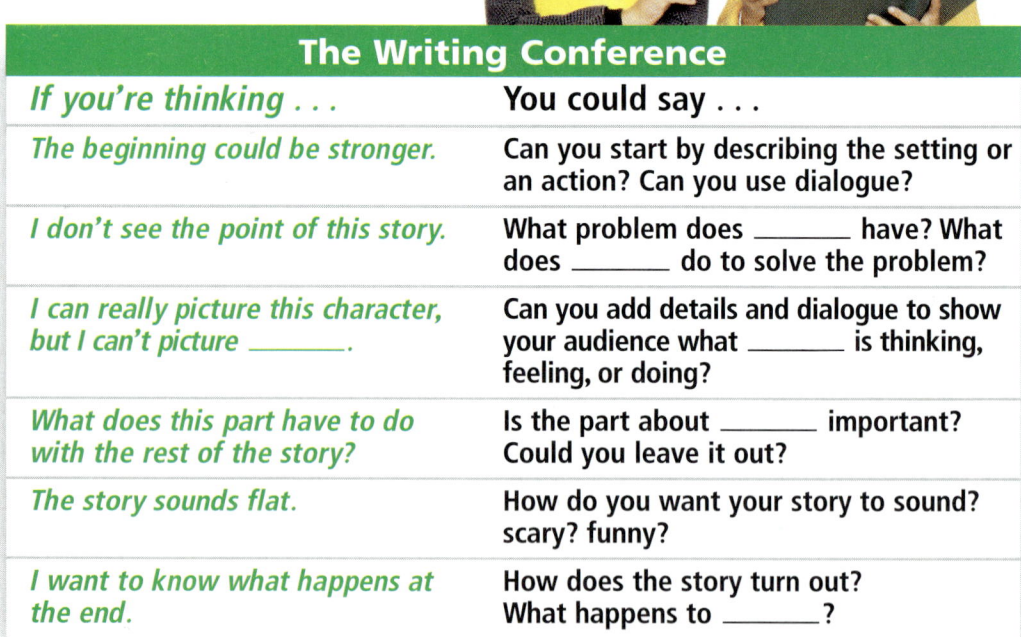

The Writing Conference

If you're thinking . . .	You could say . . .
The beginning could be stronger.	Can you start by describing the setting or an action? Can you use dialogue?
I don't see the point of this story.	What problem does _____ have? What does _____ do to solve the problem?
I can really picture this character, but I can't picture _____.	Can you add details and dialogue to show your audience what _____ is thinking, feeling, or doing?
What does this part have to do with the rest of the story?	Is the part about _____ important? Could you leave it out?
The story sounds flat.	How do you want your story to sound? scary? funny?
I want to know what happens at the end.	How does the story turn out? What happens to _____?

❸ Make additional revisions to your story, using your writing conference notes and the Revising Strategies on the next page.

Unit 9: Story

Revising Strategies

Elaborating: Word Choice Use exact words to help your readers clearly picture how things look and how actions are done.

Without Exact Words	With Exact Words
The **vehicle went** down the **road**.	The **covered wagon rumbled slowly** down the **trail**. The **sports car sped quickly** down the **track**.

▶ Find at least three places in your story where you can add exact nouns, verbs, adjectives, and adverbs. 📖 Use the Thesaurus Plus on page H81.

Elaborating: Details Use adverbs and prepositional phrases to add information to a sentence.

Without Details	Elaborated with Details
Anna styled her hair and left.	Anna styled her hair **expertly with new silver bands** and **hurriedly** left **for the party**.

▶ Add at least three adverbs or prepositional phrases to your story.

GRAMMAR LINK ▶ See also pages 248 and 260.

Sentence Fluency Avoid stringy sentences. A stringy sentence contains too many conjunctions, such as *and, or, but,* or *so.* Break it into shorter sentences.

Stringy sentence	My dog likes the car **and** she rides a lot **but** my cat doesn't like the car **so** he stays home.
Simple sentences	My dog likes the car. She rides a lot. My cat doesn't like the car. He stays home.
Compound sentences	My dog likes the car, and she rides a lot. My cat, on the other hand, doesn't like the car, so he stays home.

▶ Break stringy sentences in your story into shorter sentences.

GRAMMAR LINK ▶ See also page 47.

Revising   **339**

The Writing Process — PREWRITING · DRAFTING · REVISING · **PROOFREADING** · PUBLISHING

Proofread Your Story

Proofread your story, using the Proofreading Checklist and the Grammar and Spelling Connections. Proofread for one skill at a time. Then use a dictionary to check spellings.

Proofreading Checklist
Did I…
- ✓ indent all paragraphs?
- ✓ correct any stringy or run-on sentences?
- ✓ punctuate dialogue correctly?
- ✓ write contractions correctly?
- ✓ spell all words correctly?

Use the Guide to Capitalization, Punctuation, and Usage on page H57.

Proofreading Marks
- ¶ Indent
- ∧ Add
- ℐ Delete
- ≡ Capital letter
- / Small letter

Tech Tip Use the Find function to search for the words *and, but, or,* or *so.* Break stringy sentences into shorter sentences.

Grammar and Spelling Connections

Writing Dialogue Use quotation marks and commas to set off a speaker's exact words. Capitalize the first word. Place end punctuation inside the quotation marks.

Statement	"Sorry I'm late," apologized Sid.
Exclamation	"You're never on time!" Emily grumbled.
Question	"Where were you?" asked Joe.
Divided quotation	"Well," admitted Sid, "I overslept."

 GRAMMAR LINK See also page 194.

Spelling the |ā| and |ē| Sounds The |ā| sound is often spelled *ai, ay,* or *a*-consonant-*e*. The |ē| sound is often spelled *ee* or *ea*.

s**ai**l, pl**ay**, t**a**m**e**, f**ee**l, h**ea**t

See the Spelling Guide on page H67.

340 Unit 9: Story   Go to www.eduplace.com/kids/hme/ for proofreading practice.

PREWRITING   DRAFTING   REVISING   PROOFREADING   **PUBLISHING**

▶ Publish Your Story

❶ Make a neat final copy of your story. Be sure you fixed all mistakes.

❷ Title your story. The title should make your audience curious. "Giggles Saves the Day" is more inviting than "Visiting the Circus."

GRAMMAR TIP ▶ Capitalize the first, the last, and each important word in a title.

❸ Publish or share your story so that it appeals to your audience. See the Ideas for Sharing box.

Tips for Storytelling
- Speak clearly, slowly, and loudly enough to be understood by your audience.
- Use different voices for different characters.
- Read with expression. Pause at commas, raise your voice at the end of questions, and say exclamations with feeling.

Ideas for Sharing
Write It
- Send it to a magazine or an Internet site that publishes student writing.
- Make a story book and illustrate the events.

Say It
- Dress up as the main character and tell the story to your classmates.

Show It
- Make a diorama and attach your story to it.

▶ Reflect

Write about your writing experience. Use these questions to get started.
- What did you like best about writing your story? What was the hardest part?
- What ideas do you have for another story?
- How does this story compare to other papers you have written?

Publishing   **341**

Assessment Link

Writing Prompts

Use these prompts as story topics or to practice for a test. Decide who your audience will be, and write a story that you think they will understand and enjoy.

1 Write a story about a fifth-grade student who wakes up invisible. What does the student like and dislike about being invisible? What happens?

2 Write a story about two best friends who are after-school detectives. Who needs their help? What has happened? How do the friends solve the mystery?

3 Write a story about a talking animal that teaches a lesson to a human. Who are these characters? How do they meet? What's the lesson?

4 Choose an inanimate object—something that is not alive—such as an alarm clock, a backpack, or a baseball bat. Write a story from this object's point of view.

Writing Across the Curriculum

5 **FINE ART**

Who are the riders? Where are they going? How did the fire get started, and how long will it last? Write a story about the fire and the riders.

Prairie Fire, by Francis Blackbear Bosin

Watercolor on paper, 1953
The Philbrook Museum of Art

See www.eduplace.com/kids/hme/ for more prompts.

Assessment Link

✓ Test Practice

This prompt to write a story is like ones you might find on a writing test. Read the prompt.

> Write a story about **two best friends** who are after-school **detectives**. Who needs their help? **What has happened?** How do the friends **solve the mystery**?

These strategies can help you do a good job of responding to a prompt like this.

Remember that a story is an original narrative made up by the author.

❶ Look for clue words that tell what to write about. What are the clue words in the prompt above?

❷ Choose a plot that fits the clue words. Write the clue words and your plot.

Clue Words	My Topic
two best friends—detectives What has happened? solve the mystery	I will write about a missing backpack. The backpack will be found in a doghouse!

❸ Plan your writing. Use a story map.

Beginning:	
Middle:	
End:	

❹ You will get a good score if you remember the description of the kind of story that rings the bell in the rubric on page 337.

Test Practice **343**

Special Focus on Entertaining

Writing a Play

A **play** is a story written to be performed by actors on a stage. The author tells the story through the characters' dialogue and actions. Read the play below.

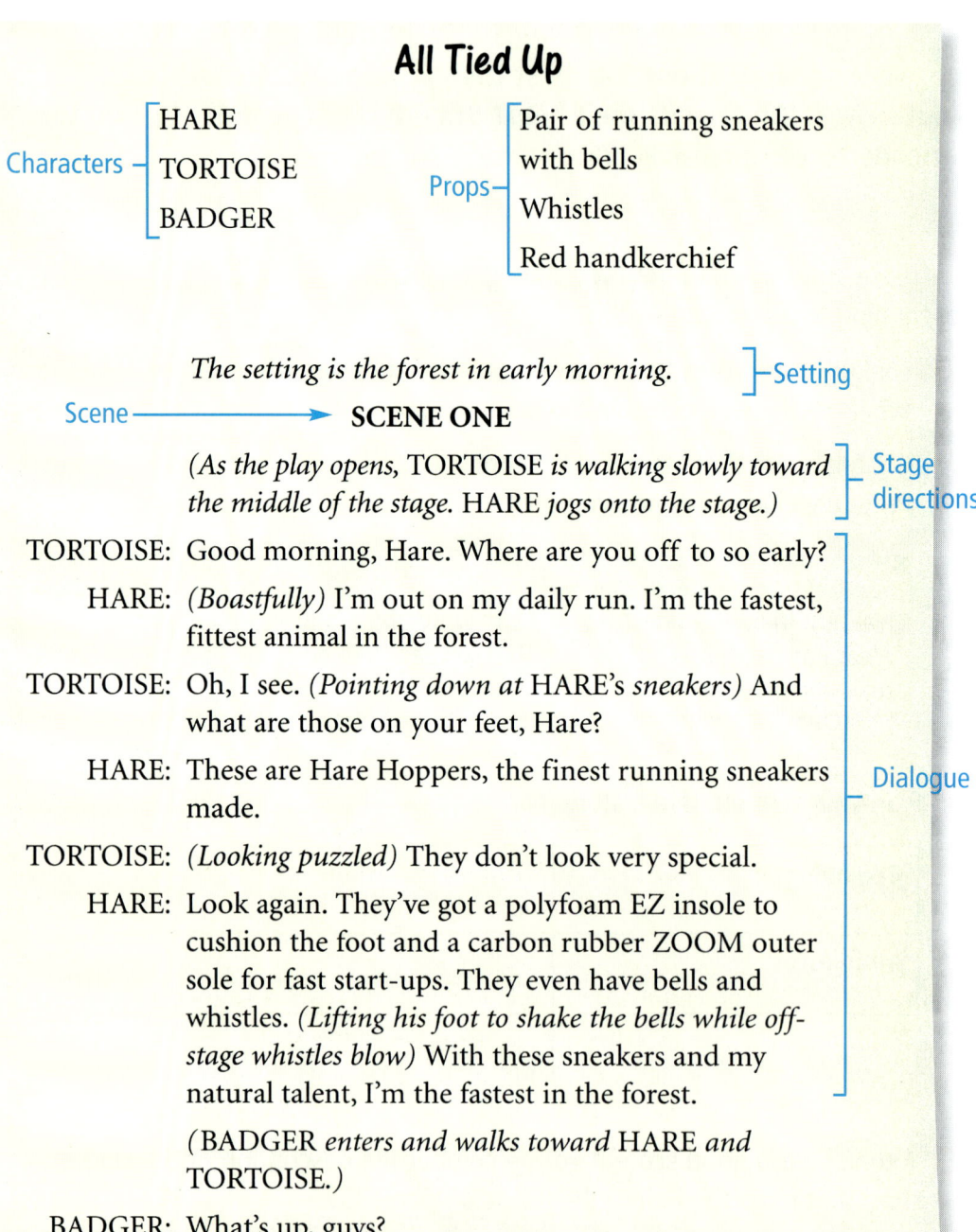

All Tied Up

Characters — HARE, TORTOISE, BADGER

Props — Pair of running sneakers with bells, Whistles, Red handkerchief

The setting is the forest in early morning. — Setting

Scene ⟶ **SCENE ONE**

(*As the play opens,* TORTOISE *is walking slowly toward the middle of the stage.* HARE *jogs onto the stage.*) — Stage directions

TORTOISE: Good morning, Hare. Where are you off to so early?

HARE: *(Boastfully)* I'm out on my daily run. I'm the fastest, fittest animal in the forest.

TORTOISE: Oh, I see. *(Pointing down at* HARE's *sneakers)* And what are those on your feet, Hare?

HARE: These are Hare Hoppers, the finest running sneakers made.

TORTOISE: *(Looking puzzled)* They don't look very special.

HARE: Look again. They've got a polyfoam EZ insole to cushion the foot and a carbon rubber ZOOM outer sole for fast start-ups. They even have bells and whistles. *(Lifting his foot to shake the bells while off-stage whistles blow)* With these sneakers and my natural talent, I'm the fastest in the forest.

(BADGER *enters and walks toward* HARE *and* TORTOISE.)

BADGER: What's up, guys?

— Dialogue

344 Unit 9: Story

TORTOISE: Hare has just been telling me about his special sneakers. He's sure he's the fastest animal in the forest.

BADGER: Then why don't we have a race to find out?

HARE: But who would race me? All the animals know I can't be beat.

TORTOISE: *(Shyly)* I'll race you.

HARE: *(Laughing)* You? You're joking!

TORTOISE: No, I'm not.

BADGER: Well then, let's have a race. Meet back here at four o'clock sharp.

(ALL *leave the stage.* HARE *runs,* BADGER *walks, and* TORTOISE *walks slowly.*)

SCENE TWO

(*Later that same day. Chalk lines on the floor mark the start and finish lines for the race.* TORTOISE *and* HARE *stand side by side at the starting line.* BADGER *stands next to them.*)

BADGER: *(Waving a red handkerchief in the air)* Are you ready? (TORTOISE *and* HARE *look at each other and then nod.*) On your mark, get set, GO! (BADGER *drops the handkerchief as he says "GO!" and then moves to the finish.*)

(HARE *runs across the stage and then exits as* TORTOISE *walks slowly across the stage. Off-stage, bells ring and whistles blow.* HARE *comes back on stage and sits down.*)

HARE: I might as well rest a while. Tortoise will never catch up. (HARE *yawns, leans back, and goes to sleep.* BADGER *tiptoes over to* HARE *and ties* HARE's *sneakers together as* TORTOISE *watches.* BADGER *holds his finger to his lips to say "Sh," and walks to the finish line.* TORTOISE *continues to inch across the stage until he or she is almost at the finish line.*)

more ▶

Writing a Play

Special Focus *continued*

BADGER: *(With enthusiasm)* Come on, Tortoise, you can do it!

HARE: *(Sitting up, noticing that* TORTOISE *is about to win the race)* Oh, no! *(Jumps up and starts to run, but stumbles)*

*(*TORTOISE *crosses the finish line.)*

HARE: *(Untying his sneakers and then walking over to* TORTOISE*)* I can't believe it! You won!

TORTOISE: *(Putting a hand on* HARE's *shoulder)* You know, my friend, slow and steady really does win the race. Sorry you were caught napping.

CURTAIN

Reading As a Writer

- The list of **characters** tells who is in the play.
  What are the names of the characters in this play?
- The **props** are the items the characters will use in the play.
  What props are used in this play?
- A **scene** presents the action that happens in one place at a certain time.
  What happens in Scene One?
- The **setting** tells where and when the action takes place.
  What is the setting for Scene Two?
- The **stage directions** tell the characters what to do.
  How does Hare come on stage at the beginning of the play?
- A character's **dialogue** tells what the character is thinking, seeing, and feeling.
  What does Hare say in Scene One that shows how he feels about himself?

How to Write a Play

❶ Choose a story idea for a short play that you think will interest or entertain your audience. Be sure you can tell the story using dialogue and action. Use only a few characters and one or two settings. When choosing, think about these points.

- What is the problem or conflict?
- What is the play's setting? Is it appropriate for the problem or conflict?

Stuck for an Idea?
Try one of these.
- a favorite tale
- a story of your own
- an event from history
- a funny or unusual experience

Some settings are very specific, such as "the principal's office" or "the laboratory of a scientific genius." However, many plays have a setting that's general, such as "a forest," "a street at dawn," or "an island."

You can use a T-chart to help you list details about your characters. Look at the sample T-chart below for Hare, Tortoise, and Badger. Notice that the characters' names are across the top and details about each character are listed below his or her name.

Hare	Tortoise	Badger
high energy	slow, but sure	trickster
boastful	shy	enthusiastic

❷ Plan your play. Use a story map like the one below to help you. Add details about your characters' actions and about the setting or settings. Think about what will happen in each scene. The plot in a play is similar to the plot in a story. However, in a play, the characters' dialogue moves the story forward. There is usually no narrator to tell the audience details about what is happening and why.

Character	Setting	Plot
		Beginning
		Middle
		End

more ▶

Special Focus *continued*

❸ Write your play.

- List your characters.
- Write stage directions telling what actions the characters will be taking at the beginning of the play.
- Use dialogue to tell the story. Be sure to write the way you think the characters would talk. The dialogue should help tell the story. Write more stage directions throughout the play to tell how characters talk and act.
- If the action moves from one place to another, divide your play into scenes. Describe the setting of each scene and give stage directions.
- End your play in a way that wraps up the action. Did you resolve the central conflict? Do the characters get what they need or want? Why or why not? When you have finished, write BLACKOUT or CURTAIN.

❹ Read your play aloud to yourself or with one or more partners.

- Read the dialogue with expression. Does the dialogue sound natural? Does it reflect the characters' personalities? Is it appropriate for your purpose and audience?
- Walk through the action. Are the stage directions helpful? Are any other directions needed?
- Is more dialogue or action needed to make the problem and the solution clear? Should anything be taken out?

Do you need some help with the dialogue? Listen to the conversations around you. Write down some common things people say.

348 Unit 9: Story

5 **Revise** your play. Ask yourself these questions.

- Is the plot clear?
- Is the play too short?
- Should any characters be taken out or added?
- Are any of the parts uninteresting or unclear?
- Do the final events make the play feel finished?

6 **Proofread** your play. Did you spell the characters' names consistently? Is the end punctuation accurate for the expression you want in the dialogue? Use the Proofreading Checklist on page 340. Use a dictionary to check your spelling.

7 **Make** a neat final copy.

8 **Perform** your play for an audience, such as your classmates or parents.

HELP See page 350–351 for guidelines on how to dramatize a character.

Here are some other suggestions:

- Conduct a readers' theater, or staged reading. There's no need to memorize the dialogue, but everyone should read with feeling.
- Videotape your play. Send it to a friend or family member.

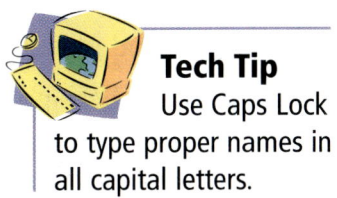

Tech Tip
Use Caps Lock to type proper names in all capital letters.

Writing a Play

COMMUNICATION LINK **Speaking**

Dramatizing

In a movie or a play, actors dramatize, or act out, a story. They bring the characters and events to life by speaking and moving as the characters would. You can dramatize a character from a story or play, or you can choose a poem or personal experience to act out.

Start Thinking

Read the example below and think about how the characters are feeling. What facial expressions and gestures would you use to act out this scene?

DAN: *(Turning on his flashlight)* It's getting dark. We'd better switch on our flashlights.

SARAH: *(Turning on her light and stepping over a root)* Yeah, watch the roots. I think we should head for the river if we want to find any beaver.

DAN: Good idea! Maybe if we're really quiet, we'll get to see one.

SARAH: OK. Let's go!

(Dan and Sarah step carefully over rocks and roots. Finally they reach the river's edge.)

DAN: *(Excitedly, pointing to the ground at his feet)* Look! Over here! Tracks in the mud!

SARAH: *(Also excited, pointing off into the woods)* See that stump? It looks like somebody's been hard at work!

350 Unit 9: Story

Think About It

How would you change your voice to express the different parts of the scene on page 350? Would you use the same facial expressions as the ones in the photograph? What other expressions might work?

Use these guidelines to help you dramatize.

Guidelines for Dramatizing

1. Put yourself in your character's shoes. Is your character courageous, generous, or kind? Why does your character act in a certain way?
2. Use your speaking voice. By changing the volume, rate, pitch, and tone of your voice, you can express your character's feelings.
3. Use facial expressions. For example, a wrinkled forehead may show that someone is puzzled or confused.
4. Use gestures. Stamping your foot and crossing your arms can mean you are unhappy and frustrated.
5. Speak clearly but naturally. Be sure your audience can hear all of your words.

Using Your Voice	
volume	means loudness
rate	means speed
pitch	means how high or how low it sounds
tone	means mood

Apply It

Choose a scene from a play or story to dramatize. Then follow the Guidelines for Dramatizing as you practice. Present the scene to a small group or to the class. You may want to wear a simple costume and use simple props.

- What was your character's mood?
- What facial expressions, gestures, and voices did you use to show different feelings?
- What worked well? What would you do differently if you were to dramatize this character again?

COMMUNICATION LINK Viewing

Comparing Stories in Print and on Film

Filmmakers often adapt, or change, stories when they film them for a movie. As a result, a story printed in a book or magazine can be quite different from the movie version. The chart below compares some of the differences between storytelling in books and in movies.

Stories in Print	Stories on Film
The writer uses words to describe all parts of the story. Readers then create pictures in their own minds.	The filmmaker uses images and sounds to show the audience the story.
The writer can let the reader into the characters' thoughts and emotions by describing them to the reader.	The filmmaker shows the audience what the characters are thinking and feeling. Actors behave and speak in specific ways.
The writer describes the setting.	The filmmaker builds a set or chooses a location to show the setting.
The writer uses words to create the mood, or feeling, of the story.	The filmmaker uses music, sound effects, and lighting to create the mood.
The writer can take as many pages as he or she likes to tell the story	The filmmaker has a limited time to tell the story, so events in the story may be cut or changed for the screen.

To compare the same story in a book and in a movie, you need to notice what has changed and what has stayed the same. These guidelines will help you.

Guidelines for Comparing a Story in Print and on Film

1 Plot
- What events happened only in the book? only in the movie?
- What events were changed for the movie? Why do you think so?

2 Characters
- Which characters appeared only in the book? only in the movie?
- In what ways was a character in the book different from the same character in the movie?
- Did character changes affect the story? How?

3 Setting and Mood
- How was the setting in the book similar to or different from the movie's setting?
- How was the mood of the story similar or different?
- How did changes in the setting and the mood affect the story?

Apply It

Choose a printed story you have read that has been made into a movie. Watch the movie. Use the guidelines above to take notes comparing the book and the movie. Then write a summary from your notes, answering the questions below.

- Which medium—printed story or film version—did you prefer? Why?
- How were the book and the movie alike? What were their biggest differences?
- If you were making a movie from the story in the book, how would you make it differently?

Books with Movie Versions
- Mary Poppins
- The Borrowers
- My Friend Flicka
- Where the Red Fern Grows
- The Adventures of Tom Sawyer

Section 2
Explaining and Informing

What You Will Find in This Section:

Getting Started
- Listening for Information 356
- Writing Informational Paragraphs 357

Unit 10 Writing to Compare and Contrast 364

Special Focus on Explaining
Writing Instructions 388

Communication Links
Listening/Speaking:
Giving and Following Instructions 394

Viewing/Media:
Comparing Visual Information 396

Unit 11

Writing a Research Report 398

Special Focus on Informing
Writing to Solve a Problem 428
Writing a News Article 430
Completing a Form 432

Communication Links
Speaking/Viewing/Media:
Giving an Oral Report 434
Viewing/Media: Evaluating the News ... 436

Getting Started: Listening

Listening for Information

When you listen to the news or call the movie theater for recorded show times, you are listening for **factual information**. **Facts** can be proved true. You can use factual information to increase your knowledge, to solve problems, and to make decisions. Here are some guidelines that will help you to listen successfully.

Guidelines for Listening for Information

▶ Identify the topic. What subject is the author talking about?
▶ Listen for the main idea. What does the author have to say about the topic?
▶ Notice facts and examples. How do they support, or explain, the main idea?
▶ Consider the source of the information. Is it reliable? Can you trust the facts to be accurate?
▶ Listen for the author's purpose. Why is the author telling about this topic?

Try It Out Listen as your teacher reads aloud from "Dancing Bees," an informational chapter by Margery Facklam that explains why bees don't need road maps! Listen for facts to answer the questions below.

- What is the topic?
- What is the main idea?
- What are some facts that elaborate the main idea?
- Why do you think Margery Facklam wrote this chapter?

356 Section 2: Explaining and Informing

See www.eduplace.com/kids for information about Margery Facklam.

Getting Started: Paragraphs

Writing Informational Paragraphs

A paragraph that gives facts is called an **informational paragraph**. The writer's purpose is to share information about a topic he or she knows well.

An informational paragraph has a topic and a main idea. The **topic** is the subject of the paragraph. The **main idea** is what the writer wants to say about the topic. What is the topic of the informational paragraph below? What is the main idea?

Remember to indent the first line of a paragraph.

Indent —
Topic sentence —
Supporting sentences —
Concluding sentence —

Cave explorers, known as spelunkers, rely on good equipment to avoid injury. Hardhats, for example, keep heads dry and protect against falling rocks. Even more important are strong ropes that prevent spelunkers from falling from steep cliffs. Most explorers consider light to be the most important safety tool. They always carry two kinds—a flashlight and a headlamp. With the right equipment, spelunkers can turn a risky activity into a fascinating adventure.

The topic is spelunking equipment. The main idea is that cave explorers rely on such equipment for safety. Which sentence states the topic and the main idea? The labels show the three parts of an informational paragraph.

- The **topic sentence** states the topic and tells the writer's main idea.
- **Supporting sentences** usually follow the topic sentence and give facts about the main idea.
- The **concluding sentence** wraps up the paragraph.

Think and Discuss What facts does the writer include in the supporting sentences in the cave paragraph?

Getting Started: Paragraphs

The Topic Sentence

 On the previous page, you saw that a **topic sentence** names the topic and tells what the writer wants to say about it. A good topic sentence will also make the reader curious to read more.

                           Main idea   Topic

Example: Despite the fact that ice and snow cover 98 percent of Antarctica, hundreds of rugged creatures still call it home.

                       Main idea

In informational paragraphs, the topic sentence usually comes first. However, it may also come at the end of the paragraph and take the place of the concluding sentence. Which is the topic sentence in the paragraph below? Which are the supporting sentences?

> The largest living animal on the snow-covered Antarctic mainland is the wingless midge, a tiny fly. Closer to the coast, however, the climate is milder and moister. Birds nest along the coast. Penguins waddle across the ice. Seals dive for fish. Migrating whales visit in summer. The harsh mainland supports only a few creatures, but the Antarctic Ocean bursts with life.

Try It Out Read the paragraph below. It is missing the topic sentence. On your own or with a partner, write the paragraph's topic and main idea. Then write two possible topic sentences.

> _____Topic sentence_____. His natural curiosity, along with scientific experiments, produced many useful inventions. Franklin invented the lightning rod, which protects buildings. He designed the Franklin stove, which produces efficient heat. Benjamin Franklin also invented bifocal glasses, which help people read things up close and see things far away with one pair of glasses. Franklin's inventions have made people's lives safer, warmer, and clearer.

358 Section 2: Explaining and Informing

Supporting Sentences

Supporting sentences usually follow the topic sentence. They give details that explain the main idea. In informational writing, some details are **facts**, such as numbers. Other details are **sensory words**, which tell how something looks, sounds, smells, feels, or tastes.

The heating process with solar power is simple, clean, and efficient. First, collectors placed on a roof or on the sunny side of a house absorb solar energy from sunlight. This energy heats water, which flows into a large storage tank. Then, when the house is chilly, cool air is pulled into this tank, warmed, and pumped throughout the house by a fan. Without using fuel burned in a dirty furnace, a home can stay toasty warm, even on the rawest winter day.

Think and Discuss What facts and sensory words are in the above paragraph? in the paragraph about Antarctica on page 358?

Ordering Details Supporting sentences in an informational paragraph are arranged in an order that makes sense.

- Details describing events, such as those in the solar power paragraph, are usually told in **time order**.
- Other kinds of details, such as those in the paragraph about spelunkers on page 357, are told in **order of importance**, from most important to least important or from least important to most important.
- Descriptive details that describe something are arranged in **spatial order**, the order in which you might look at something.

Transitional words and phrases, such as *first, also, another point, to the right, finally,* and *more important,* help readers follow the order of the details more easily. They also help readers see how ideas are connected.

See page 16 for tips on ordering details. See page 18 for more transitional words.

more ▶

Getting Started: Informational Paragraphs

Getting Started: Paragraphs

Try It Out On your own or with a partner, look at the diagram below. Use what you see and the facts provided to write some supporting sentences for the topic sentence. Link two of your sentences with a transitional word or phrase.

Topic sentence: From the Statue of Liberty, you can see for miles.

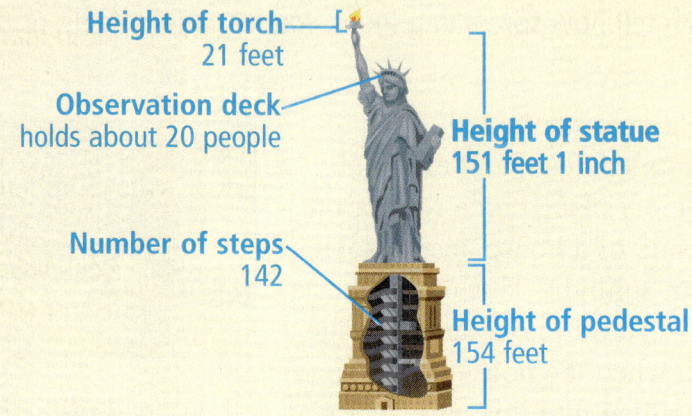

- **Height of torch** 21 feet
- **Observation deck** holds about 20 people
- **Number of steps** 142
- **Height of statue** 151 feet 1 inch
- **Height of pedestal** 154 feet

GRAMMAR TIP Remember to change the forms of the verbs **be** and **have** to agree with their subjects (examples: The torch **is/has**; the steps **are/have**).

The Concluding Sentence

The **concluding sentence** can restate the main idea or add a final comment. For example, the spelunker paragraph on page 357 ends with an interesting restatement of the main idea. The Ben Franklin paragraph on page 358 ends with a final comment.

Try It Out Read the paragraph below. It is missing the concluding sentence. On your own or with a partner, write two different concluding sentences.

Giraffes are unique in size and shape. As the tallest living creatures, they can measure 17 feet from their black hooves to their bony horns. Giraffes' skinny legs are 6 feet long, and their straight necks may be even longer. Adult males weigh about 2,600 pounds, far less than other large animals. It would take five giraffes to weigh as much as one male African elephant. _____Concluding sentence_____.

Section 2: Explaining and Informing

Paragraphs That Compare and Contrast

Some informational paragraphs compare and contrast two subjects. When you show how two subjects are alike, you **compare** them. When you show how two subjects are different, you **contrast** them. You can compare and contrast in a single paragraph. If two subjects are alike and different in many ways, however, you may need to compare and contrast them in separate paragraphs.

Each **paragraph that compares and contrasts** has a topic sentence. It has supporting sentences that explain what is the same or what is different about the two subjects. Transitional words and phrases, such as *on the other hand*, *similarly*, or *in contrast*, help connect the supporting sentences. Which sentences compare and which contrast in the paragraphs below? What transitional words can you find?

Topic sentence — It's easy to understand why toads and frogs are often mistaken for one another. They have the same body shape, and they both capture their prey with their long, sticky tongues. Like toads, frogs go through three life stages—egg, tadpole, and adult—and spend the first two stages in the water.

Supporting sentences

Topic sentence — If you observe toads and frogs more closely, however, you will notice certain differences. First, toads have a broader, flatter body and shorter, less powerful back legs than frogs. Also, their skin is dry and rough and covered with bumps, but frogs have smooth skin. Finally, most toads spend most of their adult life on land, while frogs continue to live in or near the water. Next time you read a fairy tale, see if you can tell what the princess is kissing!

Supporting sentences

Concluding sentence

Try It Out On your own or with a partner, choose one of the pairs listed below. Write at least three supporting sentences that compare and contrast the two subjects.

- a helicopter and an airplane
- fourth grade and fifth grade
- figure skating and hockey

Getting Started: Informational Paragraphs

Getting Started: Paragraphs

Paragraphs That Show Cause and Effect

A **paragraph that shows cause and effect** explains why or how one thing makes another thing happen. In this type of paragraph, the topic sentence can introduce the cause, an effect, or both. The supporting sentences give details about causes or effects. Transitional words and phrases, such as *first, because, soon after, as a result,* and *a consequence of,* show how ideas are connected. A concluding sentence wraps up the paragraph.

Read the paragraph below. What is the cause? What are the effects?

Topic sentence — When an oil tanker runs aground, a response team is alerted. Within the hour, a cleanup effort is in full swing. First, the team makes an "overflight" by helicopter to survey the scene. Once they see crude oil spilling into the ocean, they consult a special computer program to estimate the size of the spill and the direction it is traveling. If the spill is drifting toward nearby wildlife, volunteers set up a *boom,* or floating barrier, to keep the oil away. Finally, a boat is sent to spray chemicals that break the oil into small droplets so that it decomposes more easily. **Concluding sentence** — As a result of the team's quick response, the damage to the environment can be minimal.

Supporting sentences

Try It Out On your own or with a partner, identify the cause stated in the topic sentence below. Then write at least three supporting sentences that explain its effects. Use a transitional word or phrase to connect two of your sentences.

Topic sentence: When an oil spill contaminates a beach, it puts the lives of the animals that live there in danger.

Write Your Own Informational Paragraph

Now it's time for you to write your own informational paragraph. You may decide to write a paragraph that compares and contrasts, one that shows cause and effect, or one that explains what something is or does.

First, think of a topic that you know well and that you will enjoy writing about. Then make a list of details to include. After you share your ideas with a partner, you will be ready to write.

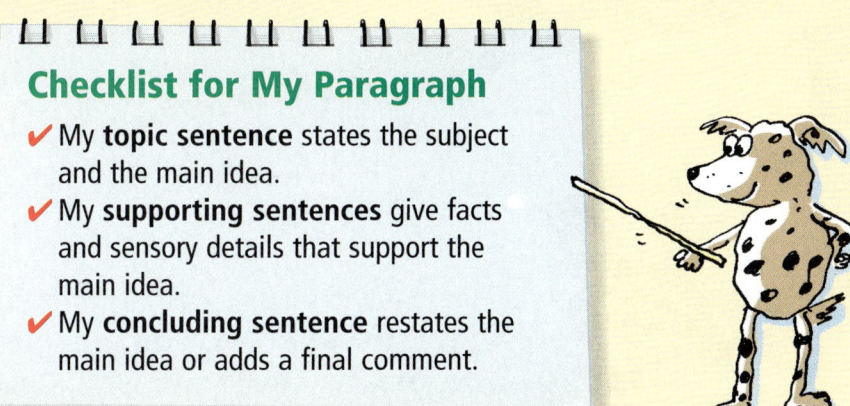

Checklist for My Paragraph
- ✔ My **topic sentence** states the subject and the main idea.
- ✔ My **supporting sentences** give facts and sensory details that support the main idea.
- ✔ My **concluding sentence** restates the main idea or adds a final comment.

Looking Ahead

Knowing how to write an informational paragraph will make it easier to write a longer composition. The diagram below shows how the parts of an informational paragraph match the parts of a longer composition.

Informational Paragraph .... **Informational Composition**

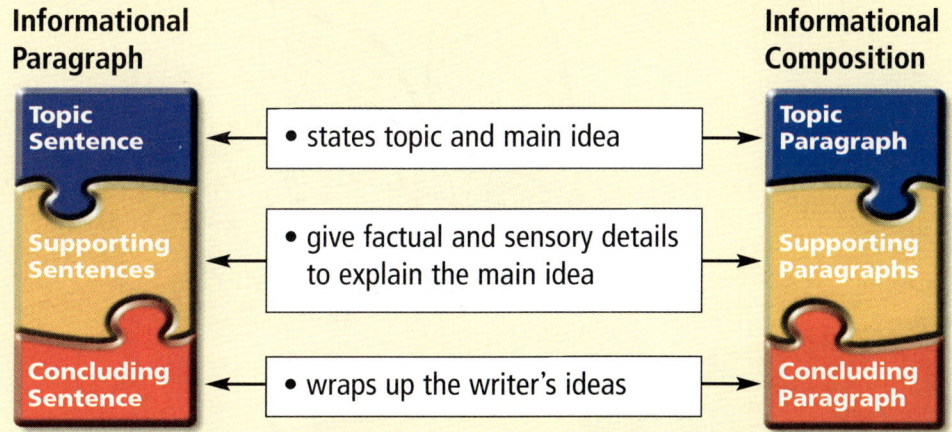

Topic Sentence	← states topic and main idea →	Topic Paragraph
Supporting Sentences	← give factual and sensory details to explain the main idea →	Supporting Paragraphs
Concluding Sentence	← wraps up the writer's ideas →	Concluding Paragraph

Getting Started: Informational Paragraphs

Unit 10

Writing to Compare and Contrast

In what *other* ways are a man in a tuxedo and a penguin alike? In what ways are they different?

In this essay, the author compares and contrasts hurricanes and tornadoes. Why did he choose these two subjects to write about?

Hurricanes and Tornadoes

from *Hurricanes and Tornadoes: When Disaster Strikes*, by Keith Greenberg

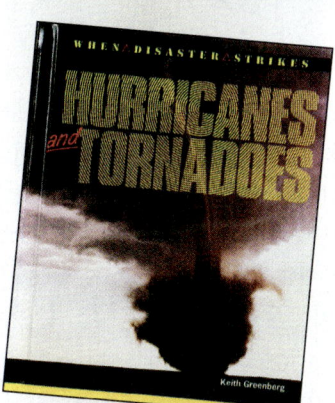

Hurricanes and tornadoes are two of the most violent and devastating types of storms that occur, as many people have had the misfortune to experience. Aside from their very destructive characteristics, hurricanes and tornadoes share a few other similarities. Both of them depend on warm, moist air to start, and both are accompanied by fierce winds, rain or hail, and low air pressure.

While hurricanes and tornadoes do have some things in common, they are two distinct types of storms. Hurricanes begin over water, and tornadoes start over land. A tornado has a shape like an upside-down cone, while a hurricane swirls around a calm center, or an eye, in a doughnutlike pattern. Although a hurricane is much larger and lasts longer, a tornado tends to be more treacherous and hits with less warning.

When storm winds start gusting to 74 miles (119 kilometers) per hour, the storm is labeled a hurricane. Hurricanes create a rising wall of water that frequently washes onto beaches, piers, and private property. Called a storm surge, this water can climb as high as 25 feet (8 meters) above sea level. The storm surge is what is responsible for the greatest number of deaths during hurricanes, when many people drown in the roaring waters. In addition to ferocious winds and flooding, hurricanes bring heavy rains and, sometimes, tornadoes.

A tornado—also known as a twister—is distinguished by spinning, funnel-shaped clouds moving along the ground, and winds up to 310 miles (499 kilometers) per hour. Anything that stands in its path—trees, cars, buildings—is in danger of being completely destroyed.

Reading As a Writer

Think About the Compare-Contrast Essay
- Why are hurricanes and tornadoes good subjects for a compare-contrast essay?
- Where does the author first name the two subjects he is writing about?
- Which sentences on page 365 tell how the two kinds of storms are alike? Which tell how they are different?
- How does the author organize his information?

Think About Writer's Craft
- Where does the author use figures of speech to describe the shape or pattern of each storm?
- What descriptive words help you to see, feel, and hear these storms?

Think About the Pictures
- How do the photographs add to your understanding of tornadoes? What information do the photographs convey that an illustration might not convey?

Responding

Write responses to these questions.
- **Personal Response** How have storms you have experienced been similar to or different from the storms described in this essay?
- **Critical Thinking** Find sentences describing the devastation hurricanes and tornadoes can cause. How can understanding a storm's potential for destruction help people protect themselves and their property?

What Makes a Great Compare-Contrast Essay?

A **compare-contrast essay** tells how two things are alike and how they are different. When you compare, you explain how the subjects are similar. When you contrast, you explain their differences.

When you write a compare-contrast essay, remember these guidelines.

▶ Choose two subjects that have something in common.
▶ Write an attention-grabbing introduction that states your subjects.
▶ Compare and contrast corresponding details for each subject.
▶ Use one method of organization from beginning to end.
▶ Use topic sentences to state your main ideas.
▶ Use transitional words and phrases to compare and contrast.
▶ Write an ending that sums up your main ideas.

GRAMMAR CHECK

Use singular verbs with singular subjects in your sentences. Use plural verbs with plural subjects.

Student Model

WORKING DRAFT

Portia Caldwell has played the piano since she was in the first grade, and recently her dad showed her a few chords on the guitar. Read Portia's draft comparing these two instruments.

Portia Caldwell

I'm writing this essay to compare and contrast the piano and the guitar. Have you ever thought about what a piano and a guitar have in common? At this moment, I know you are saying to yourself, "No, I haven't," or "They don't have anything in common."

> You state your two subjects, but will this introduction interest your readers?

You may have to look closely to see the similarities, but they are there. Like the piano, the guitar is enclosed in a shiny wooden case. You need to use two hands to play either instrument. Both the piano and the guitar have strings that vibrate to make beautiful sharp and flat notes. When played by a knowledgeable piano or guitar player, these notes can be put together to produce melodies. Classical music, contemporary, rock-and-roll, blues, and ragtime can be played using the piano as well as the guitar. The piano is a large percussion instrument. The guitar is a small flat-bodied stringed instrument.

> I like this detail about the vibrating strings.

> Does every sentence here tell a similarity?

more →

Student Model continued

The differences are easier to spot, especially in appearance. The piano has a long keyboard. The guitar has a long fretted neck. The piano stands on its own wooden legs. The guitar usually hangs from a strap ~~and must be held. In my opinion, pianos are nicer-looking than guitars, especially baby grands. I love those! Uprights are okay, but baby grands are really amazing to look at!~~

To play the piano comfortably, you must sit in an upright position so you can reach the keys and the pedals. With a guitar, you can easily sit, stand, or even stroll around while you play.

Does this paragraph need a topic sentence?

A piano player makes sounds by pushing on keys, which causes hammers to hit the strings. A guitar player uses his or her hands to strum or pluck the strings. A piano player has to be concerned with playing eighty-eight keys. A guitar player only has about six or more strings to worry about.

A piano and a guitar can be played for fun or as a profession. When I told my father about pop star Elton John and his success playing the piano, Dad reminded me about B. B. King. He learned to play his guitar, Lucille, for fun but enjoyed a successful career playing it professionally.

These are nice details about guitar players, but do these sentences belong here?

Reading As a Writer

- What questions and comments did Sal have? What revisions might Portia make?
- Which sentences describe similarities? Which describe differences?
- How are the paragraphs organized? Do any sentences need to be moved? Which ones?
- Why did Portia cross out some sentences in paragraph three?
- What could Portia do to make her essay feel less cut off at the end?

Student Model

FINAL COPY

Portia revised her essay after discussing it with classmates. Read the final version to see what changes she made.

Strings That Sing
by Portia Caldwell

What's your favorite instrument? I've always liked the piano best and have played since the first grade. Recently, my dad showed me a few chords on the guitar. While I knew there were plenty of differences between the piano and the guitar, I was surprised to discover they have a lot in common too.

You may have to look closely to see the similarities, but they are there. Like the piano, the guitar is enclosed in a shiny wooden case. You need to use two hands to play either instrument. Both the piano and the guitar have strings that vibrate to make beautiful sharp and flat notes. When played by a knowledgeable piano or guitar player, these notes can be put together to produce melodies. Classical and contemporary music, rock-and-roll, blues, and ragtime can be played using the piano as well as the guitar. A piano and a guitar can be played for fun or as a profession. When I told my father about pop star Elton John and his success playing the piano, Dad reminded me about B. B. King. He learned to play his guitar, Lucille, for fun but enjoyed a successful career playing it professionally.

The differences between the two instruments are easier to spot, especially in appearance. While the piano is a large percussion instrument, the guitar is a small

Your new introduction is much more interesting!

The transitional words you added to contrast your two subjects make these paragraphs sound much smoother.

flat-bodied stringed instrument. The piano has a long keyboard, but the guitar has a long fretted neck. Unlike the piano, which stands on its own wooden legs, the guitar usually hangs from a strap and must be held.

There are differences in how the instruments are played too. To play the piano comfortably, you must sit in an upright position so you can reach the keys and the pedals. However, with a guitar, you can easily sit, stand, or even stroll around while you play. While a piano player makes sounds by pushing on keys, which causes small hammers to hit the strings, a guitar player uses his or her hands to strum or pluck the strings. A piano player has to be concerned with playing eighty-eight keys, but a guitar player only has about six or more strings to worry about.

> This topic sentence helps introduce the subject of this paragraph.

When I first picked up that guitar, I thought I'd be starting from scratch. It turned out I was able to transfer a lot of what I already know about playing the piano to learning to play the guitar. Don't be afraid to try something that seems completely new. You just might be surprised. You probably know more about it than you think you do!

> Now your essay feels finished!

Reading As a Writer

- What did Portia do to respond to Sal's questions?
- What did Portia do to improve her introduction? her conclusion?
- What transitional words did Portia add to paragraphs three and four?
- Which sentences did Portia move? Why did she move them?

See www.eduplace.com/kids/hme/ for more examples of student writing.   Student Model   **373**

The Writing Process

PREWRITING · DRAFTING · REVISING · PROOFREADING · PUBLISHING

Write a Compare-Contrast Essay

▶ Start Thinking

 Make a writing folder for your compare-contrast essay. Copy the questions in bold print, and put the paper in your folder. Write your answers as you think about and choose your topic.

- **Who will be my audience?** Will it be someone unfamiliar with my topic? Will it be my classmates? a younger child?
- **What will be my purpose?** Do I want to define an unfamiliar subject by comparing it to something familiar? clear up confusion about two closely related subjects? show that one subject is better than another?
- **How will I publish or share my essay?** Will I publish it as a magazine article? read it aloud to classmates? make a diagram for display?

▶ Choose Your Topic

① List five pairs of familiar subjects that you could compare and contrast.

② Discuss your ideas with a partner.

- Play catch, either with or without a ball. For each pair of subjects, "throw" your partner a similarity. Your partner must then "throw the ball back" by stating a difference. Continue playing until one of you can't think of anything more to say.

③ Choose a topic. Ask yourself these questions about each pair of subjects. Then circle the pair you will write about.

- Do I know enough about both subjects?
- Can I think of at least three ways in which these subjects are alike and three ways in which they are different?

 Stuck for an Idea?

Think about these pairs.
- a book and its movie version
- an e-mail and a handwritten letter
- travel by car and travel by bus
- firefighters and EMTs

See page 386 for more ideas.

PREWRITING DRAFTING REVISING PROOFREADING PUBLISHING

▶ Explore Your Topic

Eiffel Tower and Leaning Tower

❶ **Think** about your topic as a scale. Close your eyes, and imagine dropping details that describe each subject onto the trays. Keep the scale balanced! Don't include a detail describing one subject that doesn't have a corresponding detail describing the other subject.

 **Stuck for Details?**

If you can't think of enough details or of any similarities, try another topic.

❷ **List** details about each subject. Use the Exploring Questions to help you think of details to include.

Exploring Questions
- What are they like?
- How do they look, sound, feel, taste, or smell?
- What do they do? What can you do with them?
- Where are they found?
- What do they cost?
- What are the rules or skills involved?

Tech Tip
If you have a topic that really interests you but don't have enough details, try researching it on the Internet.

more ▶
Prewriting

The Writing Process — PREWRITING · DRAFTING · REVISING · PROOFREADING · PUBLISHING

❸ **Draw** a Venn diagram. Write the name of one subject above each circle. Use Portia's diagram below as a model.

❹ **Write** details that tell how the subjects are different in the outer circles. Write details that tell how the subjects are alike in the space where the circles overlap.

❺ **Use** different colors to match details that describe the same feature for both subjects on your diagram. Cross out any details that you can't connect.

Pianos / **Guitars**

- eighty-eight keys
- must sit while playing
- large percussion instrument
- players push keys
- ~~player pianos play by themselves~~

Overlap:
- shiny wooden case
- strings
- can play classical, rock, blues
- can play for fun or as a career
- need 2 hands

- small stringed instrument
- six strings
- players pluck or strum strings
- can play sitting, standing or strolling
- ~~picks can protect your fingers~~

▲ **Portia's Venn diagram**

HELP? See page 14 for other ideas for exploring your topic.

 Go to www.eduplace.com/kids/hme/ for graphic organizers.

376 Unit 10: Compare-Contrast

Organizing Your Essay

Pick a method of organization. Here are two possible ways to present information in your essay.

Write about similarities and then differences. Tell all the ways the subjects are alike in one or more paragraphs. Then tell how they are different in separate paragraphs. The first two paragraphs in "Hurricanes and Tornadoes" are organized this way.

You may prefer to tell about differences first and then similarities. That's fine too.

Similarities	Differences	
Hurricanes/Tornadoes	**Hurricanes**	**Tornadoes**
destructive	begin over water	start over land
depend on warm, moist air	swirl around a calm center, doughnutlike	cone-shaped
fierce winds rain or hail	larger, last longer	treacherous, hit with less warning

Use feature-by-feature order. Choose two or three **features** your subjects share, such as appearance or habits. For each feature, explain all the similarities and differences you can think of. Look at the following plan for comparing and contrasting average male adult lions and tigers.

Feature	Tigers	Lions
appearance	425 pounds, 9 feet long	350–400 pounds, 9 feet long
	brownish-yellow to orange-red coat, black stripes	brownish-yellow coat
	ruff of hair around sides of face	long, thick mane

more ▶
Prewriting 377

The Writing Process

PREWRITING · DRAFTING · REVISING · PROOFREADING · PUBLISHING

Focus Skill continued

Feature	Tigers	Lions
habits	live alone	live in prides (10–35 lions)
	hunt at night	hunt at night
	avoid human beings, unless sick or wounded or if food is scarce	avoid human beings, unless sick or wounded or if food is scarce

Paragraph Tip

Group sentences that tell about one main idea, such as similarities, differences, or one particular feature, in one paragraph. Begin a new paragraph when you start to write about another main idea.

GRAMMAR TIP When you use a conjunction to combine sentences, remember to write a comma before it.

Think and Discuss Look at the final draft of Portia's essay on pages 371–373.

- Which type of organization did Portia use?

▶ Plan Your Essay

❶ **Decide** which method you will use to organize your essay.
  - similarities and then differences
  - feature-by-feature order

❷ **Make a chart** like the ones shown above to plan your essay. Add details from your Venn diagram that describe each subject.

378 Unit 10: Compare-Contrast

PREWRITING DRAFTING REVISING PROOFREADING PUBLISHING

Focus Skill

Introductions and Conclusions

Like a frisky pet, a good introduction jumps up and demands your reader's attention. In addition to creating curiosity, a good introduction will name your two subjects.

Try starting with a question or with a statement that arouses curiosity. Compare these two introductions for a feature-by-feature essay.

Weak Introduction	Strong Introduction
I like to watch TV. My favorite shows are ones that feature main characters who are around my age.	Does TV show a true picture of the average young person's looks, clothes, and behavior? To find out, let's compare and contrast real kids and kids portrayed on TV.

Write a strong conclusion. Don't just tell the last similarity or difference. Make your essay feel finished by summing up your ideas.

Weak Conclusion	Strong Conclusion
TV characters always look perfect. They never have bad days or anything out of place.	TV characters always look great and have a perfect comeback. They never have bad-hair days or mayonnaise on their chins. Real kids don't have their own hairdresser or clothes buyer. We mess up all the time! In short, TV characters are just too smooth to believe!

Try It Out

- On your own, improve the weak introduction above by beginning with a statement that arouses curiosity.

▶ Draft Your Introduction

Write three different introductions for your essay. Include a question in one and a surprising statement in another. Choose the one you like best.

Drafting **379**

Topic Sentences and Transitional Words

A good topic sentence states the main idea or the purpose of the paragraph. It tells readers what the rest of the paragraph will be about. The topic sentence in the paragraph below is underlined.

> <u>Using a phone to communicate is very different from using a computer.</u> If I call my friend Julie, and she's not home, her brother never gives her my messages. However, when I send Julie a message by e-mail, her trusty computer saves it and eventually alerts her that she has mail.

The topic sentence is often first, but it may come anywhere in the paragraph.

Follow these steps when you write your essay.

Decide what the purpose of your paragraph is. Will the paragraph describe similarities? differences? Will it explore one particular feature?

Write a topic sentence that makes this purpose clear.

Use transitional words and phrases that show how ideas within or between paragraphs are connected.

To signal similarities	as well as, both, likewise, similarly
To signal differences	but, instead, however, on the other hand, unlike

Think and Discuss

- What transitional word in the paragraph above helps the author connect her two subjects? Does this word signal similarities or differences?

▶ Draft Your Compare-Contrast Essay

❶ Write the middle paragraphs for your essay. State your main ideas in topic sentences. Use transitional words to show how ideas are connected.

❷ Create a strong conclusion that sums up your ideas.

380 Unit 10: Compare-Contrast

Evaluating Your Compare-Contrast Essay

▶ **Reread** your essay. Use this rubric to decide how to make it better. Write the sentences that describe your essay.

Rings the Bell!

- ☐ My introduction grabs the reader's attention.
- ☐ I compare and contrast corresponding details for each subject.
- ☐ I use one method of organization throughout my essay.
- ☐ A topic sentence states the main idea of each paragraph.
- ☐ I use transitional words to signal similarities and differences.
- ☐ I have ended my essay with a strong conclusion.
- ☐ There are very few mistakes in grammar, spelling, or punctuation.

Getting Stronger

- ☐ My introduction could be more interesting.
- ☐ I didn't always compare and contrast corresponding details.
- ☐ I used more than one method of organization to present my ideas.
- ☐ Some paragraphs are missing topic sentences.
- ☐ More transitional words would help connect my ideas.
- ☐ My conclusion could be stronger.
- ☐ There are a lot of mistakes.

Try Harder

- ☐ My introduction doesn't name my two subjects.
- ☐ I don't compare and contrast corresponding details.
- ☐ I don't tell how my subjects are alike and different.
- ☐ The details in my paragraphs are mixed up and don't support one main idea.
- ☐ There are no transitional words to show how the ideas are connected.
- ☐ My essay just stops. There is no conclusion.
- ☐ Many mistakes make my essay very hard to follow.

 See www.eduplace.com/kids/hme/ to interact with this rubric.

The Writing Process

PREWRITING · DRAFTING · **REVISING** · PROOFREADING · PUBLISHING

▶ Revise Your Essay

❶ Revise your essay. Use the list of sentences you wrote from the rubric. Work on the parts that you described with sentences from "Getting Stronger" and "Try Harder."

❷ Have a writing conference.

When You're the Writer Read your essay to a partner. Discuss any questions or problems you're having with it. Take notes to remember what your partner said.

When You're the Listener Tell at least two things you liked about the essay. Ask questions about anything that is unclear.

 **Revising Tip**

Use two different colors to highlight sentences that tell likenesses and differences. Then ask: Is every sentence in the right place? Do I need more sentences that compare? that contrast?

What should I say?

The Writing Conference

If you're thinking . . .	You could say . . .
The introduction could be stronger.	Could you begin with a surprising statement or a question?
I don't know what your second subject is until the end.	Can you state your two subjects in the introduction?
I don't really see how your two subjects are alike.	Can you add more details that compare?
Your ideas are great, but they are sometimes hard to follow!	Can you tell likenesses, and then differences?
This paragraph's purpose is not exactly clear.	What's the main idea here? Can you state it in a topic sentence?
The essay just stops.	Can you write a conclusion that sums up your ideas?

❸ Make other revisions to your essay, using your conference notes and the Revising Strategies on the next page.

382 Unit 10: Compare-Contrast

Revising Strategies

Elaborating: Word Choice **Antonyms** are words that have opposite meanings. Use them to make the contrast between two subjects sharper.

Without Antonyms	Elaborated with Antonyms
Water in swimming pools is calm, but water in oceans is not.	Water in swimming pools is calm, but water in oceans is often choppy.

▶ Find at least two places in your essay where you can use antonyms.

📖 Use the Thesaurus Plus on page H81. See also page H14.

Elaborating: Details Adding vivid details will clarify likenesses and differences.

Few Details	Elaborated with Details
The violin is an instrument made of wood. The trumpet is made of brass.	The violin is a delicate musical instrument made of polished wood. The trumpet is a short horn made of shiny brass.

▶ Find at least two places where you can tell more by adding details.

GRAMMAR LINK ▶ See also page 154.

Sentence Fluency Make your writing more interesting to your audience by varying the way your sentences begin. Read these sentences comparing identical twins.

Similar Beginnings	Varied Beginnings
Their hair is usually in a ponytail. Their eyes are brown. Their skin is covered with freckles.	Both girls usually wear a ponytail. Their eyes are brown, and freckles cover their skin.

▶ Vary sentence beginnings in at least two places. Does your essay sound better?

Revising 383

The Writing Process   PREWRITING   DRAFTING   REVISING   **PROOFREADING**   PUBLISHING

Proofread Your Essay

Proofread your essay, using the Proofreading Checklist and the Grammar and Spelling Connections. Proofread for one skill at a time. Use a class dictionary to check spellings.

Proofreading Checklist
Did I
- ✔ indent all paragraphs?
- ✔ choose correct verb forms?
- ✔ use commas to separate items in a series?
- ✔ correct any run-on sentences?
- ✔ correct any spelling errors?

📖 Use the Guide to Capitalization, Punctuation, and Usage on page H57.

Proofreading Marks
- ¶ Indent
- ∧ Add
- ⌒ Delete
- ≡ Capital letter
- / Small letter

Tech Tip Print out your piece and proofread it. Small mistakes are easy to miss on screen.

Grammar and Spelling Connections

Subject-Verb Agreement Use the singular form of the verb if your subject is singular. Use the plural form of the verb if your subject is plural.

Singular subjects	Our dog **yawns** and **stretches** when she's tired.
Plural subjects	Our cats, on the other hand, **hide** under the bed.

GRAMMAR LINK See also page 112.

Commas in a Series When you list three or more items in a sentence, separate them with commas. Write a conjunction before the last item.

> Both hurricanes and tornadoes are accompanied by fierce winds **,** rain or hail **,** **and** low air pressure.

GRAMMAR LINK See also page 184.

Spelling the |o͞o| or |yo͞o| Sound The |o͞o| or the |yo͞o| sound is often spelled *ue*, *ew*, or *u*-consonant-*e*. The |o͞o| sound may also be spelled *oo* or *ui*.

bl**ue**, cr**ew**, c**u**t**e**, p**oo**l, cr**ui**se

📖 See the Spelling Guide on page H67.

384   Unit 10: Compare-Contrast

 Go to www.eduplace.com/kids/hme/ for proofreading practice.

PREWRITING   DRAFTING   REVISING   PROOFREADING   **PUBLISHING**

▶ Publish Your Essay

① **Make a neat final copy** of your essay. Check to make sure that you corrected all mistakes.

Tech Tip Look for computer clip art or photos to download and use to illustrate your essay.

② **Add a title** to your essay. Choose a title that will make your reader curious, such as "Water, Mild and Wild" instead of "Streams and Rivers."

GRAMMAR TIP *Capitalize the first, the last, and each important word in a title.*

③ **Publish** or share your essay in a way that suits your audience. See the Ideas for Sharing box.

Tips for Reading Aloud

- Practice in small groups before you give your "real" performance.
- Speak clearly, slowly, and loudly enough for everyone to hear.
- Speak with expression. Highlight words in advance that you will emphasize.
- Make eye contact with your audience. Don't hide behind your paper!
- Use body language to make your points.

Ideas for Sharing

Write It
- Turn your essay into a magazine article. Add photographs or drawings.
- Place a copy of your essay in the Reading Center.

Say It
- Read it aloud in the Author's Chair.
- Give an interview about your essay.

Show It
- Find slides that support the information in your essay. Show the slides as you read your essay aloud.

▶ Reflect

Write about your writing experience. Use these questions to get started.

- What was difficult about writing your essay? What was easy?
- How does this paper compare with other papers you have written?

Assessment Link

Writing Prompts

Use these prompts as ideas for writing compare-contrast essays or to practice for a test. Decide who your audience will be, and write your essay in a way that they will understand and enjoy.

1 Compare and contrast two outdoor games or sports that you know well. What are the rules? Do players form teams? Is there special equipment?

2 Compare and contrast yourself and a close friend or family member. What are your ages? What do you look like? What are your most and least favorite foods, hobbies, music, or school subjects?

3 Choose two kinds of pets. Write a compare-contrast essay to help a friend who is trying to decide what kind of pet to adopt. Write about looks, behavior, and care required.

4 Compare and contrast two holidays or family celebrations. When do they take place? What special activities do you do? What foods are a part of the celebration?

Writing Across the Curriculum

5 **FINE ART**

Look closely at the painting. What similarities between a tidal wave and a mountain does the artist suggest? What differences? Consider size, shape, color, strength, and movement.

Color woodblock print, 1831

The Great Wave of Kanagawa, Katsushika Hokusai

 See www.eduplace.com/kids/hme/ for more prompts.

Assessment Link

✓ Test Practice

Sometimes on a test you will be asked to write a compare and contrast essay in response to a picture prompt like this.

Remember that a compare-contrast essay tells how two things are alike and how they are different.

Write an essay to **compare and contrast each form of transportation.** First look at the pictures. Then think carefully about each vehicle. What does it **look like?** How **fast** is it? What **costs** are associated with it?

Here are some strategies to help you do a good job responding to a prompt like this.

1 Look for clue words that tell what to write about. See whether the prompt suggests a particular method of organization. Write the clue words and some notes about your essay.

Clue Words	My Essay
compare and contrast each form of transportation, look like, fast, costs	I will compare and contrast cars and bikes. The prompt suggests three characteristics, so I think I'll organize my essay using the feature-by-feature method.

2 Plan your writing. Make a Venn diagram like the one shown on page 376 and list several details for each subject. Keep any suggested categories of details in mind as you write.

3 You will get a good score if you remember the description of what kind of compare-contrast essay rings the bell in the rubric on page 381.

Test Practice **387**

Special Focus on Explaining

Writing Instructions

Instructions explain how to make or do something. Read Cyrus's instructions on how to make a kazoo. Would you be able to make one of your own using these instructions?

How to Make a Kazoo

Introduction

The kazoo is a musical instrument that's easy to play. All you have to do is hum. Anyone can make one too. Here's how.

Materials

First, get all of your materials together. You'll need an empty toilet paper roll or an empty paper towel roll cut in half. You'll also need waxed paper, a ruler, a pencil, a paper punch, scissors, and a rubber band.

Steps

Next, use the ruler to measure about an inch from one end of the roll. After you have marked that spot with the pencil, use the paper punch to make a hole there.

Cut a piece of waxed paper into a circle that is big enough to fit over the end of the roll that has the hole. Finally, use the rubber band to keep the waxed paper over the end. Don't cover the hole with waxed paper.

Order word

Now you're ready to play your new kazoo. Loudly hum into the end without waxed paper. The waxed paper should be loose enough to vibrate, because that's how a kazoo works.

You can make your kazoo look and sound different. Do the same steps, but this time use aluminum foil instead of waxed paper. The foil also needs to be loose enough to vibrate.

Conclusion — Making a kazoo might be fun to do with a younger brother or sister. They'll like making their own music on an instrument they made themselves. They can try playing some of their favorite songs.

Reading As a Writer

- The **introduction** tells the purpose of the instructions. Often it also tells the reader something interesting about the subject.
  What information does Cyrus give in his introduction?
- All **materials** are listed. The correct amounts and sizes are given.
  What materials does Cyrus list?
- All of the **steps** to do the task are described clearly and in order.
  What is the first step in making a kazoo?
- **Order words**, such as *first, after, then,* or *finally,* help the reader understand the sequence of steps.
  What order words does Cyrus use?
- The **conclusion** completes the instructions. It can include other interesting information or suggestions about the topic.
  What is Cyrus's final suggestion?

more ▶

Writing Instructions

Special Focus continued

How to Write Instructions

❶ **Choose** a task that you can do well. Ask yourself these questions as you think about which task to choose.

- Can I clearly and easily explain it in one or two pages?
- Can I explain what to do in writing, or will I need to show the steps?
- Who will be my audience?

❷ **List** all of the materials needed. Then list the steps.

❸ **Make** a flow chart to show the steps in order. Add details to explain each step. To help decide what to include, ask yourself these questions.

- Why is this step important?
- What would happen if I left out this step?
- What other details, such as size, weight, or amount, do I need to add?

 Stuck for an Idea?

Here are some suggestions.

How to
- pitch a tent
- make craft dough
- transplant a plant
- take care of goldfish
- start a stamp collection
- set up a lemonade stand

Write each step and its details on a big self-stick note. Then arrange the self-stick notes until they are in the correct order.

Flow Chart for Making a Paper Kazoo

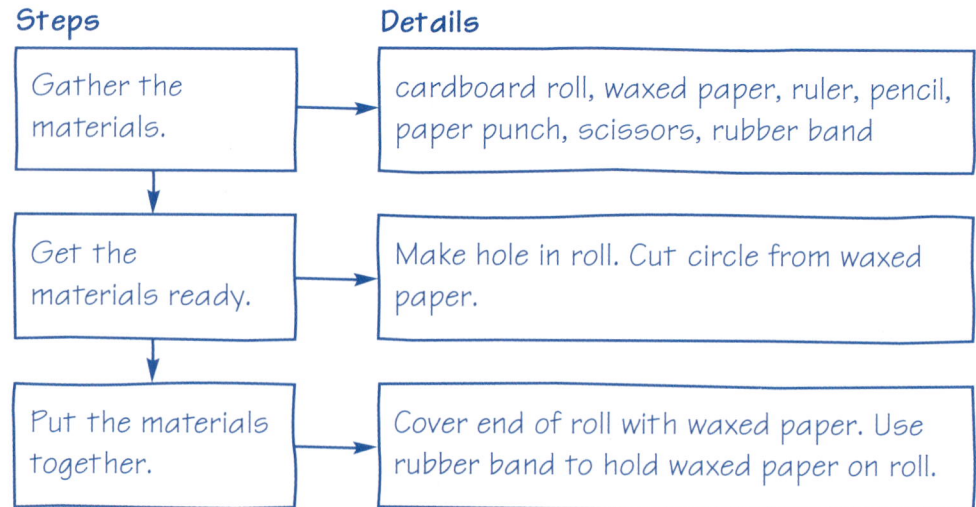

Unit 10: Compare-Contrast

④ **Think** about your audience. Who will be using these instructions? Be sure to adapt your language to suit your readers.

⑤ **Write** an introduction that tells your audience what your topic is. It should be lively enough to make readers want to know more. For example, you might state a surprising or little-known fact about your topic to capture your readers' attention.

   The introduction should also explain your purpose. In this case, the purpose is probably to inform. However, it may also be to entertain your readers, or even to persuade them to give something new a try.

⑥ **Write** a first draft of the instructions, using your flow chart or by following the self-stick notes you arranged in order.
   - Describe the materials and each step in order. Include suggestions about where to get materials that are needed.
   - Use order words to make the order clear.
   - Use details and exact words to make your instructions clear.

Order Words	
first	before
second	after
next	now
then	finally
when	later

⑦ **Write** a conclusion. A good closing is as important as a good introduction. A conclusion finishes your instructions. It can sum up the main steps or show how following your instructions relates to everyday life. You can also use the conclusion to tie the different parts of your instructions together.

more ▶

Special Focus *continued*

❽ **Revise** your draft. Use the Revising Checklist to help you evaluate and improve your instructions.

Revising Checklist
✔ How did my introduction state my topic and purpose in an interesting way?
✔ Have I listed all materials and included any necessary details about them?
✔ Did I include all steps and details?
✔ Are the steps in order?
✔ Do I need more order words?
✔ Does my conclusion wrap things up in an interesting way?

❾ **Have** a writing conference. These questions may help you during your conference.

The Writing Conference	
If you're thinking . . .	*You could say . . .*
This doesn't tell me what I'm going to learn.	Could you state the topic and purpose of the instructions more clearly?
I don't know what I need to do to complete this task.	Are all of the materials listed? Are all of the steps included? Are they in the correct order?
I don't understand how to complete this step.	Could you give more details? Could you add more exact information?
Why is this step here?	Do you need to include this information?
The instructions just stop. There's no real ending.	Could you finish by telling about how the completed product looks or sounds?

10 **Proofread** your instructions. Use the Proofreading Checklist below. Use a dictionary to check your spelling.

Proofreading Checklist

Did I
- ✓ indent all paragraphs?
- ✓ use conjunctions correctly?
- ✓ use commas to separate items in a series?
- ✓ correct any fragments or run-on sentences?
- ✓ spell all the words correctly?

📖 Use the Guide to Capitalization, Punctuation, and Usage on page H57 at the back of this book.

Proofreading Marks
- ¶ Indent
- ∧ Add
- ꟾ Delete
- ≡ Capital letter
- / Small letter

11 **Publish** or share a final copy of your instructions with your audience. Add pictures and make a booklet or a poster showing each step. Another idea would be to have two classmates demonstrate your task, using your instructions as a guide.

Writing Instructions 393

COMMUNICATION LINK   Listening/Speaking

Giving and Following Instructions

When you explain how to play a game or complete a task, you are giving instructions. It is important to give clear directions with all the steps included so the task can be completed. Are the instructions below clear and easy to follow?

> **How to Wrap a Gift**
>
> First, place the wrapping paper, with the pattern down, on a flat surface. Next, place the gift on the paper and check to see how much of the paper you will need by folding it around the gift. Then, mark where you want to cut the paper. Finally, cut, fold, and tape to wrap the gift.

Would adding numbers to the steps help? Why or why not? How might the last step give more information?

Use the guidelines below to give instructions aloud.

Guidelines for Giving Instructions

1. Write the instructions for the task, then try to follow them to make sure you have included all of the steps.
2. Explain the purpose for the instructions.
3. Give the instructions one step at a time. You can use words such as *first, next, then,* and *finally* to help show the order of the steps.
4. Speak clearly. Be aware of your pace and volume. Are you speaking too fast? Can everyone hear you?
5. If you can, demonstrate what to do.

Unit 10: Compare-Contrast

When you listen to instructions, it is important to pay attention to the speaker and to each step so you can complete the task.

Guidelines for Following Instructions

1. Listen carefully for the words that tell exactly what to do.
2. Be sure you understand the order of the steps. Listening for words such as *first, then, next,* and *finally* will help you.
3. Picture each step as you hear it. Watch carefully if there is a demonstration.
4. Ask questions about any step that is not clear.
5. If the instructions are long or complicated, take notes.

After listening to a set of directions, you may want to check your understanding by repeating them to the person who gave them to you.

Apply It

Choose something you know how to do well that you can explain in four or five steps. Give a partner instructions as you demonstrate how to do the task. Then have your partner try it as you give the instructions again. Switch roles and follow your partner's instructions.

- Were your instructions and demonstration clear?
- Could your partner complete the task, or were there steps you left out?
- Are there any questions you would like to ask to help you understand your partner's instructions?

COMMUNICATION LINK Viewing

Comparing Visual Information

To get a point across, writers may use visuals in addition to words. Photographs, diagrams, charts, drawings, and illustrations present different kinds of visual information. They often show data and ideas that are not given in words.

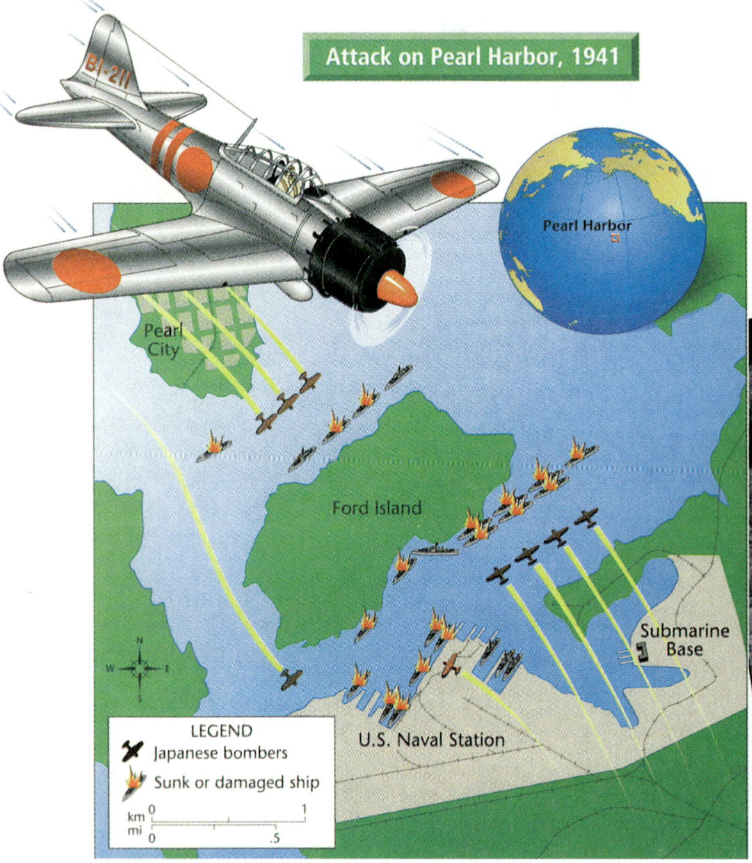

Attack on Pearl Harbor, 1941

Illustrations

Illustrations give an artist's sense of a subject. The artist chooses the focus, or center of interest. He or she also decides which details to include and which to leave out. When facts are not clear about a subject, the artist may use his or her imagination.

An illustrated map is a drawing of a place that is meant to explain facts about it. Look at the illustrated map above. Which details might have come from the artist's imagination? Which details do you think are accurate?

News Photographs

For a news photograph, the photographer wants to present the facts about a place, an event, a thing, or a person. A photograph only captures a single instant in time. The subject may change soon after the photo is taken. A photo also shows only one view of a subject. What a photo does not show may be as important as what it does show.

In the photo on page 396, the photographer focused on one main image. Why do you think he or she decided to leave out the other things happening nearby?

Guidelines for Comparing Visuals

▶ Look for the subject or center of interest of each visual. What do you think the artist or photographer is trying to show?

▶ Think about the kind of information the visuals show. Does one give more details than the other? Why?

▶ Find the purpose of the visuals. Are they intended to persuade, advertise, teach, sell, or entertain?

▶ Remember that photographers and artists can leave out information in their work. What do you think they left out of the visuals? Why?

▶ Suppose that you had been given only one of the visuals to look at. What information would you miss, if one of them were gone?

Apply It

Choose two different kinds of visuals. Use the guidelines above to help you compare them. Take notes while you look at each one. Then write a paragraph comparing them. Answer these questions.

- Did you learn more from one of the visuals than the other?
- Did either visual create a particular feeling, such as sadness or curiosity? Why do you think this is so?
- What were the main differences between the two visuals?

Comparing Visual Information **397**

Unit 11

Writing a Research Report

No one is sure why the people who lived in these cliff dwellings suddenly abandoned their homes. Some archaeologists believe...

In this article Christina Wilsdon reports on some interesting information about lions. Watch for the surprising main idea.

Scaredy Cats

by Christina Wilsdon, *originally printed in Contact*

An angry roar rumbles across the African plain. The sound alerts two lionesses. They realize that the voice belongs to a stranger trespassing on their territory. One lioness trots forward, looking for the intruder. Then she pauses briefly as she looks over her shoulder. Where did her partner go?

Oh, there she is—strolling so slowly that by the time she catches up to her sister, any fighting that breaks out might be over!

The Noble Lion . . . Not!

That scene doesn't sound much like the way we expect the King—or rather, Queen—of Beasts to act. Lions are supposed to be fearless fighters. But after years of studying lions living in Tanzania, Africa, researchers have discovered something surprising about these big cats: Lions can be cowards and bad teammates who don't pull their weight.

All for One and One for All

Working as a team is important for lions. A lion living on its own suffers a lot. It leads a lonely, scary life. Sure, it can catch food, but it's always trespassing on other lions' territories. Those lions will chase the loner away or even kill it. The only way to have a territory is to be part of a group, or pride.

That's where teamwork comes in. To take over a pride of females, a male must team up with his brothers, cousins, or pals. This band has to be strong enough to chase away or kill the males who rule that pride.

"Males rarely hang back when they go out to face danger," notes Dr. Craig Packer of the University of Minnesota. He studies lion behavior. "They need to look after their buddies." If a male loses his buddy, he may also wind up losing his whole pride and being a loner for the rest of his life—which will probably be a short one!

Chicken Cats

Females rely on teamwork, too. They band together with sisters, cousins, aunts, and daughters to raise cubs and hunt. They protect their territory from other females. But some lionesses don't do their part.

How did Packer discover the cowardly lionesses? It happened when researchers played tapes of roaring lions in another pride's territory. The scientists saw how the animals reacted to the cries of the "trespassers."

The researchers noticed that certain females were always in the lead in defending their territory. But a few lionesses always dragged their feet.

Leaders of the Pack

So, in 1992, Packer and another researcher, Dr. Robert Heinsohn, started working to find out which lionesses were leaders and which ones were "laggards," or slowpokes.

The researchers played recordings of roars to pairs of lionesses. They saw that sometimes a courageous leader would look over her shoulder at her cowardly companion as if to say, "Hey, get over here!"

The idea of a chicken-hearted lion sounds funny, but it's no joke. When real enemy lions showed up, the leader met them first and got attacked. The laggard avoided getting clobbered right away because she arrived half a minute or more later. In serious fights, this could mean the difference between life and death.

There's a limit to how many lazybones a pride can put up with. Notes Packer, "If the number of slackers is too high, then the pride will just be taken over by another pride."

Reading As a Writer

Think About the Article
- What is the main idea of this article?
- What questions about lions does the article answer?
- What sources of information might Christina Wilsdon have used to research this article?

Think About Writer's Craft
- What are the subheadings? How do they help the reader?
- Where does the writer use quotations? What do they contribute to the piece?

Think About the Pictures
- Look at the pictures on pages 399–400. Which of them might show a lioness who isn't doing her part? Use information from the article to support your answer.

Responding

Write responses to these questions.
- **Personal Response** What facts about lions did you find surprising?
- **Critical Thinking** For lions, what are the advantages to living in a pride? What might be the disadvantages?

What Makes a Great Research Report?

A research report presents facts learned through research about a particular topic.

Follow these guidelines when you write a research report.

▶ Gather information, and organize it well.

▶ Write an interesting introduction that tells the main idea.

▶ Write at least one paragraph for each main topic. Support each topic sentence with facts.

▶ Show how your ideas are connected.

▶ Use your own words. Don't copy your sources word for word.

▶ Write a conclusion that sums up your research.

▶ Include an accurate list of sources.

GRAMMAR CHECK

Capitalize all proper nouns and proper adjectives in your report.

Student Model

WORKING DRAFT

After watching a fascinating TV special about Mount Everest, Christina Clark decided to write a report about the men and the women who have tried to climb it. Here is her working draft.

Christina Clark

Working Draft

Mount Everest

Mount Everest is very dangerous. Avalanches and cold climate are two of the dangers. The summit is cold all year, and the wind and snowstorms can be extreme. Also, the air high on Everest is so thin that climbers can hardly breathe.

Some say George Leigh Mallory was the first to reach the summit of Mount Everest. It stands 29,035 feet above sea level, between Nepal and Tibet. After two unsuccessful trips, Mallory tried again. In early June of 1924, his group reached Camp Four on the north pass. Next, Mallory and Sandy Irvine tried for the summit. The last time they were seen, they were almost there, but they never returned. In 1933, Irvine's ice ax was found. In 1975, Wang Hongbao, a Chinese climber, found a man in 1920s clothing dead on the slopes, but he could not bring the body down. In May of 1999, climbers following Mallory and Irvine's route found that body again.

Edmund Hillary, of New Zealand, wanted to climb the highest mountain in the world. In 1953, he set out with a climbing party. Hunt's group was guided by Sherpas. The group was going up from the south instead of the north.

Is this related to the paragraph's main topic?

Could you break this into two paragraphs and tell more?

404 Unit 11: Research Report

Working Draft

These exact facts show that you've done excellent research.

Hunt picked Hillary and Tenzing Norgay, a Sherpa, to try for the summit. Soon after 11:30 A.M. on May 29, 1953, Hillary and Tenzing stood triumphant on the summit.

Can you write a sentence to tell the topic of this paragraph?

In 1975, a Japanese expedition leader named Junko Tabei was trapped when an avalanche slammed into her tent. Sherpas rescued her and her tent mates. Even though she was injured, Junko Tabei became the first woman to reach the summit of Mount Everest.

Reinhold Messner has the honor of being the first person to climb Mount Everest alone. Climbing on the very difficult north route, Messner took only three days to reach the summit from base camp. On April 20, 1980, Reinhold Messner stood on the top of Mount Everest. He said, "Mountains are not fair or unfair; they are just dangerous."

I really like this quotation.

Could you add a conclusion?

Reading As a Writer

- What did Sal like about this research report? What improvements did he suggest?
- What is the main idea of this report? State it in one sentence.
- What questions do you have for Christina? Where could she add more facts to help her readers?

Student Model

Christina revised her research report after discussing it with her classmates. Read her final copy to see how she improved it.

First to the Top
by Christina Clark

Mount Everest is the world's tallest mountain. It stands 29,035 feet above sea level, between Nepal and Tibet. Avalanches and the cold climate make it scary to climb. Its summit is a dangerous place. It is cold all year, and the wind and snowstorms can be extreme. Also, the air high on Everest is so thin that climbers can hardly breathe. Many people have died there in the cold, yet climbers keep trying to reach the top.

> This introduction makes me feel the danger!

Some say George Leigh Mallory was the first to reach the summit of Mount Everest. After two unsuccessful trips, Mallory tried again. In early June of 1924, his group reached Camp Four on the north pass. Next, Mallory and Sandy Irvine, another climber, tried for the summit. The last time they were seen, they were almost there, but they never returned.

> You show how your ideas are connected.

For a long time, it seemed Mallory and Irvine had disappeared forever in the snow and ice. Then, in 1933, Irvine's ice ax was found. In 1975, Wang Hongbao, a Chinese climber, found a man in 1920s clothing dead on the slopes of Everest, but he could not bring the body down before losing his own life in an avalanche. In May of 1999, climbers following Mallory and Irvine's route found that body again. Labels in the clothing were marked

406 Unit 11: Research Report

"G. L. Mallory." Did Mallory and Irvine reach the summit before they died? The answer is still a mystery.

Edmund Hillary, of New Zealand, also wanted to climb the highest mountain in the world. In 1953, he set out with a climbing party led by John Hunt, an Englishman. Hunt's group was guided by Sherpas, the mountain people of Nepal. The group was going up from the south instead of the north. Hunt picked Hillary and Tenzing Norgay, a Sherpa, to try for the summit. Soon after 11:30 A.M. on May 29, 1953, Hillary and Tenzing stood triumphant at the top of the world. They shook hands, hugged, and took pictures. When Hillary and Tenzing returned from Mount Everest, they were honored greatly.

You added helpful facts.

I like this topic sentence.

In 1975, two expeditions raced to put the first woman on the summit. In one group, a Japanese expedition leader named Junko Tabei was trapped under ice when an avalanche slammed into her tent. Sherpas rescued her and her tent mates. Even though she was injured, Junko Tabei became the first woman to reach the summit of Mount Everest.

more

Student Model continued

Reinhold Messner has the honor of being the first person to climb Mount Everest alone. Climbing on the very difficult north route, Messner took only three days to reach the summit from base camp. On April 20, 1980, Reinhold Messner stood on the top of Mount Everest.

These climbers will be remembered for conquering the treacherous mountain. As Reinhold Messner said, "Mountains are not fair or unfair; they are just dangerous." Many climbers are still eager to face that danger.

> This sums up your research report very well.

Sources

Gaffney, Timothy R. *Edmund Hillary*. Chicago: Childrens Press, 1990.

Hillary, Sir Edmund P. "Mount Everest." *World Book Encyclopedia,* 1993 ed.

"Mount Everest." *Encyclopaedia Britannica Online.* 1999. 30 Nov. 2001.

Rosen, Mike. *The Conquest of Everest*. New York: The Bookwright Press, 1989.

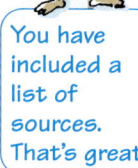

> You have included a list of sources. That's great!

Reading As a Writer

- How did Christina respond to Sal's questions?
- What did she do to improve her introduction and her conclusion?
- Where did Christina add helpful information?
- Why did she break paragraphs differently in her final copy?

 Go to www.eduplace.com/kids/hme/ for more examples of student writing.

The Writing Process — **PREWRITING** · DRAFTING · REVISING · PROOFREADING · PUBLISHING

Write a Research Report

▶ Start Thinking

Make a writing folder for your research report. Copy the questions in bold type, and put the paper in your folder. Write your answers as you think about and choose your topic.

- **Who will be my audience?** Will it be my classmates? a club?
- **What will be my purpose?** What do I want to find out about? What do I want my readers to learn?
- **How will I publish or share my research report?** Will I write a newspaper article? read my report aloud? display my report with visuals?

▶ Choose Your Topic

① **Brainstorm** topic ideas. List things you are curious about. Then circle three topics you would like to research, as shown below.

② **Discuss** your ideas with a partner. Which topics does your partner like? Why? Which ones do you like best?

③ **Ask** questions about each idea.
- Would I enjoy writing about this topic?
- Is there enough information available about this topic?
- Is it too broad? Will I find too much information?

④ **Draw** a star next to the idea you will write about. Keep your list in case you change your mind later.

HELP? Grab an Idea!
- Think about subjects of movies or books.
- Look through your school books.
- Ask an older person about events years ago.

See page 427 for more ideas.

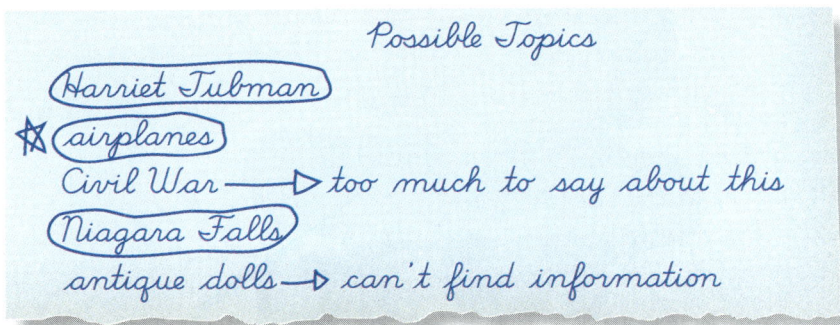

Possible Topics
- Harriet Tubman
- ★ airplanes
- Civil War → too much to say about this
- Niagara Falls
- antique dolls → can't find information

Prewriting   409

The Writing Process

PREWRITING · DRAFTING · REVISING · PROOFREADING · PUBLISHING

▶ Explore Your Topic

1 **Narrow** your topic. If it's too broad for one report, try looping.

- Write one question about your topic.
- Write three questions about your first question.
- Then choose one of these three questions, and write three questions about it. Keep going until you have a topic just right for a report. Draw a star next to it.

- How long have people been able to fly?
  - How was the airplane invented?
    - Who invented the airplane? ★
    - Who tried to fly but failed?
    - What were the first airplane companies?
  - How was the helicopter invented?
  - Who first flew a hot-air balloon?

I'd like to learn more about the Wright brothers.

 Read All About It!

Read about your topic. What parts are most interesting? Could you write a report on just those parts?

410 Unit 11: Research Report   Go to www.eduplace.com/kids/hme/ for graphic organizers.

PREWRITING · DRAFTING · REVISING · PROOFREADING · PUBLISHING

❷ **Make a K-W-S chart.** What do you already know about your topic? Write these things in the first column. What do you want to learn? Write these questions in the second column.

> Ask Who? What? When? Where? Why? and How? to come up with questions for your chart.

What I Know	What I Want to Learn	Possible Sources
Mount Everest is dangerous to climb.	What makes it so dangerous?	
Mallory almost made it to the top (check this!).	Who first successfully climbed Everest?	
Mount Everest is the tallest mountain in the world.	Exactly how tall is it?	
	Who was the first woman to reach the top of Everest?	
	~~What other mountains are a big challenge to climbers?~~	
	Where is Everest located?	

▲ Part of Christina's chart

❸ **Brainstorm** lots of questions for your chart. Then cross out any that wander off your topic. Christina had to cross off one of her questions.

The British Everest team of 1924 (Irvine and Mallory are standing on the left.) ▶

Finding the Best Information

Locating Sources

You can find information in lots of places. Talk to experts, use technology, or look in print sources.

Get in touch with people. Interview an expert, such as a college professor, an expert toolmaker, or a doctor. Call, write to, or e-mail organizations connected with your topic, such as a zoo or an antique automobile club.

 See page H9 to find out more about interviewing.

Tap into technology. Use the Internet. Try different search engines, and make links from Web sites. You can also use CD-ROM encyclopedias. See if your library has any on hand that might be useful for your research.

See page H45 for more about using the Internet.

Look at a variety of print sources.
Here are some ideas.

- **Nonfiction books** give facts about real people, places, things, and events. Use the library catalog to find books on your subject.
- **Reference books** are packed with facts. These include almanacs, atlases, encyclopedias, and special kinds of dictionaries.
  – A **biographical dictionary** gives facts about real people.
  – A **geographical dictionary** gives facts about real places.
- **Magazines** and **newspapers** have the most up-to-date information about recent events. Libraries also have old issues of magazines and newspapers. Ask your librarian how to find them.

 See page H23 for more about using the library.

Evaluating Sources

Test your information. Ask these questions about your sources.

- Did an expert provide the information? Has the person studied or worked in your topic area?
- Does the source offer plenty of facts about your exact topic?
- Is it a recent source? For some topics, you'll need up-to-date facts.
- Ask your teacher about sources from the Internet. Some sites are not created by experts and may contain mistakes.

Think and Discuss What sources might you use to answer each question?

- What's the name of the new baby lion at the city zoo?
- What countries border on Tanzania?
- What is the subject of the renowned scientist Jane Goodall's research?
- How big can an adult male lion grow to be?

▶ Explore Your Sources

❶ **Find** sources you might want to use. Look for answers to the questions you wrote on your K-W-S chart.

❷ **Evaluate** the sources. Choose at least three strong sources. Only one should be an encyclopedia. Write your sources in the third column of your chart.

❸ **Plan** an interview if you can.

If you can't find good information on your topic, choose a different topic from your list.

Go to www.eduplace.com/kids/hme/ for topic links.

Prewriting **413**

The Writing Process: PREWRITING, DRAFTING, REVISING, PROOFREADING, PUBLISHING

▶ Research Your Topic

❶ Take notes to help you remember information.

- Keep one card that lists all your sources.
- Write a question from your K-W-S chart on a note card. Then write facts that answer the question, using your own words.
- To quote exact words, enclose them in quotation marks. Give the author credit in your report.
- Write your source again on this note card. You can shorten the title.

❷ Gather interesting facts that answer your questions. Don't write down every fact that you find!

See page H28 for more about taking notes.

❸ Check that the facts in the What I Know column of your chart are correct if you plan to write about them. Take notes about them too.

❹ Write facts, not opinions. A **fact** can be proved true. An **opinion** states a feeling or a belief. Your paper should report facts.

Fact: People have been injured while trying to climb Mount Everest.

Opinion: It would be foolish to climb Mount Everest.

During research you may find new questions or change some of your first questions.

414 Unit 11: Research Report

PREWRITING · DRAFTING · REVISING · PROOFREADING · PUBLISHING

Here is part of a source that Christina used and some of her notes cards.

Edmund Hillary

At 11:30 A.M., Hillary rounded a cornice and found himself looking into Tibet. The ridge they had been climbing now fell steeply away to the North Col and the Rongbuk Glacier. To his right was a narrow ridge that led to a snow-covered crest. After chipping steps in the slope, the two climbed to the top.

Now the world fell away from them on all sides. They were on the summit of Everest—the roof of the world. They shook hands, then hugged.

50

Sources
Timothy R. Gaffney. *Edmund Hillary*. Chicago: Childrens Press, 1990.

Who first successfully climbed Everest?
—11:30 in morning, Hillary looked over into Tibet.
—Ridge led to snow-covered crest.
—Hillary and Tenzing climbed to top.
—shook hands and hugged
            E. Hillary, Gaffney, p. 50

▲ Some of Christina's note cards

HELP
Neat Note Cards
Try color-coding. Use cards of the same color for facts that answer the same question.

Prewriting **415**

The Writing Process — PREWRITING · DRAFTING · REVISING · PROOFREADING · PUBLISHING

Plan Your Report

1 **Sort** your note cards. The answers to important questions are the **main topics** of your report. Make a stack of cards for each main topic.
- Order the facts in each stack. You might use time order, order of importance, or cause and effect.
- Remove cards with unimportant facts.
- Decide which stack you'll write about first, second, and so on.

2 **Make an outline.** An outline will put your ideas in order.
- List each main topic with a Roman numeral.
- Each important supporting detail becomes a **subtopic**. List it with a capital letter.
- Give your outline a title.

Here are two of Christina's note cards and part of her outline.

Who was the first woman to reach the top of Everest?
— 1975, two groups competing
— one group from China, one from Japan
— May 4, Junko Tabei (Japanese) was trapped under ice.
— She was rescued by Sherpas.
    Conquest, Rosen, p. 24

Who was the first woman to reach the top of Everest?
— May 15, Tabei was chosen to try for summit.
— May 16, Tabei reached the top.
    Conquest, Rosen, p. 25

IV. Tabei—first woman to reach top of Everest
    A. 1975, two female teams in competition
    B. May 4, injury to Junko Tabei
    C. May 15, Tabei to try for summit
    D. May 16, reaches top

See page H30 for more about outlining.

3 **Read** your outline. If you need more facts, do more research.

416 Unit 11: Research Report

PREWRITING DRAFTING REVISING PROOFREADING PUBLISHING

Focus Skill

Writing from an Outline

Write a paragraph for each main topic. Write an interesting **topic sentence**, which states the main topic of the paragraph. Then write sentences about the supporting details that you listed as subtopics.

I. Invention of written symbols for Cherokee language
  A. Invented by Sequoyah
  B. Completed symbols for writing in 1821
  C. Taught daughter and others to read and write
  D. Sent messages between Arkansas and eastern states

A very important step for the Cherokee was inventing a written language. A famous Cherokee, Sequoyah, made up symbols to stand for the spoken language. He finished in 1821. Then he taught his daughter and other people to read and write the language. He also sent Cherokee messages between Arkansas and eastern states. Finally the Cherokee people could communicate in writing!

Use transitional words and phrases. Help your reader see the connections between facts and ideas.

Transitional Words	Transitional Phrases
first, next, also, then, besides, however, finally, now, because, although, after, later, meanwhile, when, soon, again	for example, as a result, in fact, in addition, in one case, due to, because of, in contrast, of course, for instance, even if, for that reason

Think and Discuss Look at the paragraph about Sequoyah.
- Which is the topic sentence?
- Which transitional words did the writer use?

Drafting **417**

The Writing Process

PREWRITING | DRAFTING | REVISING | PROOFREADING | PUBLISHING

Focus Skill continued

Write with voice. A research report shouldn't be a boring list of facts.

- Use descriptive words and phrases. You might elaborate with adjectives or add a prepositional phrase.
- Think of interesting comparisons. You might use a simile or a metaphor.
- Vary the length of your sentences. One short statement after another can have a humdrum effect.

Weak Voice

The Chinese watched comets. They recorded them a long time ago. The earliest record is from 1059 B.C. Comets seemed to mean a new era would begin. That is what the ancient Chinese thought.

Strong Voice

The Chinese recorded sightings of comets as long ago as 1059 B.C. They thought that comets, with their tails of light, looked like brooms. When they saw these "broom stars," people expected the old ways to be swept away. Ancient Chinese astronomers made careful observations. In fact, scientists today still find this information helpful.

Think and Discuss

- What comparison is used in the strong model above?
- What two prepositional phrases together elaborate *comets* in the strong model?

▶ Draft the Body of Your Report

The topic sentence can come at the beginning, in the middle, or at the end of a paragraph.

❶ Write a paragraph for each main topic on your outline. Include a topic sentence and sentences that tell details. Don't write your introduction and conclusion yet.

❷ Include transitional words and phrases to help your reader.

❸ Use your own voice! Show your reader how interesting your topic is.

> **GRAMMAR TIP** If you give an exact date in your report, remember to put a comma between the day and the year.

418 Unit 11: Research Report

PREWRITING DRAFTING REVISING PROOFREADING PUBLISHING

Introductions and Conclusions

Focus Skill

Write a main idea statement. Think about the research and the writing that you've done so far. Write one sentence that tells the main idea of your report.

Introduce your report. A good introduction should express the main idea in an interesting way. You might raise a question or put an unusual fact in this paragraph.

Weak Introduction
Early windmills did not look much like windmills we see today. They looked different.

Strong Introduction
Do most people know what the first windmills looked like? They had a strange appearance. One type looked like eight sails turning on a merry-go-round! Both then and now, windmills harness the wind as a source of energy.

Write a strong conclusion. In your conclusion, sum up your important points, and remind the reader of your main idea.

Weak Conclusion
Well, modern windmills are a lot different from early ones, but they are still used all over the world.

Strong Conclusion
Windmills have changed a lot since the early "merry-go-round" types. Although they now have a different design, they still help people use wind power as a source of energy.

Think and Discuss

- Suggest other ways to improve the weak models above.

Draft Your Introduction and Conclusion

1. **Write** an interesting introduction for your research report. Remember to tell the main idea. Then write a conclusion that sums up your report.

2. **Make** a list of sources. Use page 408 as a model.

Drafting 419

Evaluating Your Research Report

▶ **Reread** your research report. Which parts need improvement? Use this rubric to help you decide. Write the sentences that describe your report.

Rings the Bell!

- ☐ My report is thoroughly researched.
- ☐ An interesting introduction and conclusion present the main idea.
- ☐ The report is well organized. Good transitions connect ideas.
- ☐ Each paragraph has a topic sentence, and supporting details.
- ☐ The report gives factual information in my own words.
- ☐ My list of sources is complete and accurate.
- ☐ There are almost no mistakes in spelling or grammar.

Getting Stronger

- ☐ I used only one or two sources of information.
- ☐ The introduction and conclusion tell the main idea but are boring.
- ☐ The paragraphs are in a good order, but I need better transitions.
- ☐ Some paragraphs need topic sentences or details.
- ☐ In some places I mix opinions with facts.
- ☐ I have a list of sources, but it is incomplete.
- ☐ There are a few mistakes.

Try Harder

- ☐ I did very little research.
- ☐ The report needs an introduction and a conclusion.
- ☐ The paragraphs are not in a logical order.
- ☐ I have few topic sentences and few supporting details.
- ☐ I need to check that the report is in my own words.
- ☐ I forgot to include a list of sources.
- ☐ Mistakes make the report hard to read.

 Go to www.eduplace.com/kids/hme/ to interact with this rubric.

PREWRITING   DRAFTING   **REVISING**   PROOFREADING   PUBLISHING

▶ Revise Your Research Report

❶ **Revise** your report. Use the list of sentences you wrote from the rubric. Work on the parts that you described with sentences from "Getting Stronger" and "Try Harder."

 Paragraph Tip
Look for paragraphs crammed with ideas. Break them into smaller paragraphs, each with one main idea.

❷ **Have a writing conference**.

When You're the Writer Read your research report to a partner. Discuss any questions or problems you have. Take notes to remember what your partner said.

When You're the Listener Tell at least two things you liked about the report. Ask questions about anything that is confusing.

The Writing Conference	
If you're thinking…	**You could say…**
The introduction is boring.	Could you start with a question or an unusual fact?
This fact has nothing to do with the main idea.	Are all your facts important to your main idea?
The report jumps from one idea to the next.	Where could you add words to connect your ideas?
There isn't enough information here.	Could you do more research?
This sounds like an encyclopedia article.	Did you make sure to use your own words?
The report just stops.	What could you write at the end to sum up your research?

❸ **Use** your writing conference notes and the Revising Strategies on the next page to make other revisions you want.

Revising **421**

Revising Strategies

Elaborating: Word Choice To help your readers understand your report, define words that they might not know.

Without a Definition	With a Definition
The Washington Monument is an **obelisk**.	The Washington Monument is an obelisk. An obelisk is a tall, four-sided stone post that comes to a point at the top.

▶ Add definitions in at least two places in your report.

Elaborating: Details Give exact details, such as dates, quantities, measurements, and locations.

Unclear Details	Exact Details
The Washington Monument in Washington, D.C., **is really old and really big**.	The Washington Monument in Washington, D.C., was completed in 1884. This huge structure is 555 feet tall and weighs about 91,000 tons.

▶ Add exact details in at least two places in your report.

Sentence Fluency Make your sentences different lengths to keep them interesting. Try combining some sentences with *and, but,* or *or.*

Choppy Sentences	Smooth Sentences
The Washington Monument was dedicated in 1885. It was not opened to the public until 1888.	The Washington Monument was dedicated in 1885, but it was not opened to the public until 1888.

▶ Change the lengths of three sentences in your report.

GRAMMAR LINK *See also page 46.*

422 Unit 11: Research Report

Adding Graphics and Visuals

Graphics and visuals share information in the form of pictures, maps, charts, graphs, time lines, flow charts, or diagrams. You can add these to your written report or use them as part of an oral presentation. If visuals don't seem to fit your report, don't include them.

Pictures You can use photographs or drawings to illustrate your report. Include a map if your readers need to know about places you've described. Make your own, or make photocopies. Be sure to give credit if you use someone else's work.

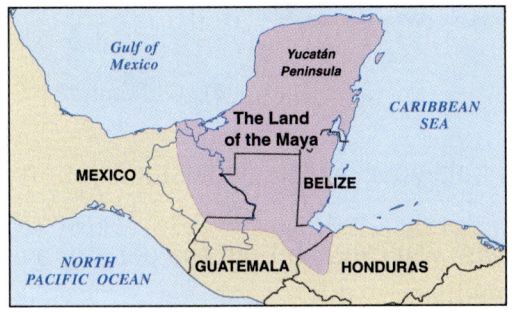

Land of the Maya

Always put a title or a caption on any visual you use.

▶ Add a picture or a map if it fits your report.

Charts, Graphs, and Time Lines You can organize complicated information by using a chart or a graph. If your report discusses events that happen over a period of time, think about adding a time line.

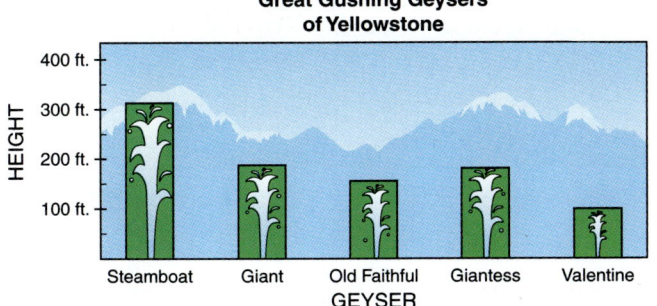

Tech Tip
If you have a computer illustration program, you can place your visuals next to the text they illustrate.

▶ Organize information in a chart, a graph, or a time line if it will enhance your paper.

more ▶

Adding Graphics and Visuals continued

Flow Charts You can show the steps in a process or how one event causes another by using a flow chart.

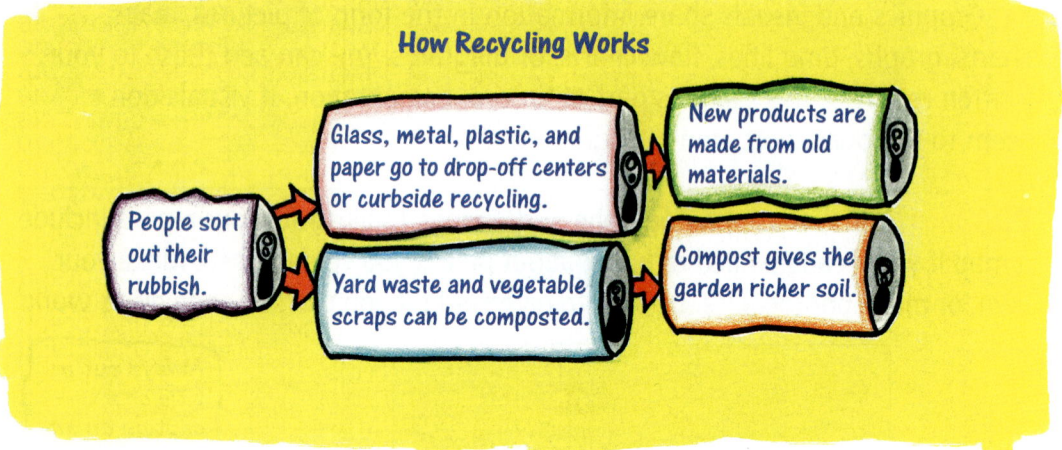

▶ Make a flow chart if it will help your readers understand your report.

Diagrams By adding a diagram, you can point out the parts of a structure or show how something is put together.

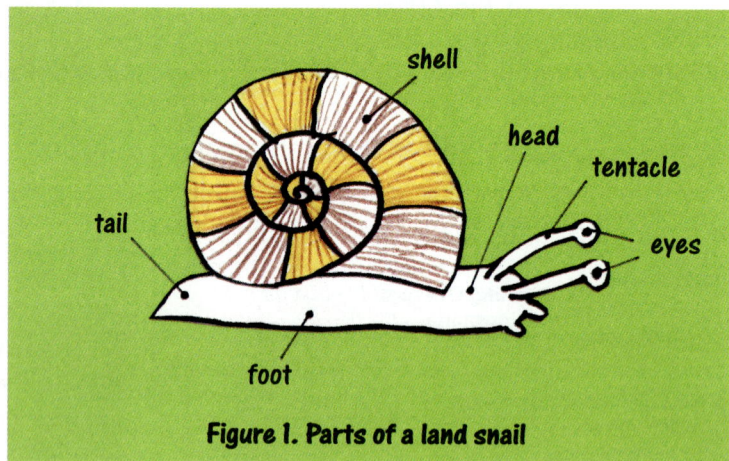

Figure 1. Parts of a land snail

▶ Create a diagram if it suits your report.

Remember that a visual cannot take the place of written text!

You will still need to write a two-page report.

424 Unit 11: Research Report

Proofread Your Research Report

Proofread your report, using the Proofreading Checklist and the Grammar and Spelling Connections. Proofread for one skill at a time. Use a class dictionary to check spellings.

Proofreading Checklist
Did I
- ✓ indent all paragraphs?
- ✓ correct any fragments or run-on sentences?
- ✓ use capital letters where needed?
- ✓ spell all words correctly?

📖 Use the Guide to Capitalization, Punctuation, and Usage on page H57.

Proofreading Marks
- ¶ Indent
- ∧ Add
- ﻪ Delete
- ≡ Capital letter
- / Small letter

Tech Tip Spelling tools can't always tell whether words are capitalized correctly.

Grammar and Spelling Connections

Proper Nouns and Adjectives Nouns that name particular people, places, and things are **proper nouns**. Adjectives formed from proper nouns are called **proper adjectives**. Capitalize proper nouns and proper adjectives.

Proper Nouns	Proper Adjectives
Africa	African elephant
Spain	Spanish language
Hawaii	Hawaiian flowers

GRAMMAR LINK See also page 182.

Spelling the |ô| Sound The |ô| sound is often spelled *aw* or *au*. It may be spelled *a* before *l*.

    dawn   haul   stalk

📖 See the Spelling Guide on page H67.

 Go to www.eduplace.com/kids/hme/ for proofreading practice.

The Writing Process — PREWRITING · DRAFTING · REVISING · PROOFREADING · **PUBLISHING**

▶ Publish Your Research Report

❶ Make a neat final copy of your research report. Check to make sure that you corrected all mistakes.

❷ Write an interesting title for your report. A title such as "The Mysteries of Mars" is more likely to get attention than "Information About Mars."

❸ Publish or share your report in a way that suits your audience. See the Ideas for Sharing box.

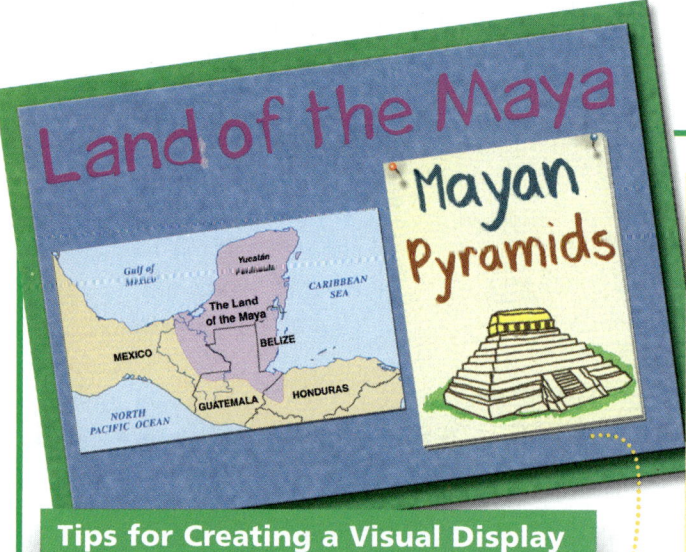

Tips for Creating a Visual Display
- Make large visuals for your report. Use nice lettering. Add hand-drawn or cutout art, or collect objects related to your topic.
- Arrange your visuals on poster board and stand them on a frame, or place them on a table. Display your report with them.

Ideas for Sharing
Write It
- Write your report as a newspaper article. See page 430 for tips.

Say It
- Present your report orally. See page 434 for tips.
- Share your report in a small group. Speak loudly enough to be heard well by everyone.

Show It
- Create a multimedia presentation. See page H47 for tips.
- ★ Make a visual display.

▶ Reflect

Write about your writing experience. Use these questions to get started.
- What have you learned about writing a research report?
- What else would you like to learn about your topic?
- How does this report compare with other papers you have written?

Assessment Link

Writing Prompts

Use these prompts as ideas for writing research reports. Think about who your audience will be, and write your report in a way that they will understand.

Writing Across the Curriculum

1 SCIENCE
Write a research report on a part of the human body, such as the ears, the brain, or the bones and muscles. You might include a diagram.

2 PHYSICAL EDUCATION
It's the Olympics! Write a report on the history of the Olympics, an unfamiliar Olympic sport, or a gold-medal winner from the past.

3 LITERATURE
Think about a biography you have read. Which parts of the person's life were most fascinating? Find out more, and write a report.

4 SCIENCE
What do you know about solar eclipses, waterspouts, or sun dogs? Write a report on a strange happening in the weather or nature.

5 MULTICULTURAL EDUCATION
Research the history of a holiday. Choose a familiar one or one that you don't know about. Write about it. You might include pictures.

6 SOCIAL STUDIES
Study and report on an ancient culture, such as the Anasazi or Aztec peoples, or a culture of Africa or India. Think about including maps.

7 MATH
Who discovered or developed mathematical ideas? Write a report on Euclid, Isaac Newton, Ibn Sina (also known as Avicenna), or another math genius.

8 MUSIC
Do you play a musical instrument? Find out about the development of that instrument over the years. Add pictures if you like.

Go to www.eduplace.com/kids/hme/ for more prompts.

Special Focus on Informing

Writing to Solve a Problem

When you write to **solve a problem**, you tell what the problem is, find and use resources to help solve it, and then explain your solution. Read how one student solved a problem.

Problem —
Problem: Where should we go on vacation?	Possible Sources of Information
• Dad wants to go to a beach.	• a travel agency
• Mom wants to go fishing.	• friends who travel often
• Emily wants to ride a giant Ferris wheel.	• books on travel
• I want to play miniature golf.	

— Resources

Summary —

I live in New York. My problem was finding a nearby place to go on vacation that my whole family would like. It had to have a beach, a giant Ferris wheel, and a miniature golf course. It also had to have good fishing.

First, I visited a travel agency in town. There I learned that North Carolina, New Jersey, and Massachusetts have nice beaches. I got a brochure about Cape Cod, Massachusetts. Cape Cod has beaches and great fishing, but no major amusement parks.

I asked some friends for advice on favorite places to travel. Their ideas didn't include places to fish.

Solution —

Finally, I found a book about Long Beach Island, New Jersey, in the travel part of a bookstore. Success at last! Long Beach Island has nice beaches, good fishing, an amusement park with a giant Ferris wheel, and two miniature golf courses. We decided to rent a house on Long Beach Island for the last week in July.

Reading As a Writer

- The **problem** is a question or a situation that needs to be solved. *What was this student's problem?*
- **Resources** are people, places, and materials that might provide information to solve the problem. *What kinds of possible resources are listed?*
- The **summary** refers back to the problem and explains the actions taken to solve the problem. *Which paragraph restates the problem?*
- The **solution** is the decision you make. *What did this family decide?*

How to Write to Solve a Problem

1. **State** your problem in one clear sentence.
2. **Write** a list of questions you want to answer.
3. **Identify** sources of information to help you. Then do the necessary research. Organize information and your sources in a chart.

Information	Source
Disneyland, Disneyworld, Valleyfair, Six Flags	friends
Cape Cod, MA: beach, fishing, no amusement park, no miniature golf	Mr. Anshan— Travel Rite Travel Agency
Long Beach Island, NJ: beach, fishing, amusement park with Ferris wheel, miniature golf	travel book from bookstore

Long Beach Island, New Jersey

4. **Solve** the problem, using the information you collected. Write a paragraph explaining your decision and why you made that choice.

Special Focus on Informing

Writing a News Article

A **news article** tells about a recent or upcoming event. It reports facts about what happened or gives information about what will happen. Read this article from a school newspaper.

Headline →

Fall Frolic Is Back!

Lead paragraph or introduction

Fall Frolic, an annual event at the Booker T. Washington School, returns to Knolls Park this Saturday from 10:00 A.M. until 2:00 P.M. There will be food, fun, and games for the whole family. Students are selling tickets now. All money raised will be used to buy new computers for the media center.

Supporting details

The Fall Frolic carnival committee is introducing several new games this year, including Radar Baseball Throw and Dunk-a-Rama. Of course, old favorites such as the Flaky Fish Pond and the Rolly-Polly Ring Toss will be back. Teddy Berke, committee chair, said, "I think people will find the new games a lot of fun."

Also new this year is the Fall Frolic Pie Toss. Coach Ed Sosa and several other faculty members have volunteered to be the "targets" for the pie toss.

Conclusion

School principal, Ms. Tabitha Horton, encourages all students to bring their families and friends to Fall Frolic. "This is really a neighborhood event," she said. "We have something for everyone."

430 Unit 11: Research Report

Reading As a Writer

- The **headline** gets the readers' attention and tells the main idea of the article. *What is the main idea of this news article?*
- The **lead paragraph** or **introduction** presents the most important facts. It answers the questions *Who? What? Where? When? Why?* and *How? Who is invited to this event? Why is the event being held?*
- The **supporting details** give a more complete picture. *What will be added to this year's event?*
- The **conclusion** wraps up the news article. It may include more details or a quotation from someone connected to the event. *How does the writer end this news article?*

How to Write a News Article

1. **Choose** a recent event for your subject. Think about the audience who will read about the event and what they would want to know.
2. **Use** a pyramid structure to outline your news article.
3. **Research** your subject. Take careful notes to answer each of the six questions. Jot down quotations from people at the event. Write the quotations exactly.
4. **Write** your article. Tell *who, what, where, when, why,* and *how* in the lead paragraph. Then write other details from the most important to the least important.

   Who?
   What? Where?
   When? Why? How?

   Supporting details

   Other, less important, details

5. **Think** of a headline that will get the readers' attention.
6. **Revise and proofread** your article. Are the facts clear? Did you use short sentences and paragraphs? Are the names spelled correctly?
7. **Make** a final copy. Work with other writers to make a class newspaper.

Special Focus on Informing

Completing a Form

When you **complete a form**, you provide specific information about yourself. You might complete a form to subscribe to a magazine, to enter a contest, to go on a field trip, or to join an after-school organization. Read this form.

Intramural Soccer Application

Directions → Complete this application. Please print.

Date → Date: September 18, 2001

Name: Kim Harris
Address: 23 Keed Rd.
           Street
           Raleigh   NC   27610
           City   State   Zip

← Writing lines

Phone: (252) 555-1951

Circle your T-shirt size: S   (M)   L

Which position do you prefer playing?

Number your choices from 1 to 4.
  _2_ forward   _3_ halfback
  _1_ fullback   _4_ goalie

Have you ever played on a soccer team before?

Circle yes or no.   (Yes)   No

If yes, for how many seasons? ___2___

What position(s) did you play? forward and fullback

← Information about you

Reading As a Writer

- The **directions** explain how to complete the form. *Should Kim write in cursive or print?*
- The **date** is the month, day, and year on which you fill out the form. *When did Kim fill out this form?*
- Some forms have **writing lines** on which you write information. Others use boxes. *What is Kim's phone number?*
- The **information about you** is often your name, address, and phone number. Some forms may ask for other information. Be sure to check with a parent or guardian if you are asked to give detailed information. *What is Kim's first choice of positions to play?*

Don't forget! Remember to read all the choices before you select one.

How to Complete a Form

1. **Read** the directions carefully.
2. **Date** the form.
3. **Complete** the form. Fill in the information about yourself by writing on the lines and circling your responses. Write your letters and numbers carefully and correctly so that they won't be misread.
4. **Proofread** for mistakes. Check that you have completed every part of the form.

Completing a Form

COMMUNICATION LINK Speaking/Viewing

Giving an Oral Report

When you do research for an oral report, you can look for different kinds of media to present. Photographs, recordings, or videos may make your topic more interesting for your audience. You can also make visual aids of your own to support your spoken ideas.

Which Media?

Models A model can show what something looks like from every side. Would your listeners better understand your topic if you made a model to show?	• dioramas, clay models, papier-mâché objects
Photographs Pictures can show historic events or unusual details. Would your report be clearer if you included a photograph or showed slides of your topic?	• posters, slides; pictures from newspapers, magazines, books 
Illustrations Does your topic contain many facts and figures that you can organize into a chart or a drawing?	• charts, graphs, diagrams, tables, fine art, cut-away diagrams
Technology Could you project a Web site that gives information or that shows pictures of your topic? Use reliable sources to help your audience understand your ideas.	• videotapes, CDs, audiotapes, CD-ROMs, the Internet, computer programs for tables and graphs 

Getting Ready

Prepare the media you have selected. If you plan to show a videotape, be sure to preset the tape to the segment you want to show. Arrange ahead of time any assistance you might need during your report, such as having lights turned off or equipment turned on.

Use the guidelines below to help you practice and give your report.

Before the Talk

- Write notes, or key words and phrases, on note cards.
- Put your notes in order.
- Practice saying words that are hard to pronounce.
- Record your entire talk. Then listen to it. Work on parts that need more practice.

Guidelines for Giving an Oral Report

▶ Stand up straight.
▶ Speak clearly and sound interested in what you are saying.
▶ Don't fidget or move around, but *do* use gestures to make a point.
▶ Be sure not to say *ah, well,* and *um.*
▶ Look at your listeners as you speak.
▶ Make sure that everyone in the audience can see or hear the materials you are using.

 See also pages H47–H49 in the Tools and Tips Handbook.

Apply It

Prepare media for a report you have already written. Use the guidelines above as you give your report. Then answer the following questions.

  Which media did you choose for your report? Why?

  Did your report hold the attention of your audience? How do you know?

  If you could present your report again, what would you do differently?

"How the War Ended"
Media to Use
1. A reading of the Gettysburg Address—CD
2. Picture of Lincoln—from library
3. Map of the last battle—the Internet

COMMUNICATION LINK   Viewing

Evaluating the News

Most people use the mass media to find out about the day's news and events. Newspapers, radio, television, and the Internet are types of mass media. They are used to get information to large numbers of people.

The News in Print

A newspaper, like other mass media, includes much more than the news. Different parts of a newspaper have different purposes. Some parts inform, others educate, and still others try to entertain or persuade.

What's in the Newspaper?	
Terms	**Explanations**
headlines	sum up the article and attract the reader's attention
news stories	tell *who, what, when, where, why,* and *how*; they can be of local, regional, national, or international interest
news photographs	show *who, what, when, where, why,* or *how*
feature stories	give in-depth information about a topic of interest to readers
illustrations	are maps, diagrams, and other drawings made to explain written information
editorials	give the opinions of the paper's editors
political cartoons	combine cartoons and text to give an opinion
reviews	give facts and opinions about books, films, concerts, or the theater
advertisements	paid for by companies to call attention to a product, service, or event
sports, weather	entertain and inform readers
comic strips, crossword puzzles	entertain readers of all ages

436   Unit 11: Research Report

The News Business

Crossword puzzles and comics are clearly not "news." Newspapers print them because they appeal to a wide audience. After all, most newspapers must make money to stay in business.

Newspapers make money in two main ways. They sell copies of the paper to readers, and they sell space in the paper for companies to advertise products and services to readers.

Use the guidelines below to help you evaluate news in print.

Guidelines for Evaluating the News

▶ Notice how the newspaper is organized. What comes first? What is included in the different sections?

▶ Look at the front page. Think about why its stories were chosen to be seen first. Which story has a large photo? Why do you think that photo was chosen?

▶ Flip through the pages, skimming the other news and feature stories. Are the stories mostly local, national, international, or all three?

▶ Look at the editorials. Where else can you find opinions in the paper?

▶ Find the parts of the paper not directly connected to news, such as travel, fashion, advice columns, want ads, and real estate. Which section of the paper has the most ads? Why? Think about why the comic strips are placed where they are.

▶ Look at the ads. Notice whether the same companies advertise in the travel and business sections. Why might this be so?

Apply It

Read or skim through a newspaper. Use the guidelines above to help you think about the news and the features you are seeing. Answer these questions.

- Why do you think the paper is divided into sections?
- Which part of the paper did you enjoy the most? Why?
- Do you think the newspaper gave you an accurate idea of what has happened recently? Explain why or why not.

Section 3
Expressing and Influencing

What You Will Find in This Section:

Getting Started
- Listening to an Opinion 440
- Writing an Opinion Paragraph 441

Unit 12 Writing to Express an Opinion 446

Special Focus on Expressing
Writing a Book Report 468
Writing a Poem 470

Communication Links
Listening/Speaking:
Having a Panel Discussion 476
Viewing/Media:
Finding Points of View in Visuals 478

Unit 13 **Writing to Persuade** 480

Special Focus on Influencing
Writing a Business Letter 503

Communication Links
Listening: Listening for
Persuasive Tactics 505

Viewing/Media:
Watching for Persuasive Tactics 507

Getting Started: Listening

Listening to an Opinion

An **opinion** tells what someone thinks, feels, or believes. An opinion cannot be proved true or false, but its strength can be evaluated by the reasons, facts, and examples that back it up. Two of the main purposes for listening to an opinion are to find out what someone else thinks and to help yourself make up your own mind. Here are some guidelines to help you be a good listener.

Guidelines for Listening to an Opinion

- Identify the topic. What subject is being discussed?
- Notice terms that signal that an opinion is being stated, such as *I think, good, bad,* and *if you ask me.*
- Listen for the opinion. What does the author believe about the topic?
- Listen for reasons. Why does the author hold this opinion?
- Listen for details. What facts or examples explain the reasons?
- Evaluate the reasons and details. Are the reasons good ones? Do the details explain the reasons?

Try It Out Listen as your teacher reads aloud an opinion essay written by a student named Lauren Tancreti and published in a magazine for young people. Listen for information to answer the questions below.

- What is the topic of Lauren Tancreti's essay?
- What does Lauren believe about Jane Addams?
- What reasons and other details does she give to back up her opinion?

440 Section 3: Expressing and Influencing

Getting Started: Paragraphs

Writing an Opinion Paragraph

A paragraph that expresses a writer's thoughts or beliefs about something is an **opinion paragraph**. An opinion paragraph has a topic and a main idea. The **topic** is the subject of the paragraph. The **main idea** is the writer's opinion about the topic. Every sentence supports the main idea. What is the topic of the opinion paragraph below? What is the main idea?

Remember, the first line of a paragraph is indented.

Indent
Opinion statement

Supporting sentences

Concluding sentence

   The aquarium is a great place for school classes to visit. First, teachers don't have to spend their field-trip money for tickets. Admission is free on Tuesdays. Also, the aquarium has a lending library. Teachers and students can borrow books, science kits, and other supplies. The best reason, though, is that the aquarium has excellent hands-on exhibits. Students can observe and handle living sea creatures such as horseshoe crabs and starfish. The aquarium knows how to please all its visitors!

In the paragraph above, the topic is the aquarium. The main idea—the writer's opinion—is that it benefits students and teachers. Which sentence gives the writer's opinion?

The labels show the three parts of an opinion paragraph.

- The **opinion statement** names the topic and expresses the main idea—the writer's opinion.
- **Supporting sentences** explain why the writer thinks or feels this way.
- The **concluding sentence** finishes the paragraph.

Think and Discuss Look again at the paragraph about the aquarium. What reasons are given in the supporting sentences?

Getting Started: Opinion Paragraphs **441**

Getting Started: Paragraphs

The Opinion Statement

 The first sentence in a paragraph usually names the topic and tells the main idea. In an opinion paragraph, this sentence is the **opinion statement**. It tells how the author feels about the topic.

                           Main idea   Topic

Example: The city made a big mistake when it tore down the old ballpark.

   Occasionally, the opinion statement appears at the end of the paragraph. When this happens, it takes the place of the concluding sentence. Which is the opinion statement in the paragraph below? Which are the supporting sentences?

>   At the newly renovated movie theater, you no longer wait in huge lines to buy refreshments. Now dozens of employees staff a gleaming snack bar. When you take your seat, you practically disappear in the plush new chairs! Forget about juggling your popcorn and your drink in your lap, for each armrest now has a cup holder and a little tray. When the movie starts, the new sound system will knock your socks off! It's loud, clear, and no longer interrupted by static. The renovation of the old movie theater is a huge success!

Try It Out On your own or with a partner, read the paragraph below. It is missing the opinion statement. First, write the topic and the main idea of the paragraph. Then write two possible opinion statements for it.

>   _____*Opinion statement*_____. First, riding my bike saves time. I can get to school, the ballpark, or my music lessons faster by riding my bike than by walking. Bike riding is also great exercise. By the time I get to school, I am ready to get started! Finally, riding my bike gives me a sense of freedom. I don't have to wait for anyone but me!

442 **Section 3:** Expressing and Influencing

Supporting Sentences

Supporting sentences usually follow the opinion statement and give strong **reasons** to support the writer's opinion. Each reason, in turn, is supported by details, such as **facts** and **examples**. The chart below shows how this works in the aquarium paragraph on page 441.

Opinion: The aquarium is a great place for classes to visit.			
Reasons	don't have to spend money	library	hands-on exhibits
Details	free on Tuesdays	can borrow science kits	can handle starfish

The paragraph below uses facts and examples in its supporting sentences.

Music is great for changing or improving your mood. Listening to dance music on headphones while I jog allows me to run farther. Playing loud music while I clean my room helps me plow right through the mess! Some scientists offer evidence that music can also help you to relax by making your blood pressure fall. Soft music at the dentist helps slow your pounding heart when the drill starts to buzz. Jazz played low keeps my parents cool when they're fighting traffic. Whether you want to pick up the pace or slow it down, music can help you find the right speed.

Think and Discuss Reread the paragraph above.
- What facts and examples are mentioned in the supporting sentences?

more ▶

Getting Started: Paragraphs

Ordering Reasons In an opinion paragraph, reasons are often organized in order of importance. They may be arranged from least important to most important or from most important to least important. **Transitional words**, such as *also, most important, in addition,* and *another,* help to connect the reasons within a paragraph and can give clues about their importance.

 See page 18 for more transitional words.

Try It Out Use the pictures in the collage or your own ideas to complete the opinion statement below. Write three sentences that support your statement. Use transitional words in at least one sentence.

Opinion statement: I would really like to learn how to _____.

The Concluding Sentence

The **concluding sentence** finishes the paragraph. This sentence can restate the main idea in a new way or make a final comment or observation. In the aquarium paragraph on page 441, the concluding sentence makes a final comment.

Try It Out Read the paragraph below. It is missing the concluding sentence. On your own or with a partner, write two different concluding sentences for the paragraph.

> If there were a contest for "Father of the Year," my dad would win first prize. First, he always has time for me. He might have a million things to do, but he drops everything when I need help. My dad also knows how to make me feel special. He's always doing unexpected little things, such as staying at soccer practice instead of just dropping me off. Finally, no one has a better sense of humor than my father. You don't stay down in the dumps for long when he's around.
> _____.
> *Concluding sentence*

Section 3: Expressing and Influencing

Write Your Own Opinion Paragraph

Now it's time to write a paragraph of your own. What do you feel strongly about? First, write an opinion statement that expresses your feeling or belief. Then think of how you can best support or explain your opinion. Make a list of reasons, facts, and examples that explain why you feel the way you do. After sharing your ideas with a partner, you are ready to write!

Checklist for My Paragraph

- ✔ My **opinion statement** names the topic and introduces the main idea—my opinion.
- ✔ The **supporting sentences** give reasons for my opinion. Details, such as facts and examples, explain my reasons.
- ✔ My **concluding sentence** restates the main idea in a new way or makes a final comment.

Looking Ahead

Knowing how to write an opinion paragraph will help you write an opinion essay. The diagram below shows how the parts of an opinion paragraph mirror the parts of an opinion essay.

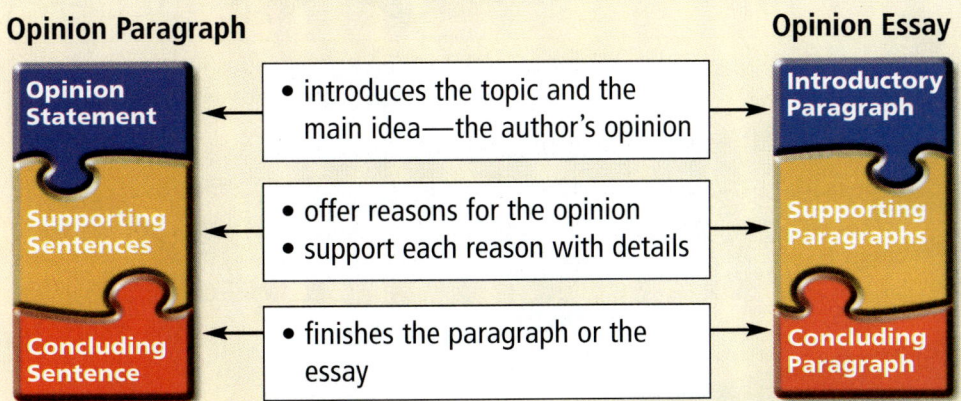

Getting Started: Opinion Paragraphs **445**

Unit 12

Writing to Express an Opinion

There's nothing I'd rather do than cover paper in colors.

Angela Shelf Medearis wrote an opinion essay about Kwanzaa, an African American holiday. How does she feel about this celebration?

Why I Love Kwanzaa

by Angela Shelf Medearis

Each year I look forward to winter because I love celebrating Kwanzaa. The first reason I love Kwanzaa is that it is an original African American cultural holiday. It was created in 1966 by Dr. Maulana "Ron" Karenga as a way of unifying the African American family and community through a celebration based on our African heritage. Kwanzaa begins on December 26 and ends on January 1. In our house, we celebrate Christmas and Kwanzaa.

Another reason I love Kwanzaa is that it involves wonderful food and presents! Food is a big part of most celebrations, and Kwanzaa is no different. Kwanzaa is sort of like an African American Thanksgiving celebration. During Kwanzaa I cook recipes that contain ingredients such as okra, peanuts, sesame, and black-eyed peas. These ingredients were brought from Africa to America and were introduced to Americans by African cooks. Including such ingredients in my Kwanzaa celebration is a way of honoring our ancestral heritage. On the last day of the celebration, we exchange handmade presents or books. I love making gifts that involve food, like homemade vinegars and cookies. I also love buying and receiving books.

See www.eduplace.com/kids/ for information about Angela Shelf Medearis.

Finally, I love Kwanzaa because it focuses on ways we can improve ourselves, help others, and secure our future as a family and as a community. We study one of the seven Kwanzaa principles each day of the celebration. These principles, called the *Nguzo Saba* in the African language of Swahili, are unity, self-determination, collective work and responsibility, cooperative economics, purpose, creativity, and faith. Each day we shout "Harambee," which is a pledge to "pull together" to achieve our goals.

More and more African American families are celebrating the holiday, and people of all races attend Kwanzaa festivals. For me, Kwanzaa has become a wonderful way to share my African American heritage with my friends, to focus on improving myself and on helping others, and to share good food and gifts with my family. Harambee!

Reading As a Writer

Think About the Opinion Essay

- How does Angela Shelf Medearis feel about Kwanzaa?
- How many reasons does the writer give for her opinion? What are they?
- What transitional words signal to readers that the writer is about to tell a new reason?
- What details support the reason in the third paragraph?
- Where does the writer sum up her feelings about Kwanzaa?

Think About Writer's Craft

- Sometimes writers repeat phrases to add emphasis and to help make smooth transitions from one thought to the next. Find a phrase that Angela Shelf Medearis repeats.

Think About the Pictures

- What do the photographs tell you about Kwanzaa that is not described in the essay?

Responding

Write responses to these questions.

- **Personal Response** What is your favorite celebration? How are your feelings about it similar to the writer's feelings about Kwanzaa? How are they different?
- **Critical Thinking** Pick one of the seven principles of Kwanzaa and explain how it is demonstrated, or shown, in the holiday.

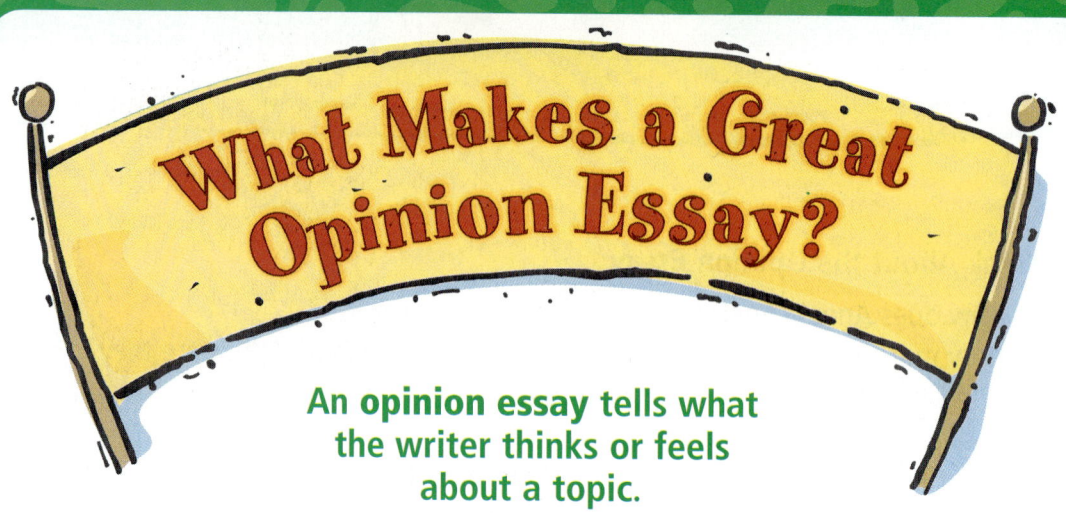

What Makes a Great Opinion Essay?

An opinion essay tells what the writer thinks or feels about a topic.

Use these guidelines when you write an opinion essay.

▶ Select a topic that matters to you. Let readers hear your voice when you write.

▶ State your opinion in the introduction in a clear and interesting way.

▶ Give three or more reasons to support your opinion.

▶ Use details, such as facts and examples, to explain each reason.

▶ Tell your most important reason first or last.

▶ Write a conclusion that sums up the ideas in your essay.

GRAMMAR CHECK

Use possessive pronouns to show ownership. Use pronouns such as *her* and *their* before nouns. Use pronouns such as *hers* and *theirs* to replace nouns in a sentence.

Student Model

WORKING DRAFT

Allison France loves living in Florida, and she has a lot of reasons for feeling that way. She wrote this draft to share her opinion.

Allison France

> Will this introduction really draw in your readers?

Working Draft

Florida

Living in Florida is great. Here are some reasons why I like Florida so much.

Florida is the twenty-seventh state. Tallahassee is its capital. Florida is a peninsula in the southeast part of the United States.

World-class theme parks are common in Florida. Disney World is a neat place to go. It has a lot of neat rides, great food, nice shows, great scenery, and lots of cool characters. They have neat rides at Universal Studios too. On my favorite ride, "Back to the Future," riders get to bolt into the future, zoom back to the Ice Age, race through an avalanche, and dodge *T. rex*! Shamu the whale attracts many visitors to Sea World. When I went there, I came face to face with sharks, eels, and barracuda, from the safety of an underwater tunnel, of course. You can never be bored in Florida!

I'd have to say that the weather is what I like best about Florida. It never snows, so no one ever has to shovel an icy walk. Here it's frequently sunny and always warm, rain or shine. Yes, we do get some rain, but as a result we are surrounded by nice plants and beautiful

> Does this reason support your opinion?

> What great elaboration! This example really shows what fun the rides are.

> This reason means the most to you. Can you tell it first or last?

more →

Student Model continued

Working Draft

flowers. All in all, you couldn't ask for better weather.

If you're looking for fun in the sun, Florida's the place to go. You can stay in a resort right on the beach! They're lined up all along the coast in Daytona, Cocoa, and New Smyrna. You can do many fun things at the beach, or just relax.

Now you know why I think Florida is the best place to live.

> Could you tell more about plants and fun at the beach?

Reading As a Writer

- What did Sal like about Allison's essay? What questions did Sal have for her?
- What reasons did Allison give for loving Florida?
- In the third paragraph, what adjectives could Allison use instead of *neat*, *great*, and *nice*?
- What might Allison do to improve her conclusion?

Student Model

Allison revised her opinion essay after discussing it with her classmates. Read her final version to see how she improved it.

There's No Place Like Home
by Allison France

What's it like living in paradise? Just imagine beautiful weather, world-class theme parks, and spectacular beaches, and you're looking at Florida, the place I call home. I couldn't imagine living anywhere else.

I'd have to say that the weather is what I like best about Florida. It never snows, so no one ever has to shovel an icy walk. It's frequently sunny and always warm, rain or shine. Yes, we do get some rain, but as a result we are surrounded by lush green plants, such as ferns, palms, and grasses, and exotic tropical flowers, like wild white azaleas that bloom along the highway. All in all, you couldn't ask for better weather.

I also love Florida for its world-class theme parks. Disney World has a lot of exciting rides, delicious international foods, entertaining shows, beautiful scenery, and lots of cool characters. They have exciting rides at Universal Studios too. On my favorite ride, "Back to the Future," riders get to bolt into the future, zoom back to the Ice Age, race through an avalanche, and dodge *T. rex*! Shamu the whale attracts many people to Sea World. When I went there, I came face to face with sharks, eels, and barracuda, from the safety of an underwater tunnel, of course. You can never be bored in Florida!

Last, but not least, if you're looking for fun in the sun, Florida's the place to go. You can stay in a resort right on

This introduction really makes me want to read the rest of your essay!

Good! You tell your most important reason first.

You did a great job of replacing dull adjectives with more exact words.

These details make me think I'm looking at a photo!

more →

Student Model continued

the beach. They're lined up all along the coast in Daytona, Cocoa, and New Smyrna. If you feel like taking it easy, you can search for seashells, build sandcastles, or doze under an umbrella. If you're looking for a little more excitement, you can ride the waves or go surfing. As you can see, there's something for everyone to enjoy!

Now that you understand what it's like living in paradise, I'm sure you won't be surprised to hear me say that even if I had my choice of any place to live, I'd still pick Florida. It's a beautiful, fun-packed place to call home!

> I can really hear your voice! This topic obviously means a lot to you.

Reading As a Writer

- How did Allison respond to Sal's questions and comments?
- Why did Allison cut the paragraph about Florida's history?
- What details did Allison add to show rather than tell about the nice plants and beautiful flowers? fun beach activities?
- What changes did Allison make to the conclusion of her final copy? Why is this conclusion better?

454 Unit 12: Opinion   See www.eduplace.com/kids/hme/ for more examples of student writing.

Write an Opinion Essay

▶ Start Thinking

Make a writing folder for your opinion essay. Copy the questions in bold print, and put your paper in your folder. Write your answers as you think about and choose your topic.

- **Who will be my audience?** Will it be my classmates? my parents? people in my community?
- **What will be my purpose?** Do I want to tell people about something that is fun? warn them about something dangerous?
- **How will I publish or share my opinion essay?** Will I create a booklet? read it aloud? make a poster?

▶ Choose Your Topic

❶ List five topics. List opinions about each one. Don't list people.

❷ Discuss your opinions with a partner.
- Can you think of reasons to support each opinion?
- Which ideas does your partner like? Why?
- Is any opinion too broad? Could you write about one part? Notice how a student broke one big topic, *holidays*, into smaller parts. Each part could be its own essay.

Need an Idea?
Tell how you feel about
- computers
- the circus
- a certain law or rule
- volunteering

See page 466 for more ideas.

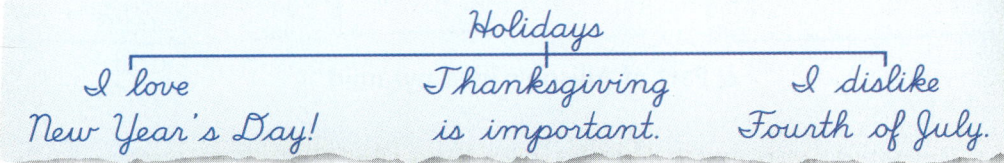

Holidays
I love New Year's Day! | Thanksgiving is important. | I dislike Fourth of July.

❸ Ask yourself these questions about each opinion. Then circle the opinion you will write about.
- Do I feel strongly about this opinion?
- Do I have enough to say about it? Can I support my reasons with details?
- Will my audience care about this opinion?

Prewriting 455

The Writing Process — PREWRITING · DRAFTING · REVISING · PROOFREADING · PUBLISHING

▶ Explore Your Opinion

Make sure you can back up your opinion with reasons before you share it with others! Strong reasons answer the question *Why?* about your opinion.

❶ Brainstorm reasons. Have a partner take the opposite point of view and challenge your opinion. Your partner's comments and questions will help you generate strong reasons.

❷ Make an idea pyramid. List at least three reasons that support your opinion. Use the idea pyramid below as a model.

▲ Part of Allison's idea pyramid

If you can't think of enough good reasons, try another topic.

Tech Tip
You can brainstorm on a computer. Just remember to start drafting in a separate document.

 See page 14 for other ideas for exploring a topic.

456 Unit 12: Opinion   See www.eduplace.com/kids/hme/ for graphic organizers.

PREWRITING DRAFTING REVISING PROOFREADING PUBLISHING

Focus Skill

Elaborating Your Reasons

Explain, or elaborate, your reasons with details. Give facts and examples.

Opinion: Science Club is fun.

Reason	Details
great activities	**examples:** field trips, experiments, speakers
lots of members	**fact:** grew to 25 members this year

Check that your details are exact and clear. Expand your details to tell more.

Reason: great activities

Details	Expanded Details
field trips	planetarium and natural history museum
experiments	tested drinking water in lab
speakers	geologist and marine biologist

Later, when you start drafting, these details will be in your supporting sentences.

Think and Discuss Look at page 447 of the published model.

- What reason for loving Kwanzaa does the writer give in the second paragraph? What details does she give to support that reason?

▶ ## Explore Your Reasons

Add details to your idea pyramid to support your reasons. Be sure to elaborate all your reasons with details.

Reason: world-class theme parks

Details:
great food
great scenery
~~warm and sunny~~
"Back to the Future" ride
Shamu the whale

Part of Allison's idea pyramid ▶

Prewriting **457**

The Writing Process

PREWRITING · DRAFTING · REVISING · PROOFREADING · PUBLISHING

Focus Skill

Organizing Your Reasons

Now that you've collected your building materials—your reasons—you need to decide on the best way to assemble them. Without a plan, it's hard to know where to begin! Follow the steps below to help you get started.

Evaluate your reasons. Which are strong? Which have the most and best supporting details? Here are three weak reasons Allison took out when she explained why she loves Florida.

Restates opinion	Florida is awesome!
Unrelated	The state flower is the orange blossom
Too general	It's a good place to have fun.

Take out any reasons that you have difficulty supporting.

Order your reasons. Which are the most important to you? You should write about the most important reason either first or last.

Use transitional words and phrases. Use these words and phrases within a paragraph to move smoothly from detail to detail. Use them between paragraphs to move smoothly from reason to reason.

Transitional words and phrases	another reason, finally, first, also, last, however, therefore, the most important reason, then, to begin with, for example

Think and Discuss Look at Allison's final copy on pages 453–454.

- Why are the reasons in Allison's final copy better than those she took out?

▶ Plan Your Essay

Reread your idea pyramid. Cross out reasons that you can't support with clear, exact details. Number the reasons in the order you will write about them.

458 Unit 12: Opinion

PREWRITING **DRAFTING** REVISING PROOFREADING PUBLISHING

▶ Draft Your Essay

❶ Write a paragraph for each reason on your pyramid. Skip every other line to allow room for changes. Don't worry about mistakes at this point.

- Write a topic sentence that tells your reason.
- Write supporting sentences that include details to explain your reason.
- Use transitional words within and between paragraphs.

GRAMMAR TIP ▶ Use a comma after introductory words in a sentence.

❷ Decide how you want your essay to sound. Will it be funny? serious? critical? Let your feelings show through when you write. Remember, the ideas are your own, and the voice you use to tell them should be too. Look at a paragraph from one student's draft.

> Opinion: The Internet is this century's best invention.
>
> Reason: planning trips
> Reason: doing research for reports
> Reason: keeping in touch with faraway friends and relatives
>
> Details: photographs reservations information

>   The Internet makes trip planning a breeze. Just sit back in your comfy chair, and you're off! First, log onto a national park's Web site. Find out how much campsites cost and whether there are any available. Then yawn, stretch, and check the calendar of activities. If you have any energy left, download a few choice photos. Finally, print this information and show it to your parents. ~~They won't believe how quickly you found stuff.~~ They'll be loading the car before you know it!

Tech Tip
Dim the screen while drafting. This will help you focus on expressing your ideas rather than avoiding mistakes.

Drafting **459**

The Writing Process

PREWRITING | **DRAFTING** | REVISING | PROOFREADING | PUBLISHING

Focus Skill

Introductions and Conclusions

Good Introductions

Make your introduction more interesting than *Science Club is an enjoyable after-school activity.* Compare these examples.

> Use your own voice! If you try too hard to sound a particular way, your writing will sound flat or awkward.

Lively opinion statement	I never thought I'd say this, but I love Science Club!
Question	Is our drinking water safe? That's just one important question that Science Club is trying to answer.
Description	Ten rain-soaked fifth-graders crouched by the bog gathering slimy algae samples. You might say "Yuck," but I say "Yeah!" Outings like this make Science Club an awesome adventure!

Good Conclusions

A good conclusion sums up your main ideas and makes your essay feel complete.

Weak Conclusion	Strong Conclusion
Science Club keeps me very busy. My friend wants me to join the Movie Club, but I don't have enough time to participate in two clubs.	Experiments, chats with scientists, and interesting trips have become regular events in my life. I never knew that learning could be so much fun!

Think and Discuss

- Why is the strong conclusion better than the weak one?
- What kind of introduction does the author use in the published model on page 447? in the student model on page 453?

▶ Draft Your Introduction and Conclusion

Write two introductions and two conclusions for your essay. Choose the ones you like better.

460 Unit 12: Opinion

Evaluating Your Opinion Essay

▶ **Reread** your opinion essay. Which parts need improvement? Use this rubric to help you decide. Write the sentences that describe your essay.

Rings the Bell!

- ☐ The introduction states my opinion in an interesting way.
- ☐ My reasons are strong and are supported with details.
- ☐ This essay really sounds like me!
- ☐ My reasons are in a clear order of importance.
- ☐ The conclusion sums up the important points.
- ☐ There are almost no mistakes in capitalization, punctuation, or spelling.

Getting Stronger

- ☐ The introduction could be more interesting.
- ☐ Some reasons are vague or unclear. Some need more details.
- ☐ In places, the writing doesn't sound like me.
- ☐ My reasons are not in a clear order of importance.
- ☐ The conclusion doesn't sum up the important points.
- ☐ Mistakes make the story confusing in some places.

Try Harder

- ☐ The introduction is dull!
- ☐ I have fewer than three reasons. I need a lot more details.
- ☐ This essay doesn't sound like me at all!
- ☐ It's hard to follow the connections between my ideas.
- ☐ This essay just ends. I didn't write a conclusion.
- ☐ There are a lot of mistakes in capitalization, punctuation, or spelling.

See www.eduplace.com/kids/hme/ to interact with this rubric.

The Writing Process

PREWRITING · DRAFTING · **REVISING** · PROOFREADING · PUBLISHING

▶ Revise Your Opinion Essay

❶ Revise your essay. Use the list of sentences you wrote from the rubric. Work on the parts that you described with sentences from "Getting Stronger" and "Try Harder"

❷ Have a writing conference.

When You're the Writer Read your opinion essay to a partner. Discuss any questions or problems you're having. Take notes to remember what your partner says.

When You're the Listener Tell at least two things you like about the opinion essay. Ask questions about any parts that are confusing.

Revising Tip

Cut apart your working draft so you can rearrange paragraphs or add new ones.

What should I say?

The Writing Conference

If you're thinking . . .	You could say . . .
The opening doesn't catch my interest.	Could you start with a description, opinion statement, or a question?
This reason doesn't seem very important.	Does this reason really explain why you think or feel this way?
This reason isn't clear.	Can you give more details to support this reason?
I can't tell where one reason stops and the next one starts.	Is each reason a separate paragraph? Can you add transitional words to connect your reasons?
This writing seems flat.	How do you really feel about this topic?
The essay just stops.	Can you sum up the important points?

❸ Make other revisions to your opinion essay. Use your writing conference notes and the Revising Strategies on the next page.

Revising Strategies

Elaborating: Word Choice **Synonyms** are words with the same or nearly the same meaning. Using synonyms for words you use a lot will make your writing more interesting and exact.

Without Synonyms	With Synonyms
I **like** flying. Takeoff is **neat**. The crew is always **nice**. If the pilot is **good**, the landing is **okay**.	I **adore** flying. Takeoff is **exciting**. The crew is always **welcoming**. If the pilot is **skilled**, the landing is **smooth**.

▶ Replace three or four words in your opinion essay with synonyms.

📖 Use the Thesaurus Plus on page H81. See also page H13.

Elaborating: Details Add details within a sentence, or write more sentences.

Without Details	With Details
You can see **many things** below.	You can see **winding rivers, huge forests, or bustling cities** below.

▶ Find at least three places in your opinion essay where you can add details.

Sentence Fluency Make your sentences different lengths to keep them from sounding choppy.

Choppy sentences	The view is delightful. We look out the window. We see sparkling water. We see rocky mountaintops.
Smoother sentences	The view is delightful. **When we look out the window, we see sparkling water and rocky mountaintops.**

▶ Try making at least three sentences different lengths. Does your essay sound less choppy?

GRAMMAR LINK ▶ See also page 191.

Revising 463

The Writing Process

PREWRITING · DRAFTING · REVISING · **PROOFREADING** · PUBLISHING

▶ Proofread Your Opinion Essay

Proofread your opinion essay, using the Proofreading Checklist and the Grammar and Spelling Connections. Proofread for one skill at a time. Use a class dictionary to check spellings.

Proofreading Checklist
Did I
- ✓ indent all paragraphs?
- ✓ correct any fragments or run-on sentences?
- ✓ write possessive pronouns correctly?
- ✓ write interjections correctly?
- ✓ correct any spelling errors?

📖 Use the Guide to Capitalization, Punctuation, and Usage on page H57.

Proofreading Marks
- ¶ Indent
- ∧ Add
- ⌒ Delete
- ≡ Capital letter
- / Small letter

Proofreading Tip
Read your essay aloud to a partner. You may notice mistakes when you hear them.

Grammar and Spelling Connections

Possessive Pronouns Possessive pronouns show ownership. Use pronouns such as *her* and *their* before nouns. Use pronouns such as *hers* and *theirs* in place of a noun.

Pronoun Before Noun	Pronoun in Place of Noun
My essay was about **our** flight to Colorado.	This essay is **mine**.

GRAMMAR LINK ▶ See also page 222.

Interjections An interjection is a word or words that show feeling or emotion. Use an exclamation point or a comma after an interjection.

    Phil: **Wow!** That ride was scary! Is there anything tamer?
    Jamie: **Well,** I suppose we could try the teacups.

GRAMMAR LINK ▶ See also page 192.

Spelling the |ō| Sound The |ō| sound is often spelled *o, o-consonant-e, oa,* or *ow.*

    g**o**, th**o**se, c**oa**st, sh**ow**

📖 See the Spelling Guide on page H67.

Unit 12: Opinion   Go to www.eduplace.com/kids/hme/ for proofreading practice.

PREWRITING DRAFTING REVISING PROOFREADING **PUBLISHING**

▶ Publish Your Opinion Essay

❶ **Make a neat final copy** of your opinion essay. Be sure to fix all errors.

❷ **Title** your essay. Think of a title that will make your readers interested, such as "The Greatest Invention" rather than "The Internet."

> **GRAMMAR TIP** ▶ Capitalize the first, the last, and each important word in the title.

❸ **Publish** or share your essay in a way that suits your audience.

Tips for Making a Stairstep Booklet

- Fold four sheets of paper to form flaps of 3, 4, 5, and 6 inches. Tuck them inside one another. Staple them on the crease.
- The top flap is your cover. The other flaps are for your reasons. Write one on each flap.
- Open the first flap. Write your introduction and the paragraph for your first reason. Continue for the other reasons. Write your conclusion after the paragraph for your third reason.
- Add drawings or magazine art on each flap.

Ideas for Sharing

Write It
- ★ Create a stairstep booklet.
- Write a letter to a newspaper. See page 503 for tips.

Say It
- Invite parents and friends for an evening of oral reading at school.
- Read your essay aloud to begin a panel discussion. See page 476 for tips.

Show It
- Make a poster with a picture for each reason.

▶ Reflect

Write about your writing experience. Use these questions to get started.
- What did you learn about writing an opinion essay?
- What was easy to do? What was most challenging?
- How does this paper compare with other papers you have written?

Publishing **465**

Assessment Link

Writing Prompts

Use these prompts as ideas for opinion essays or to practice for a test. Decide who your audience will be, and write your essay in a way that will be clear to them.

1 Name the invention you think has most improved our lives. How has this invention made our lives safer? more fun? more convenient? What would life be like without this invention?

2 Some athletes make millions of dollars each year. Do you think that is right? Why or why not? Write a letter to a local newspaper to explain your opinion.

3 Do you think it's better to be an only child or to have sisters and brothers? Tell the advantages and disadvantages of each.

4 What's your favorite movie? What did you like best about it? Write a review of the movie for someone who hasn't seen it.

Writing Across the Curriculum

5 **FINE ART**
What would it be like to live in a building like this? Write your opinion of the architect's design.

Habitat, Montreal, designed by Moshe Safdie

See www.eduplace.com/kids/hme/ for more prompts.

Assessment Link

Test Practice

This prompt to write an opinion essay is like ones you might find on a writing test. Read the prompt.

> **Name the invention you think has most improved our lives.** How has this invention made our lives safer? more fun? more convenient? What would life be like without this invention?

Here are some strategies to help you do a good job responding to a prompt like this.

Remember that an opinion essay tells what the writer thinks or feels about a topic.

❶ Look for clue words that tell what to write about. What are the clue words in the prompt above?

❷ Choose a topic that fits the clue words. Write the clue words and your topic.

Clue Words	My Topic
invention most improved our lives	I will write an essay describing how cars have made life more enjoyable and convenient.

❸ Plan your writing. Use an idea pyramid.

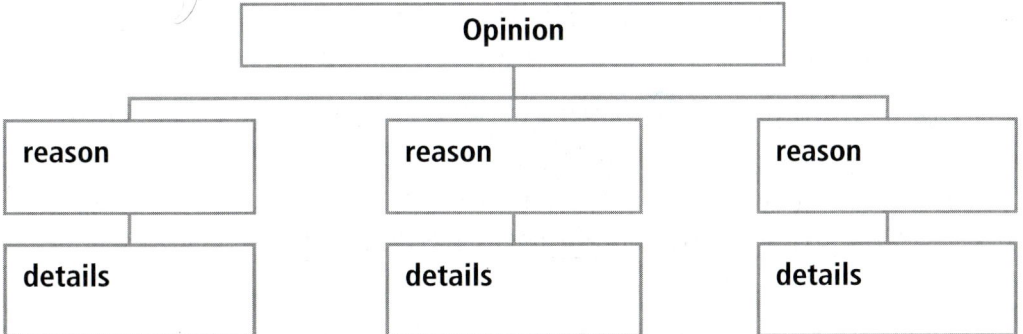

❹ You will get a good score if you remember the description of what kind of opinion essay rings the bell in the rubric on page 461.

See www.eduplace.com/kids/hme/ for graphic organizers.

Test Practice **467**

Special Focus on Expressing

Writing a Book Report

Writing a **book report** is a way to share information and opinions about a book you have read. Read Nora's report on *When Will This Cruel War Be Over?*

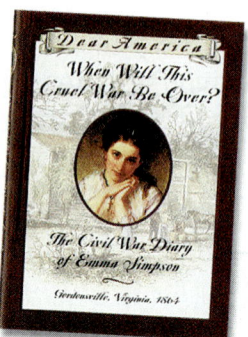

Title → *When Will This Cruel War Be Over?*
Author → by Barry Denenberg

Introduction
> If you want to learn the facts about the Civil War, read a history book. If you want to know what it was like to live during the Civil War, read *When Will This Cruel War Be Over?*

Description
> Emma Simpson is a teenager living on a plantation in Gordonsville, Virginia. Her diary tells about a year when the war turned her family's world upside down. First her brother dies. He is a soldier in the South's Confederate army. Later, Union soldiers from the North take over their house. They force Emma, her mother, her aunt, and her young cousins to live on the top floor. Emma and her family live in fear. They feel trapped and can only fix meals when the soldiers are out of the house. The soldiers stay for about two months. When the soldiers leave, they almost destroy the home.

Opinion
> This book is fascinating, especially if you like history. It is sad and exciting. Read *When Will This Cruel War Be Over?*, especially if you want to find out what happens to Emma after the soldiers leave.

Conclusion

See www.eduplace.com/kids/hme/ for more examples of book reports.

Reading As a Writer

- The **title** gives the name of the book. *What is the title of this book?*
- The **author** is the person who wrote the book. *Who is the author?*
- The **introduction** presents the subject of the report and captures the reader's interest. *How did Nora begin her report?*
- The **description** tells what the book is about.
  What is this book about? What did Nora tell about the book?
- The **opinion** tells what the reader thought of the book.
  What was Nora's opinion?
- The **conclusion** sums up the report and leaves the reader with something to think about. *How did Nora conclude her report?*

How to Write a Book Report

1. **List** the title of the book and the author's name.

2. **Introduce** the book by making the reader curious about it. You might begin with a quotation from the book, a surprising piece of information, or a question.

3. **Summarize** information that describes the book. Include at least one event from the story in your summary.

4. **Give** your opinion. Tell what you thought about this book and why.

5. **Write** a conclusion that wraps up your book report.

6. **Revise and proofread** your report. Use the Proofreading Checklist on page 464. Use a dictionary to check your spelling.

7. **Display** a neat final copy of your book report in your classroom's reading center or in the school library for others to read.

Tell About This!

Ask yourself these questions.
- What one event stands out?
- Is the story funny, sad, suspenseful, or frightening?
- Is the story fiction or nonfiction?

Writing a Book Report

Special Focus on Expressing

Writing a Poem

Poets sometimes tell a story in a poem. The story might be serious or silly, describing a real experience or something the writer made up. A good story poem will also delight the reader with its use of language.

Read these models to see how the writers spin a tale in a poem.

Daddy Fell into the Pond

Everyone grumbled. The sky was gray.
We had nothing to do and nothing to say.
We were nearing the end of a dismal day,
And there seemed to be nothing beyond.
    THEN
    Daddy fell into the pond!

And everyone's face grew merry and bright,
And Timothy danced for sheer delight.
"Give me the camera, quick, oh quick!
He's crawling out of the duckweed." Click!

Then the gardener suddenly slapped his knee,
And doubled up, shaking silently,
And the ducks all quacked as if they were daft
And it sounded as if the old drake laughed.

Oh, there wasn't a thing that didn't respond
    WHEN
    Daddy fell into the pond!

Alfred Noyes

maggie and milly and molly and may

maggie and milly and molly and may
went down to the beach(to play one day)

and maggie discovered a shell that sang
so sweetly she couldn't remember her troubles,and

milly befriended a stranded star
whose rays five languid fingers were

and molly was chased by a horrible thing
which raced sideways while blowing bubbles:and

may came home with a smooth round stone
as small as a world and as large as alone.

For whatever we lose(like a you or a me)
it's always ourselves we find at the sea.

E. E. Cummings

Special Focus continued

Instant Storm

One day in Thrift-Rite Supermart
My jaw dropped wide with wonder,
For there, right next to frozen peas,
Sat frozen French-fried thunder,
Vanilla-flavored lightning bolts,
Fresh-frozen raindrop rattle—
So I bought the stuff and hauled it home
And grabbed my copper kettle.

I'd cook me a mess of homemade storm!
But when it started melting,
The thunder shook my kitchen sink,
The ice-cold rain kept pelting,
Eight lightning bolts bounced round the room
And snapped my pancake turners—
What a blooming shame!
    Then a rainbow came
And spanned my two front burners.

X. J. Kennedy

Reading As a Writer

- In a sentence or two, sum up the story that each poem tells.
- Look at how the lines are grouped in each poem. Why do you think the poets grouped their lines in these different ways?
- In each poem, which lines end in words that rhyme? that almost rhyme?
- Which poem uses dialogue? What does it add to the poem?

How to Write a Story Poem

1 **Decide** on a story idea. Here are ideas from the poems you just read.

Tell me a story! Make me weep! Make me laugh!

- Tell about something that happened to you, as Alfred Noyes does.
- Write a story about other people, as E. E. Cummings does.
- Go on an imaginative romp, as X. J. Kennedy does. Write about your talking vacuum cleaner or the day you turned into a bird.

2 **Map** your story. Make a chart like this one, with notes about the people, the place, the events, and details about how things looked, smelled, tasted, felt, and sounded. Add dialogue if you wish.

Who, What, Where	Details
—I woke	—yellow beak
—I'd turned into a bird	—red wing, blue wing
	—funny green feet
—I laughed	—cuckoo sounds

3 **Think** about stanzas. **Stanzas** are groupings of lines, separated by a space. They can have different rhyming patterns. In two-line stanzas, which are called **couplets,** the end words usually rhyme as in the last four lines of the poem on page 471. Here are some rhyming patterns for longer stanzas.

And everyone's face grew merry and **bright**,   A
And Timothy danced for sheer **delight**.   A
"Give me the camera, quick, oh **quick**!   B
He's crawling out of the duckweed." **Click**!   B

One day in Thrift-Rite Supermart   A
My jaw dropped wide with **wonder**,   B
For there, right next to frozen peas,   C
Sat frozen French-fried **thunder**.   B

more ▶

Writing a Poem **473**

Special Focus *continued*

Decide on the number of lines to put in each stanza. Look at the poems on pages 470–472 for ideas. Then select a rhyming pattern.

❹ **Write** your poem.

- Use ideas from your chart.
- Leave a space between stanzas. Try writing a stanza about each main event.
- End your poem in a memorable way. You might tell what the story means or finish with a pleasing image, like the rainbow in "Instant Storm."

Even after you've chosen a stanza and a rhyming pattern, you can "bend the rules" a little if it helps you write a better poem.

❺ **Reread** your poem. Does each stanza have the right number of lines? Did you follow your rhyming pattern? Is any part too wordy?

> **Keep It Light!**
>
> Some words are like extra baggage. Follow these hints to keep your poem from getting bogged down in wordiness.
>
> - Cross out *very*, *really*, and *so*. Instead of *very bright*, use an exact word like *brilliant*.
> - Replace forms of *to be* and *to have* with strong exact verbs.
> - Don't use unimportant, rambling phrases. Dive into the story.

❻ **Revise** your poem. Read it aloud to a partner, and ask for feedback. Make more changes if you need to.

Decide on capitalization and punctuation in your poem. Many poets begin the first word of each line with a capital letter, even if the word does not begin a new sentence. Follow this pattern if you wish.

📖 Use the Thesaurus Plus at the back of this book.

❼ **Proofread** your poem. Use a dictionary to check spellings.

❽ **Publish** your story poem. Act it out for your class, or deliver it in a dramatic reading. Use an overhead projector to show your poem to the class, or put it on your school Internet site.

HELP? See pages 350–351 for dramatizing help.

Unit 12: Opinion

Writing an Acrostic

Do you have a favorite word? Maybe it's a food you love, the name of your pet, or your own name. You can use this word to create an interesting poem called an **acrostic**. In an acrostic, the letters that begin each line spell the subject of the poem.

Jumping up high to block the ball
Amazing save
Making a goal
Each team was surprised when I
Scored

James Alfano,
Student Writer

Happy means
A lot of
Pears falling off a
Pear tree and
You pick up the pears and make a pie.

Linda Romano,
Student Writer

Reading As a Writer

- What words did the writers choose for their acrostics?
- What event does each poem describe? What connection do you see between the event and the acrostic word?

How to Write an Acrostic Poem

1. **Pick** a word that is interesting to you. It might be the name of a person or a place, something you like to do, or any noun, verb, or adjective that tickles your imagination.

2. **Brainstorm** a list of things and experiences that the word brings to your mind. Include sensory words and phrases that describe sights, sounds, feelings, tastes, and smells. Circle the best ideas.

3. **Write** an acrostic based on the word you chose. Try not to write each line on a different topic. Focus the poem on one main event or idea.

4. **Revise and proofread** your poem. Cut unnecessary words.

5. **Publish** your acrostic.

COMMUNICATION LINK Listening/Speaking

Having a Panel Discussion

In a panel discussion, a group of people talk about a topic in front of an audience. Each member of the group is called a panelist. Panelists take turns sharing their information and ideas. Each is given a limited time period in which to speak.

A classroom panel discussion might work this way.

The moderator	• tells the audience the topic • introduces the panelists
Panelist 1	• speaks on the topic for three minutes
Panelist 2	• speaks on the topic for three minutes
Panelist 3	• speaks on the topic for three minutes
The moderator	• announces that the panelists can now discuss the topic together for ten minutes
The panelists	• talk and disagree politely
The audience	• asks questions of any or all of the panelists for ten minutes; panelists respond

When you take part in a panel discussion, you are both a speaker and a listener. Be sure that you understand the other speakers' opinions and reasons before you agree or disagree.

Unit 12: Opinion

Here are some guidelines to help you be a good panelist.

Guidelines for Being a Panelist

When You Are Speaking

- Clearly state your opinion about the topic.
- Give reasons for your opinion. Support your reasons with facts.
- Speak loudly enough so that everyone can hear you.
- Be polite when you disagree with others.

Organize your ideas before you speak. Write key ideas on note cards.

When You Are Listening

- Pay close attention to the person who is speaking. Watch the speaker's face and listen to the tone of his or her voice. Try to block out sounds that make your mind wander away from the discussion.
- As the speaker presents his or her thoughts, take notes that you can refer to if you need to ask questions.
- Try to understand each speaker's point of view. Listen to the reasons the speaker gives for his or her views. Are the reasons based on facts or opinions? Do they make sense?
- Don't interrupt another panelist. Use your notes to ask questions after the speaker has finished.

Apply It

Plan a panel discussion. Choose a topic and decide on time limits for the panelists. Research the topic and then write your opinion about it. Follow the guidelines above when you are speaking and listening. After the discussion, answer these questions.

 Need a Topic?
- favorite sports
- countries to visit
- the best seasons of the year

- Which guidelines were difficult to follow? Why do you think so?
- What kinds of topics do you think would work well for a panel discussion? Explain why.

COMMUNICATION LINK   Viewing

Finding Points of View in Visuals

Every day you see hundreds, even thousands, of visuals or images. People create these images to send messages to audiences. Each visual has a purpose. Some inform or entertain, for example. Instead of giving all the facts, though, an image may give only one viewpoint. A viewpoint is a way of thinking about a subject.

Think It Through

Look carefully at each photograph. Notice that the main focus, or center of interest, of each photo is a woman at work. The photos send different messages, however. Look at the details in the first photo. The stacks of paper and the woman's expression suggest that she is greatly overworked. The message about work in the second photo is different. What do you think it is?

Thinking Further

When a photographer takes a picture, he or she has a purpose. It may be to capture a moment of fun, to inform, or to make money. The purpose shapes the choices a photographer makes about what to shoot and how to do it.

Here are some ideas to help you find the viewpoint in visuals.

Guidelines for Finding Points of View

① Focus
- Look for the center of interest in the image. What do you notice first? bold colors? unusual shapes?

② Purpose
- Look at the whole visual. What is its purpose?

③ Audience
- If you know who the audience is, you can tell a great deal about the purpose of the visual. Are the audience voters? parents? or consumers?

Visuals have many purposes:
- to persuade or influence
- to make money
- to express an opinion
- to inform or mislead
- to entertain

④ Message
- Look for the message. What is the visual telling you about the subject? Is the message one-sided?

⑤ Viewpoint
- The people who made the visual have a way of thinking about the subject. What do you think it is?

Apply It

Find two visuals that have the same main focus but send different messages. For each one, write a caption that tells the visual's message. Then write a sentence that tells each visual's viewpoint. Use the guidelines to help you. Before you write, think about these questions.

- What feelings, such as joy or sorrow, does each image communicate?
- What is the message of the first image?
- How does the message change when you view the second photograph?

Unit 13

Writing to Persuade

Newly hatched sea turtles are always in danger, and measures to protect them are urgently needed. How can people help?

A Published Model

Gary Soto has a problem in his neighborhood. Here's how he persuaded his neighbor Terry to solve the problem. What does he want Terry to do?

Chiming In on Wind Chimes

by Gary Soto

You can walk away from the rattle of the jackhammer. You can hold your breath when a taxi screeches its brakes. You can wait for a dog to stop barking and finally settle into sleep. You can even outlast the howl of a leaf blower until the gardener goes away. With wind chimes, however, the sound is with you every day. And on days when the wind picks up and slaps the trees around, the clanking chimes destroy world peace.

Recently, while I was writing a letter to a friend, I made out a tiny sound that was interesting for about five seconds and then intensely irritating—like the old scraping of fingernails down a blackboard. I looked out the window and saw that monster metal wind chimes were hanging from my neighbor's roof. "Oh, no," I thought. And then I thought, "How can I convince Terry to take them down?"

Before I approached Terry, I came up with a tidy list of reasons for my complaint. First, wind chimes are irritating. Their sound is unpredictable—not like a song, in which you know the melody runs its course. Then, I added to my list, wind chimes ruin my concentration because I'm aware that at any moment they'll start clanging. I may be writing at my desk, but instead of concentrating on my work I'm thinking, "When will it start?" In short, I'm at the mercy of the wind.

Some might ask, "Do you have a problem with church bells, too?" No. I know they'll sound only on the hour or half-hour or when someone is getting married.

 See www.eduplace.com/kids/ for information about Gary Soto.

A Published Model

The third reason I wrote on my list was this: wind chimes are unnecessary. To refresh my mind during the day, I often take short walks. What I've discovered on those walks is that people with wind chimes are never at home. No, they're off to their offices or somewhere, leaving us poor noise-sensitive folks at home to suffer. What is so necessary about these contraptions if the person who hung them is not even around to hear them?

I was at first hesitant to approach my neighbor and ask him, politely of course, to please take down his wind chimes. But I had no choice when I saw that his wife had added yet another one by their bird feeders. "Terry," I said when he opened his door, "we have a problem."

His face expressed concern. "Was there a break-in in the neighborhood? Is anyone hurt?"

I nodded my head. "Yes," I said sadly, "your wind chimes have broken my concentration and are hurting my ears." I asked him to take them down because they were irritating, an obstruction to concentration, unnecessary, and, finally, contrary to nature. Couldn't we just enjoy the birds when they fly down to feast? Now that's music!

By the way, Terry is a scientist who works for an oil company. I knew he was a reasonable man. Would he think I was weird? a grumpy neighbor? He listened to my complaints, and the next moment the wind chimes were gone, presumably tossed in a box that now sits in his garage.

Gary Soto with wind chimes

Reading As a Writer

Think About the Persuasive Essay

- What does Gary Soto want his audience to do? Tell his goal.
- Look at the third paragraph. What is the first reason that the writer gives to support his goal?
- What possible objection does the writer introduce in the fourth paragraph? How does he answer this objection?
- In the fifth paragraph, Gary Soto writes that wind chimes are unnecessary. What facts and examples does he give to support this reason?

Think About Writer's Craft

- In the second paragraph, what comparison does the author use to describe the sound of wind chimes? How does this comparison support his goal?

Think About the Picture

- Look at the picture on page 482. How do you think Gary Soto feels about being so close to wind chimes? Use details from the photograph to support your answer.

Responding

Write responses to these questions.

- **Personal Response** Describe a time when someone you know did something that bothered you. What did you do to solve the problem? How was your experience different from Gary Soto's? How was it similar?
- **Critical Thinking** Suppose Terry disagreed with the writer. What reasons might Terry give for leaving his wind chimes up? How might he answer the writer's reasons for him to take them down?

What Makes a Great Persuasive Essay?

In a persuasive essay, a writer tries to persuade an audience to do something.

Remember to follow these guidelines when you write a persuasive essay.

- ▶ Start by telling your goal, what you want your audience to do.
- ▶ Support your goal with strong reasons that appeal to your audience.
- ▶ Support your reasons with facts and examples.
- ▶ Answer objections your audience might have.
- ▶ Order your reasons from most to least important or from least to most important.
- ▶ Use positive, confident language.
- ▶ End by summing up your reasons and repeating your call to action.

GRAMMAR CHECK

Be sure that each pronoun clearly takes the place of only one noun.

Student Model

WORKING DRAFT

Michael Le likes everything about karate, and he wants his friends to take karate lessons with him. He knows many good reasons why they should learn karate, so he wrote this draft of a persuasive essay.

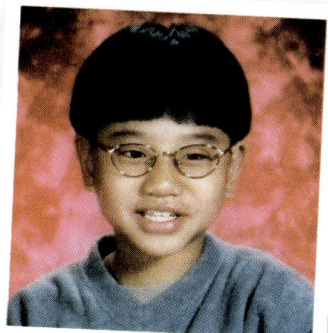

Michael Le

Karate can help you with everyday things and with dangerous people. It's also a lot of fun! ~~Before you join,~~ There are many good reasons for joining.

Karate makes you a better person. The classes will help you with respect for other people. Karate helps me with five things: effort, etiquette, character, sincerity, and self-control. Karate will help you with these things too! The classes teach what you need to do.

Karate builds up your strength, stamina, and agility. Karate does this by teaching you how to move like animals. These are such animals as the crane, the monkey, the tiger, the leopard, the dragon, and the snake. These animals all help you in self-defense.

> What is your goal? State it clearly.

> What facts and examples support this reason?

> Could you tell more about how these animals help you?

more

Student Model **485**

Student Model continued

> You sound so positive!

Here is the best part. Karate will teach you how to break boards! Yes, you heard me. You focus all of your strength into your body part, such as your hand, and use it to break the board. This proves your strength is building. If you think you're ready, you can go for more boards or maybe even bricks!

> Great! You answer a possible objection.

So you think karate is cool. I hope so. All that practice can be boring, but remember that it does help you. Well, that's all you need to hear from me about karate. Join a karate class soon!

> Could you sum up your reasons?

Reading As a Writer

- What questions did Sal ask? What revisions might Michael make?
- Which of Michael's reasons is most convincing? Why do you think so?
- What questions would you like to ask Michael?

Student Model

Michael revised his persuasive essay after discussing it with a classmate. Read his final version to see how he improved it.

Join Karate!
by Michael Le

> This beginning states your goal clearly.

Karate can help you with everyday things and with dangerous people. It's also a lot of fun! You should join karate. There are many good reasons for joining.

First of all, karate makes you a better person. We call our teacher *sensei*. My *sensei* tells stories about how to be respectful. He says that respect for other people is what karate is all about. When I make a mistake, my *sensei* helps fix it. For example, I was not doing a strike right. My *sensei* showed me how to do it and then told my dad to work on it with me. Practicing and going to class help me with five things: effort, etiquette, character, sincerity, and self-control. Karate will help you with these things too!

> You support this reason well.

Second, karate builds up your strength, stamina, and agility. Karate does this by teaching you how to move like animals. These are such animals as the crane, the monkey, the tiger, the leopard, the dragon, and the snake. You learn

more →

Student Model continued

different *forms* from them. A form is a movement that includes many techniques. The crane teaches you balance, and the monkey teaches you how to use your strength. The leopard and tiger both teach speed, the dragon teaches balance and strength, and the snake teaches twisting out of a grapple move. These animals all certainly help you in self-defense.

> Now I understand! This is a great explanation.

> Using transitional words is smart!

Last and most important is the fun part. Karate will teach you how to break boards! Yes, you heard me. You focus all of your strength into your body part, such as your hand, and use it to break the board. This proves your strength is building. If you think you're ready, you can go for more boards or maybe even bricks!

So you think karate is cool. I hope so. All that practice can be boring, but remember that it definitely does help you. Karate gives you more honor and makes you a better person. It builds up your strength, stamina, and agility. It's also a lot of fun! Well, that's all you need to hear from me about karate. Join a karate class soon!

> You sum up your goal and reasons nicely.

Reading As a Writer

- What changes did Michael make in response to Sal's questions?
- What facts and examples did Michael add to support his reason that karate can make you a better person?
- What did Michael think was his most important reason? How do you know?

See www.eduplace.com/kids/hme/ for more examples of student writing.

The Writing Process

PREWRITING · DRAFTING · REVISING · PROOFREADING · PUBLISHING

Write a Persuasive Essay

▶ Start Thinking

 Make a writing folder for your persuasive essay. Copy the questions in bold type, and put the paper in your folder. Write your answers as you think about and choose your topic.

- **What will be my purpose or goal?** What do I want to persuade someone to do? Why is this action important to me?
- **Who will be my audience?** Do I want to convince my parents? my classmates? my teacher? a leader in my city or town?
- **How will I publish or share my essay?** Will I reach my audience through a magazine or newspaper? in a flier? on a poster?

▶ Choose a Goal

❶ Make a chart to help you come up with ideas. List five actions someone should take. These are your goals. List the people who should take each action. This is your audience. Part of Michael's chart is shown below.

Goal	Audience
join karate	other kids
exercise more	my parents
buy new software	my teacher

HELP? Drawing a Blank?
Complete these sentences for goal ideas.
- My principal should change _____.
- My city or town should fix the _____.
- My parents should allow me to _____.

See page 501 for more ideas.

❷ Discuss each goal with a partner.
- Is each goal clear? Will your audience know exactly what to do?
- Is any goal too large for your audience to do?
- What reasons will you use? Will these reasons convince your audience?

❸ Ask yourself these questions. Then circle the goal you will write about.
- Do I really care about this goal?
- Will this goal interest my audience?
- Can I think of facts and examples to support my reasons for this goal?

Prewriting **489**

The Writing Process

PREWRITING | DRAFTING | REVISING | PROOFREADING | PUBLISHING

Focus Skill

Supporting Your Goal

Your reasons are like a tabletop. Your facts and examples are like the legs that hold it up. Without their support, your goal would go crashing to the floor.

Support your goal with reasons. Each reason must tell why it is important for your audience to do what you ask. Don't just restate your goal.

Goal: persuade town officials to add a traffic light near my house

Weak Reason: Restates Goal	Strong Reason: Supports Goal
You have to put a traffic light on that corner!	Driving through that intersection is dangerous.

GRAMMAR TIP Reasons are statements. They usually end with a period.

Imagine yourself having a friendly argument with your audience.

Get ready for disagreement. How might your audience object to your goal? Answer their possible objections with your reasons.

Goal	persuade my parents to buy me a new bike
Objection	My parents will say that I won't take care of a new bike.
Objection answered	I know you're worried that I won't take care of a new bike. Well, I will. I won't just drop it on the driveway, and I'll always put it away in the garage.

Think and Discuss Look at Michael's working draft on pages 485–486.

- What objection does Michael introduce? How does he answer it?

490 Unit 13: Persuasion

PREWRITING   DRAFTING   REVISING   PROOFREADING   PUBLISHING

Focus Skill continued

Support or elaborate your reasons with facts and examples. A fact can be proven. An example tells something that has happened or might happen.

Reason: Driving through that intersection is dangerous.

Weak Support	Strong Support
Opinion: There must be many accidents at corners without traffic lights. **Opinion:** Corners without traffic lights are frightening.	**Fact:** Two car accidents happened at that corner in the past month. **Example:** I saw two drivers swerve to miss each other at the last second.

Think and Discuss Look at the published model on pages 481–482.

- Find three facts or examples that Gary Soto uses to support his reasons.

▶ Explore Your Goal

❶ **Start** a web like the one below. State your goal in one short sentence. Add as many reasons as you can think of to your web.

❷ **Discuss** your goal and reasons with a partner. Think of possible objections. Answer each objection. Add each answer to your web.

If you can't list at least three strong reasons, try another goal.

❸ **Add** facts and examples to elaborate each reason.

Goal: I want other kids to join karate.
Reason: a lot of fun
Fact or Example: break boards
Fact or Example: break bricks later

▲ Part of Michael's web

HELP? See page 14 for other ideas for exploring your topic.

 Go to www.eduplace.com/kids/hme/ for graphic organizers.

The Writing Process — **PREWRITING** · DRAFTING · REVISING · PROOFREADING · PUBLISHING

Evaluating Your Reasons

Your essay needs at least three strong reasons to be convincing. Which of your reasons are the most persuasive?

Be sure each reason has enough support. Choose reasons that you can explain. Supply names, dates, or numbers whenever possible.

Be sure each reason is accurate. Don't exaggerate.

Goal: persuade town officials to add a traffic light near my house

Weak: Not an Accurate Reason	Strong: Accurate Reason
Adding a traffic light will save hundreds of lives.	Adding a traffic light will make crossing that street less dangerous.

Be sure each reason is right for your audience. We all care about different things. Choose reasons that matter to the people you want to convince.

Goal: persuade the class to watch a documentary about a journey to the Arctic

Reason for Classmates	Reason for Teacher
The documentary is so exciting! It's almost like watching an action movie!	The documentary is full of facts about the explorers. We'll learn a lot of history.

Try It Out Work with a partner.

- Think of two strong reasons to persuade your teacher to give little or no homework one night a week.
- Think of two strong reasons to persuade your classmates not to watch television or listen to the radio while doing their homework.

▶ Explore Your Reasons

❶ **Reread** your web. Which reasons are supported by the most facts and examples? Which reasons will matter most to your audience?

❷ **Choose** at least three persuasive reasons. Put a star beside them.

Unit 13: Persuasion

PREWRITING   DRAFTING   REVISING   PROOFREADING   PUBLISHING

Organizing Your Essay

Order your reasons. Do you want to start with a bang or end with one?

- You can tell your most persuasive reason first. Arranging your reasons from most to least important gets your readers' attention.
- You can tell your most persuasive reason last. Arranging your reasons from least to most important builds interest throughout your essay.

Keep to your topic. Leave out reasons that do not support your goal. Leave out facts and examples that do not support your reasons.

Make each of your reasons a paragraph. The reason itself will be your topic sentence. The facts and examples will be the supporting sentences.

Use transitional words. Transitional words link your reasons and paragraphs. They can also link the facts and examples within a paragraph.

Transitional Words	Transitional Phrases
first, finally, also, too, another, next, because, therefore, thus, however, although, similarly, besides, better, best	to begin with, first of all, in the first place, my second reason, in the third place, last of all, in addition, in conclusion, for example, above all, most important, as a result

Think and Discuss Look at Michael's final copy on pages 487–488.

- Which reason did Michael tell first? second? third?
- What transitional words and phrases did Michael use to link his reasons? to link his facts and examples?

▶ Plan Your Essay

① **Reread** your web. Cross out reasons, facts, or examples that don't support your goal.

② **Number** your reasons in the order you want to write about them.

Prewriting   **493**

The Writing Process

PREWRITING • **DRAFTING** • REVISING • PROOFREADING • PUBLISHING

Focus Skill

Introductions and Conclusions

Grab your readers and clearly state your goal in your introduction. What can you tell your audience to make them interested in your goal?

This introduction asks questions. You can also start with dialogue or a surprising statement.

Weak Introduction
Talk to a new person when it's his or her first day in school. Being friendly is a nice thing to do.

Strong Introduction
Were you scared on your first day in school? If you think a new classmate feels the way you did, just walk up and say, "Hi!"

Repeat the call to action in your conclusion. Remind your audience of what you want. Sum up your goal and reasons. How can you make your audience enthusiastic about doing what you ask?

Weak Conclusion
That's why the town should do something about the footbridge over Mill River. Besides, my dad says that you used to get really good views from that bridge.

Strong Conclusion
Fixing the footbridge over Mill River would prevent accidents, connect the bike paths in Stanford Park, and create a safe place for fishing. The bridge is really important to this town.

Think and Discuss Reread the weak and strong examples above.

- What makes the strong introduction more interesting than the weak one?
- In what ways is the strong conclusion better than the weak one?

▶ Draft Your Introduction

Write two different introductions that state your goal. Use the goal statement from your web. Then choose the introduction you think will be most interesting to your audience.

Unit 13: Persuasion

PREWRITING DRAFTING REVISING PROOFREADING PUBLISHING

Writing with Voice

Writing in your own voice will make your essay more persuasive.

Show that you care about your goal. Use language that shows your feelings, but be positive. Sounding whiny or sarcastic will turn your audience away.

Weak: Negative Voice	Strong: Positive Voice
Computers are great, but only an idiot would sit in front of one for hours. Are these people too stupid to think of anything else to do?	Using a computer is certainly enjoyable, but there is more to life than staring at a monitor. We need to get outside and talk with other people.

Write with a confident tone. Sound like a leader. Use persuasive words such as *clearly, obviously, strongly, definitely,* and *plainly.*

Weak: Not a Confident Voice	Strong: Confident Voice
I guess giving kids an allowance might teach them how to manage money. They would probably learn about what things cost.	I once thought ATMs were magic money machines. Having an allowance definitely taught me to take responsibility for my money.

Think and Discuss Compare the examples of weak and strong voice.

- What words and phrases weaken the example showing negative voice?
- What persuasive words are used in the strong examples?

▶ Draft Your Essay

1. **Write** the rest of your essay. Leave extra space between lines for changes. Don't worry about mistakes. Use a confident voice.

2. **Follow** your web. Write a conclusion that sums up your goal and your reasons.

Tech Tip
Draft your reasons in bold print. Use regular print for facts and examples. Does each reason have enough support?

Drafting **495**

Evaluating Your Persuasive Essay

▶ **Reread** your persuasive essay. Use this rubric to help you decide how to make it better. Write the sentences that describe your essay.

Rings the Bell!

- ☐ The introduction tells my goal clearly and grabs my readers.
- ☐ At least three strong reasons, listed in a clear order, support my goal.
- ☐ Facts and examples back up each reason. I answer objections.
- ☐ My voice is confident and persuasive.
- ☐ My conclusion sums up my reasons and calls my audience to action.
- ☐ I made very few mistakes in spelling, grammar, or punctuation.

Getting Stronger

- ☐ The introduction tells my goal but could be more lively.
- ☐ I have three reasons, but some aren't strong or are out of order.
- ☐ Some reasons need more support. I mention objections but don't answer them.
- ☐ My voice sounds negative or lacks confidence.
- ☐ My conclusion doesn't sum up my reasons or restate my goal.
- ☐ I made at least one mistake in every paragraph.

Try Harder

- ☐ The introduction does not tell my goal.
- ☐ My reasons are unclear and not well ordered.
- ☐ Every reason needs support. I don't mention objections.
- ☐ I don't sound as if I care at all about this goal.
- ☐ I forgot to write a conclusion.
- ☐ I made a lot of grammar, spelling, or punctuation mistakes.

496 Unit 13: Persuasion

 See www.eduplace.com/kids/hme/ to interact with this rubric.

PREWRITING DRAFTING **REVISING** PROOFREADING PUBLISHING

▶ Revise Your Persuasive Essay

❶ **Revise** your essay. Use the list of sentences you wrote from the rubric. Work on the parts that you described with sentences from "Getting Stronger" and "Try Harder."

> **Revising Tip**
> If you reorder your reasons, don't forget to change your transitional words and phrases also.

❷ **Have a writing conference.**

When You're the Writer Read your essay aloud to a partner. Ask questions about parts that gave you difficulty. Take notes to remember what your partner says.

When You're the Listener Begin by sharing at least two things you like about the essay. Ask questions about any parts that seem confusing.

What should I say?

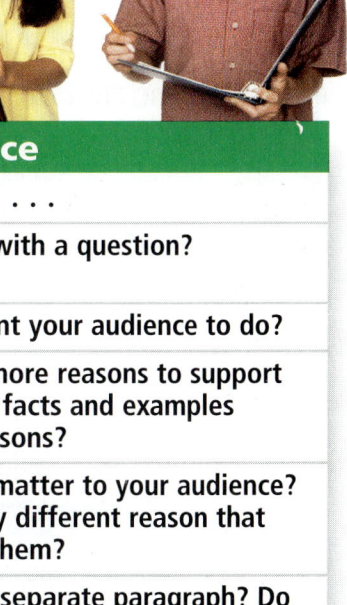

The Writing Conference

If you're thinking . . .	You could say . . .
The introduction could be more interesting.	Could you start with a question?
I don't understand the goal.	What do you want your audience to do?
Why would anyone want to do that?	Could you give more reasons to support your goal? What facts and examples support your reasons?
That reason is not very convincing.	Will this reason matter to your audience? Is there a slightly different reason that might convince them?
The reasons are all mixed up. I'm confused.	Is each reason a separate paragraph? Do all the other sentences tell facts and examples that support this one reason?
The writer sounds uncertain.	Could you use more persuasive words?

❸ **Make** more revisions to your persuasive essay. Use your conference notes and the Revising Strategies on the next page.

Revising **497**

Revising Strategies

Elaborating: Word Choice The feelings a word suggests are called its **connotations**. Use words with connotations that support your goal and reasons.

Weak: Wrong Connotation	Strong: Right Connotation
I was late because I had to **stroll** through a snowstorm.	I was late because I had to **trudge** through a snowstorm.
A nature walk will be relaxing. We will **trudge** through the woods, looking at plants and animals.	A nature walk will be relaxing. We will **stroll** through the woods, looking at plants and animals.

▶ Find at least two places in your essay where you can use a better word to support your goal and reasons.

📖 Use the Thesaurus Plus on page H81. See also page H15.

Elaborating: Details Use vivid, descriptive details to make your facts and examples come alive for your audience.

Without Details	With Details
When we stood on the footbridge, we could **see a lot**.	When we stood on the footbridge, we could **see the waterfall and the red cliffs**.

▶ Find at least two places in your essay to add descriptive details.

Sentence Fluency Be sure every sentence expresses a complete thought. Avoid sentence fragments, especially fragments with *because* or *since*.

Weak: Sentence Fragment	Strong: Complete Sentence
My parents should let me buy an iguana. **Because I can learn a lot from observing its unusual habits.**	My parents should let me buy an iguana **b**ecause I can learn a lot from observing its unusual habits.

▶ Check your writing for sentence fragments. Complete each fragment you find.

 See also page 32.

PREWRITING DRAFTING REVISING **PROOFREADING** PUBLISHING

▶ Proofread Your Persuasive Essay

Proofread your essay, using the Proofreading Checklist and the Grammar and Spelling Connections. Proofread for one skill at a time. Use a class dictionary to check spellings.

Proofreading Checklist
Did I
- ✔ indent all paragraphs?
- ✔ use complete sentences?
- ✔ use commas correctly?
- ✔ use pronouns clearly?
- ✔ correct any spelling errors?

📖 Use the Guide to Capitalization, Punctuation, and Usage on page H57.

Proofreading Marks
- ¶ Indent
- ∧ Add
- ⌐ Delete
- ≡ Capital letter
- / Small letter

Proofreading Tip
Read your paper backward so that you focus on the spelling of each word.

Grammar and Spelling Connections

Commas in a Series Use a comma after each item in a list except the last.

> Repairing the bridge would benefit pedestrians **,** cyclists **,** and fishermen.

GRAMMAR LINK See page 184.

Using Pronouns Clearly Be sure that each pronoun clearly takes the place of only one noun. If it is not clear which noun the pronoun stands for, replace the pronoun with a noun.

Unclear	Clear
Mary and Angela both finished their essays. **She** took the most time.	Mary and Angela both finished their essays. **Mary** took the most time.

GRAMMAR LINK See page 225.

Spelling the Final |ər| Sounds The final |ər| sounds in two-syllable words are often spelled *ar, or,* or *er*: lun**ar**, hum**or**, clov**er**   📖 See the Spelling Guide on page H67.

Go to www.eduplace.com/kids/hme/ for proofreading practice.

The Writing Process

PREWRITING DRAFTING REVISING PROOFREADING **PUBLISHING**

Publish Your Persuasive Essay

1. **Make a neat final copy** of your essay. Be sure you fixed all mistakes.
2. **Title** your essay. Choose an attention-getting title, such as "A Slam-Dunk Breakfast" rather than "Eating a Good Breakfast."
3. **Publish** or share your essay in a way that fits both your goal and your audience. See the Ideas for Sharing box.

Tips for Creating a Persuasive Poster
- Choose a poster title that states your goal.
- Find photos or make drawings to illustrate each of your reasons clearly.
- Attach your essay to the center of the poster.
- Run string from each reason to its illustration.
- Display your poster where it will be seen by your audience.

Ideas for Sharing
Write It
- Send your essay as a letter to a newspaper. See page 503 for tips.

Say It
- Present it as a speech. See page H5 for tips.

Show It
- Display your essay on a poster, and illustrate each reason.
- Make slides that illustrate your reasons. Read your essay as you show your slides.

Reflect

Write about your writing experience. Use these questions to get started.

- What was most difficult about writing a persuasive essay? What was easiest?
- What advice would you give someone who is writing a persuasive essay for the first time?
- How does this paper compare with other papers you have written?

Assessment Link

Writing Prompts

Use these prompts as ideas for persuasive essays or to practice for a test. Some of them will work well for other subjects you study. Decide who your audience will be, and write your essay to convince them.

1 Choose a rule in your school or classroom that you disagree with. Try persuading your principal or your teacher to change it.

2 Is there a hobby or a sport you love to do? Write an essay persuading your friends to try it.

3 Does your school have a school mascot? If not, suggest one and persuade students to accept it. If there is one, persuade students to change it.

4 Your town is considering replacing your school with a brand-new building on the other side of the town. Write a letter arguing for or against this proposal.

Writing Across the Curriculum

5 **SOCIAL STUDIES**
Choose a town or a state you have visited. Persuade your classmates to go there. Give reasons, facts, and examples to support your goal.

6 **LITERATURE**
Choose a book that you have enjoyed. Persuade your friends to read it too. Support your reasons with details from the book.

7 **HEALTH**
Persuade your classmates to give up junk food for a week. Use facts about junk food to support your reasons. Discuss healthy snacks students might try instead.

8 **MATHEMATICS**
Persuade your classmates that geometry is both fun and useful. Use facts and examples from your own experience with geometry.

See www.eduplace.com/kids/hme/ for more prompts.

Assessment Link

✓ Test Practice

This prompt to write a persuasive essay is like ones you might find on a writing test. Read the prompt.

Remember, in a persuasive essay, a writer tries to persuade an audience to do something.

> Is there **a hobby or a sport you love to do**? Write an **essay persuading your friends to try it**.

Here are some strategies to help you do a good job responding to a prompt for a topic like this.

❶ Look for clue words that tell what to write about. What are the clue words in the prompt above?

❷ Choose a topic that fits the clue words. Write the clue words and your topic ideas.

Clue Words	My Topic
a hobby or a sport you love to do, essay persuading your friends to try it	I will write an essay persuading my friends to try skiing.

❸ Plan your writing. Use a web.

```
                    ┌─ fact or example
           reason ──┤
          /         └─ fact or example
         /
        /           ┌─ fact or example
Goal ──── reason ───┤
        \           └─ fact or example
         \
          \         ┌─ fact or example
           reason ──┤
                    └─ fact or example
```

❹ You will get a good score if you remember the description of what kind of persuasive essay rings the bell in the rubric on page 496.

Unit 13: Persuasion   Go to www.eduplace.com/kids/hme/ for graphic organizers.

Special Focus on Influencing

Writing a Business Letter

A **business letter** is usually written to a person you do not know. It can be written to request information, to express an opinion, to order a product, or to persuade someone to do something. Read Yesenia's business letter.

Heading
>289 Second Avenue
>Hammond, IL 61929
>February 20, 2001

Inside address
>Ms. Suki Lang, Director
>YMCA
>653 Neil Street
>Chicago, IL 60601

Greeting → Dear Ms. Lang:

Body
>I read in a book that if I wanted information on baby-sitting, I should write to my local YMCA. I was wondering if you have any information or tips on how to baby-sit. Do you have a class I could sign up for? I would like to baby-sit my two younger sisters and other neighborhood children as well. From baby-sitting, I hope to earn enough money to buy a computer.
>
>If you would please send me any information you have, I would appreciate it. Thank you for your time and help.

Closing → Cordially,
Signature → *Yesenia Lopez*
Yesenia Lopez

more ▶
Writing a Business Letter **503**

Special Focus continued

Reading As a Writer

- The **heading** contains the writer's address and the date.
  What is Yesenia's address?
- The **inside address** gives the person's name and title, and the name and address of that person's business or organization.
  What organization is included in the address?
- The **greeting** begins with *Dear*, followed by a title of respect, such as *Ms.* or *Mr.*, and a last name. A colon follows it. Capitalize each word. If you do not know whose name to write, use *Dear Sir or Madam*.
  To whom is Yesenia writing?
- The **body** is the main part of the letter. It tells the writer's purpose. It has at least one paragraph. *What is Yesenia's purpose for writing?*
- The **closing,** such as *Cordially, Sincerely,* or *Yours truly,* is a polite expression that finishes the letter. A comma follows it.
  What closing did Yesenia use?
- The **signature** is the writer's full name as written by the writer.
  Why do you think giving both first and last names is important?

How to Write a Business Letter

1. **Think** about your purpose for writing.
2. **Make notes** first about what you want to say. Then organize your ideas.
3. **Write** a draft of the letter. Include all six parts of a business letter. Be brief and to the point. Keep your language polite and formal.
4. **Revise** your business letter so that your purpose is clear.
5. **Proofread** your letter, using the Proofreading Checklist on page 499. Make sure you have spelled all proper names correctly.
6. **Make** a neat final copy of your letter. Add your signature.
7. **Address** the envelope. Make sure the names and addresses on the letter match those on the envelope. Put a stamp on the envelope and mail it.

COMMUNICATION LINK | Listening

Listening for Persuasive Tactics

When a speaker is trying to persuade you, he or she wants you to do something. Listen for reasons the speaker gives. Then ask yourself why you should take the action the speaker wants. Watch out for persuasive tactics that can tug on your feelings and keep you from thinking clearly.

Look at the situations shown below.

Other Tactics

Sometimes a speaker may use the fact that he or she is older than you to convince you to do something. Other times, a speaker may use taunts or dares, claiming that you can't do something, just so that you will try to prove that you can. What other tactics are familiar to you?

more ▶

Listening for Persuasive Tactics

COMMUNICATION LINK continued

Decide for Yourself

Think about what you hear. Then decide for yourself what to do.

- **Think about the goal.** What does the speaker want you to do? Why is this goal important to him or her?
- **Think about the reasons.** Why does the speaker think you should do this? Does each reason make sense to you? Do the reasons go against any rules you shouldn't break?
- **Think about the support.** How does the speaker explain each reason? Does the speaker just repeat an opinion or does he or she give facts and examples?

Guidelines for Listening for Persuasive Tactics

1. Listen for promises. Is the speaker claiming that something good will happen to you if you do what he or she asks? Do you think this promise will be kept? Why?

2. Listen for flattery. Is the speaker telling you how wonderful you are? Does the speaker mean it? Is being wonderful a good reason for doing what the speaker asks?

3. Listen for taunts or dares. Is the speaker asking you to prove you can do something? Is the speaker claiming you are afraid of doing something? Is what the speaker says fair?

Apply It

For the next week, listen carefully when someone tries to talk you into doing something. Take notes on what you hear.

- What did each speaker want you to do?
- What reasons did each speaker give? What facts and examples did each speaker give?
- Did each speaker use any persuasive tactics? Which ones did he or she use?

COMMUNICATION LINK — Viewing

Watching for Persuasive Tactics

Mass media are used to get information to large numbers of people. Television, radio, the Internet, billboards, and magazines are types of mass media.

Advertising is a big part of mass media. Companies pay money to place ads to be seen or heard by large audiences.

Tactics You've Seen

The people who make ads have a specific audience in mind. They create ads to appeal to the feelings of the audience. They choose music they think the audience will like. They may use bright colors and fast-action images. Actors in the ads may be asked to look happy or to act out a funny role.

The purpose of ads is to persuade. Ads are made to get people to buy products, use services, or vote for candidates. Many ads use persuasive tactics, or methods, that don't tell the whole story. Look at the examples below. You've probably seen similar examples on television or in magazines.

Bandwagon	Everyone else has one, so you should too.	
Superstars	Your favorite sports or movie star loves this product, so you will too.	
Exaggeration	If the product sounds better than it is, you might just buy it.	Can Do ANYTHING!
Flattery	You are wonderful. You deserve this product. You're too smart to be fooled by that one.	
Before and After	Your hair looks bad. Use the product and—wow! Your hair looks great.	

more ▶

Watching for Persuasive Tactics

Stop and Think

When you look at an advertisement, remember that you are seeing only what the people who made it want you to see. They often leave out facts, or they only tell you good opinions.

Most ads want you to feel before you think. You might buy the product if you believe it will make you look better, feel happier, or become popular. If you ask questions and think about the product first, you might find reasons not to buy it.

Look at the ad shown below for golf gloves.

Advertisers know that famous people are admired. People want to be like them and may believe that using products that movie or sports stars use will do this. Is the product "the best" just because the star says so?

Focus on the Words

Ads must grab the attention of the viewer. They need to have a lot of "punch" so viewers remember them. As a result, ad writers must choose words carefully.

- Words must be "catchy," or easy to remember.
- Words in print need to be easy to read. Words spoken in a television or radio ad must be easy to understand.
- A few words are better than long paragraphs.
- The words should make the audience feel good about the product.

A few words may not give much information in an ad, but a few words can tug on emotions.

When you look at an ad, notice how it tries to persuade you. Here are some guidelines to follow.

Guidelines for Looking at Media Advertising

▶ Look carefully at the advertisement. Who made it? What does it want you to do?

▶ Study the images, music, and speech used. How do they make you feel?

▶ Read the text of the ad. Does the ad use facts or opinions? Does it tell you all there is to know? Do the words focus on the product or on a mood or an idea?

▶ Study the ad to see which persuasive tactics were used, if any. Why do you think the tactic was chosen?

▶ Ask yourself what the ad wants you to believe. Ask yourself if the ad is fair and truthful. Make up your own mind about what you see.

Apply It

Watch the commercials that air during a television program you like. Videotape the ads if you can. Follow the guidelines above and take notes on one commercial. Then answer these questions.

- What product or service is being advertised?
- Is the commercial fun and entertaining? What do you like about it?
- Watch the commercial without the sound. What do you notice?
- Listen to the sound without watching. What do you notice?
- If you could talk to the people who made the commercial, what questions would you ask?

Look through several children's magazines. Find an ad that uses one of the persuasive tactics described in this lesson. Share the ad with your classmates and talk about the tactics it uses. Then create an ad of your own using the same tactic.

Watching for Persuasive Tactics

Tools and Tips

What You Will Find in This Part:

Listening and Speaking Strategies H4

Building Vocabulary H11

Research and Study Strategies H20

Test-Taking Strategies H33

Using Technology H37

Writer's Tools H50

Guide to Capitalization,
Punctuation, and Usage H57

Spelling Guide H67

Diagramming Guide H72

Thesaurus Plus H81

Index I-1

Listening and Speaking Strategies

Taking and Leaving Messages

People keep in touch by using the telephone. If you answer a call for someone else, take a message. If you make a call and no one answers, you can leave a message on an answering machine. Read this conversation and Keisha's message. What information did she write?

MR. BAY: Hello, Keisha. This is Mr. Bay. May I speak to your father?
KEISHA: I'm sorry, he can't come to the phone right now. May I take a message?
MR. BAY: Yes, please ask him to call me at 555-2197.
KEISHA: I'll tell him to call Mr. Bay at 555-2197.

Saturday, 10:15 a.m.
Dad, please call Mr. Bay at 555-2197.
Keisha

Keisha included all of the information that her father would need in her message. When you take or leave messages, follow these guidelines.

Guidelines for Taking and Leaving Messages

 When you take a message, write the caller's name, the telephone number, and the message. Ask questions if any part of the message is not clear, and retell the message to be sure you have taken it correctly. Include the day and time that you take the call.

 When you leave a message, give your name, your telephone number, and a brief message, including the day and time you called.

❸ Be polite. Speak slowly and clearly.

Apply It

A. Follow the guidelines and practice taking notes as your teacher reads a telephone message.
B. Role-play giving and taking telephone messages with a classmate.

Giving a Talk

When you give a talk, you speak about a certain topic. You need to plan, prepare, and practice your talk before you present it. Follow these guidelines when you give a talk.

Guidelines for Giving a Talk

1 **Plan** your talk.

- Decide if the purpose of your talk will be to inform, to persuade, or to entertain. The tone of your talk, such as humorous or serious, should match your purpose.

- Think about your audience. Should you use formal or informal language? How much do the listeners know about your topic?

2 **Prepare** your talk.

- Find the information you need. Gather any graphics or visuals, such as maps, pictures, or objects, that you want to show.

- Jot down notes or key words on note cards. Be sure to use words that are appropriate for your audience.

> Kennedy Space Center
> - full name: John F. Kennedy Space Center of the National Aeronautics and Space Administration (NASA)
> - location: Merritt Island, Florida, near Cape Canaveral (show map)
> - what they do: test, repair, and launch all manned U.S. space missions

- Be sure your talk has a beginning, a middle, and an end. Put notes in the order you will talk about them. You might want to highlight key words.

more ▶

Giving a Talk continued

3 **Practice** your talk.

- Give your talk to a friend or family member, using your notes and your visual aids. Revise your talk after listening to their comments.

> **Tips for Using Visual Aids**
> - Make sure any lettering is large enough for your audience to read.
> - Practice using any machines, such as an overhead projector or a slide projector, before you give your talk.
> - Don't block the visuals from the view of the audience.

- Practice how you say your words. Think about the rate, volume, pitch, and tone of your voice.

> **Speaking Tips**
> - Don't talk too fast or too slowly.
> - Talk loudly enough to be heard, and remember to talk more loudly in a big room than in a small space.
> - Speak with expression.

HELP? Talk About Talk

Rate: how fast or slowly you talk
Volume: how loud or soft your voice is
Pitch: how high or low your voice is
Tone: how happy, sad, funny, or angry you sound

- Practice until you have almost memorized your talk.

4 **Present** your talk.

- Remember to use your voice and visual aids in the same way you practiced.
- Project your voice. Avoid saying *um, ah,* and *well*.
- Make eye contact with people in your audience.

Apply It

Give a talk about a funny experience, an opinion you have, or another topic that interests you. Then follow the guidelines as you **plan, prepare, practice,** and then **present** your talk.

Understanding Nonverbal Cues

Look at the students pictured below. Imagine they are talking about having to take part in a new school sport—tennis. How do you think each one feels about it?

Just like words, your face and body movements or positions can let others know what you think or how you feel. This "body language" is known as **nonverbal cues**.

Using Nonverbal Cues

You can use nonverbal cues to support what you are saying. Here are some examples.

- Use facial expressions to match your message.
- Use hand motions to stress a point when persuading.
- Use your hands to show sizes and shapes.
- Point to show a direction or an object. (Don't point to people!)
- Make eye contact to show you're aware of your listeners.

more ▶

Understanding Nonverbal Cues *continued*

You can use nonverbal cues to send a message without words. Here are some examples.

- Smile and nod your head to show interest and understanding. Look puzzled when something is not clear.
- Put your arm around a family member to show affection or around a friend to show comfort.
- Give a thumbs up to show support.
- Give a high-five to show friendship.
- Smile to show friendliness. Frown to show unhappiness.
- Sit back to show you're relaxed. Lean forward to show special interest.

Warning! Nonverbal cues can give away your true feelings or send the wrong message!

Observing Nonverbal Cues

Watch others' nonverbal cues. A pained look on someone's face may show that you said something that hurt. Someone looking at the ground while talking may be shy or embarrassed. Someone slouching or staring into space may be bored. If you are aware of a person's nonverbal cues, you will know better how to react appropriately.

Guidelines for Nonverbal Cues

1. Always have good eye contact when speaking.
2. Use nonverbal cues to support your words.
3. Use nonverbal cues to show what you think or feel without words.
4. Watch others' nonverbal cues as clues to their thoughts and feelings, and respond appropriately.

Apply It

With your class or in a small group, take turns demonstrating different nonverbal cues. Discuss what message each nonverbal cue sends.

Interviewing

One way to get facts for a report or a news article is to **interview** someone who knows that information. An interview is a kind of conversation. One person asks questions and the other person answers them. The **interviewer** is the person who asks the questions.

To get all the facts you want during an interview takes careful planning. The guidelines below will help you.

Guidelines for Interviewing

1. Decide what you want to know.

2. Think of questions that will help you get the information you want to know. Try to think of questions that begin with *Who, What, Where, When, Why,* or *How.* Do not ask questions that can be answered *yes* or *no.*

3. Write your questions in an order that makes sense. Leave space after each question for writing notes during the interview.

4. Before you ask your first question, tell the person the reason for your interview.

5. Ask your questions clearly and politely. Pay close attention to the answers.

6. Take notes to help you remember the answers. You may want to write the person's exact words if it is an important piece of information. Write these words as a quotation and use quotation marks.

7. If you don't understand something, ask more questions about it.

more ▶

Interviewing continued

The following notes were taken during an interview with a person who plays the steel drums.

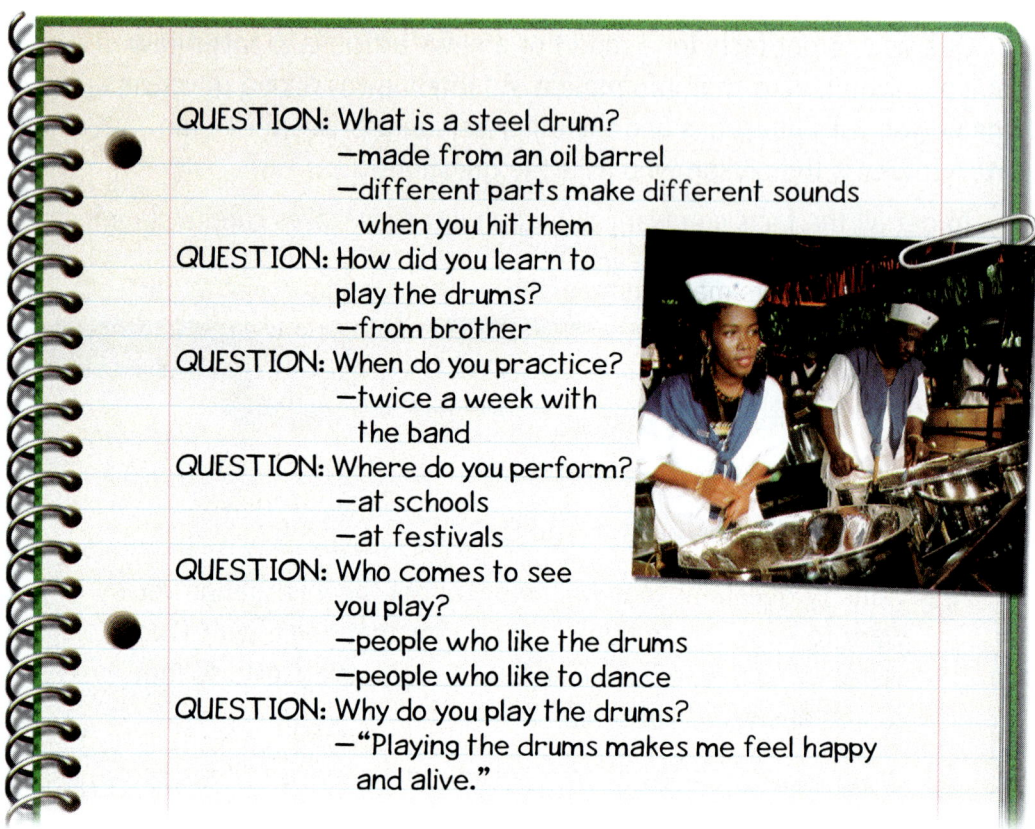

QUESTION: What is a steel drum?
— made from an oil barrel
— different parts make different sounds when you hit them
QUESTION: How did you learn to play the drums?
— from brother
QUESTION: When do you practice?
— twice a week with the band
QUESTION: Where do you perform?
— at schools
— at festivals
QUESTION: Who comes to see you play?
— people who like the drums
— people who like to dance
QUESTION: Why do you play the drums?
— "Playing the drums makes me feel happy and alive."

Think and Discuss

- What kinds of questions did the interviewer ask?
- Do any of the questions call for *yes* or *no* answers? Why not?
- Work with a partner. Make up three more questions you could ask during the interview with the person who plays the steel drums.

Apply It

A. Pair up with a classmate. Tell each other a topic that you know about. Then interview each other, using questions each of you has written about the other person's topic. Follow the guidelines.

B. Interview a parent, a relative, or a neighbor about that person's job, hobby, or other interest. Use the guidelines. Share your questions and what you learned with your class.

Building Vocabulary

Similes and Metaphors

Writers often describe something by comparing it to something else. The comparison creates a vivid picture in the reader's mind.

The sentence below uses the word *like* or *as* to compare two things. **A comparison that uses *like* or *as* is called a simile.**

  The moon is like a glowing pearl.

Sometimes writers make comparisons without using *like* or *as*. Instead of saying that one thing is *like* another, they say that one thing *is* another. **A comparison of two different things without using the word *like* or *as* is called a metaphor.**

  The moon is a glowing pearl.

Here are some more similes and metaphors.

  Simile: The winter wind sounded like a sad whistle.

  Metaphor: The winter wind was a sad whistle.

  Simile: His mean words felt as sharp as thorns.

  Metaphor: His mean words were thorns.

How do similes and metaphors help you picture what a writer is describing?

Apply It

Complete each sentence with a metaphor or simile. Use the kind of comparison shown in parentheses.

1. Tyler swam _____. (simile)
2. The kite was _____. (metaphor)
3. The cat's eyes were _____. (metaphor)
4. The water made a sound _____. (simile)
5. Diana raced across the field _____. (simile)
6. The clouds were _____. (metaphor)

Idioms

You have probably heard people use the expression *raining cats and dogs.* This expression is called an idiom. **An idiom is a phrase that has a special meaning as a whole.** The meaning of an idiom is different from the meanings of its separate words. The idiom *raining cats and dogs* does not mean that cats and dogs are falling from the sky. It means "raining heavily."

Sometimes the context of an idiom makes its meaning clear. Can you figure out the meaning of this idiom?

Gerald is a good dancer, but Tanya has two left feet.

No one can really have two left feet. What the writer means is that Tanya is clumsy on her feet.

Apply It

Write a word or a phrase from the word box to replace each underlined idiom.

1. Benjamin has his hands full. He can't take on more work.
2. We all read our speeches, but Tamako knew hers by heart.
3. I can't make heads or tails of this story.
4. After our long tiring day, we hit the sack early.
5. He didn't like their teasing, so he told them to knock it off.

is busy
stop
went to bed
make sense
from memory

Synonyms

Synonyms are words that have almost the same meaning. One way to vary your writing is to use synonyms. Look at how a writer used two different words for *slippery*.

As I caught the egg, it broke in my hand, and the slick goo slid through my fingers. Just then, Bongo raced past and skidded on the slimy floor.

Notice how the synonyms *slick* and *slimy* help vary the writing. They have nearly the same meaning, but they look and sound different.

Here are some other synonyms for *slippery*.

oily   greasy   smooth   waxy   slithery

When you write, use a synonym dictionary, or thesaurus, to look up synonyms. The word-processing program on your computer may have an electronic thesaurus to help you find synonyms.

Apply It

Rewrite each sentence. Replace each underlined word with its synonym from the word box. You may use a dictionary.

1. At night the campers were <u>bothered</u> by mosquitoes.
2. The puppy <u>jumped</u> onto her bed and licked her face.
3. The science fiction story <u>excited</u> her imagination.
4. A large skunk <u>walked</u> down the alley.
5. The bus driver <u>stared</u> at the rude, noisy passenger.
6. He had been so surprised by the question that he hadn't <u>answered</u>.
7. The bird's egg was <u>spotted</u> with tiny brown dots.
8. The <u>joyful</u> winner held up her golden trophy.

bounded	responded
elated	speckled
glared	stimulated
irritated	waddled

Building Vocabulary

Antonyms

Antonyms are words that have opposite meanings. You can use antonyms to show how things are different from each other. In the following sentence, *rough* is an antonym of *smooth*.

She sanded the rough wood until it was smooth.

Here are some more antonyms.

cheerful   grumpy

Antonyms		
top—bottom	arrive—depart	boring—interesting
admire—scorn	wild—tame	friend—enemy

Apply It

One of the two words following each sentence is an antonym for the underlined word in the sentence. Complete the sentence, using the antonym. You may use a dictionary.

1. I will allow you to walk in the garden, but I _____ you to pick the flowers. (permit, forbid)
2. He rebuilt the wobbly fence to make it _____. (stable, rickety)
3. She had no doubt in her mind and answered the question with _____. (certainty, hesitation)
4. The bird rose high into the sky and then slowly _____. (soared, descended)
5. Stop that childish behavior and be _____! (mature, juvenile)
6. The movie was serious, but it had some _____ parts. (grave, hilarious)

Word Connotations

The words you use can often create feelings and reactions. **The associations that a word brings to mind are called its connotations.** Read the sentences below.

When Ms. Orlando arrived, she saw Phillip relaxing on the lawn instead of raking.

When Ms. Orlando arrived, she saw Phillip loafing on the lawn instead of raking.

Relaxing has a positive connotation. It suggests that Ted was resting. *Loafing* has a negative connotation. *Loafing* would suggest that Ted was lazy. In order to convey the meaning you intend, it is important to know the connotations of the words you use.

Connotations	
Positive	clever, curious, cautious
Negative	tricky, nosy, timid

Apply It

Complete each sentence with one of the two words that follow it. Write the sentence. Then write whether the word you chose has a positive or negative connotation.

1. Janine was _____ about the food she ate. (careful, fussy)
2. The _____ morning air made us feel like walking quickly. (chilly, crisp)
3. A _____ sound came from the old piano. (delicate, weak)
4. The stranger's eyes were a _____ gray. (soft, dull)
5. Once she made a decision, she was _____ about it. (firm, rigid)

Prefixes

A **prefix** is a word part that you add to the beginning of a word. The word to which you add a prefix is called the **base word**.

The boy was really comfortable in the big chair. When his brother joined him, they were both **un**comfortable.

Like a base word, a prefix has a meaning. The prefix *un-* means "not" or "the opposite of." *Uncomfortable* means "the opposite of *comfortable*."

Here are some other prefixes and their meanings.

Prefix	Meaning	Example	Meaning
mis-	wrong, incorrectly	**mis**spell	to spell incorrectly
re-	again	**re**make	to make again
pre-	before, in advance	**pre**school	before school

Apply It

A. Copy each underlined word. Then underline the prefix and write the meaning of the word.
 1. They had misheard the directions.
 2. She rewrote the letter several times.
 3. I observed an unusual bird.
 4. Preheat the oven before you mix the batter.
 5. He retold the story to every friend and relative.

B. Add the prefix *un-*, *mis-*, *re-*, or *pre-* to each of these words. Use every prefix at least once. Check your words in a dictionary. Then use each one in a sentence of your own.
 6. build
 7. view
 8. read
 9. understood
 10. clean

Tools and Tips: Building Vocabulary

Suffixes

A suffix is a word part added to the end of a base word.

The queen held great power, but the king was even more power**ful**.

Each suffix has its own meaning. The suffix *-ful* means "full of." *Powerful* means "full of power."

Here are some other suffixes and their meanings.

Suffix	Meaning	Example	Meaning
-able	able to be	wear**able**	able to be worn
-er	one who does	walk**er**	one who walks
-ish	like, somewhat	green**ish**	somewhat green
-less	without	fear**less**	without fear
-ness	quality of being	kind**ness**	quality of being kind

A word can have both a prefix and a suffix.

un + manage + able = unmanageable

By adding the prefix *un-* and the suffix *-able* to the base word *manage*, a word is formed that means "not able to be managed."

Apply It

A. Copy each underlined word. Then underline the suffix and write the meaning of the word.
  1. The trail seemed endless.
  2. Then I fell off the horse and looked foolish.
  3. Luckily my clothes were washable.

B. Add a suffix from this lesson to each of these words. Check your words in a dictionary. Then use each word in a sentence.
  4. baby
  5. bend
  6. smooth
  7. thought
  8. work

Building Vocabulary

Suffixes **H17**

Word Roots

One way to learn and remember new words is by looking at their parts. Prefixes, suffixes, and base words are all parts of words. Sometimes the main part of a word is called a word root. **A word root has a special meaning but cannot stand alone as a word.**

Word Root	Meaning	Example
port	to carry	portable
spect	to look or see	inspect
ped	foot	pedal
loc	to place	local
mit	to send	transmit
ject	to throw	reject

Apply It

Write the word root in each word. Then write the meaning of each word. You may use a dictionary. You can also find meanings quickly if you have an electronic dictionary.

1. project
2. pedestrian
3. permit
4. transport
5. emit
6. porter
7. location
8. eject
9. import
10. spectacle
11. biped
12. spectator

Regional and Cultural Vocabulary

Which word or words do you use to name this insect? Depending on where you live, you might call it a darning needle, a mosquito hawk, a dragonfly, or a snake feeder. People in different regions of the country sometimes use different words for the same thing. Here are more examples of words that reflect regional differences.

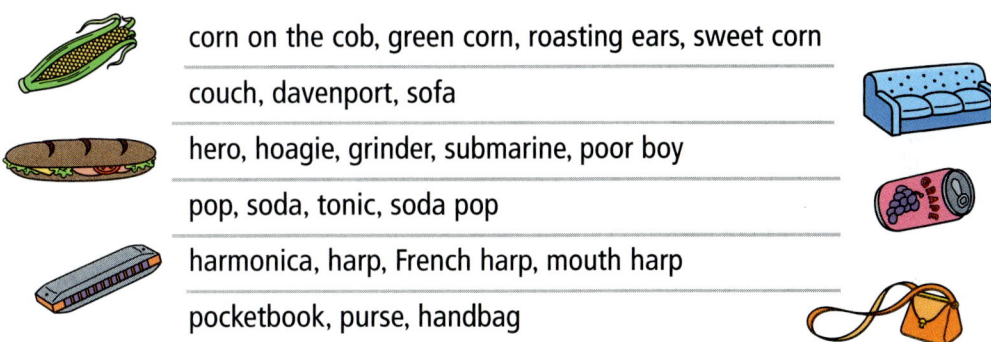

corn on the cob, green corn, roasting ears, sweet corn

couch, davenport, sofa

hero, hoagie, grinder, submarine, poor boy

pop, soda, tonic, soda pop

harmonica, harp, French harp, mouth harp

pocketbook, purse, handbag

People of different cultures and in other countries might also use different words to name the same thing. The game of soccer in the United States is called football by people in other countries, such as Great Britain. In Great Britain, a baby carriage is called a pram, and French fries are called chips. Friends are called mates in Australia and amigos in Hispanic cultures. In Hawaii, people say aloha to greet one another, but in Hebrew, the greeting is shalom.

Apply It

Choose a word from the examples above to complete each sentence. Use the word that comes most naturally to you. Discuss your choices with classmates.

1. Mom keeps money, keys, and stamps in her _____.
2. A _____ is a sandwich made from deli meats served on a long roll.
3. We were thirsty, so Dad bought us each a can of fizzy _____.
4. The butter melted on the hot _____.
5. The two _____ traded baseball cards.

more ▶

Research and Study Strategies

Using a Dictionary

Entry Words and Guide Words

Entry Words Each main word listed in your dictionary is called an **entry word**. It is printed in heavy, dark type.

Guide Words At the top of each page in a dictionary are **guide words**. The guide word on the left tells the first entry word on the page. The one on the right tells the last entry word. In the sample dictionary page below, *mine* and *minstrel* are the guide words. Any entry words that fall alphabetically between these two words will appear on this page.

Guide words ────────

Entry word ──────────

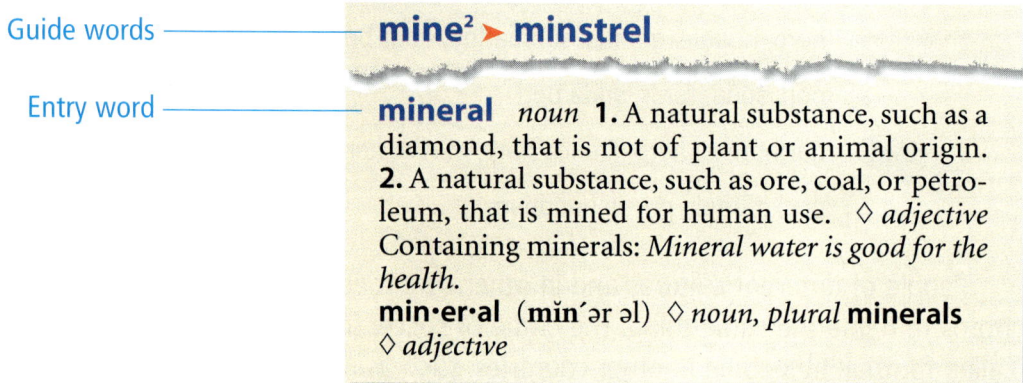

mine² ▶ **minstrel**

mineral *noun* **1.** A natural substance, such as a diamond, that is not of plant or animal origin. **2.** A natural substance, such as ore, coal, or petroleum, that is mined for human use. ◊ *adjective* Containing minerals: *Mineral water is good for the health.*
min·er·al (mĭn′ər əl) ◊ *noun, plural* **minerals** ◊ *adjective*

Other Forms of Words Entry words are usually listed in their simple forms, without endings such as *-ed, -ing, -s, -er,* and *-est.* Suppose you are looking for the word *mingled* on the sample dictionary page. The basic form of *mingled* is *mingle.* Find *mingle* as an entry word. Another form of the word, *mingling,* is also listed in the entry.

mingle *verb* **1.** To mix or become mixed; combine: *The sound of chimes mingled with the ringing of the doorbell.* —See Synonyms at **mix. 2.** To join in company with others: *We mingled with the crowd during the play's intermission.*
min·gle (mĭng′gəl) ◊ *verb* **mingled, mingling**

Other forms ──────────

H20 Tools and Tips: Research and Study Strategies

Definitions

When you come across an unfamiliar word in your reading, first use the context of the sentence to figure out its meaning. If these words do not help you, look up the word in a dictionary.

Words with More Than One Meaning Many words have more than one meaning. Read the meanings for *harbor*.

Part of speech

Definitions

Parts of Speech Some words can be used as more than one part of speech. The entry above gives two meanings for *harbor* used as a noun and two meanings for *harbor* used as a verb.

Homographs Two or more different words that have the same spelling but different meanings are called **homographs**. Homographs come from different word roots, or sources. In the entries for *mint*, each homograph is marked with a raised number.

Raised number

First homograph

Second homograph

more ▶

Using a Dictionary   **H21**

Using a Dictionary continued

Pronunciations

Look at this picture of a flying reptile that lived during the dinosaur age. Can you pronounce the creature's name?

Syllables · Accent marks
pter·o·dac·tyl (tĕr´ə dăk´ təl)
Phonetic respelling

If you look up *pterodactyl* in your dictionary, you will find the listing shown above. Notice that the entry word is broken into four syllables.

Phonetic Respelling Following the entry word is a phonetic respelling that tells you how to pronounce the word. The consonant letters stand for the common sounds of those letters. A pronunciation key shows the sounds for the vowels.

Pronunciation Key On every page or every other page of a dictionary, there is a pronunciation key. One is shown below.

ă pat	ĭ pit	oi oil	th bath
ā pay	ī ride	ŏŏ book	th bathe
â care	î fierce	ōō boot	ə ago,
ä father	ŏ pot	ou out	item
ĕ pet	ō go	ŭ cut	pencil
ē be	ô paw, for	û fur	atom
			circus

Schwa Sound Look at the phonetic respelling of *pterodactyl*. In the second syllable, you see this mark: ə. Find it in the pronunciation key. After ə are five words: **a**go, it**e**m, penc**i**l, at**o**m, and circ**u**s. The dark letters in those words stand for the ə sound, called the **schwa sound**.

Accent Marks When a word has more than one syllable, one of those syllables is said with more **stress**, or force. The dark accent mark after the third syllable of *pterodactyl* means that *dăk* is spoken with more stress than the other word parts.

Notice the light accent mark after the first syllable of *pterodactyl*. That syllable is said with more stress than the second and fourth syllables, but it is not spoken as forcefully as the third syllable.

Using the Library

How Libraries Arrange Books

Libraries arrange books into two main categories, fiction and nonfiction.

Fiction books are stories made up by the author. They are arranged alphabetically by the author's last name in one section of the library.

Nonfiction books contain factual information. They are in a separate section and are grouped by subject, such as government, music, or travel. Each subject has its own range of call numbers, which tell where a book is located on the shelves. A specific call number is printed on the spine of each book.

Searching for Books

Using an electronic or traditional card catalog will enable you to find any book a library owns when you know the title or author. It will also help you find a selection of books when you just have a subject in mind.

Using an Electronic Catalog There are many different electronic catalogs, but all are easy to use if you follow the directions on the computer screen. Enter the book's title, the author's name, or the subject of the book. Don't enter the words *A, An,* or *The* at the beginning of a title.

The computer will search its database of materials in the library's system for your request. When you make an author entry, you will get a list of all the books the author has written. When you make a subject entry, you will get a list of all books related to that subject. To see an information screen about a particular book, choose an item from the list.

Electronic input screen

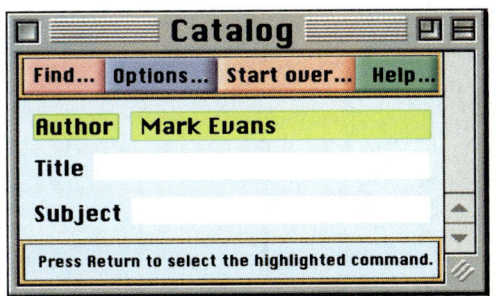

Author information list

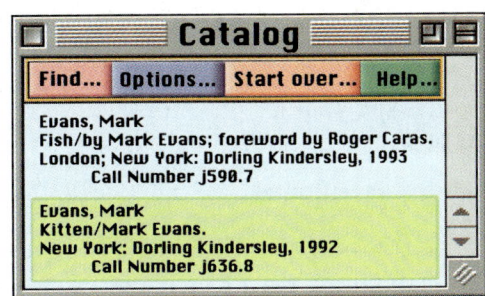

more ▶

Using the Library continued

When you enter a book title, you will automatically receive an information screen if the library owns the book. An information screen will give you a book's title and author. If the book is nonfiction, the screen may also display a call number.

Book information screen —

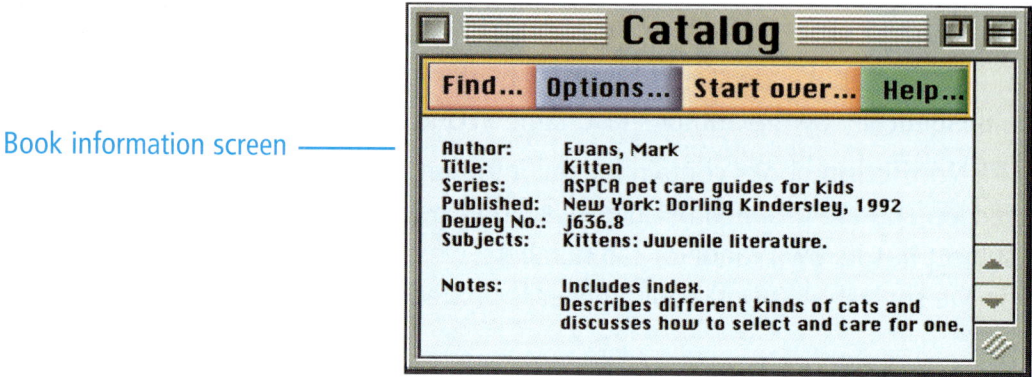

Using a Card Catalog
A traditional card catalog can also help you to find a book. This type of catalog lists an author card and title card for every book. Some books have a subject card too. The cards are filed alphabetically in long wooden drawers. To help you find the book, write the title, the author, and the call number. Here is a set of author, title, and subject cards for one book.

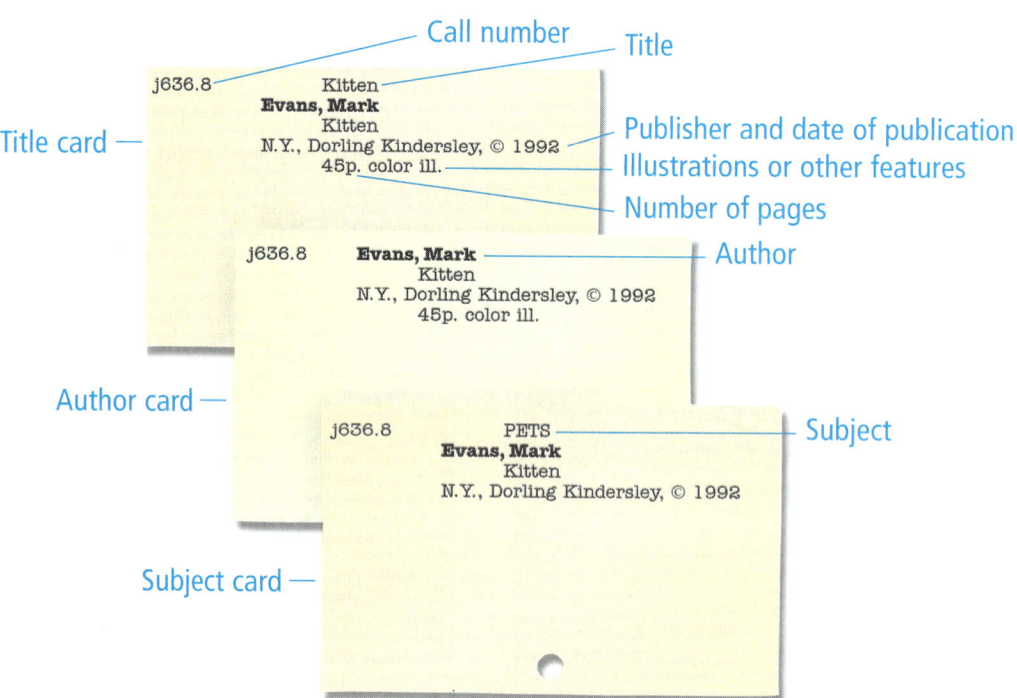

Tools and Tips: Research and Study Strategies

Reference Materials

The library can provide information on almost any subject. Here is a list of nonfiction reference materials in print that can help you. Most of these materials can also be found as electronic versions on CD-ROMs or on electronic databases in your library. (See "The Internet" on pages H45–H46 for more about using computers to find information.)

Encyclopedia An encyclopedia is a set of books that have articles about people, places, things, and events. The articles are arranged in alphabetical order in volumes. Each volume is lettered with the beginning letter or letters of the topics in that book. Guide words at the tops of pages help locate key words related to a topic.

Atlas An atlas is a book of maps. The atlas index provides the page number of each map and also gives the exact location of cities and towns.

Almanac An almanac is published once a year and has facts and other information on important people, places, and events. The index in the front lists every subject covered in the almanac. The most current almanac has the most accurate information.

Thesaurus Like dictionaries, most thesauruses list entry words in alphabetical order. In a thesaurus, however, these words are followed by lists of synonyms and antonyms. Writers use a thesaurus to find words that will make their writing more interesting.

More Dictionaries There are many special dictionaries that deal with specific topics. For example, there are dictionaries of geography or biographies that you can use to search for detailed information.

Periodicals Most libraries subscribe to magazines and newspapers from all over the country. Recent issues are usually available for use, but back issues are often bound into books and stored. Use the *Reader's Guide to Periodical Literature* to find an article on a specific topic in a back issue of any magazine.

Using Visuals

Tables

Facts can be shown on tables, or charts, that make it easy to see how different kinds of information fit together. The table below shows the average, or typical, temperatures of some cities in the United States.

Average Temperatures in U.S. Cities	January	July
Denver, Colorado	30°F (−1°C)	73°F (23°C)
Fairbanks, Alaska	−12°F (−24°C)	61°F (16°C)
Honolulu, Hawaii	72°F (22°C)	80°F (27°C)
New York, New York	32°F (0°C)	77°F (25°C)
Phoenix, Arizona	51°F (11°C)	91°F (33°C)

This table has captions across the top and along the left side. The top captions are *January* and *July*. The side captions name five cities.

The lines that go across are called **rows**. The lines that go up and down are called **columns**. To use the table, trace across the row and down the column that you are interested in. The entry where the row and column meet will give you the information you need.

Bar Graphs

The bar graph below shows how long certain zoo animals usually live. Like the table above, this graph has captions. Notice that ages in years are shown by lines that cross the entire length of the graph. To figure out how long an animal lives, look where a bar meets a number line.

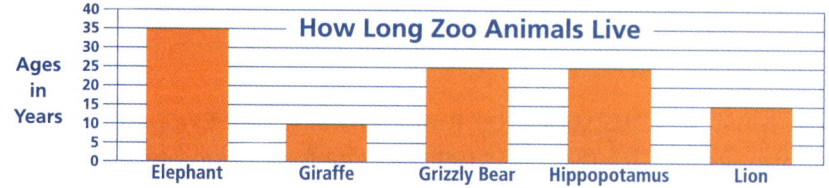

A bar graph shows how different things compare to one another at the same time. The bars can go up and down or sideways.

Maps

A map is a drawing or chart of all or part of the earth's surface, including features such as mountains, rivers, boundaries, and cities.

Legend Every map has a legend, which usually appears in a box near the map. The legend explains the map's **symbols,** the marks that stand for various things. For example, a star is a symbol for a state capital.

Distance Scale A distance scale is usually shown below the legend. It shows how a particular distance on the map relates to real distance in miles or kilometers.

Compass Rose Another important part of a map is the compass rose. Arrows show the directions *north, south, east,* and *west.*

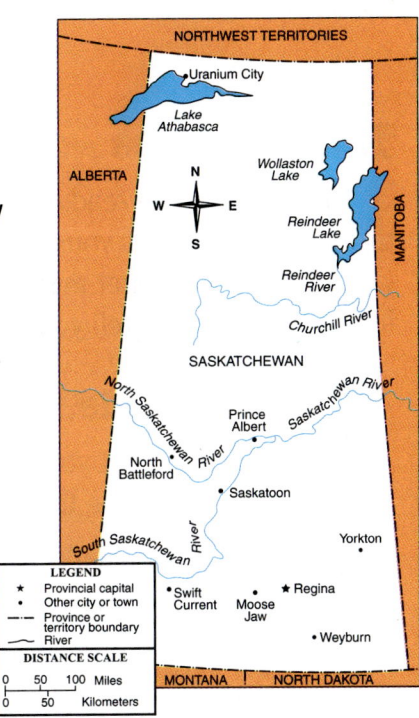

Diagrams

A diagram shows how something is put together or how it works. To understand a diagram, read the captions and all the labels.

If a diagram uses unfamiliar words, check the text near it for definitions. If you found this owl diagram in a book and did not understand the term *facial disk,* you would read the paragraphs near the diagram. You might discover that a facial disk is the ring of short feathers surrounding the owl's eyes.

Using Visuals

Research and Study Skills

Taking Notes

Whether you are reading, listening to a speaker, or watching a movie, taking notes will help you remember what you read, hear, or see. Good notes will help you remember much more than what you actually write down. The following guidelines tell you important things to remember when taking notes.

Guidelines for Taking Notes

1. Don't copy what you read. Summarize main ideas in your mind, and restate them in your own words.
2. Use quotation marks to give credit for someone's exact words.
3. Write only key words and phrases, not entire sentences.
4. Below each main idea, list the details that support it.
5. Keep careful records of the sources you are using.

Here is text from an encyclopedia entry about Robert E. Lee. A card with notes is also shown. Notice that the card lists the source of the information.

LEE, ROBERT EDWARD (1807–1870), American soldier and educator, was born at "Stratford," Westmoreland Co., Va., on Jan. 19, 1807. On account of business losses and ill health, his father, Gen. "Light-Horse Harry" Lee, moved with his family to Alexandria, Va. Here young Robert attended school until appointed to the United States Military Academy at West Point, from which he graduated in 1829, standing second in his class.

Lee's early life
- born January 19, 1807
- father was "Light-Horse Harry" Lee
- grew up in Alexandria, Virginia — Facts
- attended West Point
- graduated second in class in 1829 — Volume number
Collier's Encyclopedia, 1999 Volume 14, page 440. — Page number(s)
— Source

Taking Notes While Listening When you take notes while reading, you can always look back and check facts to see if you missed anything. When listening to a speaker, you have just one chance to hear what is being said. Use the following guidelines to help you take good notes while listening.

Guidelines for Taking Notes While Listening

1. Keep your mind on what the speaker is saying.
2. Pay careful attention to the speaker's introduction and conclusion. A good speaker will outline the speech in an introduction and sum up the main points in the conclusion.
3. Listen for cue words, such as *first, the main point,* and *most important,* that signal important information.
4. Don't write everything. Write only key words or phrases.
5. Go over your notes after the speech to make sure you have included all of the main points.
6. Note the speaker's name, the location, and the date of the speech.

Taking Notes While Viewing It takes practice to view something, think about it, and take notes all at the same time. Unless you are watching a video, you can't stop the action and watch the film again. In addition to the general guidelines for taking notes, the following guidelines will help improve your note-taking skills.

Guidelines for Taking Notes While Viewing

1. Prepare for the film or event by reading related material ahead of time.
2. Look and listen carefully during the introduction.
3. Be selective. Don't write everything. Listen for important ideas and write only the key words.
4. Use symbols and abbreviations, such as *w/* for *with* and *#* for *number*.
5. Even though you can't watch while taking notes, listen to the dialogue and learn new information.
6. As soon as the film is over, go over your notes and fill in missing details while they are still fresh in your mind.
7. Be sure to record the title of the film.

Research and Study Skills continued

Outlining

An **outline** is a useful tool for sorting out main ideas and supporting details when you are reading or writing. When you use an outline to organize a piece of writing, it helps you plan the best order for your ideas.

An outline has a title and is made up of main topics, subtopics, and details. A **main topic** tells a main idea. **Subtopics** give supporting facts or details for the main topics. **Details** give more information about a subtopic. Use the following guidelines to write an outline.

Guidelines for Writing an Outline

1. Use a Roman numeral followed by a period to show each main topic.
2. Use a capital letter followed by a period to show each subtopic.
3. Use a number followed by a period to show each detail.

Here is an example of a topic outline. Note that the outline has a title. Usually the topics, marked with Roman numerals, are answers to questions about the subject.

```
            Help for Blind People ———— Title
I. Help with reading and learning ———— Main topic
    A. Braille         ⎫
    B. Talking books   ⎬ ———— Subtopics
    C. Enlarged-print books ⎭
        1. Each letter enlarged by special machine ⎫
        2. Readers feel large letters              ⎬ ———— Details
II. Help for moving about
    A. Special walking cane
    B. Trained dog
    C. Sonar device
```

Topics, subtopics, and details can be words, phrases, or sentences. The first word in each entry begins with a capital letter. There should always be at least two main topics, two subtopics under a main topic, or two details under a subtopic.

Summarizing

Summarizing helps you remember key points when you are reading or studying. A summary includes only the most important information.

Summarizing an Article Suppose that you read a lengthy article. Writing a summary can help you understand and remember details in the article. Read this summary of "Scaredy Cat," found on pages 399–402.

> Not all lions are brave and tough! Lions need to work together in groups to survive and do well, but some lions are not very good team players. Some of them will react quickly to trouble, but others will not be so eager. Scientists have found that most of the cowards are female lions who do not follow the leads of their fellow lionesses. This can put the leader in real trouble if she goes out to meet a threat and finds herself alone.

Notice that this summary begins with a clear statement of the main idea. The other sentences give details that support this main idea. The following guidelines should help you to write your own summary of an article.

Guidelines for Summarizing an Article

1. State the main idea of the article clearly and briefly.
2. Look for key words and important names, dates, and places from the article.
3. Use these facts to write sentences that support the main idea.
4. Be sure to explain events or steps in the correct order.
5. Use as few words as possible. Put the facts into your own words without changing the meaning of what you have read.

Research and Study Skills continued

Summarizing a Story When summarizing a story, briefly retell what happens, making sure to include all the important characters and events. Read the following summary of "The Woman Who Outshone the Sun," the story found on pages 320–324.

> Villagers who live near a river depend on it for water and food. In the village lives an unusual woman who loves the river. The river loves her in return. Many people fear the woman because she looks and acts different. They treat her unkindly and force her to leave her home. As she leaves, the river goes with her. Suddenly everyone realizes that without the river there is no water to drink or food to eat. They panic and beg the woman to return the river. She agrees only after they promise to show kindness to each other.

Notice that this summary includes the main events of the story. It also describes the characters' actions and their results. Use the following guidelines when you summarize a story.

Guidelines for Summarizing a Story

1. Decide what is the most important feature of the story. If it is a mystery, you might write about the plot. If the story is about friendship, you might write about the characters.

2. Write clear, brief sentences stating the most important ideas. Include important names, dates, and places from the story but don't include other details.

3. Be sure to give enough information so that the summary makes sense. The order of events in a summary should be the same as the order in the story.

4. To catch the tone or mood of the story, describe a specific character's actions or give a direct quotation.

Open-Response Questions continued

Birds have their own warm coats made of feathers. However, they have a special problem because they have no "leggings" to warm their feet and legs. Only a few birds whose feet and legs can stand very low temperatures, such as the ptarmigan, live in the Arctic.

There's one kind of animal you won't find, though—snakes and other reptiles. These cold-blooded animals would freeze as stiff as statues in an Arctic winter!

Summarize why **arctic animals are able to survive the cold winters.**

Read these two answers to the instruction. Which one is a better answer?

The Arctic is at the top of the world. It's really, really cold there. Sometimes it gets as cold as 60 degrees below zero. A lot of furry animals live there but no snakes! There are the the polar bear, the arctic fox, seals, walrus, and the lemming. If you don't know what a lemming is, it's an arctic mouse. Birds and insects live there too because they don't freeze.

Animals in the Arctic have different ways that help them survive the cold winters. Some animals, such as the polar bear, have thick coats of fur. Water animals like seals have fur and blubber. Some small animals live in tunnels in the snow. The birds have feathers and special feet and legs that don't get too cold. These are the ways the animals stay alive in winter.

The first answer names the kinds of animals in the Arctic, but it doesn't tell about why they are able to survive. It also gives facts about the Arctic that the question doesn't ask for.

The second answer uses clue words from the instruction in the topic sentence, such as *survive* and *cold winters*. The other sentences summarize the main points about how the animals survive the cold. This answer gives only the information asked for.

Tools and Tips: Test-Taking Strategies

Open-Response Questions

Sometimes on a test you must read a passage and then write answers to questions about it. Remember these guidelines to help you write a good answer.

Guidelines for Answering an Essay Question

1. Read the question carefully. Find clue words that tell what kind of answer to write, such as *explain*, *compare*, *contrast*, and *summarize*.
2. Look for other clue words that tell what the answer should be about.
3. Write a topic sentence that uses clue words from the question. Write other sentences that give details to support the topic sentence.
4. Answer only the question that is asked.

Read the following passage and follow the instructions at the end.

Animals in the Arctic

The Arctic is the region at the top of the world. Because it lies so far north, it has very cold, long winters. The temperature can drop to sixty degrees below zero!

Even though the Arctic has bitter winters, many kinds of animals make their home there year round. If you went for a walk on the tundra, you might see caribou, a polar bear, or an arctic fox. These animals have thick fur coats that keep them warm. Some animals that live part-time in the water, such as seals and walrus, also have fur. They also have a thick layer of blubber under their skin to help warm them in the icy water.

The arctic hare, a kind of rabbit, and the lemming, an arctic mouse, are small furry animals that protect themselves from the cold by living in tunnels under the snow.

more ▶

Word Analogies continued

Guidelines for Completing Word Analogies

1. Figure out how the first two words are alike.
2. If the analogy uses colons, say it as a sentence.
3. If you are asked to choose the second pair of words from a list, choose the pair that has the same relationship as the first pair.
4. If you are asked to fill in the last word, write a word that will make the second pair of words have the same relationship as the first pair.

Practice

A. Choose the pair of words that best completes each word analogy.

1. *Bark* is to *dog* as
   a. *scratch* is to *cat*.
   b. *tail* is to *pig*.
   c. *hoot* is to *owl*.
   d. *bark* is to *tree*.

2. *Chair* is to *furniture* as
   a. *car* is to *automobile*.
   b. *shirt* is to *clothing*.
   c. *paper* is to *book*.
   d. *dog* is to *poodle*.

3. *Day* is to *night* as
   a. *tall* is to *short*.
   b. *happy* is to *glad*.
   c. *car* is to *engine*.
   d. *horse* is to *pony*.

4. *Quiet* is to *silent* as
   a. *unhappy* is to *joyful*.
   b. *eager* is to *bored*.
   c. *sloppy* is to *messy*.
   d. *hour* is to *minute*.

B. Write the word that best completes each analogy.

5. Chef : cook :: pilot : _____.
   a. eat   b. write
   c. build   d. fly

6. Month : year :: classroom : _____.
   a. teacher   b. school
   c. chalk   d. study

7. Pie : slice :: door : _____.
   a. doorknob   b. house
   c. tall   d. window

8. Hurry : rush :: jump : _____.
   a. fall   b. swim
   c. leap   d. high

Test-Taking Strategies

Word Analogies

Many tests ask you to complete **word analogies** that show how two pairs of words are alike.

Wet is to *dry* as *hot* is to <u>cold</u>.

In this example, *wet* and *dry* are opposites. *Cold* completes the word analogy correctly because it means the opposite of *hot*. Now both pairs of words show opposites.

Often a word analogy is set up with colons. To help you answer it, think of it as a sentence.

Wet : dry :: hot : _____

Wet is to dry as hot is to _____.

This chart shows some ways words can be related.

Word Relationship	Example
antonyms (opposites)	*Fast* is to *slow* as *narrow* is to *wide*.
synonyms (same meanings)	*Surprising* is to *amazing* as *unhappy* is to *sad*.
a part to the whole thing	*Toe* is to *foot* as *finger* is to *hand*.
a whole thing to one of its parts	*Car* is to *wheel* as *airplane* is to *wing*.
a thing to a category that it belongs to	*Banana* is to *fruit* as *carrot* is to *vegetable*.
a person to something he or she does	*Farmer* is to *planting* as *doctor* is to *healing*.
a thing to one of its characteristics	*Ball* is to *round* as *knife* is to *sharp*.

more ▶

Word Analogies

Using Technology

Technology Terms

Computer Terms

Your school may be equipped with computers, or you may have your own. Try to become familiar with the following terms to understand how the computer works.

CD-ROM	A flat, round, plastic disk where computer data or music can be stored and read with a laser; many computers have built-in CD-ROM drives.
cursor	The blinking square, dot, or bar on a computer screen that shows where the next typed character will appear.
disk drive	A device that can read information from a disk or write information onto a disk; you insert a disk into a disk drive through a thin slot.
document	A written or printed piece of writing.
floppy disk	A somewhat flexible plastic disk coated with magnetic material and used to store computer data.
font	Any one of various styles of letters in which computer type can appear.
hard copy	A computer document that is printed on paper.
hard drive	A computer disk that cannot be easily removed from the computer; hard disks hold more data and run faster than floppy disks.
hardware	The parts of a computer system, including the keyboard, monitor, memory storage devices, and printer.
keyboard	A part of the computer containing a set of keys.
menu	A list of computer commands shown on a monitor.

more ▶

Technology Terms *continued*

modem	A part of a computer that allows it to communicate with other computers over telephone lines. It can be a separate device or inside the computer.
monitor	A part of a computer system that shows information on a screen.
printer	A part of a computer system that produces printed documents.
software	Programs that are used in operating computers.

Word-Processing Commands

These commands are often used in word processing. You can give each command by typing a series of keys or by selecting it from a menu.

Close	Closes the displayed document.
Copy	Copies selected, or highlighted, text.
Cut	Removes selected, or highlighted, text.
delete	Removes selected, or highlighted, text.
Find	Locates specific words or phrases in a document.
New	Opens a new document.
Open	Displays a selected document.
Paste	Inserts copied or cut text in a new location in the same document or in another document.
Print	Prints the displayed document.
Quit	Leaves the program.
return	Moves the cursor to the beginning of the next line.
Save	Stores a document for later use.
shift	Allows you to type a capital letter or a new character.
Spelling	Activates the spelling tool.
tab	Indents the cursor to the right.

Using E-mail

Writing an e-mail is different from writing a letter or talking on the phone. Follow these guidelines to write good e-mail messages.

Guidelines for Using E-mail Effectively

1. Give your message a specific title in the subject line. The person receiving your message should know the subject before opening it.

2. Use short paragraphs. Long paragraphs are difficult to read onscreen.

3. Skip a line instead of indenting when you begin a new paragraph. Your message will be easier to read onscreen.

4. Remember that special type, such as italics or underlining, may not show up on the other person's screen.

5. Be careful how you use humor. The other person can't hear your tone of voice and may not be able to tell when you're joking.

6. Even though an e-mail may seem more casual than a letter, you should still follow the rules of good writing.

7. Proofread your messages, and fix all capitalization, punctuation, usage, and spelling mistakes.

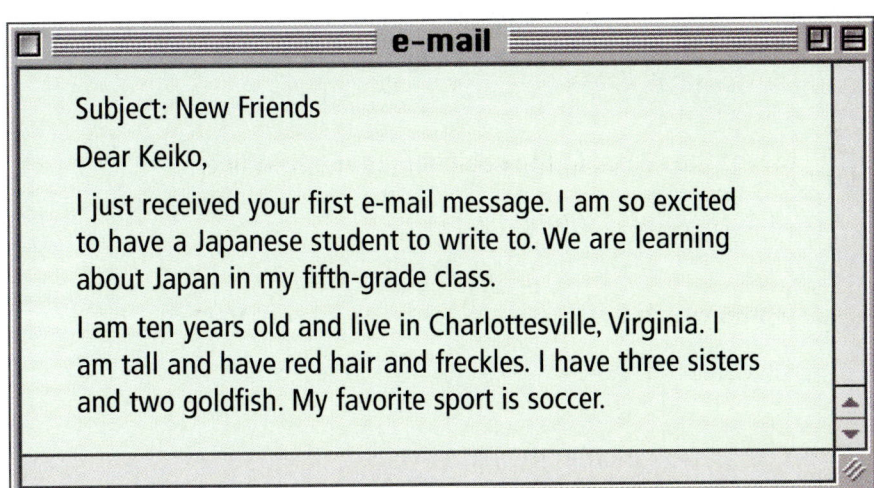

Subject: New Friends

Dear Keiko,

I just received your first e-mail message. I am so excited to have a Japanese student to write to. We are learning about Japan in my fifth-grade class.

I am ten years old and live in Charlottesville, Virginia. I am tall and have red hair and freckles. I have three sisters and two goldfish. My favorite sport is soccer.

Using a Spelling Tool

Your word-processing program's spelling tool can help you proofread your writing. Having a spelling tool on your computer doesn't mean you don't have to know how to spell, though.

Look at this paragraph. Do you see any misspelled words? If you do, you're smarter than a spelling tool because it didn't find any of the mistakes.

A spelling tool can't tell the difference between homophones.

A spelling tool can't find a misspelled word that is the correct spelling of another word.

A spelling tool doesn't know whether two words are supposed to be one word.

Summer Vacation

This summer my family and I went on a vacation to the beech. I can still remember the scent of the ocean and the feel of the sand under my bare feet. I spent ours helping my little sister build a sandcastle with a pail and a shovel. One day we saw a pair of star fish. There is no place like the beach!

Think of a spelling tool as a proofreading partner. The spelling tool can help you find mistakes in your writing, but you still need to proofread to make sure the spelling tool didn't miss anything.

Computers and the Writing Process

Computers can help you plan, draft, revise, proofread, and publish your writing more efficiently. Here are some ideas for using a computer in the writing process.

PREWRITING

Type your thoughts as you think of them. Don't worry about finishing your sentences or grouping ideas. You can use the Cut and Paste features to make changes later.

Dim the screen to help you concentrate on your thoughts rather than on correctness.

Create outlines, charts, or graphic organizers to help you plan your writing.
Tip: Some word-processing programs have ready-to-use graphic organizers that you just fill in.

```
Document
Benjamin Franklin's Career
  I. What Ben Franklin printed
      A. City laws
      B. Notices of meetings and events
      C. The Pennsylvania Gazette
 II. Other jobs Ben Franklin had
      A. Statesman
      B. Scientist
      C. Inventor
      D. Writer
```

DRAFTING

Save your prewriting notes and ideas under a new file name, and then expand a list or outline into a draft.

Double-space your draft so that you can write revisions on your printout.

Boldface or underline words you may want to change later.

Save early and often!

Using Technology

more ▶

Computers and the Writing Process continued

REVISING

Save a copy of your file under a new name before you begin making changes.

Have a conference with a partner right at the computer. Read your draft aloud and discuss any questions or problems you have. Then insert your partner's comments in capital letters. Later you can decide which comments you agree with.

Use the Find and Replace functions to check for overused words. Enter words such as *and*, *then*, *pretty*, or *nice* in the Find function. When the word is found, highlight it and click Replace. You can also simply boldface the word and revise it later.

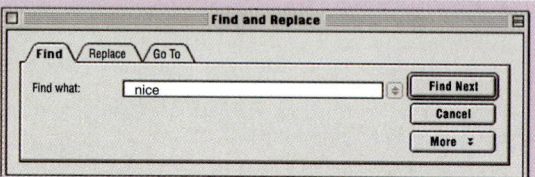

Use the Cut and Paste functions to make changes. Move or delete words, sentences, or paragraphs with just a few clicks. **Tip:** If you're unsure about cutting something, just move the text to the end of your document. You can always cut those "throwaways" later.

Use the electronic thesaurus in your word-processing program to find synonyms. Be careful to choose a synonym that has the meaning you want.

Rewrite problem sentences or paragraphs under your original text. Boldface your new text and compare the different versions. Delete the version you don't want.

PROOFREADING

Check your spelling with your word processor's spelling tool. Then check for errors a spelling tool won't catch! See "Using a Spelling Tool" on page H40.

Turn your sentences into a list. Place the cursor after each end punctuation mark and press Return. Now you can easily spot sentences that are too long or too short, run-on sentences, and fragments. You can also make sure that each sentence begins with a capital letter. When you're finished proofreading, simply delete the extra returns.

PUBLISHING

Computers make publishing your writing a snap. Here's how you can create professional-looking final products.

Choose your fonts carefully. Designers suggest using no more than three fonts per page.

Helvetica   Century   Times Roman

Choose a type size that can be read easily, but remember, type that is too big can look silly. Twelve-point type is usually a good choice.

8 pt
12 pt
16 pt

Use bullets to separate the items on a list or to highlight a passage. Typing Option + 8 usually produces a bullet.

Design your title by changing the type size or font. Make a separate title page, if you like, and use your word processor's Borders and Shading functions to make the page fancy.

Add art to your paper or report.

- **Use the computer's Paint or Draw features** to create your own picture.
- **Cut and paste** clip art, which comes with some software.
- **Use a scanner** to copy images such as photographs onto your computer. You can then insert them electronically into your document.

If you don't have the equipment to create electronic art, simply leave a space in your document, print out a hard copy, and draw or paste in a picture.

Other key combinations will make special pictures and symbols called dingbats. See how many you recognize.

Using Technology

more ▶

Computers and the Writing Process

Computers and the Writing Process *continued*

PUBLISHING

Create tables, charts, or graphs to accompany your writing. For example, you can chart or graph the results of a class survey on birthdays.

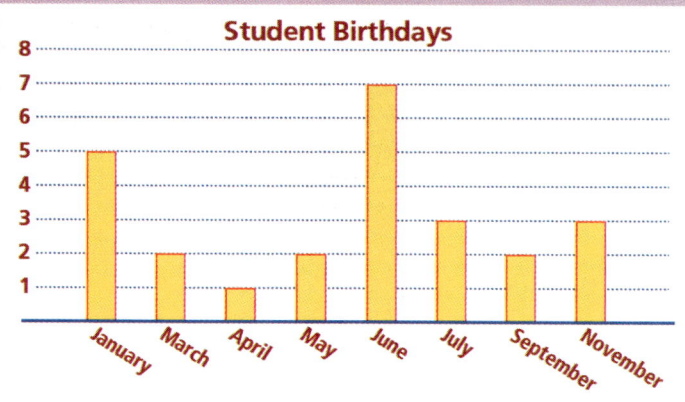

Choose your paper. White paper is always fine, but sometimes you may want to try colored paper or stationery with borders or pictures. **Tip:** Check with an adult before changing the printer paper. Paper that is too thick or heavy can jam your printer.

Create newsletters, magazines, or brochures using word-processing templates. Look at examples of real newspapers and magazines to see what kind of type to use, how big to make titles, and where to put pictures. Try combining electronic files to create a class newsletter that contains articles written by each of your classmates.

Organize your writing in electronic folders. Create separate folders to store poems, stories, research reports, and letters. You can also make a folder for unfinished pieces. Think of your computer as a giant storage cabinet!

Start an electronic portfolio for special pieces of your writing. You can create a portfolio folder on your hard drive or copy your files onto a floppy disk. Add pieces you choose throughout the year.

The Internet

What Is the Internet?

The **Internet** is a network of computers that connects people, businesses, and institutions all over the world. It lets computer users communicate with other computer users quickly and easily. Here are some of the many things you can do on the Internet.

- Do research. You can watch a volcano erupt, take a tour of the Smithsonian, or hear music from the Revolutionary War. You can search for current articles or historical documents.

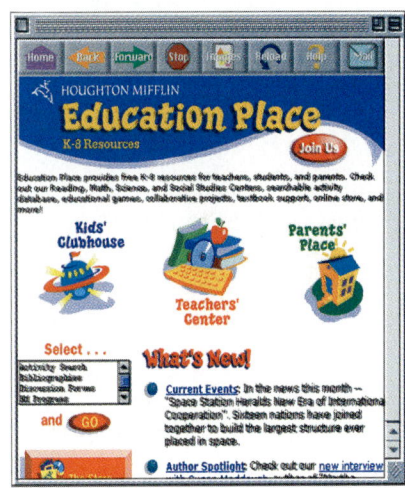

- Visit an electronic bulletin board or a chat room, where users "meet" to discuss specific topics. Here you can join an online book club, chat with other students who enjoy playing basketball, or debate current events.

- Send e-mail to your friends and family. Anyone who is online is reachable. See "Using E-mail" on page H37.

Tech Tip
Visit Education Place at www.eduplace.com/kids/hme/ for fun activities and interesting information.

more ▶

The Internet *continued*

- Use special software to create your own Web site. You design the page, write the text, and choose links to other sites. Your school may also have its own Web site where you can publish your work.

Tips for Using the Internet

Although the Internet can be a great way to get information, it can be confusing. Use these tips to make the most of it!

- Search smart! Use a search engine to help you find Web sites on your topic or area of interest. Type in a key word or search by topics. Most search engines give tips on searching. Some search engines are designed just for kids.

- Write down the source of any information you find on the Internet just as you would for a book. Along with the author, title, date of the material, and online address (URL), make sure you include the date you found the information. Information on the Internet can change daily.

- Check your sources carefully. The Internet is full of information, but not all of it is reliable. Web sites published by well-known organizations may be more trustworthy than those published by individuals.

- Protect your privacy. Never give your full name or address in a chat room.

Creating an Electronic Multimedia Presentation

An electronic multimedia presentation is a combination of words, pictures, and sound. It lets you express much more than you could with just words. For example, an electronic multimedia presentation on rain forests could contain descriptions of the plants found in a rain forest, recordings of animal sounds, photographs of the Amazon rain forest, and a video of flying squirrels.

Equipment

Here is what you need:

- a personal computer with a large memory
- high-quality video and audio systems
- a CD-ROM drive
- a multimedia software program

Check with your school librarian or media specialist to find out what equipment is available.

Parts of an Electronic Multimedia Presentation

An electronic multimedia presentation may include text, photos and video, sound, and animation.

Text The text of your presentation may include informative summaries, descriptions, directions, or photo captions. How the text appears on screen is also important. You can adjust the font, size, and color of your text. **Tip:** Don't make your letters too small or put too many words on a single screen. Text should be easy to see and to read.

more ▶

Creating an Electronic Multimedia Presentation continued

Photos and Videos Pictures can be powerful, so choose them carefully. Here are some ways you can include pictures.

- Include video you film yourself.
- Scan in photos or artwork.
- Generate your own computer artwork.

Animation Computer animation lets you create objects and then bring them to life. Here are some things you can do with animation.

- Tell a story with animated figures.
- Show an experiment being performed.
- Track changes in a chart or graph.
- Show how something is put together.
- Show how something grows.
- Display an object from all sides.

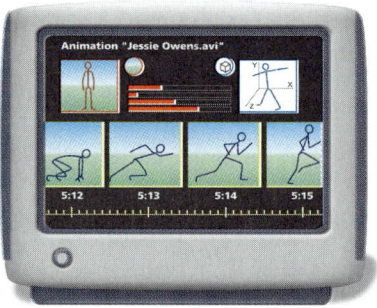

Sound Sound can help make an image or text come alive. Imagine viewing a video of the track star Jesse Owens. Then imagine viewing the same image while listening to the cheers of the crowd and the crackle of the announcer's voice. Here are some suggestions for using sound in your multimedia presentation.

- Add appropriate background sounds—birds calling, water dripping, bells ringing.
- Use music to set a mood.
- Include songs that represent a time in history or emphasize a theme.
- Include a button to let users hear the text read aloud.
- Include audio to accompany video clips.

Designing an Electronic Multimedia Presentation

The process of designing an electronic multimedia presentation is similar to that of creating a piece of writing, but here are some additional things to consider.

Types of Media If you are planning a presentation on the moon, you might come up with the following list:

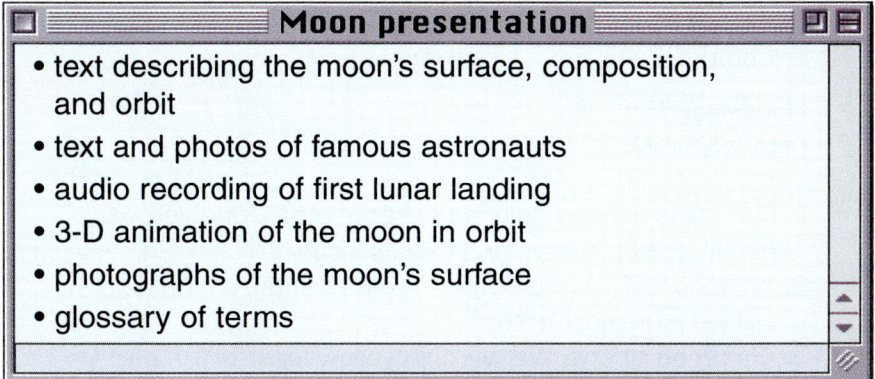

Order of Presentation Will the presentation have a specific order, or will you allow the user to choose his or her own path? A diagram, such as the one below, will help you plan.

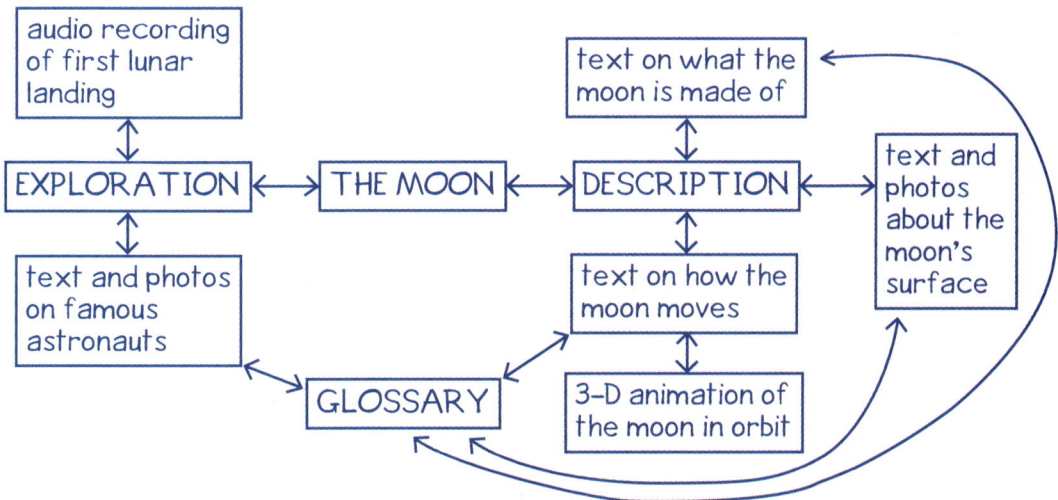

Designing and creating a multimedia presentation can be challenging and fun! **Tip:** As always, cite your sources and write text in your own words.

Writer's Tools

Keeping a Learning Log

A **learning log** is a notebook for keeping track of what you learn in different subjects. It is a place to write facts as well as your thoughts about each subject.

Getting Started Write the date at the top of the page. Then use words, charts, or pictures to help you remember what you have learned. An example from one student's learning log is shown below.

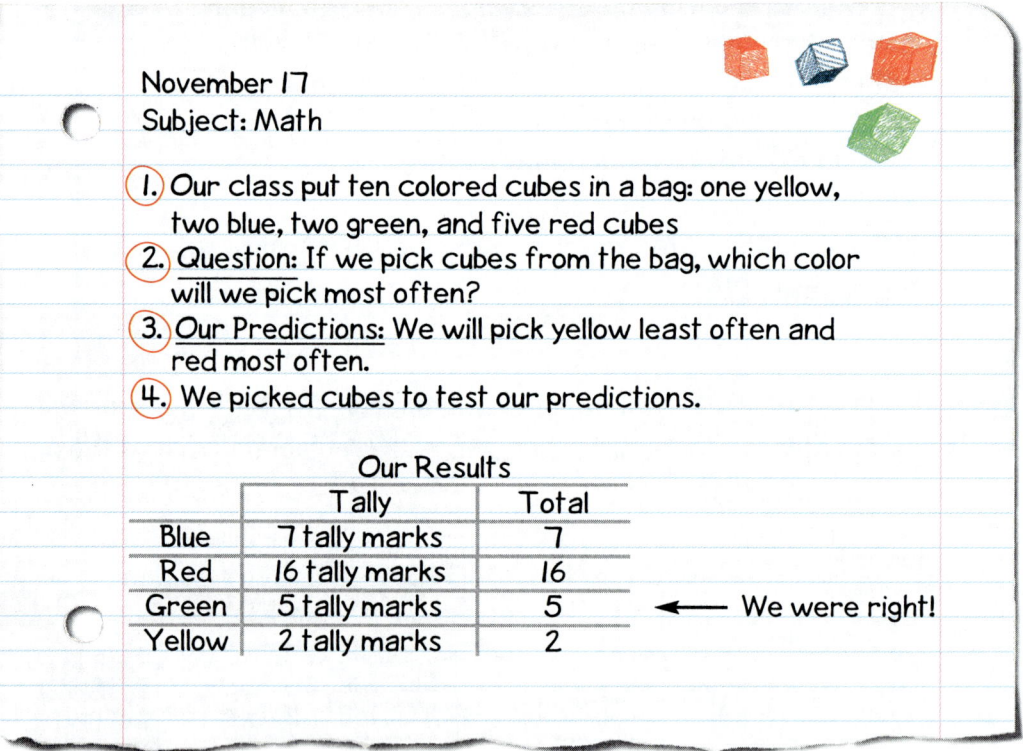

Try It Out Here are some suggestions for using a learning log.

- Make a vocabulary list for one subject. Include definitions.
- With a small group, record coin flips. Show the results in a bar graph.
- Work with classmates to record and graph weather data for a week.
- Explain how multiplication is similar to addition. How is it different?
- Describe your observations during a nature walk.
- Record what you know about your state. What do you want to know?
- Summarize what you have learned in a lesson in school.

Tools and Tips: Writer's Tools

Keeping a Writer's Notebook

A **writer's notebook** is a kind of notebook you can keep just for writing. You can record words you like, write about authors you enjoy, and make notes about ideas for stories, essays, or poems. Relax and write freely about anything that interests you. You never know what might be useful later!

When Do I Use It? Open your writer's notebook whenever you have a writing assignment. Look there for topic ideas, exact words, details, and dialogue, even facts and examples to support a goal or an opinion. Parts of pages from one student's notebook are shown below.

Words I Like

parched	alarming	appetizing	astounded	bulky
creepy	husky	scorch	cranky	sloshing
splatter	creep	gallop		

Grandpa's Stories

Last night my grandpa told me all these stories about growing up on a farm. He had to do chores like feeding thirty cows and carrying heavy buckets of water. Then he went to a one-room schoolhouse, and there wasn't a bus. Sometimes he and his sister rode one pony together. His sister was older so she got to steer, which always made him mad. In warm weather, he didn't wear shoes. I can't imagine going to school without any shoes.

Try It Out Start your own writer's notebook. Try some of these suggestions.

- Write your thoughts or feelings about a new rule at school.
- Copy a favorite sentence or two from a book you enjoyed. Be sure to include information about the source.
- List reasons why you like a sport or other activity.
- Record a funny thing you heard someone say.
- Write details about a place you like.
- List new words.

Graphic Organizers

Are you stuck for an idea to write about? Are you confused about how to organize your ideas? Try using these graphic organizers to help you explore and plan your ideas.

Clusters or webs are good for brainstorming topics, exploring ideas, or organizing information. Write your topic in a center circle. Write details about your topic, circle them, and connect them to the center circle. Add more details to each circle.

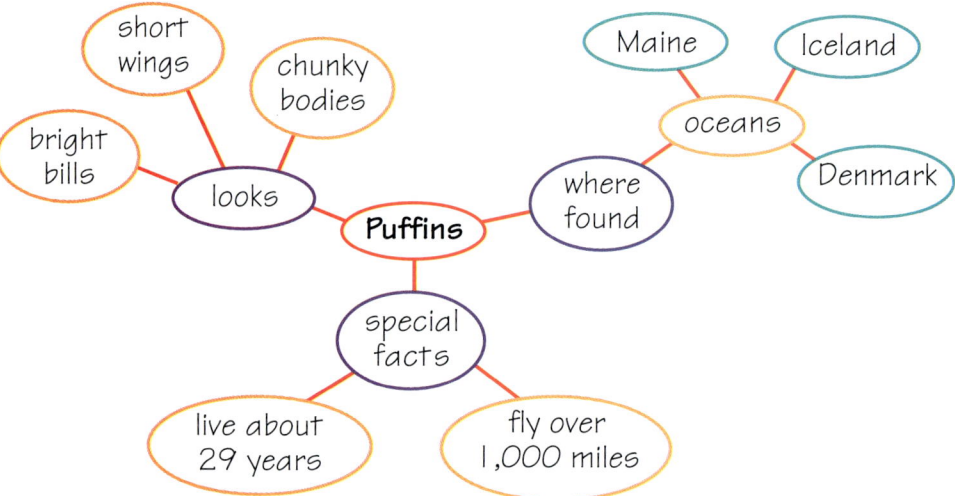

Inverted triangles can help you narrow topics that are too big. Write a broad topic in the first section of the triangle. Then write one part of that topic below it. Then write one part of the second topic. Keep going until you get a focused topic.

You can also use an inverted triangle to organize your details from most to least important.

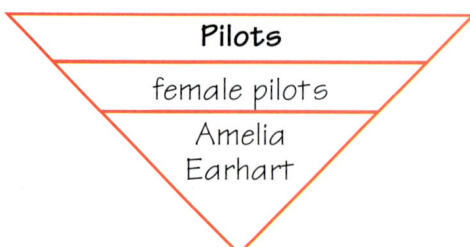

Planning charts ask you to think about your purpose, your goals, and your audience before you begin to write. These decisions will affect how you end up writing about your topic.

My Topic _____

My Purpose	My Goals	My Audience
Circle one or more.	*Name at least one.*	*Answer these questions.*
• to tell a story • to explain • to persuade • to share • to plan • to learn • other _____ _____ _____		1. Who is my audience? 2. What do they already know about my topic? 3. What do I want them to know? 4. What part of my topic would interest them most?

Observation charts organize details gathered through your five senses. Use them to add details to your writing. Try to write notes in each column. Depending on your topic, you may have more details in one column than in another, or no details at all.

My Trip to the Beach				
Sight	**Sound**	**Touch**	**Taste**	**Smell**
umbrellas choppy water kites	crashing waves kids shouting boat motor	sizzling sand slimy jellyfish	gritty sandwiches	salty air

 Go to www.eduplace.com/kids/hme/ for graphic organizers.

Graphic Organizers continued

T-charts organize information into two groups. Use T-charts to list details about two people, places, or things. They are also helpful for exploring two sides of an argument, showing likenesses and differences, listing materials and steps for instructions, or showing two points of view.

Draw a large *T*. Write your subjects at the top. Write details about each subject in the column below it. You may want to match the information in the columns.

Summer	Winter
swimming	sledding
bathing suit	boots
watermelon	hot chocolate

E-charts show a main idea and its details. Write the main idea and underline it. Then draw an *E* next to it. Write details that support the main idea on each line of the *E*.

my grandma is special
- tells funny stories
- wears crazy hats
- cooks yummy paella

KWL charts show what you already know about a topic, what you want to know about it, and what you learn after doing research.

Grizzly Bears		
What I Know	What I Want to Know	What I Learned
hibernate are very dangerous	Do they eat when they hibernate? What do they eat?	don't eat for several months eat soapberries and salmon

ISP charts show **information (I), sources (S),** and, if appropriate, the **page references (P)** where you found the information.

I	S	P
Adult grizzlies weigh about 850 pounds!	Know-It-All Encyclopedia	246
Mother grizzlies will adopt strays or orphaned grizzlies.	Mr. Ed Ucation, tour guide at the Natural History Museum	139

Step-by-step charts help you to plan your instructions. List the materials that are needed to follow your instructions. Then write each step in order. Include details your audience needs to know to complete each step.

Materials	
Steps	**Details**
Step 1	
Step 2	
Step 3	
Step 4	
Step 5	

Writer's Tools

more ▶
Graphic Organizers

Graphic Organizers continued

Story maps help you to gather details for your stories. Write notes about your character, setting, and plot.

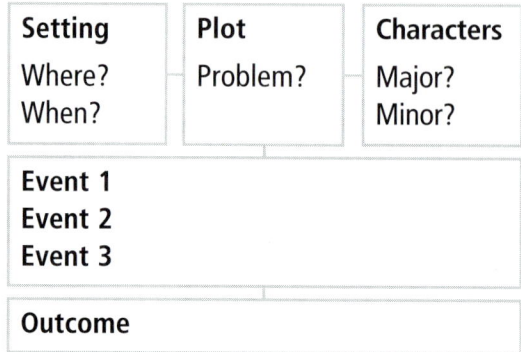

Time lines show events in order and tell when they happened. Draw an arrow, and write events along it in order from left to right. Add dates for each event.

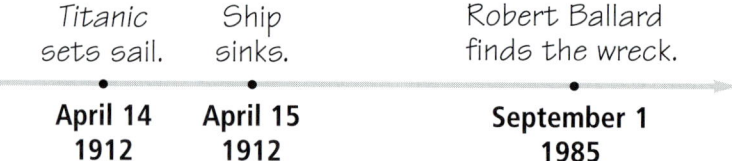

Venn diagrams are used to compare and contrast two subjects. Write details that tell how the subjects are different in the outer circles. Write details that tell how the subjects are alike where the circles overlap.

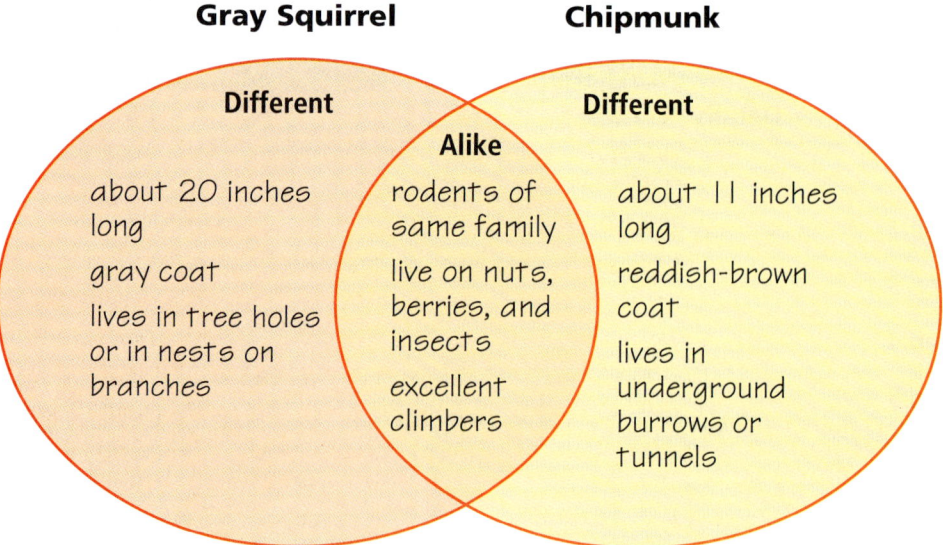

Guide to Capitalization, Punctuation, and Usage

Abbreviations

Abbreviations are shortened forms of words. Most abbreviations begin with a capital letter and end with a period. Use abbreviations only in special kinds of writing, such as addresses and lists.

Titles	Mr. *(Mister)* Mr. Juan Albino Mrs. *(Mistress)* Mrs. Frances Wong Ms. *(Any Woman)* Leslie Clark	Sr. *(Senior)* John Helt Sr. Jr. *(Junior)* John Helt Jr. Dr. *(Doctor)* Dr. Janice Dodds
	Note: *Miss* is not an abbreviation and does not end with a period.	
Words used in addresses	St. *(Street)* Blvd. *(Boulevard)* Rd. *(Road)* Rte. *(Route)* Ave. *(Avenue)* Apt. *(Apartment)* Dr. *(Drive)* Pkwy. *(Parkway)*	Mt. *(Mount or Mountain)* Expy. *(Expressway)*
Words used in business	Co. *(Company)* Corp. *(Corporation)*	Inc. *(Incorporated)* Ltd. *(Limited)*
Other abbreviations	Some abbreviations are written in all capital letters, with a letter standing for each important word. P.D. *(Police Department)* P.O. *(Post Office)* J.P. *(Justice of the Peace)* R.N. *(Registered Nurse)*	
	The United States Postal Service uses two capital letters and no period in each of its state abbreviations. AL *(Alabama)* IL *(Illinois)* MO *(Missouri)* AK *(Alaska)* IN *(Indiana)* MT *(Montana)* AZ *(Arizona)* IA *(Iowa)* NE *(Nebraska)* AR *(Arkansas)* KS *(Kansas)* NV *(Nevada)* CA *(California)* KY *(Kentucky)* NH *(New Hampshire)* CO *(Colorado)* LA *(Louisiana)* NJ *(New Jersey)* CT *(Connecticut)* ME *(Maine)* NM *(New Mexico)* DE *(Delaware)* MD *(Maryland)* NY *(New York)* FL *(Florida)* MA *(Massachusetts)* NC *(North Carolina)* GA *(Georgia)* MI *(Michigan)* ND *(North Dakota)* HI *(Hawaii)* MN *(Minnesota)* OH *(Ohio)* ID *(Idaho)* MS *(Mississippi)* OK *(Oklahoma)*	

more ▶

Guide to Capitalization, Punctuation, and Usage *continued*

Abbreviations *continued*

Other abbreviations (continued)	OR *(Oregon)* TN *(Tennessee)* WA *(Washington)* PA *(Pennsylvania)* TX *(Texas)* WV *(West Virginia)* RI *(Rhode Island)* UT *(Utah)* WI *(Wisconsin)* SC *(South Carolina)* VT *(Vermont)* WY *(Wyoming)* SD *(South Dakota)* VA *(Virginia)*
	Initials are abbreviations that stand for a person's first or middle name. Some names have both a first and a middle initial. E.B. White *(Elwyn Brooks White)* T. James Carey *(Thomas James Carey)*

Titles

Italicizing/ Underlining	**The important words and the first and last words in a title are capitalized. Titles of books, magazines, TV shows, movies, and newspapers are italicized or underlined.** *Oliver Twist* (book) *Cricket* (magazine) *Nova* (TV show) *Star Wars* (movie) *The Phoenix Express* (newspaper)
Quotation marks with titles	**Titles of short stories, songs, articles, book chapters, and most poems are set off by quotation marks.** "The Necklace" *(short story)* "Home on the Range" *(song)* "Three Days in the Sahara" *(article)* "The Human Brain" *(chapter)* "Deer at Dusk" *(poem)*

Quotations

Quotation marks with commas and periods	**Quotation marks are used to set off a speaker's exact words. The first word of a quotation begins with a capital letter. Punctuation belongs *inside* the closing quotation marks. Commas separate a quotation from the rest of the sentence.** "Where," asked the stranger, "is the post office?" "Please put away your books now," said Mr. Emory. Linda whispered, "What time is it?" "It's late," replied Bill. "Let's go!"

Capitalization

Rules for capitalization	
	Capitalize the first word of every sentence.
	What an unusual color the roses are!
	Capitalize the pronoun *I*.
	What should I do next?
	Capitalize proper nouns. If a proper noun is made up of more than one word, capitalize each important word.
	Emily G. Messe District of Columbia Lincoln Memorial
	Capitalize titles or their abbreviations when used with a person's name.
	Governor Bradford Senator Smith Dr. Ling
	Capitalize proper adjectives.
	We ate at a French restaurant. She is French. That is a North American custom.
	Capitalize the names of days, months, and holidays.
	My birthday is on the last Monday in March. We watched the parade on the Fourth of July.
	Capitalize the names of nationalities, races, religions, languages, organizations, buildings, and companies.
	Able Supply Company Chinese Central School American Kennel Club Protestant African American
	Capitalize the first, last, and all important words in a title. Do not capitalize words such as *a, in, and, of,* and *the* unless they begin or end a title.
	From the Earth to the Moon *The New York Times* "The Rainbow Connection" "Growing Up"
	Capitalize the first word of each main topic and subtopic in an outline.

	1. Types of libraries
	      A. Large public library
	      B. Bookmobile

	Capitalize the first word in the greeting and the closing of a letter.
	Dear Marcia, Yours truly,

more ▶

Guide to Capitalization, Punctuation, and Usage

Guide to Capitalization, Punctuation, and Usage *continued*

Punctuation

End marks	There are three end marks. A period (.) ends a declarative or imperative sentence. A question mark (?) follows an interrogative sentence. An exclamation point (!) follows an exclamatory sentence.
	The scissors are on my desk. *(declarative)* Look up the spelling of that word. *(imperative)* How is the word spelled? *(interrogative)* This is your best poem so far! *(exclamatory)*
Apostrophe	To form the possessive of a singular noun, add an apostrophe and *-s*.
	doctor's boss's grandmother's family's
	For a plural noun that ends in *s*, add only an apostrophe.
	sisters' families' hound dogs' Smiths'
	For a plural noun that does not end in *s*, add an apostrophe and *-s* to form the plural possessive.
	women's mice's children's geese's
	Use an apostrophe in contractions in place of dropped letters. Do not use contractions in formal writing.
	isn't *(is not)* can't *(cannot)* won't *(will not)* wasn't *(was not)* we're *(we are)* it's *(it is)* I'm *(I am)* they've *(they have)* they'll *(they will)* could've *(could have)* would've *(would have)* should've *(should have)*
Colon	Use a colon after the greeting in a business letter.
	Dear Mrs. Trimby: Dear Realty Homes:
Comma	A comma tells your reader where to pause. For words in a series, put a comma after each item except the last. Do not use a comma if only two items are listed.
	Clyde asked if we had any apples, peaches, or grapes.
	Use commas to separate two or more adjectives that are listed together unless one adjective tells how many.
	The fresh, ripe fruit was placed in a bowl. One red apple was especially shiny.

Punctuation continued

Comma (continued)	
	Use a comma before the conjunction in a compound sentence.
	Some students were at lunch, but others were studying.
	Use commas after introductory words such as *yes, no, oh*, and *well* when they begin a sentence.
	Well, it's just too cold out. No, it isn't six yet.
	Use a comma to separate a noun in direct address.
	Jean, help me fix this tire. How was your trip, Grandpa? Can you see, Joe, where I left my glasses?
	Use a comma between the names of a city and a state and between a city and a country.
	Chicago, Illinois Sydney, Australia
	Use a comma after the greeting in a friendly letter.
	Dear Deena, Dear Uncle Rudolph,
	Use a comma after the closing in a letter.
	Your nephew, Sincerely yours,

Problem Words

Words	Rules	Examples
a, an, the	These words are articles.	
a, an	Use *a* and *an* before singular nouns. Use *a* before a word that begins with a consonant sound. Use *an* before a word that begins with a vowel sound.	a banana an apple
the	Use *the* with both singular and plural nouns. Use *the* to point out particular persons, places, or things.	the apple the apples The books that I like are long.
can	*Can* means "to be able to do something."	Nellie can read quickly.
may	*May* means "to be allowed or permitted."	May I borrow your book?
good	*Good* is an adjective.	The weather looks good.

more ▶

Guide to Capitalization, Punctuation, and Usage   **H61**

Guide to Capitalization, Punctuation, and Usage continued

Problem Words continued

Words	Rules	Examples
well	*Well* is usually an adverb. It is an adjective only when it refers to health.	She swims well. Do you feel well?
its	*Its* is a possessive pronoun.	The dog wagged its tail.
it's	*It's* is a contraction of *it is*.	It's cold today.
let	*Let* means "to permit or allow."	Please let me go swimming.
leave	*Leave* means "to go away from" or "to let remain in a place."	I will leave soon. Leave it on my desk.
raise	*Raise* means "to move something up," "grow something," or "increase something."	Our principal raises the flag. Julio and Myra raise rabbits. The bus line raised its prices.
rise	*Rise* means "to get up or go up."	This ski lift rises quickly.
sit	*Sit* means "to rest in one place."	Please sit in this chair.
set	*Set* means "to place or put."	Set the vase on the table.
teach	*Teach* means "to give instruction."	He teaches us how to dance.
learn	*Learn* means "to receive instruction."	I learned about history.
their	*Their* is a possessive pronoun.	Their coats are on the bed.
there	*There* is an adverb. It may also begin a sentence.	Is Carlos there? There is my book.
they're	*They're* is a contraction of *they are*.	They're going to the store.
two	*Two* is a number.	I bought two shirts.
to	*To* means "in the direction of."	A squirrel ran to the tree.
too	*Too* means "more than enough" and "also."	I ate too many cherries. Can we go too?
who	Use the pronoun *who* as a subject.	Who can solve the math problem?
whom	Use the pronoun *whom* as a direct object.	Whom did she ask for an autograph?
your	*Your* is a possessive pronoun.	Are these your glasses?
you're	*You're* is a contraction for *you are*.	You're late again!

Tools and Tips: Guide to Capitalization, Punctuation, and Usage

Adjective and Adverb Usage

Adjective or adverb?	Adjectives describe nouns or pronouns. Adverbs describe verbs.
	Lena is a **quick** runner. *(adjective)* Lena runs **quickly**. *(adverb)*
Comparing	To compare two things or actions, add *-er* to adjectives and adverbs or use the word *more*.
	This plant is **taller** than the other one. It grew **more** quickly.
	To compare three or more things or actions, add *-est* or use the word *most*.
	This plant is the **tallest** of the three. It grew **most** quickly.
	Use *more* or *most* with an adjective or adverb that has two or more syllables, such as *careful* or *politely*. Do not add *-er* or *-est* to long adjectives or adverbs.
	agreeable–more agreeable–most agreeable slowly–more slowly–most slowly
good, bad	The adjectives *good* and *bad* have special forms for making comparisons.
	good–better–best bad–worse–worst

Negatives

	Do not use double negatives in a sentence.
	INCORRECT: We didn't go nowhere.
	CORRECT: We didn't go anywhere.

Pronoun Usage

Agreement	A pronoun must agree with the noun to which it refers.
	Kee bought a **newspaper**. Mary read it. **Jeff and Cindy** came to dinner. **They** enjoyed the meal.
Double subjects	Do not use a double subject—a noun and a pronoun—to name the same person, place, or thing.
	INCORRECT: The food it was delicious.
	CORRECT: The food was delicious.

more ▶

Guide to Capitalization, Punctuation, and Usage continued

Pronoun Usage continued

I, me	Use *I* as the subject of a sentence and after forms of *be*. Use *me* after action verbs or prepositions such as *to*, *in*, and *for*. (See subject and object pronouns below.)
	Jan and **I** are going to the show. She is taking **me**. Will you hold my ticket for **me**?
	When using *I* or *me* with nouns or other pronouns, always name yourself last.
	Beth and **I** will leave. Give the papers to Ron and **me**.
Possessive pronouns	A possessive pronoun shows ownership. Use *my*, *your*, *his*, *her*, *its*, *our*, and *their* before nouns.
	My report was about our trip to the zoo.
	Use *mine*, *yours*, *his*, *hers*, *its*, *ours*, and *theirs* to replace nouns in a sentence.
	Hers was about a visit to the museum.
Subject and object pronouns	Use subject pronouns as subjects and after forms of the verb *be*.
	He composed many works for the piano. I am **she**. The most talented singers are **we**.
	Use object pronouns after action verbs and prepositions like *to* and *for*.
	Clyde collected old coins and sold **them**. (direct object) Let's share these bananas with **her**. (object of preposition)
	Use the pronoun *who* as a subject. Use the pronoun *whom* as an object.
	Who traveled around the world? **Whom** did they see? To **whom** did they speak?
Demonstrative pronouns	A pronoun that points out something is called a demonstrative pronoun. It must agree in number with the noun it points out or with its antecedent. Use *this* and *these* to point to things nearby. Use *that* and *those* to point to things farther away.
	This is a jellyfish. **These** are sand dollars. **That** is a shark. **Those** are striped bass.

Pronoun Usage *continued*

Compound subjects and compound objects	To decide which pronoun to use in a compound subject or a compound object, leave out the other part of the compound. Say the sentence with the pronoun alone. Lu and _____ ride the bus. *(we, us)* **We** ride the bus. Lu and **we** ride the bus. I saw Dad and _____. *(he, him)* I saw **him**. I saw Dad and **him**.
We and us with nouns	Use *we* with a noun that is a subject or a noun that follows a linking verb. INCORRECT: Us girls are the stagehands. CORRECT: **We** girls are the stagehands. INCORRECT: The ushers are us boys. CORRECT: The ushers are **we** boys. Use *us* with a noun that follows an action verb or that follows a preposition such as *to, for, with,* or *at*. INCORRECT: Dr. Lin helped we players. CORRECT: Dr. Lin helped **us** players. INCORRECT: She talked to we beginners. CORRECT: She talked to **us** beginners.

Verb Usage

Agreement: subject-verb	A present tense verb and its subject must agree in number. Add *-s* or *-es* to a verb if the subject is singular. Do not add *-s* or *-es* to a verb if the subject is plural or if the subject is *I*. The road bend**s** to the right. Mr. Langelier teach**es** fifth graders. These books **seem** heavy. I **like** camping. Change the forms of *be* and *have* to make them agree with their subjects. He **is** taking the bus today. **Have** you seen Jimmy? They **are** going swimming. Mary **has** a large garden.
Agreement: compound subjects	A compound subject with *and* takes a plural verb. **Jason**, **Kelly**, and **Wanda** have new dictionaries.

more ▶

Guide to Capitalization, Punctuation, and Usage *continued*

Verb Usage *continued*

could have, should have	Use *could have, would have, should have, might have, must have*. Avoid using *of* with *could, would, should, might,* or *must*.
	She **could have** (*not* could of) spoken louder. Juan **would have** (*not* would of) liked this movie. We **should have** (*not* should of) turned left. I **might have** (*not* might of) left my wallet on my desk. It **must have** (*not* must of) rained last night.
Irregular verbs	Irregular verbs do not add *-ed* or *-d* to form the past tense. Because irregular verbs do not follow a regular pattern, you must memorize their spellings. Use *has, have,* or *had* as a helping verb with the past tense.

Verb	Past	Past with helping verb
be	was	been
begin	began	begun
blow	blew	blown
bring	brought	brought
choose	chose	chosen
come	came	come
fly	flew	flown
freeze	froze	frozen
go	went	gone
have	had	had
know	knew	known
make	made	made
ring	rang	rung
run	ran	run
say	said	said
sing	sang	sung
speak	spoke	spoken
steal	stole	stolen
swim	swam	swum
take	took	taken
tear	tore	torn
think	thought	thought
wear	wore	worn
write	wrote	written

Spelling Guide

Words Often Misspelled

You probably use many of the words on this list when you write. If you cannot think of the spelling of a word, you can always use this list. The words are in alphabetical order.

A
again
all right
a lot
also
always
another
anyone
anything
anyway
around

B
beautiful
because
before
believe
brought
buy

C
cannot
can't
caught
clothes
coming
could
cousin

D
didn't
different
don't

E
enough
every
everybody
everyone
everything

F
family
field
finally
friend

G
getting
girl
goes
going
guess

H
happened
happily
haven't
heard
here

I
I'd
I'll
I'm
instead
into
its
it's

K
knew
know

L
letter

M
might
millimeter
morning
mother's
myself

O
o'clock
off
once
other

P
people
pretty
probably

R
really
right

S
Saturday
school
someone
sometimes
stopped
suppose
sure
swimming

T
than
that's
their
then
there
there's
they
they're
thought
through
to

tonight
too
tried
two

U
until
usually

W
weird
we're
where
whole
would
wouldn't
write
writing

Y
your
you're

Words Often Misspelled

Spelling Guidelines

1. A short vowel sound before a consonant is usually spelled with just one letter: **a, e, i, o,** or **u**.

staff	grasp	slept	dwell	mist
split	fond	crush	bulb	

2. The |ā| sound is often spelled **ai, ay,** or **a-consonant-e**. The |ē| sound is often spelled **ee** or **ea**.

claim	sway	stake	fleet	greet	lease
brain	stray	male	speech	seal	beast

3. The |ī| sound is often spelled **i, igh,** or **i-consonant-e**. The |ō| sound is often spelled **o, o-consonant-e, oa,** or **ow**.

mild	thigh	strike	stole	loaf	sow
slight	stride	stroll	hose	boast	flow

4. The |o͞o| or the |yo͞o| sound is often spelled **ue, ew,** or **u-consonant-e**. The |o͞o| sound may also be spelled **oo** or **ui**. The |o͝o| sound is often spelled **oo** or **u**.

hue	brew	flute	boom	wood	put
clue	fume	troop	cruise	brook	bush
dew	duke	mood	bruise	poor	pull

5. The |ou| sound is often spelled **ou** or **ow**. The |ô| sound is often spelled **aw, au,** or **a** before **l**. The |oi| sound is spelled **oi** or **oy**.

ounce	coward	claw	fawn	fault	bald	joint	loyal
sour	scowl	hawk	haunt	stalk	moist	royal	

6. The |ûr| sounds are often spelled **ir, ur, er, ear,** or **or**. The |îr| sounds are often spelled **eer** or **ear**.

squirm	blur	stern	pearl	worm	smear
chirp	hurl	germ	earl	steer	rear

7. The |ôr| sounds are often spelled **or, ore,** or **oar**. The |âr| sounds are often spelled **are** or **air**. The |är| sound is usually spelled **ar**.

lord	tore	bore	hare	snare	flair	scar	barge
torch	sore	soar	fare	lair	harsh	carve	

8. Homophones sound alike but have different spellings and meanings.

loan lone	flea flee	berry bury

9. The final |ər| sounds in two-syllable words are often spelled **ar, or,** or **er.**

lun**ar**	burgl**ar**	maj**or**	clov**er**	thund**er**
pill**ar**	hum**or**	tract**or**	bann**er**	

10. The final |l| or |əl| sounds in two-syllable words are often spelled **le, el,** or **al**.

sing**le**	whist**le**	bush**el**	norm**al**	loc**al**
ang**le**	jew**el**	ang**el**	leg**al**	

11. Compound words may be spelled as one word, as a hyphenated word, or as separate words.

railroad	afternoon	ninety-nine	seat belt
watermelon	classmate	baby-sit	post office

12. A word with the VCCV syllable pattern is divided between the consonants.

at	tend	of	fer	traf	fic	tun	nel
sur	vive	es	cape	em	pire	wit	ness

13. If the consonants in a VCCV word are different and form a cluster or spell one word, divide the word before or after the two consonants.

a	fraid	de	gree	se	cret	ma	chine
rock	et	chick	en	oth	er	pack	age

14. If the first vowel sound in a VCV word is long, divide the word into syllables before the consonant.

pi	lot	fe	ver	sto	len	ba	sic
be	have	na	tion	de	tail	pre	fer

15. If the first vowel sound in a VCV word is short, divide the word into syllables after the consonant.

cab	in	hab	it	tal	ent	mod	ern
van	ish	rap	id	rec	ord	shad	ow

more ▶

Spelling Guidelines continued

16. When two different consonants in a VCCCV word spell one sound or form a cluster, divide the word into syllables before or after those two consonants.

| dis \| trict | al \| though | com \| plain | or \| phan |
| mon \| ster | or \| chard | dol \| phin | com \| plex |

17. When two vowels in a VV pattern spell two vowel sounds, divide the word into syllables between the vowels.

| po \| em | gi \| ant | li \| on | sci \| ence |
| cru \| el | di \| al | cre \| ate | qui \| et |

18. The **-ed** or **-ing** ending may simply be added to some words. A final **e** is usually dropped before adding **-ed** or **-ing**.

| arrest**ed** | attend**ing** | seek**ing** | borrow**ed** | ris**ing** | freez**ing** |
| offer**ed** | direct**ing** | await**ing** | squeez**ing** | amus**ing** | provid**ing** |

19. In one-syllable words ending with a single vowel and consonant, the consonant is usually doubled when **-ed** or **-ing** is added. In two-syllable words ending with an unstressed syllable, the final consonant is usually not doubled.

wi**nn**ing	bra**gg**ing	shi**pp**ed	stu**nn**ed	suffering	covered
hi**tt**ing	wra**pp**ed	whi**pp**ed	cho**pp**ed	gathering	wandered
swi**mm**ing	dro**pp**ed	be**gg**ed	spo**tt**ed	visiting	ordered

20. A suffix is a word part added to the end of a base word.

| dread**ful** | breath**less** | count**less** | active**ly** | settle**ment** | soft**ness** |

21. The final |ē| sound in a two-syllable word is often spelled **y** or **ey**.

| read**y** | sorr**y** | beaut**y** | monk**ey** | hock**ey** |
| lonel**y** | hobb**y** | turk**ey** | vall**ey** | |

22. Final |ĭj| sounds are often spelled **age**. Final |tĭv| sounds are often spelled **tive**. Final |tĭs| sounds are often spelled **tice**.

bagg**age**	post**age**	langu**age**	crea**tive**	prac**tice**
lugg**age**	voy**age**	cap**tive**	defec**tive**	jus**tice**
sav**age**	yard**age**	na**tive**	detec**tive**	no**tice**

23. The |k| sound in a one-syllable word is often spelled **k** or **ck**. In a two-syllable word, it is often spelled **k, ck,** or **c**. The |ng| sound before **k** is spelled **n**.

shar**k**	trac**k**	ja**c**ket	musi**c**	ju**nk**	bla**nk**
ris**k**	la**ck**	atta**ck**	a**c**tive	dri**nk**	si**nk**
stru**ck**	mista**k**e	publi**c**	topi**c**	ra**nk**	bla**nk**et

24. The final |j| sound is usually spelled **dge** or **ge**. The final |s| sound is often spelled **ce**.

lo**dge**	bri**dge**	do**dge**	chan**ge**	chan**ce**	glan**ce**	fen**ce**
e**dge**	ri**dge**	stran**ge**	ca**ge**	twi**ce**	sin**ce**	

25. Final |n| or |ən| sounds may be spelled **ain**. Final |chər| sounds may be spelled **ture**. Final |zhər| sounds may be spelled **sure**.

capt**ain**	mount**ain**	fix**ture**	expo**sure**
fount**ain**	crea**ture**	lec**ture**	trea**sure**
curt**ain**	adven**ture**	mea**sure**	plea**sure**

26. Prefixes are added to beginnings of words or word roots. Suffixes are added to ends of words.

decide	**un**known	**ex**cuse	pain**ful**	care**less**
improve	**com**fort	**pre**fix	move**ment**	

27. The suffix **-ion** changes verbs to nouns. Sometimes the spelling changes.

correct	reduce	explode
correc**tion**	reduc**tion**	explo**sion**

28. If a word ends with a consonant + **y**, change the **y** to **i** when adding **-es, -ed, -er,** or **-est**.

hobb**ies**	sp**ied**	nois**ier**	tin**iest**	lonel**iest**
abilit**ies**	cop**ied**	earl**ier**	happ**iest**	

29. The suffixes **-able, -ible, -ant,** and **-ent** are added to words or word roots.

suit**able**	valu**able**	horr**ible**	vac**ant**	differ**ent**
comfort**able**	poss**ible**	serv**ant**	stud**ent**	

30. Some words have unexpected spellings.

| acre | special | lamb | says | guide | knight |

Spelling Guidelines   H71

Diagramming Guide

A diagram of a sentence is a set of lines that show how the words of that sentence are related. You will begin by diagramming the most important words in the sentence. In beginning lessons, sentences contain words that you do not yet know how to diagram. Work only with the words that you are asked to diagram. You will learn about the others as you work through the lessons.

Simple Subjects and Simple Predicates

The simple subject and the simple predicate are written on a horizontal line called the **base line**. The simple subject is separated from the simple predicate by a vertical line that cuts through the horizontal line.

Find the simple subject and the simple predicate in the sentence below.

Wheat has lost its Number 1 place.

Study this diagram of the simple subject and the simple predicate from the sentence above.

```
  Wheat  |  has lost
```

Find the simple subject and the simple predicate in this sentence. Note that the subject, *you*, is understood.

Guess the largest crop.

Study the diagram of this sentence.

```
  (you)  |  Guess
```

Practice

Diagram only the simple subjects and the simple predicates in these sentences.

1. Rice has gained first place.
2. It must have a hot, wet climate.
3. Name some rice exporters.
4. The biggest growers are in the Rice Bowl.
5. This area stretches from Japan to Indonesia.

Compound Subjects

Each part of a compound subject is written on a separate horizontal line. The word *and* is written on a vertical dotted line that joins the horizontal lines.

Find the compound subject in this sentence.

India and China grow the most rice.

Study this diagram of the compound subject.

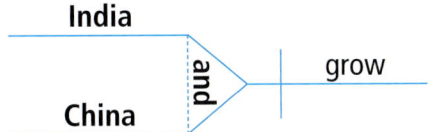

A compound subject can have more than two parts. Find the compound subject in this sentence.

Japan, Burma, and South Korea export more.

Study the diagram of this sentence. Note that the conjunction *and* is placed on the dotted line that connects the parts of the compound subject.

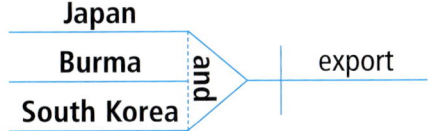

The word *or* can also join the parts of a compound subject.

Does Brazil or the United States grow more rice?

Although the sentence above is a question, it is diagrammed just like a statement. Study the diagram.

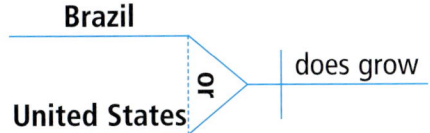

Practice

Diagram the subjects and the predicate in each of these sentences.

1. Rice and corn supplied Native Americans.
2. Quebec, the Midwest, and Louisiana had wild rice.
3. Europe and colonial America liked white rice better.
4. Is rice, potatoes, noodles, or tortillas your favorite food?

more ▶

Diagramming Guide continued

Compound Predicates

Each part of a compound predicate is written on a separate horizontal line. The words *and, or,* and *but* are written on a vertical dotted line that joins the horizontal lines.

Find the compound predicate in this sentence.

We dressed and raced outside.

Study this diagram of the compound predicate.

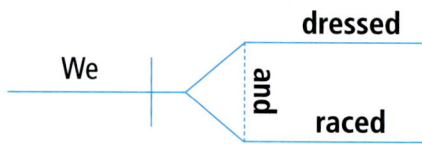

A sentence may have both a compound subject and a compound predicate.

My twin and I stumbled, slipped, and skidded along.

Study this diagram. Note where each *and* is placed.

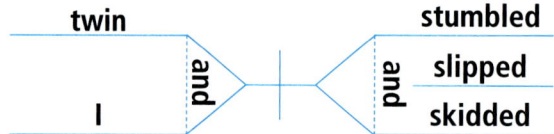

Practice

Diagram only the subjects and the predicates in each sentence. Either or both may be compound.

1. Our yard sparkled and shone after the winter storm.
2. Each branch and twig had grown and had changed.
3. Pine needles looked and felt like diamond spikes.
4. Trees groaned and complained to the wind.
5. The heavy ice bent, broke, or cracked many branches.

Direct Objects

A direct object is diagrammed on the base line after the verb. A vertical line is placed between the verb and the direct object. Notice that it does not cut through the base line.

Find the direct object in this sentence.

Paul needed some new clothes.

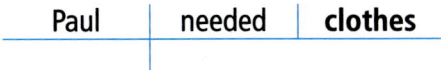

A verb can have more than one direct object. Find the compound direct object in this sentence.

Yesterday he bought boots and a jacket.
Study this diagram of the compound direct object.

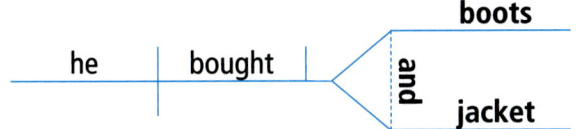

Each verb in a compound predicate can have its own direct object. Read this sentence. Find each verb and its direct object.

He liked the boots but disliked the jacket.
Study the diagram of the compound predicate and its separate direct objects.

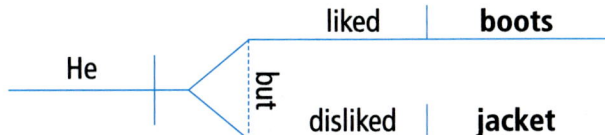

Practice

Diagram only the subjects, the verbs, and the direct objects in these sentences.

1. First, Paul found boots.
2. Then he saw a red wool jacket.
3. It had a hood and yarn cuffs.
4. Paul paid half and charged the rest.
5. Later he changed his mind and returned the jacket.

more ▶

Diagramming Guide *continued*

Linking Verbs

A linking verb is diagrammed differently from an action verb. A slanting line, not a vertical one, follows a linking verb.

Remember, a linking verb joins the subject of a sentence with a word in the predicate. The word after the slanting line may name the subject or describe what it is like.

Find the linking verb in this sentence.

A cold feels horrible.

Now study this diagram. Notice that the slanting line points back toward the subject but does not cut through the base line.

cold | **feels** \ horrible

More than one word can follow a linking verb to describe the subject. Find the two words that describe the subject of this sentence.

Sally is miserable and cranky.

Study how these compound parts are diagrammed.

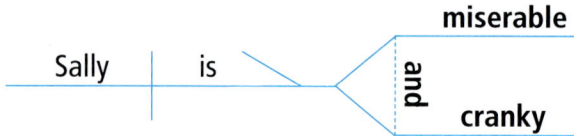

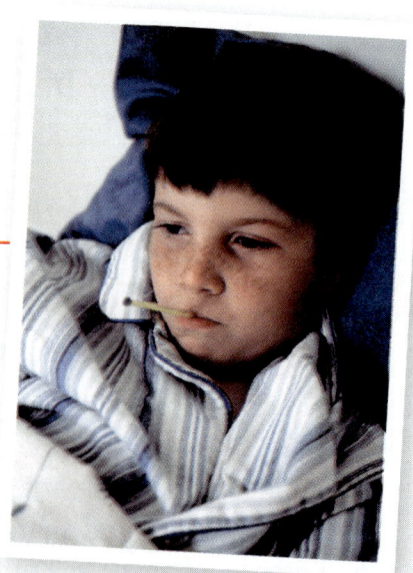

Practice

Diagram each linking verb and the two parts of the sentence that it joins.

1. Meals are not fun for a cold sufferer.
2. Food was tasteless yesterday.
3. Today my nose is red.
4. I am feverish and dizzy.
5. This head cold is a real pain.

Adjectives

Adjectives are diagrammed on a slanting line right below the word that they describe.

Find the adjectives in this sentence.

I have brown, curly hair.

Study this diagram of the sentence.

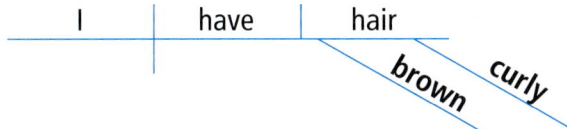

The words *a, an,* and *the* are diagrammed like adjectives.

My older sister has a long ponytail.

Study this diagram of the sentence.

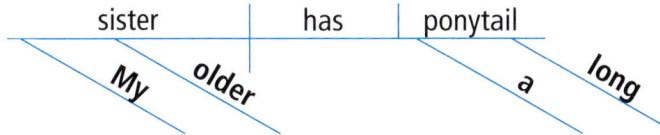

More than one adjective can describe the same word. Sometimes the word *and, or,* or *but* joins adjectives.

A long, braided, or straight hairstyle is not for me!

Note the position of the word *or* in this diagram.

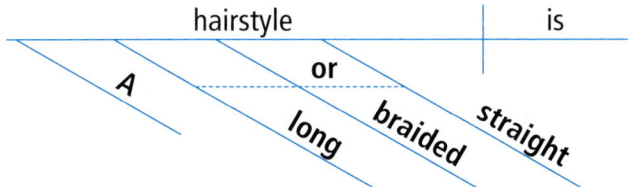

Practice

Diagram all the words in these sentences.

1. This magazine has funny costumes.
2. See the blue, pink, and green wig!
3. That outfit wins the ugly prize.
4. I like that red satin cape.
5. You have unusual taste.

more ▶

Diagramming Guide continued

Adverbs

Adverbs are diagrammed in the same way that adjectives are. An adverb is placed on a slanting line below the word that it describes. Find the adverb and the verb that it describes in the following sentence.

We patiently watched the tadpoles.

Study this diagram of the sentence.

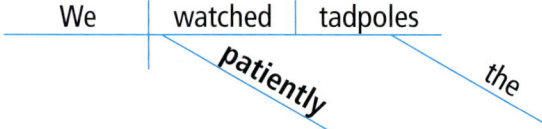

An adverb can appear anywhere in a sentence. It is not always right next to the word that it describes. Find the adverb in this sentence.

Soon the tadpoles became frogs.

Study this diagram of the sentence.

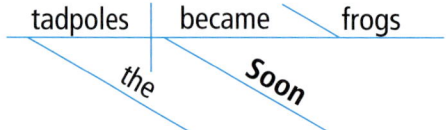

Several adverbs can describe the same word. In this sentence, find the adverbs and the words that they describe.

Then they changed swiftly and completely.

Notice the position of the word *and* in this diagram.

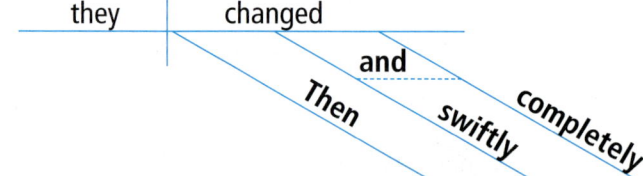

Practice

Diagram all of the words in these sentences.

1. Recently a box arrived.
2. We put a heater nearby.
3. It had twelve eggs inside.
4. Monday we heard one faint peep.
5. Now all the chicks peep constantly and happily.

Prepositional Phrases

A prepositional phrase is diagrammed below the word that it describes. Prepositional phrases that tell where, when, or how often describe verbs. On the other hand, a prepositional phrase that tells what kind, how many, or which one describes a noun.

Find the prepositional phrase in this sentence. What word does it describe?
I like stories about twins.

Study this diagram of the sentence. Notice that the preposition is written on a slanting line below the word that it describes.

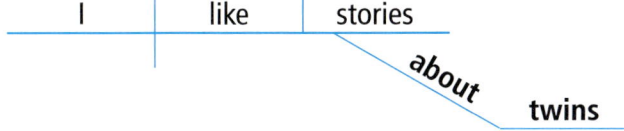

Find the prepositional phrase in this sentence. What word does it describe?
We have two sets in our family.

Study the diagram of this prepositional phrase.

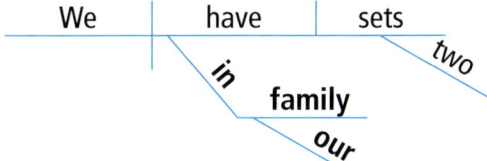

Practice

Diagram all of the words in the following sentences.

1. Jamie lives near me.
2. He plays with some twins.
3. Once we wrote invitations for his party.
4. Jamie drew a funny picture on one invitation.
5. The two girls laughed about it.

more ▶

Diagramming Guide continued

Nouns in Direct Address

Diagram a noun in direct address on a short line above and just to the left of the base line.

Find the noun in direct address in this sentence.

Students, today we are having a quiz.

Study this diagram of the sentence.

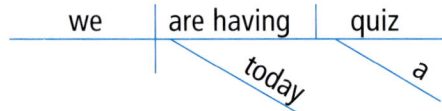

A noun in direct address is diagrammed in the same way no matter where the word appears in the sentence. Find the noun in direct address in this sentence.

Share that book with Aaron, Suzie.

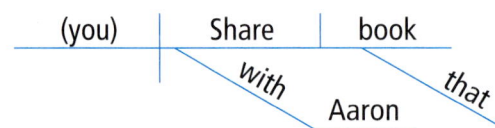

Practice

Diagram all of the words in these sentences.

1. Mr. Savchick, I have a problem.
2. My only pencil, sir, just broke.
3. You may use this pen, Liz.
4. Listen carefully, class.
5. Everyone, I will read each question twice.

Thesaurus Plus

How to Use This Thesaurus

Why do you use a thesaurus? One reason is to make your writing more exact. Suppose you wrote the following sentence:

The thin ballerina twirled gracefully.

Is *thin* the most exact word you can use? To find out, use your Thesaurus Plus.

Look up Your Word Turn to the Thesaurus Plus Index on page H88. You will find

thin, *adj.*

Entry words are printed in blue type. Because *thin* is blue, you can look up *thin* in the Thesaurus Plus.

Use Your Thesaurus The main entries in the Thesaurus Plus are listed in alphabetical order. Turn to *thin*. You will find

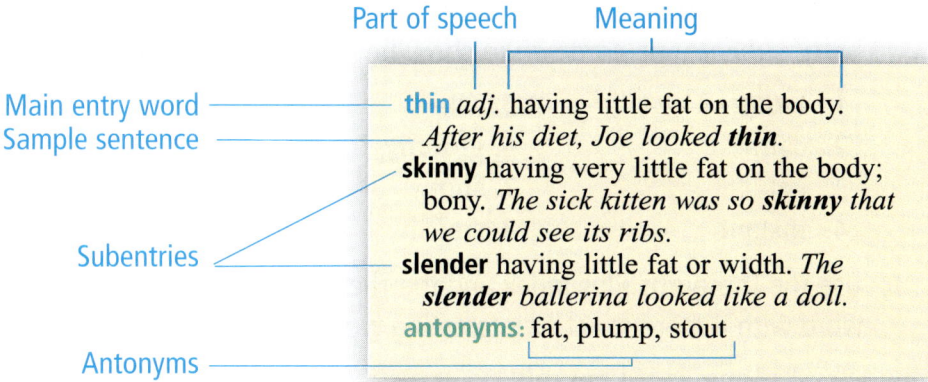

Which word might better describe the ballerina in the sentence at the top of the page? Perhaps you chose *slender*.

more ▶

How to Use This Thesaurus **H81**

How to Use This Thesaurus continued

Other Index Entries There are two other types of entries in your Thesaurus Plus Index.

① The slanted type means you can find other words for *splendid* if you look under *nice*.

splendid **nice**, *adj.*
spotless **clean**, *adj.*
spring **jump**, *v.*
sputter **say**, *v.*
spy **look**, *v.*

② The regular type tells you that *start* is the opposite of *finish*.

start **finish**, *v.*

Practice

A. Write each word. Look it up in the Thesaurus Plus Index. Then write *main entry*, *subentry*, or *antonym* to show how it is listed.

1. required
2. calm
3. get
4. instant
5. ask
6. gloomy
7. shout
8. smash

B. Use the Thesaurus Plus Index and the Thesaurus Plus. Replace each underlined word with a more exact or interesting word. Write the new sentence.

9. As long as it kept raining, we stayed inside.
10. It was really too cold to go out anyway.
11. Later we looked at a great rainbow.
12. We were nervous about the weather.
13. We had to start planning our museum trip.
14. Clara was worried that there was little time.
15. Jim thought she was being comical.
16. Jim's thoughts angered Clara.
17. Mrs. Lee helped us to create a plan.
18. We decided to stick to her plan.
19. We were grateful for Mrs. Lee's help.
20. Everyone was now happy.

H82 Tools and Tips: Thesaurus Plus

Thesaurus Plus Index

A

abandon leave, *v.*
able good, *adj.*
abnormal common, *adj.*
absurd funny, *adj.*
accept argue, *v.*
accomplish do, *v.*
achieve do, *v.*
achieve succeed, *v.*
acquire get, *v.*
act do, *v.*
active, *adj.*
actual real, *adj.*
additional further, *adj.*
admirable good, *adj.*
admirable nice, *adj.*
after before, *adv.*
agree, *v.*
agree argue, *v.*
agreeable nice, *adj.*
alarming scary, *adj.*
allow let, *v.*
also, *adv.*
alternative choice, *n.*
amaze surprise, *v.*
amiable nice, *adj.*
amusing funny, *adj.*
ancient new, *adj.*
angry, *adj.*
annoyed angry, *adj.*
answer ask, *v.*
antique new, *adj.*
anxious nervous, *adj*
appealing nice, *adj.*
appealing pretty, *adj.*
appetizing good, *adj.*
appreciative grateful, *adj.*
approve agree, *v.*
approve argue, *v.*
argue, *v.*
arid wet, *adj.*
arrive leave, *v.*
artificial real, *adj.*

as long as while, *conj.*
ask, *v.*
assemble gather, *v.*
assert think, *v.*
astonish surprise, *v.*
astound surprise, *v.*
at the end last, *adv.*
attain do, *v.*
attractive pretty, *adj.*
audacious bold, *adj.*
avoid look, *v.*
awful good, *adj.*

B

bad good, *adj.*
bark say, *v.*
be worthy of deserve, *v.*
beautiful pretty, *adj.*
before, *adv.*
begin finish, *v.*
begin start, *v.*
believe think, *v.*
bellow say, *v.*
besides also, *adv.*
big, *adj.*
blubber laugh, *v.*
boast, *v.*
bold, *adj.*
bored eager, *adj.*
boring, *adj.*
brag boast, *v.*
brave, *adj.*
break, *v.*
bright dark, *adj.*
bright shiny, *adj.*
brilliant pretty, *adj.*
build make, *v.*
bulky big, *adj.*
bumpy rough, *adj.*
bury hide, *v.*
buy get, *v.*

C

cackle laugh, *v.*
calm, *adj.*
calm angry, *adj.*
calm nervous, *adj.*
calm upset, *adj.*
capable good, *adj.*
careful, *adj.*
caring good, *adj.*
carry bring, *v.*
cause effect, *n.*
cautious bold, *adj.*
cautious careful, *adj.*
change, *v.*
changeable faithful, *adj.*
charge price, *n.*
charitable good, *adj.*
charming nice, *adj.*
charming pretty, *adj.*
cheerful happy, *adj.*
chief, *adj.*
chilly cold, *adj.*
chipper lively, *adj.*
choice, *n.*
chortle laugh, *v.*
chuckle laugh, *v.*
clash argue, *v.*
clean, *adj.*
clear, *adj.*
close finish, *v.*
close start, *v.*
cloudy clear, *adj.*
cloudy unclear, *adj.*
coarse rough, *adj.*
cold, *adj.*
cold-hearted nice, *adj.*
collect gather, *v.*
colossal big, *adj.*
come leave, *v.*
comfortable upset, *adj.*
comical funny, *adj.*
commence finish, *v.*
commence start, *v.*

more

Thesaurus Plus Index continued

common, *adj.*
companionable nice, *adj.*
complete do, *v.*
complete finish, *v.*
complex easy, *adj.*
comply with agree, *v.*
composed upset, *adj.*
conceal hide, *v.*
conceive think, *v.*
conclude finish, *v.*
confuse do, *v.*
confusing unclear, *adj.*
connect join, *v.*
conscientious careful, *adj.*
consent agree, *v.*
consent argue, *v.*
consequence effect, *n.*
consider think, *v.*
considerate good, *adj.*
considerate nice, *adj.*
construct make, *v.*
contemplate look, *v.*
contemptible nice, *adj.*
continue change, *v.*
convert change, *v.*
convince persuade, *v.*
cool cold, *adj.*
cost price, *n.*
courageous brave, *adj.*
courteous good, *adj.*
courteous nice, *adj.*
cowardly brave, *adj.*
crack break, *v.*
crass nice, *adj.*
crave wish, *v.*
create, *v.*
cross angry, *adj.*
crow boast, *v.*
cruel good, *adj.*
cry laugh, *v.*
cry say, *v.*
cry shout, *v.*
cute pretty, *adj.*

D

damp wet, *adj.*
danger, *n.*
dank wet, *adj.*
daring bold, *adj.*
dark, *adj.*
dark shiny, *adj.*
dash run, *v.*
dazzling pretty, *adj.*
deceitful honest, *adj.*
decent good, *adj.*
decide, *v.*
decode do, *v.*
dehydrated wet, *adj.*
delicious good, *adj.*
delighted angry, *adj.*
delightful nice, *adj.*
delightful perfect, *adj.*
deny agree, *v.*
depressing funny, *adj.*
deserve, *v.*
design create, *v.*
desire wish, *v.*
destroy create, *v.*
destroy make, *v.*
deter persuade, *v.*
determine decide, *v.*
dewy wet, *adj.*
different same, *adj.*
difficult easy, *adj.*
dim dark, *adj.*
dim shiny, *adj.*
direct honest, *adj.*
dirty clean, *adj.*
disagree argue, *v.*
disagreeable good, *adj.*
diseased healthy, *adj.*
disgusting good, *adj.*
disgusting pretty, *adj.*
dismantle make, *v.*
dismiss look, *v.*
displeased angry, *adj.*
displeasing nice, *adj.*
dissuade persuade, *v.*
distinct unclear, *adj.*
disturbed upset, *adj.*

do, *v.*
drag pull, *v.*
dream think, *v.*
drenched wet, *adj.*
dripping wet, *adj.*
droll funny, *adj.*
dry boring, *adj.*
dry wet, *adj.*
dull boring, *adj.*
dull shiny, *adj.*

E

eager, *adj.*
earlier before, *adv.*
earn get, *v.*
easy, *adj.*
edgy nervous, *adj.*
effect, *n.*
effect source, *n.*
effortless easy, *adj.*
emerald green, *adj.*
employment job, *n.*
enchanting nice, *adj.*
end finish, *v.*
end source, *n.*
end start, *v.*
endanger protect, *v.*
energetic active, *adj.*
energetic lively, *adj.*
enormous big, *adj.*
enormous little, *adj.*
enraged angry, *adj.*
equal same, *adj.*
essential necessary, *adj.*
establish create, *v.*
evaluate think, *v.*
evil good, *adj.*
excellent good, *adj.*
excellent nice, *adj.*
excellent perfect, *adj.*
excited calm, *adj.*
exciting boring, *adj.*
exclaim say, *v.*
execute do, *v.*
expense price, *n.*
experienced good, *adj.*

expert good, *adj.*
explore, *v.*
extraordinary common, *adj.*

F

fail do, *v.*
faint unclear, *adj.*
faithful, *adj.*
fake, *n.*
fake real, *adj.*
false faithful, *adj.*
familiar strange, *adj.*
fantastic great, *adj.*
fast quick, *adj.*
fat, *adj.*
fat thin, *adj.*
faulty perfect, *adj.*
fearless brave, *adj.*
feel think, *v.*
few many, *adj.*
few some, *adj.*
filthy clean, *adj.*
finally last, *adv.*
fine good, *adj.*
fine nice, *adj.*
finish, *v.*
finish do, *v.*
finish start, *v.*
first last, *adv.*
fit healthy, *adj.*
flavorful good, *adj.*
flawed nice, *adj.*
flawed perfect, *adj.*
flooded wet, *adj.*
foggy clear, *adj.*
forget think, *v.*
form make, *v.*
frank honest, *adj.*
frantic calm, *adj.*
fraud fake, *n.*
freezing cold, *adj.*
fresh new, *adj.*
friendly good, *adj.*
friendly nice, *adj.*
frightened brave, *adj.*

frightening scary, *adj.*
fulfill do, *v.*
fuming angry, *adj.*
funny, *adj.*
furious angry, *adj.*
further, *adj.*
fuzzy unclear, *adj.*

G

gape look, *v.*
gather, *v.*
gawk look, *v.*
gaze look, *v.*
general common, *adj.*
generous good, *adj.*
gentle nice, *adj.*
get, *v.*
giant big, *adj.*
gifted good, *adj.*
gigantic big, *adj.*
giggle laugh, *v.*
give, *v.*
glad happy, *adj.*
glamorous pretty, *adj.*
glance, *v.*
glance look, *v.*
glare look, *v.*
gleaming shiny, *adj.*
glimpse glance, *v.*
glimpse look, *v.*
glistening shiny, *adj.*
gloomy funny, *adj.*
glorious pretty, *adj.*
glower look, *v.*
good, *adj.*
gorgeous pretty, *adj.*
gracious nice, *adj.*
grateful, *adj.*
great, *adj.*
great big, *adj.*
green, *adj.*
gripe say, *v.*
groan say, *v.*
grow, *v.*
growl say, *v.*
grumble say, *v.*

grunt say, *v.*
guard protect, *v.*
guarded careful, *adj.*
guffaw laugh, *v.*

H

handsome pretty, *adj.*
handy useful, *adj.*
happy, *adj.*
hard easy, *adj.*
harmful good, *adj.*
hasty quick, *adj.*
haul pull, *v.*
hazard danger, *n.*
healthful good, *adj.*
healthy, *adj.*
heartless good, *adj.*
heedless careful, *adj.*
helpful useful, *adj.*
hide, *v.*
hilarious funny, *adj.*
hinder let, *v.*
hiss say, *v.*
hobby job, *n.*
holler say, *v.*
holler shout, *v.*
homely pretty, *adj.*
honest, *adj.*
honest good, *adj.*
honorable good, *adj.*
hot cold, *adj.*
howl laugh, *v.*
howl say, *v.*
huge big, *adj.*
humorous funny, *adj.*
hunter green green, *adj.*
hurdle jump, *v.*

I

icy cold, *adj.*
ideal perfect, *adj.*
identical same, *adj.*
ignore look, *v.*
ignore see, *v.*

Thesaurus Plus Index continued

ignore think, *v.*
ill healthy, *adj.*
imagine think, *v.*
immense big, *adj.*
impostor fake, *n.*
in addition also, *adv.*
inactive lively, *adj.*
incompetent capable, *adj.*
indifferent eager, *adj.*
inefficient useful, *adj.*
inferior good, *adj.*
inferior great, *adj.*
inquire ask, *v.*
insincere honest, *adj.*
instant moment, *n.*
insulting nice, *adj.*
interested eager, *adj.*
interesting boring, *adj.*
invent create, *v.*
investigate explore, *v.*
irate angry, *adj.*
irritated angry, *adj.*

job, *n.*
join, *v.*
judge think, *v.*
jumbo big, *adj.*
jump, *v.*

keen eager, *adj.*
kelly green green, *adj.*

large big, *adj.*
large little, *adj.*
last, *adv.*
later before, *adv.*
laugh, *v.*
laughable funny, *adj.*
law-abiding good, *adj.*
lax careful, *adj.*

lazy active, *adj.*
lazy lively, *adj.*
leap jump, *v.*
leave, *v.*
leisure job, *n.*
let, *v.*
light dark, *adj.*
lime green, *adj.*
little, *adj.*
little big, *adj.*
lively, *adj.*
lively active, *adj.*
lively boring, *adj.*
locate put, *v.*
look, *v.*
lose get, *v.*
lovely nice, *adj.*
lovely pretty, *adj.*
loving good, *adj.*
loyal faithful, *adj.*
ludicrous funny, *adj.*
luscious good, *adj.*

mad angry, *adj.*
main chief, *adj.*
make, *v.*
make do, *v.*
mammoth big, *adj.*
manufacture make, *v.*
many, *adj.*
march walk, *v.*
marvelous great, *adj.*
massive big, *adj.*
masterful good, *adj.*
mature grow, *v.*
mean good, *adj.*
mean nice, *adj.*
meaning, *n.*
mend break, *v.*
merit deserve, *v.*
meticulous careful, *adj.*
microscopic big, *adj.*

mighty big, *adj.*
mindful careful, *adj.*
miniature big, *adj.*
miniature little, *adj.*
minor chief, *adj.*
minor important, *adj.*
misleading honest, *adj.*
misty clear, *adj.*
moan say, *v.*
moist wet, *adj.*
moment, *n.*
monotonous boring, *adj.*
moral good, *adj.*
more further, *adj.*
mouth-watering good, *adj.*
mumble say, *v.*
murky dark, *adj.*
murmur say, *v.*
mutter say, *v.*

nasty good, *adj.*
necessary, *adj.*
nervous, *adj.*
nervous upset, *adj.*
new, *adj.*
nice, *adj.*
nonsense meaning, *n.*
nonsensical unreasonable, *adj.*
normal common, *adj.*
normal strange, *adj.*
notice see, *v.*
nourishing good, *adj.*
novel new, *adj.*
numerous many, *adj.*
nutritious good, *adj.*

O

obedient good, *adj.*
observe see, *v.*
obtain get, *v.*
obvious unclear, *adj.*
offensive nice, *adj.*

offensive pretty, *adj.*
offer give, *v.*
old new, *adj.*
olive green, *adj.*
omit do, *v.*
operate, *v.*
ordinary common, *adj.*
ordinary great, *adj.*
original new, *adj.*
outstanding good, *adj.*
overlook look, *v.*
overlook see, *v.*

parched wet, *adj.*
part join, *v.*
particular careful, *adj.*
patch break, *v.*
peaceful angry, *adj.*
peaceful calm, *adj.*
peek glance, *v.*
peek look, *v.*
peep look, *v.*
peeved angry, *adj.*
perfect, *adj.*
perform do, *v.*
peril danger, *n.*
permit let, *v.*
persuade, *v.*
phony fake, *n.*
place put, *v.*
placid nervous, *adj.*
play job, *n.*
pleasant nice, *adj.*
pleased upset, *adj.*
plump fat, *adj.*
plump thin, *adj.*
pointlessness
  meaning, *n.*
polished rough, *adj.*
polite good, *adj.*
poor good, *adj.*
praiseworthy good, *adj.*
preference choice, *n.*
present give, *v.*
pretty, *adj.*

prevent let, *v.*
previously before, *adv.*
price, *n.*
principal chief, *adj.*
probe explore, *v.*
produce create, *v.*
produce do, *v.*
produce grow, *v.*
proper nice, *adj.*
protect, *v.*
protection danger, *n.*
protective careful, *adj.*
prudent careful, *adj.*
pull, *v.*
push pull, *v.*
put, *v.*

quake shake, *v.*
qualified good, *adj.*
quarrel argue, *v.*
question ask, *v.*
quick, *adj.*
quit do, *v.*
quit leave, *v.*

race run, *v.*
radiant pretty, *adj.*
raging calm, *adj.*
raise grow, *v.*
rapid quick, *adj.*
rare common, *adj.*
ravishing pretty, *adj.*
real, *adj.*
receive give, *v.*
reflect think, *v.*
refreshing nice, *adj.*
refuse agree, *v.*
regular common, *adj.*
remain change, *v.*
remove put, *v.*
repair break, *v.*
repellent nice, *adj.*

reply ask, *v.*
repulsive pretty, *adj.*
required necessary, *adj.*
resolve decide, *v.*
resolve do, *v.*
result effect, *n.*
return leave, *v.*
reveal hide, *v.*
revolting pretty, *adj.*
ridiculous funny, *adj.*
risk danger, *n.*
roar laugh, *v.*
roar say, *v.*
rough, *adj.*
rude nice, *adj.*
run, *v.*
run walk, *v.*

S

sad funny, *adj.*
sad happy, *adj.*
safety danger, *n.*
same, *adj.*
satisfied upset, *adj.*
saturated wet, *adj.*
say, *v.*
scan look, *v.*
scary, *adj.*
scatter gather, *v.*
scowl look, *v.*
scream say, *v.*
screech say, *v.*
scrumptious good, *adj.*
second-rate good, *adj.*
security danger, *n.*
sedate calm, *adj.*
see, *v.*
selection choice, *n.*
sense meaning, *n*
separate gather, *v.*
separate join, *v.*
serene calm, *adj.*
serious funny, *adj.*
set put, *v.*
several many, *adj.*
several some, *adj.*

Thesaurus Plus Index continued

shake, v.
sharp unclear, adj.
shatter break, v.
shiny, adj.
shiver shake, v.
shout, v.
shout say, v.
shove pull, v.
show hide, v.
shriek laugh, v.
shudder shake, v.
shun look, v.
sick healthy, adj.
sidesplitting funny, adj.
sigh say, v.
significance meaning, n.
significant important, adj.
simple easy, adj.
sizable big, adj.
skilled good, adj.
skillful nice, adj.
skinny fat, adj.
skinny thin, adj.
slack careful, adj.
slender fat, adj.
slender thin, adj.
slim fat, adj.
slow quick, adj.
sluggish active, adj.
small big, adj.
small little, adj.
smash break, v.
smooth rough, adj.
snap say, v.
snarl say, v.
snicker laugh, v.
snigger laugh, v.
snoop look, v.
soaked wet, adj.
sob laugh, v.
sodden wet, adj.
soggy wet, adj.
soiled clean, adj.
solemn funny, adj.
solve do, v.
some, adj.

sopping wet, adj.
soppy wet, adj.
sorrowful happy, adj.
sound healthy, adj.
source effect, n.
speculate think, v.
speedy quick, adj.
spirited lively, adj.
splendid nice, adj.
spotless clean, adj.
spring jump, v.
sputter say, v.
spy look, v.
stammer say, v.
stand still walk, v.
stare look, v.
start, v.
start finish, v.
stop finish, v.
stop let, v.
stop start, v.
stout fat, adj.
stout thin, adj.
strange, adj.
strange common, adj.
strict careful, adj.
stride walk, v.
stroll run, v.
stroll walk, v.
study explore, v.
study think, v.
stunning pretty, adj.
stunt grow, v.
superb nice, adj.
superior good, adj.
supply give, v.
surprise, v.
sweet nice, adj.
swift quick, adj.
sympathetic nice, adj.

take give, v.
take away put, v.
talented good, adj.
task job, n.
tasty good, adj.
teammate opponent, n.
teeny big, adj.
terrible nice, adj.
terrific great, adj.
terrifying scary, adj.
thankful grateful, adj.
thin, adj.
thin fat, adj.
think, v.
thorough careful, adj.
thoughtful good, adj.
thoughtless careful, adj.
tiny big, adj.
tiny little, adj.
titter laugh, v.
tow pull, v.
tranquil calm, adj.
transform change, v.
transparent clear, adj.
treacherous faithful, adj.
tremble shake, v.
troubled upset, adj.
true faithful, adj.
true real, adj.

U

ugly pretty, adj.
unappealing pretty, adj.
unattractive pretty, adj.
unclear, adj.
uncomplicated easy, adj.
undo do, v.
uneven rough, adj.
unimportant chief, adj.
unite join, v.
unkind good, adj.
unnecessary important, adj.
unscramble do, v.

unselfish good, *adj.*
unusual common, *adj.*
unworthy good, *adj.*
upright good, *adj.*
upset, *adj.*
upset angry, *adj.*
upstanding good, *adj.*
use operate, *v.*
useful, *adj.*
useless useful, *adj.*

valiant brave, *adj.*
varied boring, *adj.*
vicious nice, *adj.*
view look, *v.*
view see, *v.*
vigilant careful, *adj.*
vile nice, *adj.*

wail laugh, *v.*
walk, *v.*
walk run, *v.*
warm cold, *adj.*
wary careful, *adj.*
watchful careful, *adj.*
water-logged wet, *adj.*
wee big, *adj.*
weep laugh, *v.*
weird strange, *adj.*
well healthy, *adj.*
well-mannered good, *adj.*
well-mannered nice, *adj.*
wet, *adj.*
wettish wet, *adj.*
while, *conj.*
whimper laugh, *v.*
whimper say, *v.*
whimsical funny, *adj.*
whine say, *v.*
whisper say, *v.*
whisper shout, *v.*
wicked good, *adj.*

wild calm, *adj.*
win get, *v.*
wish, *v.*
witty funny, *adj.*
wonderful great, *adj.*
work do, *v.*
work job, *n.*
work operate, *v.*
work out do, *v.*
worried upset, *adj.*
worthless important, *adj.*
worthless useful, *adj.*

yell say, *v.*
yell shout, *v.*
yummy good, *adj.*

Thesaurus Plus Index **H89**

Thesaurus Plus

A

active *adj.* full of movement. *Tennis is an **active** sport.*
energetic full of strength and energy. *My **energetic** friend Janet is always busy.*
lively full of life, alert. *The **lively** puppy kept tugging at his leash.*
antonyms: lazy, sluggish

agree *v.* to express willingness. *My parents **agreed** to get a dog.*
consent to say yes. *Did Judy **consent** to your plan?*
approve to say officially that something is correct or should be done. *The principal **approved** of the field trip.*
comply with to follow a request or a rule. *Please **comply with** the rules when you visit the museum.*
antonyms: deny, refuse

also *adv.* too. *Peter likes that album, but he likes this one **also**.*
in addition plus, as well. *We went to the park and to the zoo **in addition**.*
besides together with, over and above. *Tom plays two instruments **besides** the guitar.*

How Angry Were You?

angry *adj.* feeling or showing displeasure.

1. slightly angry: *displeased, annoyed, irritated, peeved*
2. very angry: *upset, cross, mad*
3. extremely angry: *furious, enraged, irate, fuming, outraged*

antonyms: calm, peaceful, delighted, happy, pleased

argue *v.* to give reasons for or against something, especially to someone with a different opinion. *Jo favored a town pool, but Jean **argued** against it.*
quarrel to have a fight with words. *We **quarreled** about who was smarter.*
clash to be against one another on an issue. *Employers and employees **clashed** during a recent strike.*
disagree to have a different opinion. *The senators **disagreed** with each other.*
antonyms: accept, agree, consent

ask *v.* to put a question to. *I will **ask** Donna to come with me.*
question to try to get information from. *Please **question** him about his plans.*
inquire to try to find out information. *We **inquired** about her address.*
antonyms: reply, answer

B

before *adv.* in the past. *He was excited since he hadn't been to Texas **before**.*
earlier sooner or at a past time. *The game ended **earlier** than usual.*
previously taking place in the past. ***Previously** she wore her hair long.*
antonyms: after, later

Word Bank

big *adj.* of great size or importance.

huge	colossal
immense	mammoth
large	enormous
mighty	gigantic
jumbo	sizeable
bulky	great
massive	
giant	

antonyms: little, tiny, miniature, small, wee, petite, microscopic

chief

boast *v.* to praise oneself, one's belongings, or one's actions. *Sara always boasts about how fast she runs.*
brag to use words about oneself to show off. *Leroy bragged about everything.*
crow to utter a cry of delight or victory. *Pat grinned and crowed, "I won!"*

bold *adj.* not timid or fearful. *Mary Read was a bold woman.*
daring brave enough to take on a big challenge; adventurous. *Two daring climbers reached the top at last.*
audacious not afraid of any risk. *One audacious bear came up to our tent.*
antonym: cautious

boring *adj.* not interesting. *The TV show was boring so I fell asleep.*
dull lacking excitement. *Not one player scored during the dull soccer match.*
dry tiresome. *It was hard to finish reading the lengthy, dry report.*
monotonous not interesting because always the same. *Monotonous songs repeat the same words over and over.*
antonyms: exciting, lively, interesting, varied

brave *adj.* able to face danger or pain without fear. *You seemed brave when the doctor set your broken leg.*
courageous able to face difficult situations. *That pilot is courageous.*
valiant acting with great courage. *The valiant soldiers risked their lives.*
fearless without fright. *The fearless cat stood still as a dog ran toward it.*
antonyms: cowardly, frightened

break *v.* to separate into pieces as the result of force or strain. *A beam broke under the weight of the snow.*
shatter to come apart suddenly into many pieces. *The delicate cup shattered against the floor.*
smash to crush into pieces. *The car smashed into the orange crates.*
crack to come apart with a sharp sound. *Dale cracked the bat when he hit the ball.*
antonyms: mend, patch, repair

C

calm *adj.* without excitement or motion. *The calm water looked like a mirror.*
peaceful without worry or trouble. *Their argument spoiled our peaceful day.*
tranquil quiet and undisturbed. *We found a tranquil picnic spot.*
sedate composed; dignified. *He remained sedate during the trial.*
antonyms: excited, frantic, raging, wild

Shades of Meaning

careful *adj.* giving serious thought and attention to what one is doing.

1. alert for danger or trouble:
   cautious
   vigilant
   watchful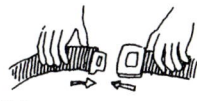
2. wise and thoughtful:
   prudent, studious, mindful
3. paying attention to details:
   meticulous, conscientious, particular, thorough, strict
4. showing lack of trust:
   wary, guarded, protective

antonyms: heedless, careless, thoughtless, slack, lax

change *v.* to make or become different. *I like how you changed your hair.*
convert to put something to a new use. *They converted the barn into a house.*
transform to alter completely the form of something. *We know how to transform fuel into energy.*
antonyms: continue, remain

chief *adj.* highest in rank or importance. *The chief product of the state is wheat.*
main most important. *The main library is bigger than its branches.*

more ▶

choice

principal leading all others. *The panda's principal food is a kind of bamboo.*
antonyms: minor, unimportant

choice *n.* the act of choosing or deciding. *Please make your choice now.*
selection the act of picking one or a few out of several. *I tried on eight pairs of shoes before I made my selection.*
preference a liking for one thing over another. *My color preference is red.*
alternative decision between two or more possibilities. *The alternative is between walking or riding to school.*

clean *adj.* free from dirt, stains, and clutter. *Dad needs a clean shirt.*
spotless completely free of dirt. *The hospital operating room is spotless.*
antonyms: dirty, filthy, soiled

clear *adj.* free from clouds, dust, or anything that would make it hard to see through. *The sky was so clear that we could see the Milky Way.*
transparent able to be seen through easily. *We watched the sharks through a transparent tank.*
antonyms: cloudy, foggy, misty

cold *adj.* at a low temperature. *Cold water is the most refreshing drink of all.*
chilly not warm enough for comfort. *If you feel chilly, you can sit in the sun.*
cool at a somewhat low temperature. *The cool wind felt good in the sun.*
icy feeling like ice. *How do birds stay alive in such icy winds?*
freezing producing icy conditions. *The freezing rain made driving difficult.*
antonyms: hot, warm

common *adj.* often found or occurring; familiar. *A common response to a kind host is a thank-you note.*
familiar well known because it is often seen or heard. *The bus route home is very familiar.*
ordinary not unusual in any way. *On an ordinary day, I eat cereal.*

normal of the usual kind; natural. *It was not our normal school schedule.*
general widespread; prevalent. *The students had a general feeling of excitement before the big game.*
regular usual or standard. *They said our regular teacher was ill.*
antonyms: abnormal, extraordinary, rare, strange, unusual

create *v.* to bring into being. *Spiders create webs to trap insects.*
establish to begin or set up. *The settlers soon established a small town.*
invent to make something that did not exist before. *No one is sure who really invented the camera.*
produce to bring forth, manufacture. *How many cars do they produce?*
design to make a plan or a drawing for something. *An art student designed the school's new sign.*
antonym: destroy

D

danger *n.* the chance of great harm or loss. *There was no danger of getting lost if we stayed on the path.*
hazard something that could cause harm. *A blocked door can be a fire hazard.*
risk the possibility of harm in an activity. *The risk of an accident increases on icy roads.*
peril a condition that can threaten lives. *Anyone out in this storm will be in great peril.*
antonyms: safety, security, protection

dark *adj.* without light or sun. *It was so dark that we turned on the lights.*
dim not well lit. *Do not read in such dim light.*
murky very gloomy. *Evans was afraid to step into the murky cell.*
antonyms: bright, light

decide *v.* to make up one's mind. *I **decided** to buy the red bike.*
determine to make a firm decision. *Dr. Tsao **determined** to do all that he could to save the cat.*
resolve to make a firm plan. *I **resolve** to eat a good breakfast every day.*

deserve *v.* ought to have or receive. *An animal lover like Paul **deserves** a pet.*
merit earn the right to something. *June's courage **merits** high praise.*
be worthy of be good or valuable enough to receive. *The animal shelter **is worthy of** your support.*

Shades of Meaning

do *v.*

1. to carry out an action: *perform, execute, produce, make, work, act*
2. to solve something: *unscramble, solve, work out, decode, resolve*

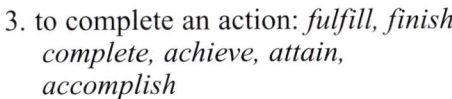

3. to complete an action: *fulfill, finish, complete, achieve, attain, accomplish*

antonyms: omit, undo, fail, quit

eager *adj.* full of strong desire. ***Eager** campers set up their camp early.*
keen full of enthusiasm and interest. *Ben is a **keen** football fan.*
interested involved or concerned with. *Peg is an **interested** committee member.*
antonyms: bored, indifferent

easy *adj.* not difficult. *Tad solved the **easy** puzzle quickly.*
simple not complicated. *Use a **simple** drawing of a few lines.*
uncomplicated not hard to understand, deal with, or solve. *We followed Dad's **uncomplicated** directions with ease.*
effortless easily done. *The athlete made weightlifting seem **effortless**.*
antonyms: complex, difficult, hard

effect *n.* something brought about by a cause. *The moon has an important **effect** on the ocean tides.*
consequence a direct outcome of something. *The fine performance was a **consequence** of practice.*
result something that happens because of something else. *The broken branches are the **result** of the storm.*
antonyms: cause, source

explore *v.* to look into or through closely. *Katie **explored** every inch of her closet for her missing shoe.*
study to examine closely and carefully. *Doris **studied** her notes before class.*
probe to search into thoroughly. *An investigator **probed** Rick's background.*
investigate to research carefully. *Who will **investigate** the jewel's disappearance?*

faithful *adj.* worthy of trust. *Ben knew his **faithful** friend would keep quiet.*
loyal offering constant support to a person, country, or cause. *The spy insisted that he was **loyal** to his country.*
true trustworthy and devoted. *Ariel was a **true** friend when I needed her.*
antonyms: changeable, treacherous, false

fake *n.* someone or something that is not what he, she, or it pretends to be. *We realized that the actor's moustache was a **fake**.*
fraud a person who lies about himself or herself. *That **fraud** claimed that he got us free tickets, but he did not!*
phony an insincere person. *Pete tries to act friendly, but he is a **phony**.*
impostor a person who pretends to be another person. *Was that woman really the queen or only an **impostor**?*

more ▶

fat

fat *adj.* having much or too much body weight. *We put our **fat** dog on a diet.*
plump rounded and full in shape. *Her baby brother has **plump** cheeks.*
stout large and heavy in build. *Al is slim, but his brother Ben is **stout**.*
antonyms: skinny, slender, slim, thin

finish *v.* to get done. *When you **finish** cleaning, you may go for a bike ride.*
end to bring or come to the final moments. *The first half **ended** when the whistle blew.*
complete to get to the end of something. *I **completed** the test as the bell rang.*
stop to come to a halt. *The engine **stopped** when the car ran out of gas.*
conclude to be or cause to be over. *Ms. Wang **concluded** her speech.*
close to come to or bring to an end. *The play **closed** with a joke.*
antonyms: begin, commence, start

How **Funny** Was It?

funny *adj.* causing laughter or amusement.

1. somewhat funny: *amusing, droll, whimsical, witty*
2. quite funny: *humorous, laughable, comical*
3. extremely funny: *ridiculous, hilarious, sidesplitting, ludicrous, absurd*

antonyms: serious, sad, solemn, gloomy, depressing

---

further *adj.* added or other. *The news station released **further** storm bulletins.*
more greater in size, quantity, extent, or degree. *We need **more** ice for the bowl.*
additional extra. *Take **additional** socks in case one pair gets wet.*

G

gather *v.* to bring or come together in one place. *They **gathered** around the campfire and sang songs.*
assemble to bring or come together as a group. *The band members must **assemble** in the auditorium at noon.*
collect to bring things together. *Tina has **collected** twenty different baseball hats in only one year.*
antonyms: scatter, separate

get *v.* to receive. *Did you **get** any payment for your work in the garden?*
earn to gain by working or by supplying a service. *Jay **earns** five dollars a week by baby-sitting for families in his neighborhood.*
obtain to gain by means of planning or effort. *Carol took a test to **obtain** her driver's license.*
win to receive as a prize or reward. *Did Joe **win** a prize in the school essay contest?*
acquire to gain by one's own efforts. *Ed worked many hours to **acquire** his typing skill.*
buy to gain by paying a price for. *Ana used her allowance to **buy** a gift for her mother.*
antonym: lose

give *v.* to hand over to another. *Sara **gave** her sister a small music box for her birthday.*
offer to put forward to be accepted or refused. *Jan **offered** Ina half of her sandwich and apple.*
supply to make available something that is needed. *Blood **supplies** oxygen to the brain.*
present to make a gift or award to. *Coach Hart **presented** the trophy to the captain of our basketball team.*
antonyms: receive, take

healthy

Shades of Meaning

good *adj.*

1. well-behaved: *polite, obedient, well-mannered, courteous*
2. trustworthy: *honest, decent, honorable, law-abiding, upstanding, upright, moral*
3. aiding one's health: *healthful, nutritious, nourishing*
4. pleasant-tasting: *delicious, tasty, flavorful, mouth-watering, yummy, appetizing, luscious, scrumptious*
5. having much ability: *skilled, able, capable, talented, gifted, masterful, expert, qualified, experienced*
6. kind: *considerate, caring, thoughtful, generous, unselfish, friendly, loving, charitable*
7. better than average: *outstanding, excellent, fine, superior, praiseworthy, admirable*

antonyms: *awful, unkind, harmful, bad, evil, wicked, disagreeable, disgusting, unworthy, cruel, mean, nasty, heartless, inferior, poor, second-rate*

glance *v.* to look briefly. *I **glanced** at him quickly.*
glimpse to get a brief view of. *She only **glimpsed** the passing car.*
peek to look briefly. *He **peeked** around the corner.*

grateful *adj.* feeling or showing thanks. *The Smiths were **grateful** when their neighbors helped rebuild their barn.*
appreciative expressing or feeling gratitude. *The **appreciative** man thanked Lori for finding his cat.*
thankful showing an understanding of how fortunate one is. *Dad was **thankful** that no one was hurt.*

great *adj.* remarkable. *Pearl took **great** pictures of the baseball game.*
terrific excellent. *A **terrific** swimmer like Natalie should make the team.*
fantastic extraordinary. *There is a **fantastic** view of the ocean from here!*
wonderful astonishing. *This is a **wonderful** museum.*
marvelous notably superior. *Your speech was **marvelous**.*
antonyms: inferior, ordinary

Shades of Green

green *adj.* having the color of grass; a mix of blue and yellow.

olive: light yellowish-green, like green olives
lime: bright yellowish-green, like limes
kelly: bright green, like grass or clover
emerald: bright, slightly dark green, like emeralds
hunter: dark green, like pine trees and cucumbers

grow *v.* to become or cause to become larger. *Rain helped the plants **grow** tall.*
raise to promote the development of. *Kate **raised** her puppy with love.*
produce to bring forth; yield. *Kansas **produces** wheat.*
mature to develop fully. *Has the fruit **matured** enough to be picked?*
antonym: stunt

happy *adj.* showing or feeling pleasure or joy. *Tina was **happy** because she got the lead part in the play.*
cheerful being in good spirits. *It is pleasant to be near **cheerful** people.*
glad pleased. *Sam was **glad** to be home.*
antonyms: sad, sorrowful

healthy *adj.* free from disease or injury. *The **healthy** plants grew tall.*
fit being in good physical shape. *Drew feels healthy and **fit**.*

more ▶

hide

sound having no damage or disease. *The old house still had a **sound** frame.*
well not sick. *Even during the flu season, Molly stayed **well**.*
antonyms: diseased, ill, sick

hide *v.* to keep or put out of sight. *The cat **hid** under the bed.*
conceal purposely to keep from being seen or known. *Allan **concealed** his sadness behind a happy face.*
bury to cover from view. *The dog **buried** another bone under the rose bush.*
antonyms: reveal, show

honest *adj.* straightforward; truthful. *The **honest** witness told the truth in court.*
direct to the point. *I will be **direct** and not waste time.*
frank free and open in expressing thoughts or feelings. *In a **frank** talk, I told Lina how I felt.*
antonyms: deceitful, insincere, misleading

job *n.* something that must be done. *Would you prefer the **job** of scrubbing or waxing?*
work things that must be done. *You have enough **work** to keep you busy.*
task an assignment or a chore. *Adam's **task** was to sweep the hall.*
employment an activity by which one earns money or to which one devotes time. *Teaching is a wonderful form of **employment**.*
antonyms: play, hobby, leisure

join *v.* to put together or attach. *We all **joined** hands to form a circle.*
connect to link things together. *A bridge **connects** the two cities.*
unite to bring together to form a whole. *The thirteen colonies were **united**.*
antonyms: part, separate

jump *v.* to rise up or move through the air. *The cow in the nursery rhyme **jumps** over the moon.*
hurdle to go over a barrier. *The horse **hurdled** the fence and galloped away.*
leap to jump or cause to jump quickly or suddenly. *Carl **leaped** away from the falling tree.*
spring to move upward or forward in one quick motion. *I **spring** out of bed when my alarm rings.*

last *adv.* after all the others. *Add the ice **last** so that it does not melt.*
finally after a long while. *After waiting two hours, the train **finally** arrived.*
at the end at the conclusion. *Flo stumbled **at the end** of her speech.*
antonym: first

Shades of Meaning
laugh *v.* to make sounds to express amusement.
1. to laugh quietly: *giggle, chuckle, titter*   2. to laugh in a mean or sly way: *snicker, snigger*   3. to laugh loudly: *cackle, chortle, guffaw, roar, shriek, howl* 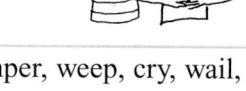
antonyms: whimper, weep, cry, wail, sob, blubber

leave *v.* to go away from. *Please **leave** this dangerous place at once!*
abandon to go away from because of trouble or danger; to desert. *The crew **abandoned** the sinking ship.*
quit to depart from. *Phil wants to **quit** Seattle and move to Tulsa.*
antonyms: arrive, come, return

let *v.* to give permission to. *Ron took the leash off his dog and **let** her run free.*
allow to say yes to. *Please **allow** me to go to Jenny's party.*

moment

permit to consent to. *The state law **permits** sixteen-year-olds to drive cars and motorcycles.*
antonyms: prevent, stop, hinder

little *adj.* not big in size or quantity. *Leroy is six feet tall, but he looks **little** next to that thirty-foot statue.*
tiny extremely reduced in size. *Dan could not read the **tiny** print without his glasses.*
small reduced in size. *I cannot wear this coat because it is too **small**.*
miniature reduced from its usual size. *Ella built a **miniature** city with toothpicks and glue.*
antonyms: enormous, large

lively *adj.* full of energy, active. *They were out of breath after dancing a **lively** polka.*
chipper full of cheer. *Ike felt **chipper** on this lovely morning.*
energetic full of strength and action. *The **energetic** children played on the swings all morning.*
spirited full of life. *Our team played a **spirited** game and won.*
antonyms: inactive, lazy

Shades of Meaning

look *v.* to focus one's eyes or attention on something.

1. to look quickly: *glimpse, glance, scan*
2. to look secretively: *spy, peep, peek, snoop*
3. to look long and thoughtfully: *gaze, contemplate, view*
4. to look steadily and directly: *stare, gape, gawk*
5. to look with anger or displeasure: *glower, glare, scowl*

antonyms: overlook, dismiss, ignore, avoid, shun

make *v.* to shape or put together out of materials or parts. *Mrs. Lewis **made** that rug from pieces of old clothes and curtains.*
build to put up something with materials or parts. *Dad **built** a tree house in our yard.*
construct to make by fitting parts together. *Will the town **construct** a bridge over the river?*
form to shape. *Ali **formed** a bird out of her piece of clay.*
manufacture to put things together with machines. *That factory **manufactures** many popular toys and games.*
antonyms: destroy, dismantle

many *adj.* adding up to a large number. *Jay learned to identify the **many** different birds on the island.*
several more than two but not a large number. *The power was out for **several** hours after the storm.*
numerous made up of a large number. ***Numerous** people lined up outside the factory to apply for a job.*
antonym: few

meaning *n.* the intended thought or message of something. *Ms. Clark explained the **meaning** of the poem to her puzzled students.*
significance the special message or intention. *What is the **significance** of the maple leaf on the Canadian flag?*
sense the many ideas implied by a word. *The **sense** of a word usually depends on its use in a sentence.*
antonyms: nonsense, pointlessness

moment *n.* a very short period of time. *Please wait just a **moment**, and a salesperson will help you.*
instant a second in time. *In an **instant**, before anyone could blink, the clown had disappeared.*

more ▶

necessary

necessary *adj.* having to be done. *It is **necessary** that you complete this form.*
essential very important, basic. *Regular brushing is **essential** to healthy teeth.*
required called for or needed. *The exam **required** careful thinking.*

nervous *adj.* shaken and jittery because of fear or challenge. *The **nervous** actor forgot his lines.*
anxious upset or fearful about something uncertain. *Olive feels **anxious** about her exam.*
edgy tense. *Bill was **edgy** the night before the exam and could not sleep.*
antonyms: calm, placid

new *adj.* never used, worn, or thought of before. *We finally bought a **new** car.*
fresh just made, grown, or gathered. *These are **fresh** beans, straight from Grandfather's garden.*
original not copied from or based on anything else. *The brilliant inventor came up with another **original** idea.*
novel strikingly different. *The detective's **novel** method of investigation was successful.*
antonyms: old, ancient, antique

Shades of Meaning
nice *adj.*
1. pleasing: *pleasant, agreeable, appealing, delightful, refreshing, lovely, charming, enchanting*
2. good: *fine, skillful, admirable, splendid, superb, excellent*
3. kind: *sweet, companionable, gentle, sympathetic, friendly, amiable, mild*
4. polite: *gracious, considerate, proper, well-mannered, courteous*
antonyms: insulting, offensive, displeasing, repellent, terrible, flawed, vile, mean, contemptible, vicious, rude, cold-hearted, crass

operate *v.* to run. *Can you **operate** a bulldozer?*
work to perform a function. *Who knows how to **work** the computer?*
use employ for some purpose. *Did you **use** my saw to build the bookcase?*

perfect *adj.* having no errors, flaws, or defects. *A **perfect** day for sailing is sunny and slightly breezy.*
ideal thought of as being the best possible. *Casey has an **ideal** job that allows her to travel.*
excellent of the highest quality. *The chef made our **excellent** meal from the freshest ingredients.*
delightful very pleasing. *A **delightful** breeze cooled the hot beach.*
antonyms: faulty, flawed

persuade *v.* to cause someone to do or believe something by pleading, arguing, or reasoning. *I **persuaded** Jim to clean my room for me.*
convince to cause someone to feel certain. *I **convinced** my mother that I was telling the truth.*
antonyms: dissuade, deter

Word Bank
pretty *adj.* pleasing to the eye or ear.
attractive beautiful radiant cute appealing brilliant charming handsome dazzling gorgeous ravishing glorious stunning lovely glamorous
antonyms: ugly, unattractive, homely, offensive, unappealing, disgusting, repulsive, revolting

price *n.* the amount of money asked or paid for something. *The price of this shirt is $10.95.*
charge a fee asked or paid, particularly for a service. *Is there a charge for washing the car windshield and windows, or is it a free service?*
cost amount of payment for a product or a service. *The cost of a concert ticket has increased ten dollars.*
expense something paid out. *Can we afford the expense of piano lessons?*

protect *v.* to keep safe from harm or injury. *Calvin wears a helmet to protect his head when he rides his bike or goes roller skating.*
guard to defend or keep safe from danger. *The police guarded the museum against theft.*
antonym: endanger

pull *v.* to apply force to in order to draw someone or something in the direction of the force. *I pulled the door toward me as hard as I could.*
drag to draw along the ground by force. *Jim dragged the heavy trash barrel across the lawn.*
haul to draw along behind, usually with great effort. *The horse hauled the heavy wagon up the mountain.*
tow to draw along behind with a chain or a rope. *With a strong rope, the big boat towed our canoe into the harbor.*
antonyms: push, shove

put *v.* to cause to be in a particular position. *Put your bike in the shed.*
place to lay something in a certain space. *Place your hands on your hips.*
locate to establish something in a certain area. *Locate your garden in a sunny place.*
set to cause to be in a particular location. *Set your books on the table.*
antonyms: remove, take away

quick *adj.* done or happening without delay. *We took a quick trip to the store just before dinner.*
fast moving or acting with speed. *Traveling by plane is faster than traveling by car.*
hasty in a hurried way. *Jim scribbled a hasty note and then ran out the door.*
rapid marked by speed. *The rapid subway train zoomed through the tunnel.*
swift able to move at great speed. *You will need a swift horse if you want to get to the farm before dinner.*
speedy able to get from one place to another in a short time. *A speedy little rabbit outran my dog.*
antonym: slow

real *adj.* not imaginary, made up, or artificial. *This apple looks real, but it is wax.*
actual existing or happening. *Tory's visit to the palace was an actual event, not just a dream.*
true in agreement with fact. *Whether or not you believe it, the story is true.*
antonyms: artificial, fake

rough *adj.* full of bumps and ridges. *The carpenter sanded the rough wood.*
bumpy covered with lumps. *The bumpy road made us bounce in our seats.*
coarse not polished or fine. *The surface of sandpaper is coarse.*
uneven not level. *Because the floor was uneven, the table didn't sit straight.*
antonyms: smooth, polished

run *v.* to move quickly on foot. *Please do not run in the halls.*
dash to move with sudden speed. *We dashed out the door to get the mail.*
race to rush at top speed. *Leon raced to catch the bus.*
antonyms: walk, stroll

same

same *adj.* being the very one. *This train is the same one that I rode last week.*
equal being alike in any measured quantity. *We got equal test scores.*
identical exactly alike. *The twins were identical; no one could tell them apart.*
antonym: different

Shades of Meaning

say *v.* speak aloud.

1. to say quietly or unclearly: *whisper, murmur, mutter, sigh, mumble, grunt*
2. to say in an excited or nervous way: *exclaim, cry, stammer, sputter*
3. to say loudly: *yell, scream, screech, shout, holler, bellow, roar, howl*
4. to say in an angry way: *snarl, snap, growl, bark, hiss*
5. to say in a complaining way: *whine, moan, groan, grumble, whimper, gripe*

scary *adj.* causing fear. *Your story was so scary that I was afraid to walk home.*
alarming causing a feeling of approaching danger. *The police siren was alarming to drivers.*
frightening causing sudden, great fear. *The frightening noise was thunder.*
terrifying causing overpowering fright. *The elephant made a terrifying noise.*

see *v.* to take in with the eyes. *Julie could not see the bird in the tree.*
notice to pay attention to. *Ron entered quietly, but we noticed he was late.*
observe to watch carefully. *The cat observed the bird in the tree.*
view to look at. *We viewed the city from the top of the mountain.*
antonyms: ignore, overlook

shake *v.* to move back and forth or up and down with short, quick movements. *The leaves on the oak tree shook in the wind.*
quake to move suddenly, as from shock. *The ground quaked when the herd of cattle moved by.*
shiver to move without control, as from cold or nervousness. *The child shivered in the cold rain.*
shudder to move with sudden, sharp movements, as from fear or horror. *Al shuddered when he read the story.*
tremble move back and forth gently or slightly, as from cold or fear. *My lips trembled as I began my speech.*

shiny *adj.* reflecting light. *Craig's shiny new bike sparkled in the sun.*
bright giving off strong rays of light. *Bright sun can be harmful to your eyes.*
gleaming glowing with light. *The gleaming runway lights showed the pilot where to land.*
glistening sparkling. *The sun turned the lake into a glistening pool of light.*
antonyms: dark, dim, dull

shout *v.* to call out at the top of one's voice. *The fans at the football game shouted, "Go, team, go!"*
yell to make a loud outcry, often in anger. *Helen yelled, "Your dog is eating my glove!"*
cry to utter a special sound or call. *Jeremy cried out in sudden pain.*
holler to call out to. *"Sue, come in for dinner!" I hollered.*
antonym: whisper

some *adj.* being an unspecified number or amount of. *Joanne invited some friends to play volleyball.*
few a small number of. *Few people today get enough exercise.*
several more than two but not a large number. *Carl moved several blocks away, but we can still walk there easily.*

H100 Tools and Tips: Thesaurus Plus

upset

start *v.* to take the first step in an action. *Joan turned to page one and **started** to read her book.*
begin to get a process underway. *I will **begin** my homework right after school.*
commence to perform the first part of an action. *The graduation ceremony **commences** at noon.*
antonyms: close, end, finish, stop

strange *adj.* different; unfamiliar. *I felt **strange** on my first day at the new school.*
weird odd or peculiar. *My brother has a **weird** sense of humor.*
odd out of the ordinary. *I read a story about an **odd** animal with three bumps!*
peculiar hard to understand or explain. *There is nothing **peculiar** about a green apple, but what do you think about a purple orange?*
unusual rare or different from what might be expected. *Her **unusual** name was hard to say.*
antonyms: normal, familiar, common, ordinary

surprise *v.* to cause to feel wonder because of the unexpected. *The sudden thunder **surprised** the picnickers in the park.*
amaze to fill with wonder or awe. *The skilled juggler **amazed** the crowd.*
astonish to startle greatly. *The unexpected news **astonished** the world.*
astound to strike with great wonder. *People were **astounded** by the speed of the new plane.*

thin *adj.* having little fat on the body. *After his diet, Joe looked **thin**.*
skinny having very little fat on the body; bony. *The sick kitten was so **skinny** that we could see its ribs.*
slender having little fat or width. *The **slender** ballerina looked like a doll.*
antonyms: fat, plump, stout

Shades of Meaning

think *v.*

1. to use one's mind:
   consider
   evaluate
   reflect
   study

2. to have an opinion:
   feel
   judge
   assert
   believe

3. to suppose:
   imagine
   conceive
   dream
   speculate

antonyms: forget, ignore

unclear *adj.* not easy to see, hear, or understand. *Those complicated directions are **unclear**.*
fuzzy blurred. *The TV picture was too **fuzzy** to see any details.*
confusing mixed up. *The recipe was so **confusing** that we could not follow the steps.*
cloudy hazy; not clear. *The powder made the water **cloudy**.*
faint not distinct or bright. *The star was only a **faint** speck in the sky.*
antonyms: distinct, obvious, sharp

upset *adj.* sad or unsettled. *I was **upset** when I heard the bad news.*
worried uneasy because of fear. *Janet was **worried** about getting lost.*
nervous shaken and jittery because of fear or challenge. *Dean was **nervous** because he had to give a speech.*
troubled concerned because of pain, fear, or sadness. *Phil was **troubled** by his father's illness.*
disturbed being bothered or feeling

more ▶

useful

unsettled. *They were **disturbed** by some noisy fire engines.*
antonyms: calm, comfortable, pleased, satisfied, composed

useful *adj.* being of service. *A rake is **useful** for cleaning up the yard.*
handy convenient, easy to use. *A wastebasket is a **handy** thing to have in each room of the house.*
helpful providing assistance. *I found this book **helpful** when I was looking for facts about the battle.*
antonyms: inefficient, useless, worthless

walk *v.* to move on foot at a steady pace. *Gabriel can **walk** to the store to get milk.*
march to move forward with regular and measured steps. *The band **marched** around the stadium as they played.*
stride to take long steps. *You **stride** so fast I cannot keep up with you.*
stroll to go forward in a slow, relaxed way. *Shall we **stroll** through the park after dinner?*
antonyms: run, stand still

while *conj.* at the same period of time as. *I was waiting at the airport for Lois **while** she was waiting at the train station for me.*
as long as for an entire length of time. *We vowed to remain friends **as long as** we lived.*

wish *v.* to want, hope for. *What sights do you **wish** to see in the city?*
desire to want strongly. *More than anything else, Jan **desired** to travel around the world.*
crave to long for intensely. *The thirsty runners **craved** a cool drink.*

How Wet Was It?

wet *adj.* covered or moistened with liquid.

1. extremely wet:
   drenched, saturated, soaked, water-logged, sopping, flooded
2. quite wet:
   dripping, soppy, soggy, sodden
3. slightly wet:
   moist, damp, dank, dewy, wettish

antonyms: parched, arid, dry, dehydrated

Index

A

Abbreviations, 196–197, 200, 203, 213, 274, H57–H58
Acrostics, 475
Addresses, 318, 504
Adjectives
articles, 156–157, 166, 173, 175, 274
choosing different, 164
combining sentences with, 155
comparing with, 158–159, 160–161, 166–167, 173, 176–177, 274
demonstrative, 156–157, 166, 173, 175, 274
distinguishing from adverbs, 252–253, 268
identifying, 152–153, 166, 173, 174, 252–253, 268, 273, 275, 278
proper, 162–163, 165, 167, 173, 178, 201, 208, 274, 425
Adverbs
choosing different, 266
comparing with, 250–251, 268, 270, 277
distinguishing from adjectives, 252–253, 268
distinguishing from prepositions, 264–265, 269, 295
identifying, 246–247, 252–253, 264–265, 267, 268–269, 275, 276, 278
as negatives, 254, 268, 279
writing with, 164
Affixes. *See* Suffixes

Agreement, subject-verb, 112–113, 114–115, 131, 143–144, 172, 273
Almanac, using, 412
Analogies, tests, H33–H34
Analyzing information, 478–479
Announcements, making, 181
Antonyms, 383
Apostrophes
in contractions, 116–117, 122–123, 131, 145, 172, 226–227, 234, 242, 254–255
in possessives, 74–77, 78–79, 83, 85, 88, 93–94
Appositives, 69, 79
Articles, 156–157, 166, 173, 175, 274
Atlas, using, 412
Audience, 12–13, 26, 304, 308, 330, 347, 374, 385, 409, 426, 431, 455, 476, 484, 489
Auxiliary verbs. *See* Verbs, helping

B

Book report, writing a, 468–469
Brainstorming. *See* Prewriting
Business letters, writing a, 503–504

C

Capitalization
of abbreviations, 196–197, 200, 203, 213, 274
of book titles, 198–199, 206, 214, 274
of first word in sentence, 32, 52, 57, 180–181, 207, 274
of proper adjectives, 162–163, 178, 182–183, 201, 204–205, 208, 274, 425
of proper nouns, 54, 66–67, 84, 86, 90, 168–169, 182–183, 201, 204–205, 208, 425
and punctuation and usage, guide to, H57–H66
of quotations, 194–195, 202, 204, 212, 274
Card catalog, 412, H24
Cause and effect, 77, 362
Characters
analyzing, 350–351
creating, 331, 333, 347
in plays, 344–349
See also Literary terms
Charts, making
flow, 390
general, 429, 431, 473
T-chart, 347
types, H53–H55
Chronological order. *See* Sequence
Combining sentences. *See* Sentences, combining
Commas
with adjectives, 152–153
combining sentences with, 186–187, 190–191
with introductory words, 188–189, 190–191, 202, 210
in quotations, 194–195, 212
in sentences, 46–47, 48–49, 54, 62, 68–69, 86, 205
in series, 184–185, 186–187, 201, 205, 209, 237, 384, 499

Index I-1

Index continued

Communication
dramatic interpretation, 348, 350–351, H7
electronic, H39, H45–H46
nonverbal, 351, H7
oral presentations, 434–435, H47–H49
producing, 436–437, H47–H48
skills, 1–10, 288, 317–318, 350–351, 352–353, 356, 388–397, 396–397, 430–431, 434–437, 476–477, 478–479, 505–506, H4, H5–H6, H7–H8, H9–H10. *See also* Composition
visual, 352–353, 396–397, 478–479, 507–509. *See also* Discussions; Speaking; Listening; Media

Comparison, degrees of, 158–159

Comparison and contrast, 16, 45, 121, 159, 229, 251, 263, 352–353, 361, 374–387

Complex sentence. *See* Sentences, types of

Composition
beginnings/introductions, 18, 307, 334, 379, 419, 460, 494
collaborate with others, 13, 22–23, 304, 311
complete sentences, 24–25
conclusions, 309, 335, 379, 419, 460, 494
elaborated sentences, 20–21, 69, 154, 186–187, 248–249, 260–261, 307, 309, 312, 333, 339, 383, 418, 422, 457, 463, 498
endings, writing, 18–19, 309, 335, 380
evaluating, 310, 337, 381, 420, 461, 492, 496
exact words, using, 17, 21, 309, 333, 391
letters
business, 503–504
friendly, 317–318
kinds of, 317–318
parts of, 317–318, 503–504
modes
descriptive, 9–11, 13, 15, 17, 19, 21, 23, 25, 27, 33, 45, 67, 71, 75, 101, 123, 159, 181, 223, 251, 257, 361
expository, 39, 77, 105, 117, 119, 125, 127, 157, 197, 217, 259, 357–363, 368, 369–373, 365–367, 374–385, 386, 387, 388–393, 399–402, 403, 404–408, 409–426, 427, 428–429, 430–431, 432–433
expressive, 35, 73, 97, 99, 153, 193, 195, 221, 344–349, 397, 441–445, 447–449, 450, 451–454, 455–456, 466, 467, 468–469, 470–475
narrative, 37, 41, 103, 107, 109, 121, 185, 189, 219, 227, 247, 251, 265, 289–293, 295–297, 298, 299–303, 304–314, 315, 316, 317–318, 320–324, 325, 326–329, 330–341, 342, 343, 344–349
persuasive, 43, 49, 65, 113, 115, 161, 183, 199, 229, 231, 253, 255, 263, 481–483, 484, 485–488, 489–500, 501, 502, 503–504
paragraph, 18–19, 289–293, 357–363, 441–445
steps in writing
drafting, 18–19, 307–309, 334–336, 379–380, 391, 417–419, 459–460, 494–496
prewriting, 12–17, 304–306, 330–332, 374–378, 390, 409–416, 455–458, 489–493
proofreading, 24–25, 313, 340, 384, 393, 425, 464, 499
publishing, 26–27, 314, 341, 385, 393, 426, 465, 500
revising, 20–23, 311–312, 338–339, 382–383, 391, 421–424, 462–463, 497–498
topic sentence, writing a 18, 357–358, 360, 361, 363, 380, 417, 459
types of
acrostic poem, 475
ad, 49, 255
award certificate, 117
biography, 41
book report, 468–469
business letter, 113, 503–504

I-2 Index

captions, 101
cause and effect, 77, 362
character sketch, 67
children's story, 107
classification, 455–465
classificatory, 455–465
compare-contrast, 361, 363, 365–367, 368, 369–373, 374–385, 386, 387, 396–397
descriptions, 9–11, 13, 15, 17, 19, 21, 23, 25, 27, 33, 45, 67, 71, 75, 101, 123, 159, 181, 223, 251, 257, 361
dialogue, 195, 344–349
expository paragraph. *See* informational paragraph
friendly letter, 317–318
informational paragraph, 357–363
instructions, 127, 259, 388–393
interview, 157, 189
invitation, 263, 318
jokes, 73, 153
journal, 71, 99
letters, 121, 185, 227, 231, 317–318, 503–504
list, 115, 197, 199
magazine article, 229
museum sign, 257
narrative paragraph, 289–293
news report, 33, 223, 430–431
opinion essay, 447–449, 450, 451–454, 455–465, 466, 467
opinion paragraph, 441–445

personal narrative, 251, 295–297, 298, 299–303, 304–314, 315, 316
persuasive essay, 481–483, 484, 485–488, 489–500, 501, 502
play, 344–349
poetry, 109, 193, 247, 470–475
post card, 35
radio announcement, 181
research report, 399–402, 403, 404–407, 409–426, 427
review, 43, 161, 183, 253
safety tips, 117
schedule, 105
science report, 45
script, 75, 123
speech, 39, 125
story, 37, 103, 219, 265, 320–324, 325, 326–329, 330–341, 342, 343
thank-you letter, 221, 318
travel brochure, 65
writing to solve a problem, 428–429
Computer, using in writing, 349, H41–H44. *See also* Technology
Conclusions, writing, 18–19, 292, 309, 335, 360, 380, 444, 460, 469, 494
Conference. *See* Writing conference
Conflict. *See* Problem, in plot
Conjunctions
coordinating, 44–45,

46–47, 51–52, 61, 68, 85, 87, 110, 170, 186–187
subordinating, 191, 209
Connotation, 498, H15
Content areas, writing in
art, 342, 386, 466
health, 501
literature, 315, 427, 501
math, 315, 427, 501
multicultural education, 427
music, 427
P.E., 315, 427
physical education, 15, 427
science, 315, 427
social studies, 427, 501
Contractions, 116–117, 122–123, 131, 145, 148, 172, 226–227, 242, 254–255, 273
Contrast. *See* Comparison and contrast
Conventions
grammar, 32–45, 51–52, 53, 55–61, 64–67, 70–77, 82–83, 84–85, 87–88, 89–94, 96–109, 116–121, 130–131, 136–142, 145–147, 152–153, 156–157, 162–163, 166–167, 170–173, 174–175, 178, 216–223, 226–231, 238–244, 246–247, 256–259, 272–275, 276, 280–281
mechanics, 34–35, 48–49, 52, 62, 66–67, 74–77, 82–83, 84–85, 87–88, 90, 93–94, 116–117, 122–123, 131–132, 145, 148, 170–173, 180–185,

Index **I-3**

Index continued

Conventions, continued
188–189, 192–199, 201–203, 207–214, 226–227, 242, 272–275
spelling, 70–71, 72–73, 106–107, 118–119, 120–121, H67–H71
usage, 44–45, 48–49, 51–52, 61–62, 87–88, 104–105, 112–115, 118–127, 130–132, 140, 143–144, 146–150, 158–161, 166–167, 170, 172–173, 176–177, 216–223, 228–231, 238–241, 243–244, 250–255, 262–265, 272–275, 277–279, 282–283

Creative activities, 81, 129, 163, 217, 314, 341, 475

Creative writing, 73, 97, 107, 109, 123, 153, 189, 247

Critical thinking, 11, 297, 324, 402, 449, 483

D

Descriptions
using exact words, 17, 71, 418
the writing process and, 12–27, 418
See also Composition, types of

Details
elaborating with, 14, 309, 312, 331, 333, 339, 383, 418, 422, 457, 463, 498
listening for, 288, 311, 338, 356, 382, 421, 440, 462, 497

using, 16, 17, 21, 291, 293, 305, 331, 347, 359, 375, 376, 390–391

Diagramming guide, H72–H80

Diagrams, 424, H27

Dialogue
punctuating, 194–195, 200, 202, 212, 274, 325
writing, 298, 301, 303, 310, 325, 327, 329, 333
See also Literary terms and Composition, types of

Dictionary, using
definitions, H21
entry words, H20
guide words, H20
pronunciation key, H22
syllabication, H22

Direct objects. *See* Object, direct

Directions. *See* Instructions

Discussion
group, 3–5
panel, 476–477

Double negatives, 254–255, 268, 269, 275, 279

Drafting, 18–19, 307–309, 334–336, 379–380, 391, 417–419, 459–460, 494–496

Drafts, revising
for coherence, 339
by combining, 46–47, 68–69, 78–79, 191, 312
by elaborating, 21, 312, 339, 498
for sentence fluency, 46–47, 68–69, 78–79, 110–111, 154–155, 186–187, 190–191,

224–225, 248–249, 260–261, 312, 339, 383, 422, 463, 498
for word choice, 21, 80, 128, 154–155, 164, 266, 312, 339, 422, 463, 498
See also Revising

Dramatizing guidelines, 351
present interpretations, 350–351
speaking voice, 351

E

E-mail, using, H39

Editing. *See* Proofreading

Elaborating, 20–21, 69, 154, 186–187, 248–249, 260–261, 307, 309, 312, 333, 339, 383, 418, 422, 457, 463, 498

Encyclopedia, using, 412–413

End marks. *See* Exclamation points; Periods; Question marks

Enrichment, 50, 81, 129, 165, 200, 233, 267

Envelopes, addressing, 318

Evaluating
analyze published models, 9–11, 295–297, 320–324, 365–367, 399–402, 447–449, 481–483
analyze student models, 299–303, 326–329, 369–373, 404–408, 451–454, 485–488
information, 413, 436–437, 492
meaning by interpreting visual images, 396–397, 478–479
respond to others'

writing, 11, 297, 324, 367, 402, 449, 483
using criteria, 298, 325, 337, 310, 368, 381, 403, 420, 450, 461, 484, 496

Exact nouns. *See* Nouns, exact

Exact verbs. *See* Verbs, exact

Exact words. *See* Words, exact

Exclamation point, 34–35, 56, 180–181, 192–193, 207, 211

Exclamations, 34–35, 56, 180–181, 207

Exclamatory sentences. *See* Sentences, types of

Expository composition. *See* Composition, modes

F

Fact and opinion, 291, 356, 359, 414, 420

Form, completing a, 432–433

Formal language, 30

Fragments. *See* Sentence fragments

Future tense. *See* Verb tenses

G

Graphic organizers
charts, 14–15, 347, 378, 390, 410, 411, 423, 424, 429, 489, H53, H54, H55
clustering, 14, 17, 304, 391, H52
diagram, 424
e-chart, H54
flow charts, 390, 424
graphs, 423
idea pyramid, 456–458
inverted triangle, H52

ISP chart, H55
K-W-L chart, H54
K-W-S chart, 411
step-by-step chart, H55
story map, 332, 347, H56
T-chart, 473, H54
time line, 423, H56
Venn diagram, 376, 387, H56
webs, H52

Graphs, 423, H26

Group discussions. *See* Discussions

H

Haiku, 50

Helping verbs. *See* Verbs, helping

Homophones, 233, 266

I

***I*, in compound subject,** 220–221, 234, 240

Ideas, 12–13, 304–305, 318, 330, 347, 374–378, 409–411, 417, 455–456

Idioms, H12

Illustrations
evaluating, 396–397
using, 423

Indenting paragraphs, 24–25, 289, 357, 441

Informal language, 30, 116–117, 317–318

Information
completing a form, 432–433
listening for, 356
locating sources, 412–413, 428–429, H23–H25

Informative writing. *See* Expository writing; Instructions; Research reports

Instructions
following, 394–395, 433
giving, 394–395
sequence of, 389–391
writing, 388–393

Interjections, 192–193, 200, 202, 211, 464

Internet, using, 17, 27, 51, 82–83, 87, 130–131, 166, 170, 201, 203, 234–235, 268, 272, 288, 303, 310, 315–316, 329, 332, 337, 342, 373, 376, 381, 384, 408, 410, 413, 420, 425, 427, 447, 454, 456–457, 461, 466, 468, 481, 488, 491, 496, 502, H45–H46

Interrogative sentences. *See* Sentences, types of

Interviews, 157, 189, 412, H9–H10

Introduction, writing an, 389, 391, 419, 431, 460, 469, 494

Invitations, 263

L

Letters
parts of, 317–318, 503–504
types of
business, 503–504
friendly, 317–318
invitation, 318
thank-you, 318

Linking verbs. *See* Verbs

Listening
for author's purpose, 288, 356, 440
critical, 505–506
for details, 288, 311, 338, 356, 382, 421, 440, 462, 497

Index   I-5

Index continued

Listening continued
  for fact and opinion, 440
  to follow instructions, 394–395
  guidelines for, 5, 356, 395, 477
  for information, 356, 395
  to interpret nonverbal cues, H7–H8
  to interpret perspectives, 440
  to a narrative, 288
  for persuasive techniques, 505–506
  and taking notes, 288, 356, 440, H29
  to understand ideas, 288, 311, 338, 356, 382, 421, 440, 462, 497
  See also Oral language activities

Listing, 13–15, 304, 374, 389, 409

Literary terms
  character, 331, 346, 352–353
  couplet, 473
  dialogue, 346, 347, 348
  metaphor, 312
  mood, 336, 352–353
  plot, 332, 334, 347, 353
  scene, 346
  setting, 288, 332, 346, 347, 352, 353
  simile, 312
  stanza, 473

Literature
  responding to, 11, 296, 324, 367, 449, 472, 483
  types of
    description, 9–11
    essay, 365–367, 447–449, 481–483
    personal narrative, 295–296
    poetry, 470–472
    story, 320–324

M

Main idea
  keeping to, 291, 334
  listening for, 288, 356, 440
  of paragraphs, 18–19, 289, 290, 357, 419, 441–442

Main topics, in outlines, 416

Maps, 267

Mechanics, 34–35, 48–49, 52, 62, 66–67, 74–77, 82–83, 84–85, 87–88, 90, 93–94, 116–117, 122–123, 131–132, 145, 148, 170–173, 180–185, 188–189, 192–199, 201–203, 207–214, 226–227, 242, 272–275
  See also Conventions

Media
  comparing print and film, 352–353
  comparing visual information, 396–397
  evaluating news, 436–437
  interpreting, 436–437, 507–509
  persuasive techniques, 507–509
  points of view in visuals, 478–479
  using, 434–435

Messages, taking and giving, H4

Metaphor. *See* Literary terms

Modifiers. *See* Adjectives; Adverbs

Mood. *See* Literary terms

N

Narrative. *See* Composition, modes; Literature, types of; Personal narrative; Stories

Negatives, 254–255, 268–269, 275, 279

News story, writing a, 33, 223, 430–431

Newspaper, 436–437

Nonfiction. *See also* Literature, types of

Nonverbal cues, 6, 350–351, 385, 394, 435, H7–H8

Notes, taking, 288, 353, 356, 414–416, 440, H28–H29

Nouns
  common, 66–67, 82, 88, 90, 170, 272
  exact, 80
  identifying, 64–65, 81, 82, 89
  irregular, 72–73, 82, 88, 92
  plural, 70–71, 72–73, 82–83, 85–86, 88, 91–92, 171, 272
  possessive, 74–77, 78–79, 83, 85, 88, 93–94, 171, 272
  proper, 66–67, 82–83, 84, 86, 88, 90, 170, 201, 208, 272
  regular, 64–65
  singular, 70–71, 82, 91

O

Object pronouns. *See* Pronouns

Objects
  direct, 98–99, 130, 137, 171, 272

Opinions, 440–445, 447–467, 469

Opposites. *See* Antonyms

Oral language activities, 434–435
  See also Discussions;

Listening; Speaking
Order, 16, 292, 359, 416, 444
Order words, 292, 306, 334, 389, 391, 394
Organization, 12, 16–17, 306, 318, 363, 377–378, 390, 423, 458, 493
Outlines, 416–417, 431

P

Panel discussion, having a, 476–477
Paragraphs
  main idea of, 18–19, 441
  organizing ideas into, 18–19, 289–293, 357–363, 418, 441–445, 459–460, 493
  topic sentence, 18, 357–358, 361, 363, 380, 417, 459
  types of
    cause and effect, 362
    compare and contrast, 361
    expressive, 67
    informational, 357–363
    lead, 431
    narrative, 289–293
    opinion, 441–445
Periods, 34–35, 56, 180–181, 196–197, 207, 213
Personal narrative
  activities for writing, 315
  using voice, 298, 308
  the writing process and, 304–314
  See also Composition, types of
Persuasion, 481–496, 507–509
Photographs
  evaluating, 397, 498–499
  using, 434

viewing, 6
Play, writing a, 344–349
Plot. *See* Literary terms
Plural nouns. *See* Nouns
Poetry, 165, 109, 470–474
  See also Literature, types of
Points of view, in visuals, 478–479
Possessive nouns. *See* Nouns
Possessive pronouns. *See* Pronouns
Predicate. *See* Sentences, predicates
Prefixes, H16
Prepositional phrases, 258–259, 260–261, 264–265, 267, 268–269, 275, 281–283
Prepositions, 256–257, 258–259, 260–261, 264–265, 267, 268–269, 275, 280–281, 283
Prewriting
  activities, 330, 409
  brainstorming, 14–15, 330, 409, 455–456
  clustering, 14, 304
  discussing, 13, 304, 330, 374, 409, 455, 489
  drawing, 14, 305
  graphic organizers, using, 14, 17, 304, 332, 347, 376, 378, 390, 410–411, 456–458, 489, 491
  interviewing, 14
  listing, 13–15, 304, 374, 409, 453
  taking notes, 414
  See also Composition, steps in writing
Problem, in plot, 332, 347
Problem solving, 428–429

Pronouns
  agreement, 224–225
  objective case, 218–219, 220–221, 234, 236, 239, 262–263, 269, 275, 282
  possessive, 222–223, 234, 236, 241, 275, 464
  subject, 216–217, 220–221, 224–225, 234, 236, 238–239, 269, 275, 499
Pronunciation key. *See* Dictionary, using a
Proofreading
  capitalization, 24–25, 183, 195, 197, 199, 201, 203, 425
  grammar and usage, 24–25, 49, 52, 54, 71, 73, 75, 83, 105, 107, 111, 113, 115, 119, 121, 123, 125, 127, 132, 157, 159, 161, 201, 221, 227, 229, 231, 235, 251, 253, 255, 263, 269, 313, 340, 384, 425, 464, 499
  punctuation, 24–25, 49, 52, 54, 83, 85–86, 49, 169, 181, 185, 189, 193, 195, 197, 199, 201, 203
  for spelling, 24–25, 71, 73, 83, 117, 133–135, 206, 227, 313, 318, 340, 384, 393, 425, 464, 499
  See also Composition, steps in writing
Proper adjectives. *See* Adjectives
Proper nouns. *See* Nouns
Publishing, 26–27, 314, 341, 385, 393, 426, 465, 500
  See also Composition, steps in writing

Index continued

Punctuation
   of quotations, 194–195, 202–203, 212
   of sentences, 32–33, 46–49, 51–52, 54, 62, 201, 274
   using appropriate end, 32–33, 51–52, 54, 56–57, 180–181, 206, 274

Punctuation marks. *See* Apostrophes; Commas; Exclamation points; Periods; Question marks; Quotation marks

Purpose
   identifying
     for listening, 288, 356, 440, 505–506
     for speaking, 394, 434
     for writing, 12–13, 304, 330, 374, 380, 391, 409, 455, 489
   for writing
     to entertain, 344–349
     to explain, 357, 361, 362, 374, 388–393
     to express, 441–445, 455, 468–469, 470–475
     to influence, 489, 503–504
     to inform, 357, 361, 362, 409, 428–429, 430–431, 432–433
     to narrate, 304, 317–318
     to persuade, 489, 503–504
     to record ideas and reflections, 26, 314, 341, 385, 426, 465, 500, H51
     to solve a problem, 428–429

Q

Question marks, 34–35, 56, 180–181, 207

Questions
   asking and answering, 12, 14, 304, 330, 370, 409, 410, 411, 413, 455, 489
   open-response, H35–H36

Quotation marks, 194–195, 198–199, 200, 202, 212, 214, 274

Quotations, 194–195, 200, 202, 212, 274

R

Record knowledge
   learning log, H50

Reference works. *See* Almanac, using; Atlas, using; Dictionary, using; Encyclopedia, using; Maps

Reflecting, 26, 314, 341, 385, 426, 465, 500

Regular verbs. *See* Verbs

Reports. *See* Research reports

Research reports
   documenting sources, 414–415
   writing, 399–402, 403, 404–408, 409–426, 427

Reviewing
   written works, 412

Revising. *See* Composition, steps in; Drafts, revising

Root words. *See* Word roots

Rubrics, 310, 337, 381, 420, 461, 492, 496

Run-on sentences. *See* Sentences

S

Scene. *See* Literary terms

Sensory words and details, 15, 291, 359

Sentence fluency, 46–47, 68–69, 78–79, 110–111, 154–155, 186–187, 190–191, 224–225, 248–249, 260–261, 312, 339, 383, 422, 463, 498

Sentence fragments, 32–33, 55, 87, 170, 272

Sentences
   activities for writing, 35, 46–47, 50, 119, 181
   capitalization of first word in. *See* Capitalization, of first word in sentence
   combining, 46–47, 68–69, 78–79, 85, 110–111, 155, 186–187, 190–191, 248–249, 260–261
   diagramming, H72–H80
   predicates, 36–37, 51, 57, 87, 170
     combining, 271, 312
     simple, 36–37, 40–41, 51, 53, 57, 59, 87, 170, 272
   punctuating, 34–35, 51, 56
   run-on, 48–49, 52, 62, 88, 170, 201, 207, 272
   subjects, 36–37, 51, 53, 57, 87, 170
     compound, 68–69
     double, 228–229, 234, 243, 275
     simple, 38–39, 42–43, 51, 58, 87, 272
   types of
     complete/incomplete, 32–33, 36–37, 51, 55, 57, 87
     compound/complex, 46–47, 48–49, 62

declarative, 34–35, 51, 56, 60, 87, 170, 207
exclamatory, 34–35, 51, 56, 87, 170, 207, 272
imperative, 34–35, 42–43, 51, 56, 60, 87, 170, 207, 272
interrogative, 34–35, 51, 56, 87, 170, 207, 272
Sequence, 16, 292, 306, 332, 334, 359, 377, 416, 443, 458, 493
Sequence of events, 292, 306, 332, 334
Setting. *See* Literary terms
Short story. *See* Personal narrative; Stories
Simile. *See* Literary terms
Simple predicates. *See* Sentences, predicates
Simple subjects. *See* Sentences, subjects
Singular nouns. *See* Nouns
Six traits. *See* Conventions; Ideas; Organization; Sentence Fluency; Voice; Word Choice
Speaking
being a good listener and speaker, 5, 350–351, 435, H4, H9
choose and adapt for audience, 350–351, 476–477
clarify messages, 3–6, 22–23, 311, 338, 382, 421, 435, 462, 497, H4, H9
dramatizing, 349, 350–351, 394, 477
giving instructions, 394
having discussions, 476–477
reading a play, 350–351
using correct rate/

volume/pitch/tone, 350–351, 394, 435, 476–477, H5–H6
See also Oral language activities
Spelling
plural nouns, 70–71, 72–73, 82–83, 85–86, 88, 91–92
proofreading for, 24–25, 71, 73, 83, 117, 133–135, 206, 318, 425, 464
verbs, 104–107, 118–119, 140–141, 143
Stanza, 473–474
Statements. *See* Sentences, declarative
Stories
activities for writing, 343
comparing, in print and on film, 352–353
narrative, 320–324
oral traditions, 320–324
parts of, 332
sequencing, 332, 334
using voice, 336
the writing process and, 330–341
See also Literature, types of; Personal narrative
Story poems, 470–474
Subject (of a sentence). *See* Sentences, subjects
Subject pronouns. *See* Pronouns
Subject-verb agreement. *See* Agreement
Subtopics, 416–417
Suffixes, H17
Summarizing, 97, 181, 429, 469, H31–H32
Supporting details/ sentences, 14–19, 289, 291–292, 357, 359, 360, 362, 417, 441, 443–444,

484, 490–491
Synonyms, 463, H13

T

Technology, using, 13, 26, 313, 340, 349, 384, 425, H37–H49
Tenses of verbs. *See* Verb tenses
Test taking, 53–54, 84–85, 133–135, 168–169, 204–206, 236–237, 270–271, 316, 343, 387, 467, 502
Thesaurus Plus, H81–H102
Thinking skills, comparing and contrasting, 16, 45, 121, 159, 229, 251, 263, 252–253, 361, 374–387
Titles
book, 198–199, 203, 206, 214, 274
for people, 196–197, 203
writing, 198–199, 203, 206, 214, 274, 314, 341, 385, 426, 465
Tone, 298, 308, 350–351, 484, 495
Topic
choosing a, 12–13, 374
exploring, 14–15, 375, 410–411
identifying, 289, 356, 391, 440
keeping to, 306, 493
narrowing, 410–411
Topic, main, 416–417, 418, 441
Topic sentence, 18, 290, 357–358, 361, 363, 380, 417, 459
Transitional words and phrases, 18, 359–360, 361–362, 380, 417–418, 444, 458, 493

Index *continued*

U

Usage
adjective, 164–165, 173
can, may, 126–127, 173, 273
conjunctions, 44–45
could of, avoiding, 122–123
good, bad, 160–161, 167, 173, 177
good, well, 252–253, 278
I, me, 220–221, 240
its, it's, 233
let, leave, 124–125, 173, 273
prepositional phrases, 258–261
pronoun, 216–225, 262–263
regular/irregular verbs, 118–121
sit, set, 126–127, 173, 273
subject-verb agreement, 112–115
us, we, 230–231, 235, 244, 275
verb phrases, 122–123
verb tenses, 104–105

V

Verb phrases, 100–101, 122–123, 132, 138, 146, 148, 172
Verb tenses
future, 108–109, 111, 131, 142, 172, 273
past, 106–107, 109, 111, 114–115, 118–119, 120–121, 129, 130, 141, 146–147, 172, 273
present, 104–105, 109, 111, 112–113, 114–115, 130, 140, 143, 172, 273
Verbs
action, 96–97, 98–99, 102–103, 130, 136–137, 138–139, 171, 272
exact, 128
helping, 100–101, 118–119, 122–123, 130, 138, 146–147, 171, 273
irregular, 118–119, 120–121, 131, 146–147, 172, 273
writing clearly with, 110–111, 112–113, 124–125, 126–127, 149–150
Viewing
guidelines for, 6, 397, 437, 479, 509
interpreting visual images, 352–353, 396–397, 478–479, 507–509
media, 436–437, 478–479
stories on film, 352–353
watching for persuasive tactics, 507–509
See also Visual images
Visual aids, using, 396–397, 423, 426, 434–435
Visual images
comparing, 352–353
interpreting, 6, 352–353, 396–397, 478–479, 507–509
organizing, 396–397, 423, 426, 434–435
using, 396–397, 423, 426, 434–435
Vocabulary
adjectives, choosing different, 164
adverbs, choosing different, 232
antonyms, H14
connotations, word, H15
homophones, 232
idioms, H12
nouns, exact, 80
prefixes, H16
regional and cultural, H19
similes and metaphors, H11
suffixes, H17
synonyms, H13
verbs, exact, 128
word roots, H18
Voice
writing with, 308, 298, 336, 350–351, 418, 450, 459, 495
speaking, 351
Word choice
exact nouns, 80
exact verbs, 128
exact words, 17, 21, 164, 333
metaphors, 312
similes, 312
synonyms, 463
Word roots, H18
Words
exact, 17, 21, 80, 164, 333
Writing. *See* Composition; Creative writing
Writing across the curriculum. *See* Content areas, writing in
Writing conference, 22–23, 311, 338, 382, 421, 462, 497
Writing process. *See* Composition, steps in writing
Writing prompts, 315–316, 342–343, 386–387, 427, 466–467, 501–502

Acknowledgments *continued*

"Scaredy Cats" by Christina Wilsdon from *3-2-1 Contact* magazine, July/August 1996 issue. Copyright ©1996 by Children's Television Workshop. Reprinted by permission of Children's Television Workshop. All rights reserved.

From *The Woman Who Outshone the Sun: The Legend of Lucia Zenteno* by Rosalma Zubizarreta, Harriet Rohmer and David Schecter. Story copyright ©1991 by Children's Book Press and Rosalma Zubizarreta. Pictures copyright ©1991 by Fernando Olivera. Reproduced with permission of the publisher, Children's Book Press, San Francisco, CA.

Poetry

"Daddy Fell into the Pond" by Alfred Noyes. Copyright 1952 by Alfred Noyes. Reprinted with permission of Andrews and McMeel Publishing. All rights reserved.

"Instant Storm" by X. J. Kennedy first published in *One Winter Night in August and Other Nonsense Jingles.* Copyright ©1975 by X. J. Kennedy. Published by Atheneum Books, a division of Simon & Schuster Books for Young Readers. Reprinted by permission of Curtis Brown, Ltd.

"maggie and milly and molly and may" from *Complete Poems 1904–1962* by E. E. Cummings, edited by George J. Firmage. Copyright ©1956, 1984, 1991 by the Trustees for the E. E. Cummings Trust. Used by permission of Liveright Publishing Corporation.

"A Perfect Hit" by Linda Romano from *Moving Windows: Evaluating the Poetry Children Write* by Jack Collom. Copyright ©1985 by Teachers & Writers Collaborative. Reprinted by permission of Teachers & Writers Collaborative. All rights reserved.

Book Report

When Will This Cruel War Be Over?: The Civil War Diary of Emma Simpson by Barry Denenberg. Copyright ©1996 by Barry Denenberg. Reprinted by permission of Scholastic, Inc.

Student Handbook

Definitions of "floppy disk," "harbor," "mineral," "mingle," and "printer" from *The American Heritage® Children's Dictionary* by the editors of the American Heritage® Dictionaries. Copyright ©1998 by Houghton Mifflin Company. Reproduced by permission of *The American Heritage® Children's Dictionary.*

Definition of "hard disk" from *The American Heritage® Student Dictionary.* Copyright ©1998 by Houghton Mifflin Company. Reproduced by permission of *The American Heritage® Student Dictionary.*

Pronunciation key on page 25 from *The American Heritage® Children's Dictionary* by the editors of the American Heritage® Dictionaries. Copyright ©1998 by Houghton Mifflin Company. Reproduced by permission of *The American Heritage® Children's Dictionary.*

From "Robert Edward Lee" from *Collier's Encyclopedia,* Volume 14, page 440. Copyright ©1997 by Atlas Editions. All rights reserved. Used by permission.

One Minute Warm-up

5/1 *Bat* by Caroline Arnold, photographs by Richard Hewett, published by Morrow Junior Books, 1996. Used by permission.

5/1 *Flying Free: America's First Black Aviators* by Philip S. Hart, published by Lerner Publications Company, 1992. Used by permission.

5/1 *Project Puffin: How We Brought Puffins Back to Egg Rock* by Stephen W. Kress as told to Pete Salmansohn, published by Tilbury House, Publishers, 1997. Used by permission.

5/2 *Children of the Wild West* by Russell Freedman, published by Clarion Books, 1983. Used by permission.

Acknowledgments *continued*

5/2 *Mae Jemison: Space Scientist* by Gail Sakurai, published by Childrens Press, 1995. Used by permission.

5/2 *Market!* by Ted Lewin, published by Lothrop, Lee & Shepard Books, 1996. Used by permission.

5/3 *A Child's Glacier Bay* by Kimberly Corral with Hannah Corral, photographs by Roy Corral. Copyright ©1998. Reproduced with permission of Alaska Northwest Books, an Imprint of Graphic Arts Center Publishing Company.

5/3 *Earthquake Terror* by Peg Kehret, published by Cobblehill Books, 1996. Used by permission.

5/3 *Growing Up in Ancient Rome* by Mike Corbishley, illustrated by Chris Molan, published by Quarto Children's Books, 1994. Used by permission.

5/3 *Lives of the Athletes: Thrills, Spills (and What the Neighbors Thought)* by Kathleen Krull, illustrated by Kathryn Hewitt, published by Harcourt Brace & Company, 1997. Used by permission.

5/3 *Me, Mop and the Moondance Kid* by Walter Dean Myers, illustrated by Rodney Pate. Copyright ©1988 by Walter Dean Myers. Used by permission of Dell Publishing, a division of Random House, Inc.

5/3 *The Counterfeit Tackle* by Matt Christopher, illustrated by Foster Caddell, published by Little, Brown and Company, 1965. Used by permission.

5/3 *The Hundred Penny Box* by Sharon Bell Mathis, illustrated by Leo & Diane Dillon, published by Viking Penguin, 1975. Used by permission.

5/4 *Elena* by Diane Stanley, published by Hyperion Books for Children, 1996. Used by permission.

5/4 *The Golden Lion Tamarin Comes Home* by George Ancona. Copyright ©1994 by George Ancona. Reprinted with the permission of Simon & Schuster Books for Young Readers, an imprint of Simon & Schuster Children's Publishing Division.

5/5 *A Very Young Musician* written and photographed by Jill Krementz. Copyright ©1991 by Jill Krementz. Reprinted with the permission of Simon & Schuster Books for Young Readers, an imprint of Simon & Schuster Children's Publishing Division.

5/5 *Introducing Mozart* by Roland Vernon, illustrated by Ian Andrew. Copyright ©1996 by Belitha Press Limited. Used by permission.

5/5 *On Call Back Mountain* by Eve Bunting, illustrated by Barry Moser. Published by The Blue Sky Press, an imprint of Scholastic Inc. Jacket illustration copyright ©1997 by Barry Moser. Used by permission.

5/5 *Yang the Second and Her Secret Admirers* by Lensey Namioka, illustrated by Kees de Kiefte, published by Little, Brown and Company, 1998. Used by permission.

5/6 *Athletes* by Laurie Lindop. Copyright ©1996 by Laurie Lindop. Used by permission of The Millbrook Press.

5/6 *Darnell Rock Reporting* by Walter Dean Myers. Copyright ©1994 by Walter Dean Myers. Used by permission of Random House Children's Books, a division of Random House, Inc.

5/6 *McBroom Tells the Truth* by Sid Fleischman, illustrated by Walter Lorraine, published by Little, Brown and Company, 1981. Used by permission.

5/7 *Anne of Green Gables* by L. M. Montgomery, illustrated by Jody Lee, published by Grosset & Dunlap, 1983. Used by permission.

5/7 *Crinkleroot's Guide to Walking in Wild Places* by Jim Arnosky. Copyright ©1990 by Jim Arnosky. Reprinted with the permission of Simon & Schuster Books for Young Readers, an imprint of Simon & Schuster Children's Publishing Division.

5/7 *Discovering the Inca Ice Maiden: My Adventures on Ampato* by Johan Reinhard, published by National Geographic Society, 1998. Used by permission.

5/7 *Summer Reading Is Killing Me!* by Jon Scieszka, illustrated by Lane Smith, published by Viking, 1998. Used by permission.

Student Writing Model Contributors
James Alfano, Portia Caldwell, Christina Clark, John Coghlan, Allison France, Ben Helmick, Mike Jones, Nora Kelly, Michael Le, Yesina Lopez, Cyrus Manjooran, Chris Rivera

Credits

Illustrations

Special Characters illustrated by: Sal, the Writing Pal by LeeLee Brazeal; Pencil Dog by Jennifer Beck Harris; Enrichment Animals by Scott Matthews.
John Bendall-Brunello: 107, 156 (top), 198, 246 (top)
Lisa Chiba: 160 (top)
Chris Demarest: 232, 290, 292, 331, 334, 414, 495
Eldon Doty: 64 (top), 106 (top), 158, 195
Cynthia Fisher: 81 (center), 233 (bottom), 248, 267 (bottom)
Kate Flanagan: 118
Bonnie Gee: H18
Jim Gordon: 252
Sharon Harker: H12
Jennifer Harris: 40, 42 (bottom), 112 (top), 218
True Kelley: 32, 42 (top)
Rita Lascara: H19
Jared Lee: 74 (top), 192
Patrick Merrell: 220
John Meza: 112 (bottom), 219
Trevor Pye: 106 (bottom)
Chris Reed: 122, 189, 228, 246 (bottom)
Michael Reid: 23, 505
Tim Robinson: 74 (bottom)
Ellen Sasaki: 1-4, 6, 7, 34, 48, 102
Lauren Scheuer: 80, 126, 164, 200 (center, bottom), 266, 289, 307, 309, 456, 458, 470-472
Alfred Schrier: 128
Rémy Simard: 66, 156 (bottom), 188, 262
Michael Sloan: 76
Susan Spellman: H22, H25
George Ulrich: 108, 196, 264, H90, H91, H93-H98, H101, H102
Matt Wawiorka: 50 (center), 165 (center), 490, 494
Toby Williams: 114, 123
Amy L. Young: 64 (bottom), 160 (bottom), 184
Debra Ziss: 233 (center)

Maps

Ortelius: 57, 423

Photographs

iii © Tim Davis/Tony Stone Images. **iv** © Carl Schneider/FPG International. **v** © Warren Bolster/Tony Stone Images. **vi** © Vladimir Pcholkin/FPG International. **vii** © Joe McBride/Tony Stone Images. **ix** © David Scott Smith/Stock Connection. **x** © Galen Rowell. **xi** (t) © Mug Shots/The Stock Market. (b) © Randy Wells/Tony Stone Images. **xiii** (t) © Terry Vine/Tony Stone Images. (b) © Kennan Ward/The Stock Market. **9** © David Samuel Robbins/CORBIS. **10** (l) © Kevin

Acknowledgments continued

Schafer/CORBIS. (r) © Michael and Patricia Fogden/CORBIS. **11** © Claus Meyer/Minden Pictures. **31** © Tim Davis/Tony Stone Images. **32** © Mark E. Gibson/Visuals Unlimited. **33** © CORBIS. **34** © Art Wolfe/Tony Stone Images. **36** © Will & Deni McIntyre/Tony Stone Images. **37** © Michelle Garrett/CORBIS. **38** © Charles E. Mohr/Photo Researchers, Inc. **39** © Phil Schofield/AllStock/Picture Quest. **40** © Frank Driggs Collection/Archive Photos. **44** © SuperStock, Inc. **46** (t) © Robert Maier/Animals Animals. (c) © SuperStock, Inc. (b) © SuperStock, Inc. **48** © Spencer Grant/PhotoEdit. **55** © Chris Cole/The Image Bank. **56** © PhotoDisc, Inc. **58** © Stephen Simpson/FPG International. **60** (t) © Elle Schuster/The Image Bank. (b) © Bruce Byers/FPG International. **61** © Siede Preis/PhotoDisc, Inc. **63** © Carl Schneider/FPG International. **65** (l) © PhotoDisc, Inc. (r) © Andrew Ward/Life File/PhotoDisc, Inc. **67** © Hulton-Deutsch Collection/CORBIS. **68** (t) © Bettmann/CORBIS. (b) © National Aviation Museum/CORBIS. **69** Courtesy NASA. **70** © Paul Kenward/Tony Stone Images. **72** © Mitch Reardon/Tony Stone Images. **76** © Rudi VonBriel/PhotoEdit. **77** © Rim Light/PhotoLink/PhotoDisc, Inc. **88** © PhotoDisc, Inc. **89** © Gordon & Cathy Illg/Earth Scenes. **90** © SuperStock, Inc. **92** © Dale Spartas/Tony Stone Images. **93** © PhotoDisc, Inc. **94** © Paul Chesley/Tony Stone Images. **95** © Warren Bolster/Tony Stone Images. **96** © Archive Photos. **98** © P.H.O.N. E./Saola/The Gamma Liaison Network. **99** © Digital Vision/Picture Quest. **100** © SuperStock, Inc. **101** © CORBIS. **102** © Tony Freeman/PhotoEdit. **103** © Marty Snyderman. **104** © S. Cordier/Explorer/Photo Researchers, Inc. **108** © Marc Epstein/Visuals Unlimited. **109** © Jeremy Woodhouse/PhotoDisc, Inc. **110** © William D. Griffin/Animals Animals. **113** © Yoav Levy/Phototake/Picture Quest. **114** © Inga Spence/Visuals Unlimited. **115** © PhotoDisc, Inc. **116** © Aneal F. Vohra/Unicorn Stock Photo. **118** © Charles Gupton/AllStock/Picture Quest. **120** © Anthony Mercieca/Photo Researchers, Inc. **121** © Philippe Colombi/PhotoDisc, Inc. **122** © Jack Dykinga/Tony Stone Images. **124** © David Young-Wolff/PhotoEdit. **125** © PhotoDisc, Inc. **136** © Hulton-Deutsch Collection/CORBIS. **137** © Culver Pictures. (Frame) provided by MetaTools. **138** © Spencer Grant/PhotoEdit. **139** © AP/Wide World Photos. **140** © Joe Atlas/Artville. **141** © Comstock, Inc. **142** © C.C. Lockwood/Animals Animals. **143** © Robert Pearcy/Animls Animals. **144** (t) © Comstock, Inc. (b) © E. Webber/Visuals Unlimited. **145** © SuperStock, Inc. **146** © Gary W. Griffen/Animals Animals. **147** © Joe Atlas/Artville. **148** © PhotoDisc, Inc. **149** © Robert Ginn/Unicorn Stock Photo. **150** © David Young-Wolff/PhotoEdit. **151** © Chip Simons/FPG International. **152** © Art Wolfe/Tony Stone Images. **154** (t) © Tom Brakefield/CORBIS. (cl) © John Cancalosi/Stock Boston. (cr) © Norbert Rosing/Animals Animals. (bl) © Renee Lynn/Tony Stone Images. (br) © Vincent DeWitt/Stock Boston. **155** © Jeff Greenberg/Photo Network. **159** © Paul Chesley/Tony Stone Images. **162** © Bill Aron/PhotoEdit. **164** © Peter Johansky/Index Stock Imagery/Picture Quest. **171** © John Gillmoure/The Stock Market. **172** © Will Hart/PhotoEdit. **174** © David C. Fritts/Animals Animals. **175** © Jeremy Walker/Tony Stone Images. **176** Image provided by MetaTools. **177** © PhotoDisc, Inc. **178** (t) © Comstock, Inc. (b) © David R. Frazier Photolibrary. **179** © Vladimir Pcholkin/FPG International. **180** © Bob Daemmrich/Tony Stone Images. **181** © PhotoDisc, Inc. **182** © The Granger Collection, New York. **183** © Telegraph Colour Library/FPG International. **185** © Joe Atlas/Artville. **188** © PhotoDisc, Inc. **190** © PhotoDisc, Inc. **191** © David Young-Wolff/PhotoEdit. **192** © PhotoDisc, Inc. **194** © Mark Snyder/Tony Stone Images. **196** © Joe Carini/The Image Works. **197** © Digital Vision/Picture Quest. **199** © Steve Cole/PhotoDisc, Inc. **207** © David Young-

Wolff/PhotoEdit. **208** (t) © *Reading Le Figaro,* Christie's Images, London/Bridgeman Art Library, London/SuperStock, Inc. (b) © Monkmeyer/Rogers. **210** (t) © Frank Siteman/PhotoEdit. (b) © PhotoDisc, Inc. **211** © Phyllis Greenberg/Animals Animals. **212** © C. T. Tracy/FPG International. **215** © Phil Schermeister/CORBIS. **216** © George Chan/Tony Stone Images. **222** © Larry Ulrich/Tony Stone Images. **223** © Michael Newman/PhotoEdit. **224** (t) © PhotoDisc, Inc. (ct) © Steve Starr/Stock Boston. (cb) © Arthur Tilley/FPG International/Picture Quest. (b) © Bob Daemmrich/Stock Boston. **225** © Michael K. Daly/The Stock Market. **226** © Rosanne Olson/AllStock/Picture Quest. **227** © PhotoDisc, Inc. **228** (l) (c) © PhotoDisc, Inc. (r) © Comstock, Inc. **229** © Bettmann/CORBIS. **230** (tl) (tr) © PhotoDisc, Inc. (b) © Frank Grant/International Stock Photo. **231** © PhotoDisc, Inc. **238** (t) Image provided by MetaTools. (c) © Joe Atlas/Artville. (b) © Comstock. **239** © Wolfgang Kaehler/CORBIS. **240** © Zig Leszczynski/Animals Animals. **241** © Dave Bartruff/CORBIS. **243** © Kennan Ward/CORBIS. **244** © David Young-Wolff/PhotoEdit. **245** © Joe McBride/Tony Stone Images. **247** (l) (c) © PhotoDisc, Inc. (r) © Stockbyte. **250** © Jeremy Walker/Tony Stone Images. **252** © Bonnie Kamin/PhotoEdit. **254** © Joanna B. Pinneo/Aurora/Picture Quest. **255** © PhotoDisc, Inc. **256** © The Granger Collection, New York. **257** © CORBIS. **258** © Robert Goldstein/Photo Researchers, Inc. **263** © PhotoDisc, Inc. **264** © Felicia Martinez/PhotoEdit. **265** © Comstock, Inc. **272** © PhotoDisc, Inc. **273** © PhotoDisc, Inc. **274** © Joe Atlas/Artville. **276** © Jeff Greenberg/Photo Researchers, Inc. **278** © Joe Atlas/Artville. **279** © PhotoDisc, Inc. **280** (t) © Aldo Brando/Tony Stone Images. (b) © Michael Andrews/Earth Scenes. **282** © Ron Sanford/Allstock/Picture Quest. **283** © Buddy Mays/CORBIS. **286** © David Roth/Tony Stone Images. **286-7** © David Scott Smith/Stock Connection. **287** (b) © Allan Davey/Masterfile. **288** © Michael Yamashita/CORBIS. **291** © Jeff Greenberg/PhotoEdit. **294** © David Roth/Tony Stone Images. **300** © Breck P. Kent/Animals Animals. **319** © Allan Davey/Masterfile. **332** © Yann Arthus-Bertrand/CORBIS. **333** (t) © Kathi Lamm/Tony Stone Images. (b) © Mary Kate Denny/PhotoEdit. **342** © *Prairie Fire* by Francis Blackbear Bosin. Watercolor on paper, 1953, The Philbrook Museum of Art. **354** © Galen Rowell. **354-5** © Mug Shots/The Stock Market. **355** (b) © Randy Wells/Tony Stone Images. **356** © Kim Taylor/Bruce Coleman/Picture Quest. **357** © Arne Hodalic/CORBIS. **358** © K. Sandved/OSF/Animals Animals. **359** © SuperStock, Inc. **360** © Stan Osolinski/FPG International. **361** (l) © Davis Barber/PhotoEdit. (r) © PhotoDisc, Inc. **362** © Ben Osborne/Tony Stone Images. **364** © Galen Rowell. **365** © Mark Perlstein/Black Star/Picture Quest. **366** (l) © Jim Zuckerman/CORBIS. (r) © CORBIS. **376** © Galen Rowell. **378** (t) © VCG/FPG International. (b) © Joseph Van Os/Image Bank. **386** © *The Great Wave of Kanagawa,* Katsushika Hokusai (1760-1849). Color woodblock print, 1831, Christie's Images/The Bridgeman Art Library. **396** © CORBIS. **398** © Randy Wells/Tony Stone Images. **399** © Wolfgang Kaehler/CORBIS. **400** © Joe McDonald/CORBIS. **401** © Karl Ammann/CORBIS. **404** © Galen Rowell/CORBIS. **407** © Galen Rowell/CORBIS. **411** © Captian John Noel/Hulton Getty Picture Library. **413** © Hunter Freeman/Tony Stone Images. **415** © Archive Photos. **416** © John van Hasselt/Sygma. **419** © Hideo Kurihara/Tony Stone Images. **429** Photo Courtesy of Fantasy Island Amusement Park. **433** © David Young-Wolff/PhotoEdit. **434.** (computer inset) Courtesy National Park Service, Gettysburg Military Park. (b) © CORBIS. **438-9** © Terry Vine/Tony Stone Images. **439** (b) © Kennan Ward/The Stock Market. **441** © Paul A. Souders/CORBIS. **442** (t) Image provided by MetaTools. (b) © Tony Freeman/PhotoEdit. **443** © Pascal Crapet/Tony Stone Images. **446** © Roy Morsch/The Stock Market. **447** © Jennifer Binder. **448** (l) © David Young-Wolff/PhotoEdit/Picture Quest. (r) © Felicia

Acknowledgments

Acknowledgments *continued*

Martinez/PnotoEdit/Picture Quest. **452** © James Randkley/Tony Stone Images. **454** © Baron Wolman/Tony Stone Images. **459** © Grant V. Faint/The Image Bank. **466** © *Habitat, Montreal*. Designed by Moshe Safdie/Photo Milton and Joan Mann, Cameramann International, Ltd. **478** (t) © Bruce Ayres/Tony Stone Images. (b) © Dan Bosler/Tony Stone Images. **480** © Kennan Ward/The Stock Market. **500** (tl) © Tony Duffy/Allsport USA. (tr) (bl) (br) © PhotoDisc, Inc. **508** © Stephen Simpson/FPG International/Picture Quest. **509** © Michael Newman/PhotoEdit. **H8** © Spencer Grant III/Stock Boston/Picture Quest. **H10** © Pablo Corral V/CORBIS. **H11** © Craig Aurness/CORBIS. **H14** © Joel Benjamin. **H33** (tl) © Comstock. (tr) (bl) © PhotoDisc, Inc. (br) © CMCD/PhotoDisc, Inc. **H48** (t) © Bettmann/CORBIS. (b) Brown Brothers. **H53** © Telegraph Colour Library/FPG International. **H54** © Mark Newman/Stock Connection/Picture Quest. **H55** © Johnny Johnson/Animals Animals. **H74** © Wolfgang Kaehler/CORBIS. **H76** © Index Stock Photography. **H79** © CORBIS. **H80** Image provided by MetaTools.

Cover Photograph

Tim Davis/Tony Stone Images.